VOLUME



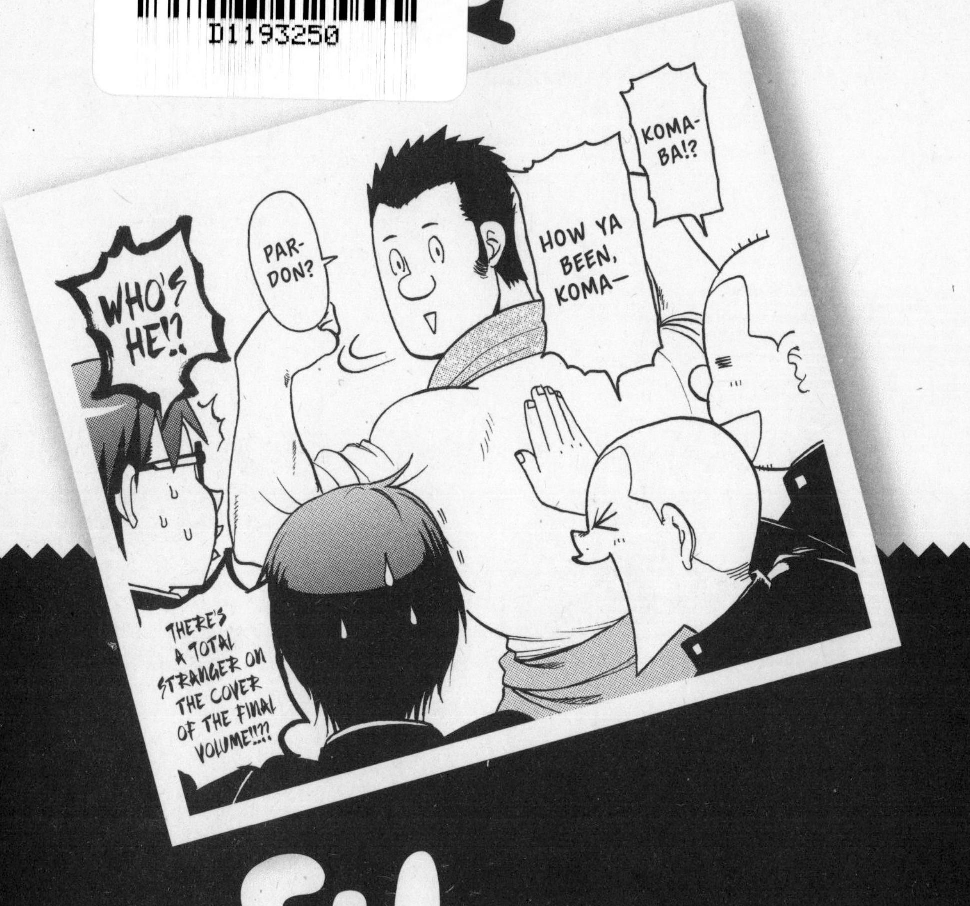
KOMA-BA!?
HOW YA BEEN, KOMA—
PAR-DON?
WHO'S HE!?
THERE'S A TOTAL STRANGER ON THE COVER OF THE FINAL VOLUME!!??

# Silver Spoon

HIROMU ARAKAWA

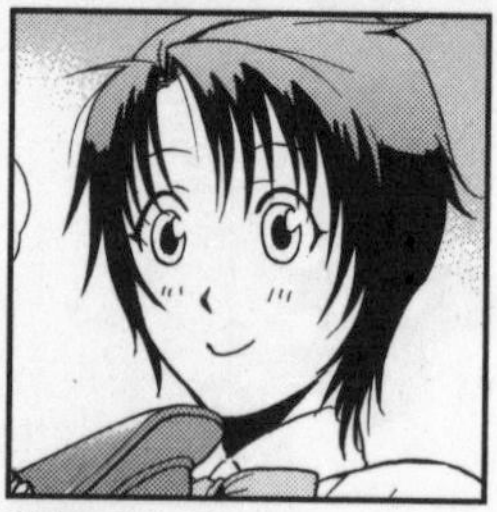

## AKI MIKAGE

A third-year student at Ooezo Agricultural High School, enrolled in the Dairy Science Program. She set her sights on attending Ooezo University of Animal Husbandry to get a job working with horses, and she successfully got in through their recommendation exam.

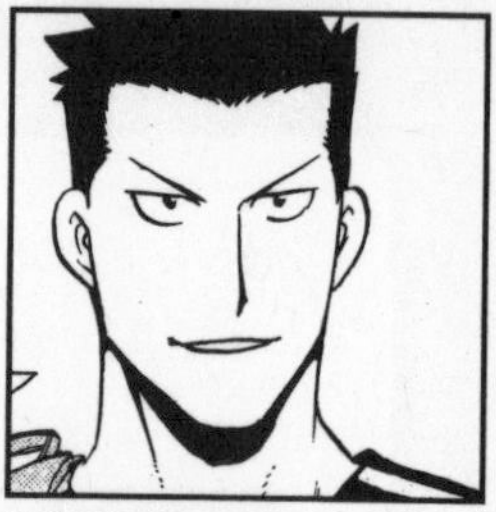

## ICHIROU KOMABA

A former student at Ooezo Agricultural High School who dropped out when his family's dairy farm went out of business. Now he's working jobs far from home to realize his dream of owning his own ranch.

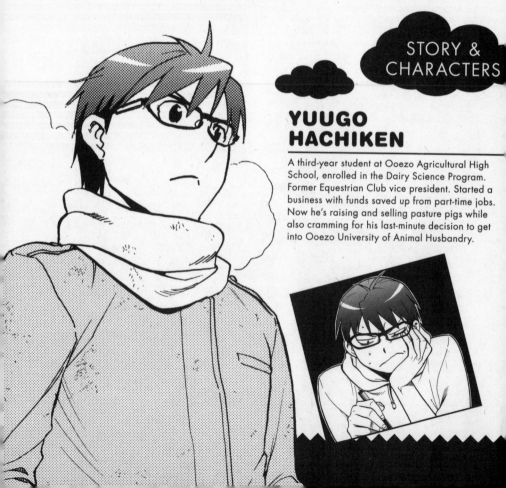

# STORY & CHARACTERS

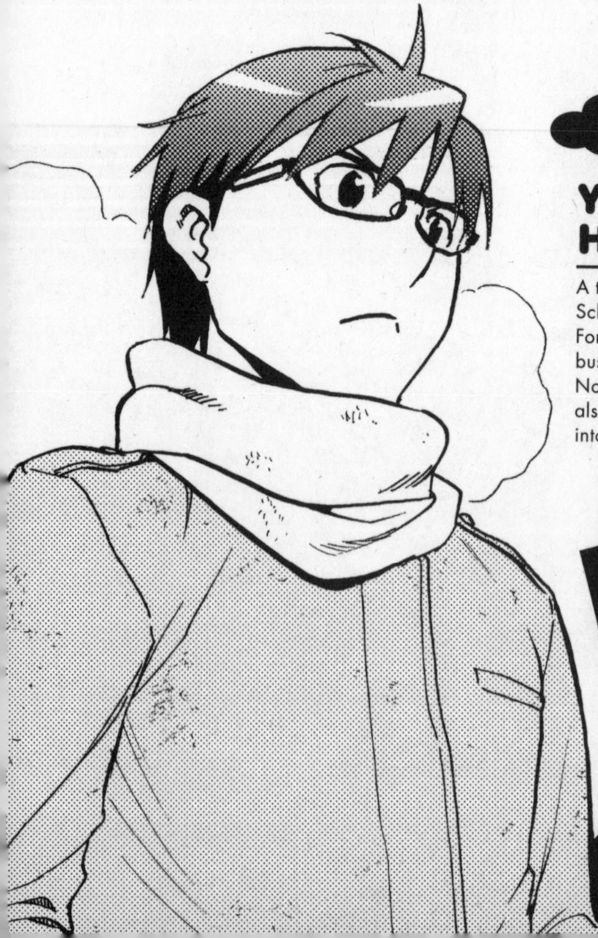

## YUUGO HACHIKEN

A third-year student at Ooezo Agricultural High School, enrolled in the Dairy Science Program. Former Equestrian Club vice president. Started a business with funds saved up from part-time jobs. Now he's raising and selling pasture pigs while also cramming for his last-minute decision to get into Ooezo University of Animal Husbandry.

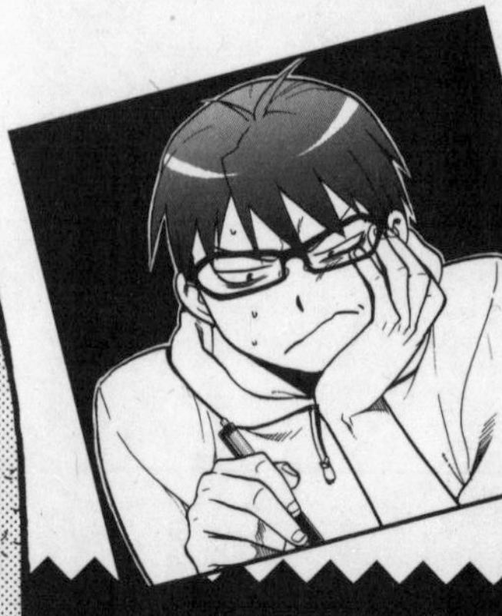

## SHINNOSUKE AIKAWA

A third-year student at Ooezo Agricultural High School, enrolled in the Dairy Science Program. To reach his goal of becoming a veterinarian, he aspires to be accepted at Ooezo University of Animal Husbandry.

## SHINEI OOKAWA

A graduate of Ooezo Agricultural High School. He hadn't found permanent employment at the time of his graduation, but he has since started a company with Hachiken and become its president.

# The Story Thus Far:

Hachiken and his classmates' final year of high school is approaching its end, and their time at Ooezo Agricultural High School is now almost over. Mikage has passed her Ooezo University of Animal Husbandry recommendation exam and is one step closer to her dream, thanks in part to Hachiken's support over the last three years. Now Hachiken and Mikage can finally relax and enjoy some time together as a couple...or so they thought. This time, it's Hachiken who's applying to Ooezo U at the presidential orders of Ookawa-senpai! Can Hachiken overcome the exam and father traumas that originally drove him to enroll at Ezo Ag...!? Meanwhile, in a land far away, what kind of future does Komaba see as he scrimps and saves for a war chest of his own...?

## AYAME MINAMIKUJOU

Aki's childhood friend. Has resolved to get into college to compete with her. Hachiken's older brother, Shingo, is now overseeing her college prep.

CONTENTS

Silver Spoon

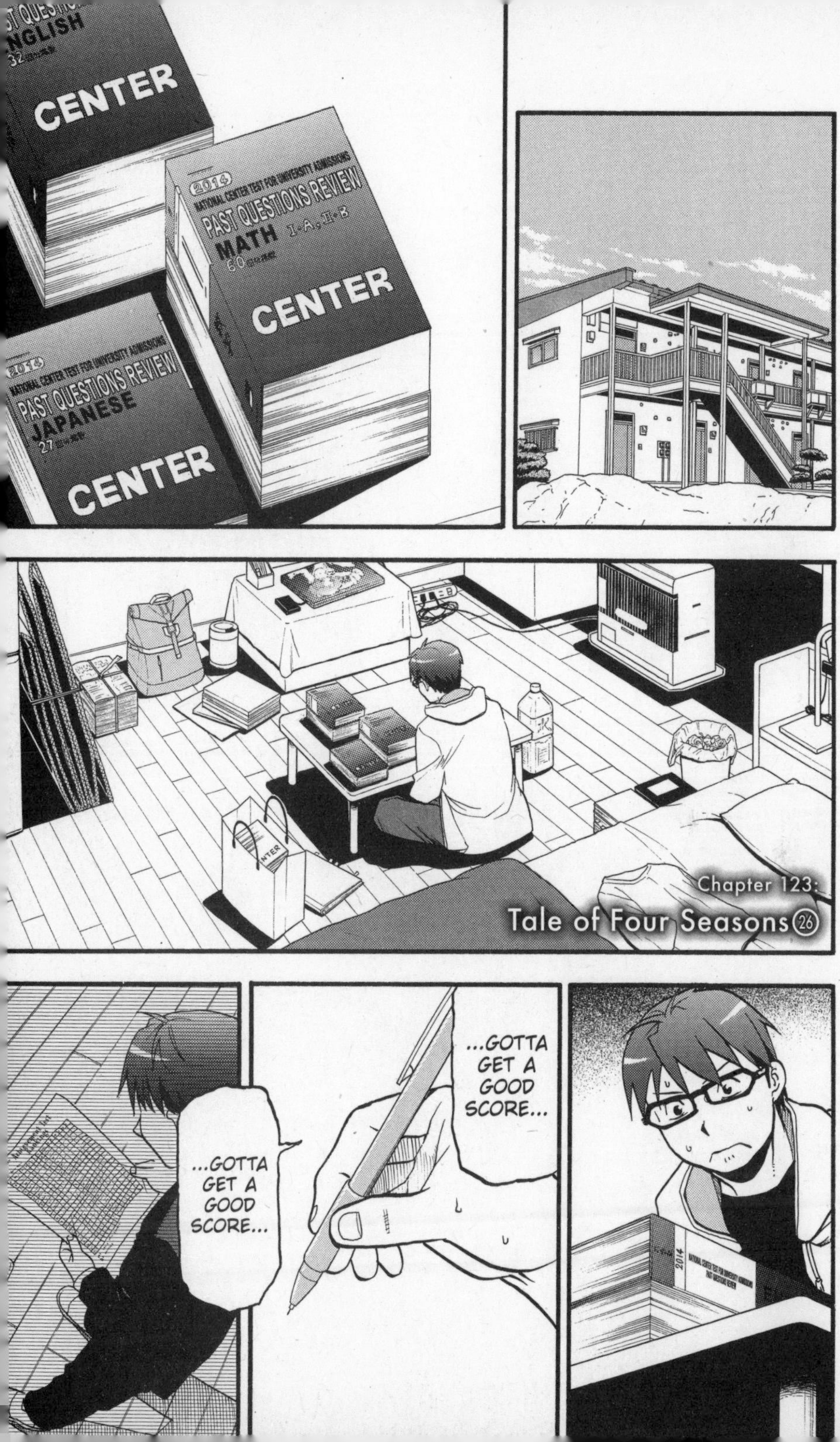
ENGLISH
CENTER
2014
NATIONAL CENTER TEST FOR UNIVERSITY ADMISSIONS
PAST QUESTIONS REVIEW
MATH I·A, II·B
CENTER
2014
NATIONAL CENTER TEST FOR UNIVERSITY ADMISSIONS
PAST QUESTIONS REVIEW
JAPANESE
CENTER
Chapter 123:
Tale of Four Seasons ㉖
...GOTTA GET A GOOD SCORE...
...GOTTA GET A GOOD SCORE...

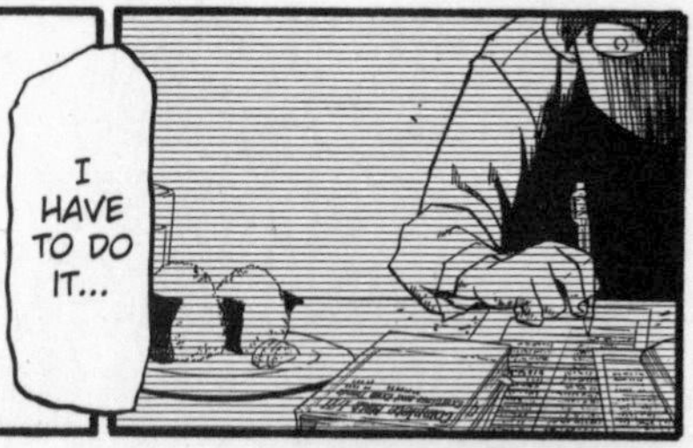
I HAVE TO DO IT...

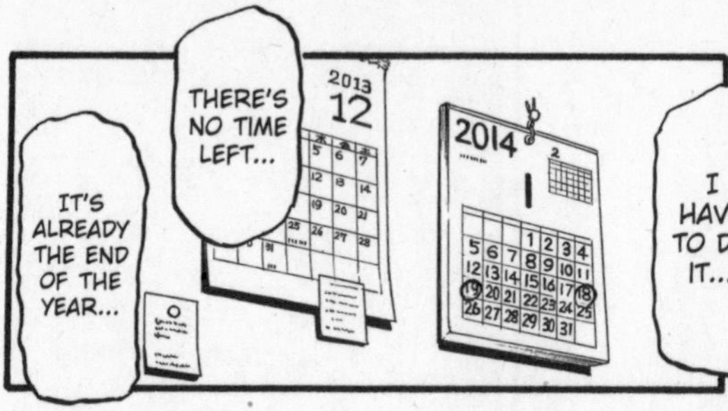
THERE'S NO TIME LEFT...
IT'S ALREADY THE END OF THE YEAR...
2013
12
2014
1

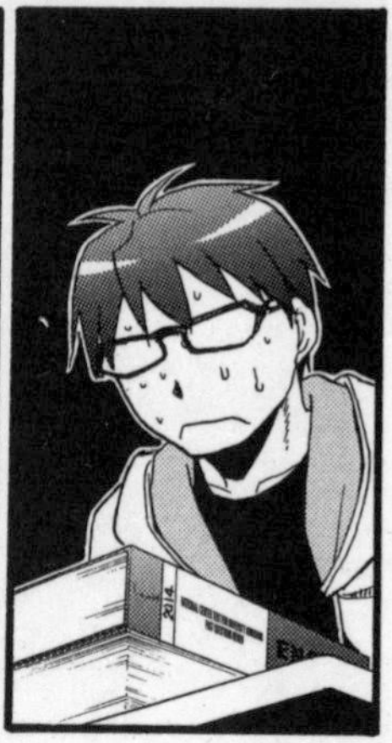

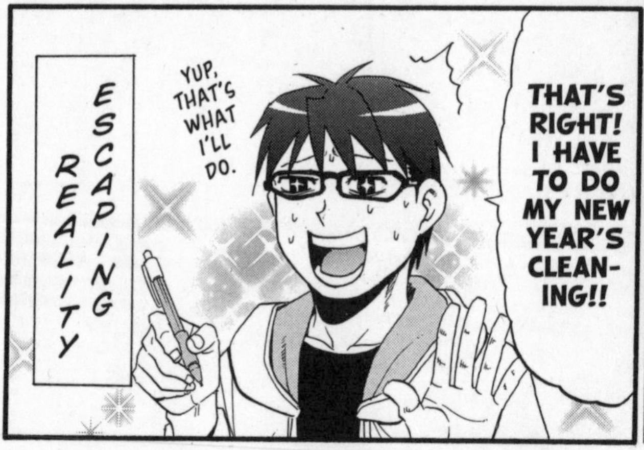
THAT'S RIGHT! I HAVE TO DO MY NEW YEAR'S CLEANING!!
YUP, THAT'S WHAT I'LL DO.
ESCAPING REALITY

## Chapter 123:

# Tale of Four Seasons ㉖

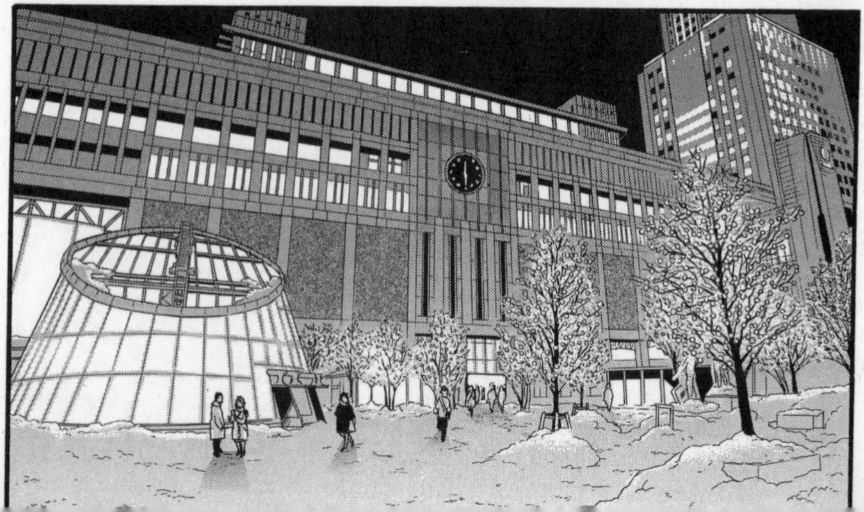

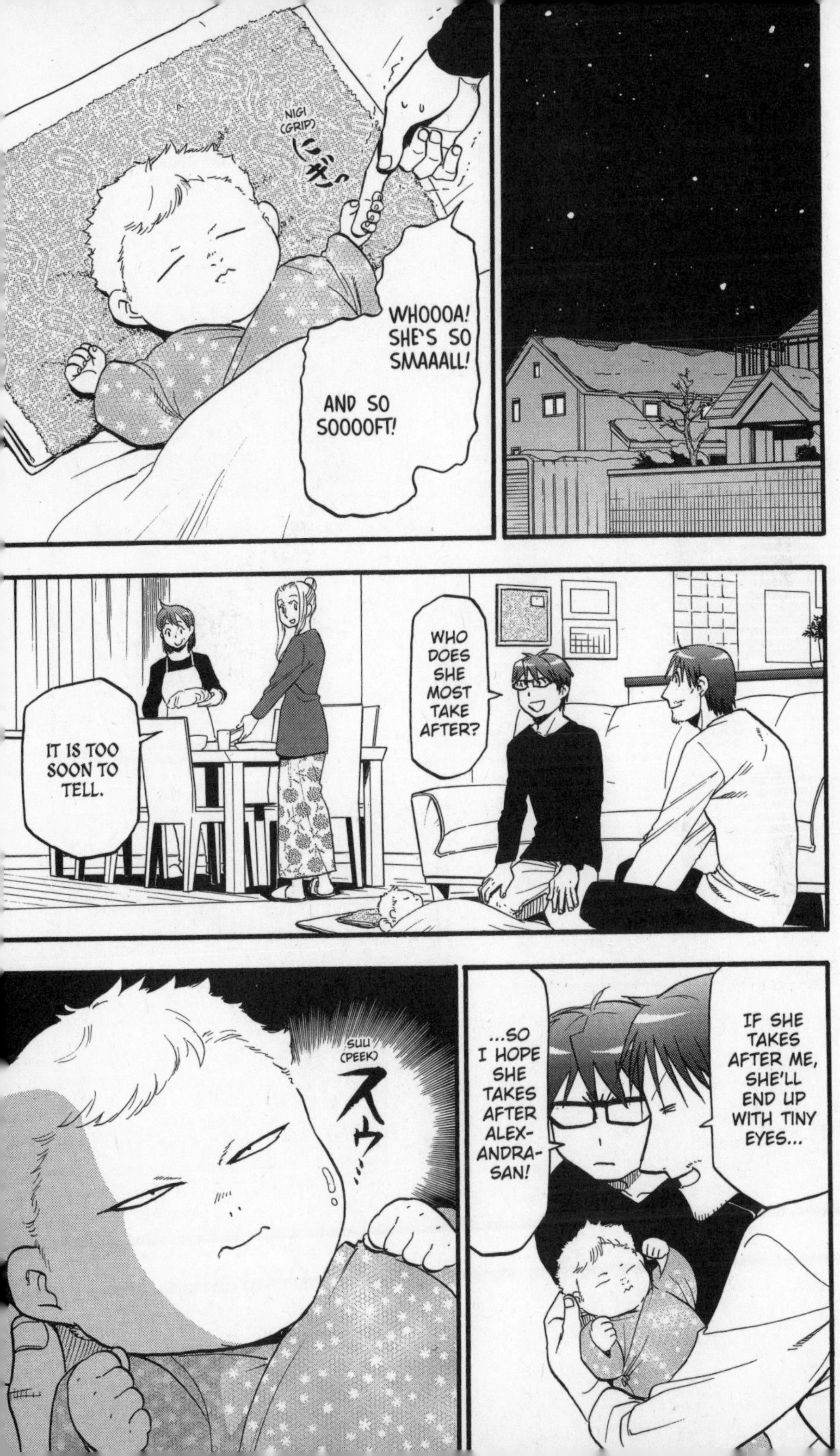
NIGI (GRIP)
WHOOOA! SHE'S SO SMAAALL!
AND SO SOOOOFT!
WHO DOES SHE MOST TAKE AFTER?
IT IS TOO SOON TO TELL.
IF SHE TAKES AFTER ME, SHE'LL END UP WITH TINY EYES...
...SO I HOPE SHE TAKES AFTER ALEX-ANDRA-SAN!
SUU (PEEK)

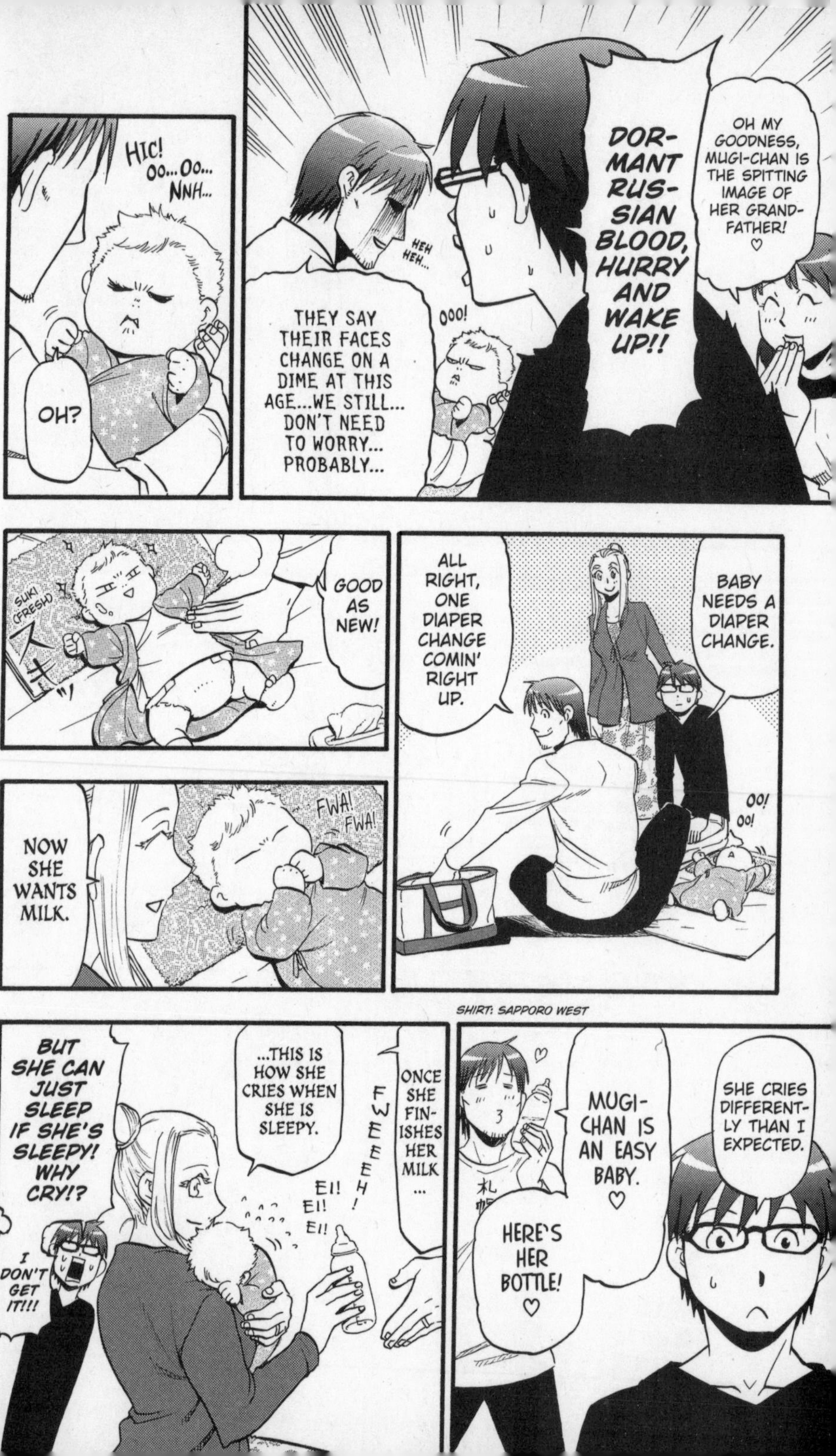
OH MY GOODNESS, MUGI-CHAN IS THE SPITTING IMAGE OF HER GRANDFATHER! ♡
DORMANT RUSSIAN BLOOD, HURRY AND WAKE UP!!
HEH HEH...
OOO!
THEY SAY THEIR FACES CHANGE ON A DIME AT THIS AGE...WE STILL... DON'T NEED TO WORRY... PROBABLY...
HIC! OO...OO... NNH...
OH?
BABY NEEDS A DIAPER CHANGE.
ALL RIGHT, ONE DIAPER CHANGE COMIN' RIGHT UP.
OO! OO!
GOOD AS NEW!
SUKI (FRESH)
FWA! FWA!
NOW SHE WANTS MILK.
SHIRT: SAPPORO WEST
SHE CRIES DIFFERENTLY THAN I EXPECTED.
MUGI-CHAN IS AN EASY BABY. ♡
HERE'S HER BOTTLE! ♡
ONCE SHE FINISHES HER MILK...
...THIS IS HOW SHE CRIES WHEN SHE IS SLEEPY.
FWEEEEH!
EI! EI! EI!
BUT SHE CAN JUST SLEEP IF SHE'S SLEEPY! WHY CRY!?
I DON'T GET IT!!!

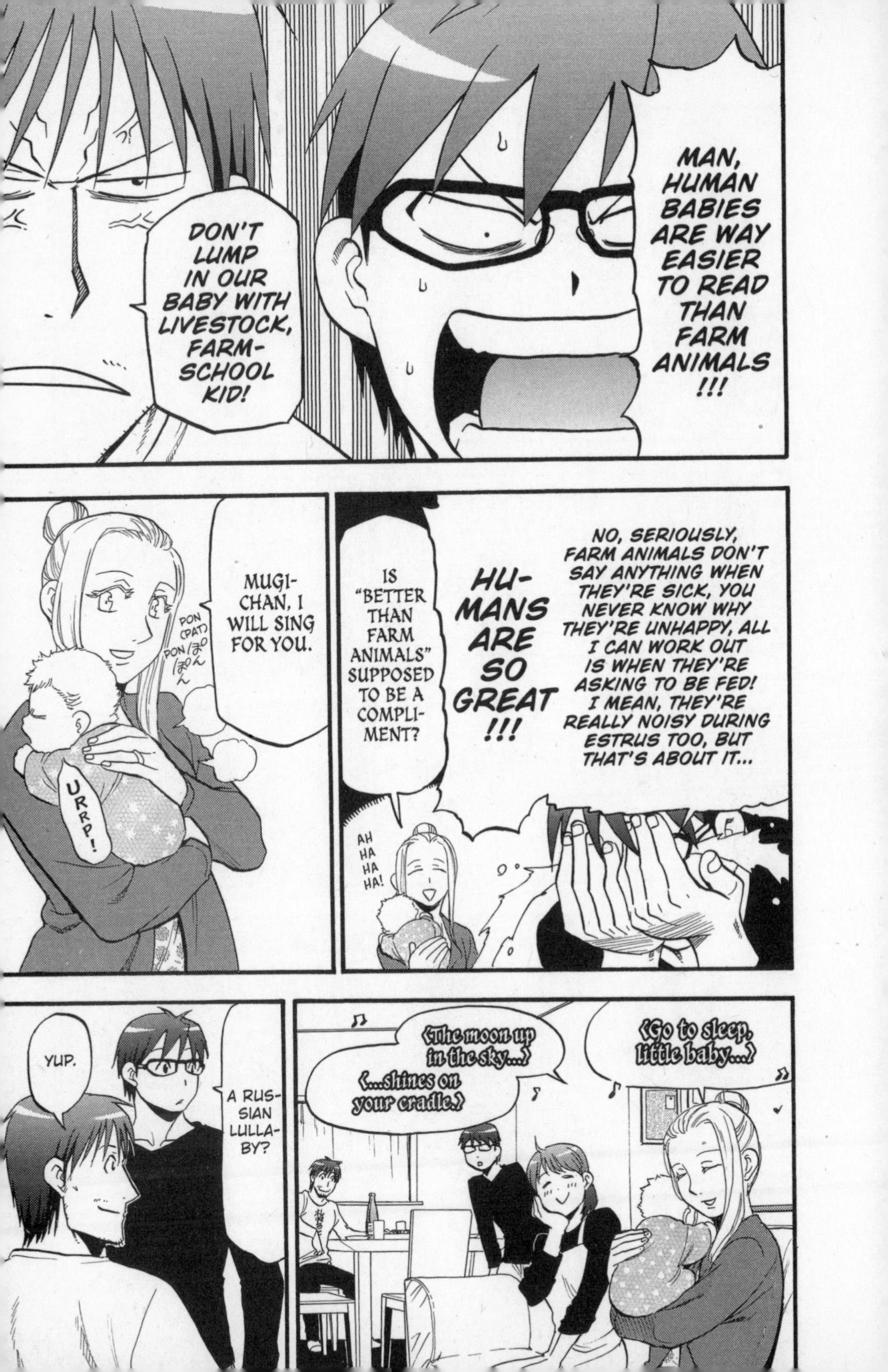
MAN, HUMAN BABIES ARE WAY EASIER TO READ THAN FARM ANIMALS!!!
DON'T LUMP IN OUR BABY WITH LIVESTOCK, FARM-SCHOOL KID!
NO, SERIOUSLY, FARM ANIMALS DON'T SAY ANYTHING WHEN THEY'RE SICK, YOU NEVER KNOW WHY THEY'RE UNHAPPY, ALL I CAN WORK OUT IS WHEN THEY'RE ASKING TO BE FED! I MEAN, THEY'RE REALLY NOISY DURING ESTRUS TOO, BUT THAT'S ABOUT IT...
HU-MANS ARE SO GREAT!!!
IS "BETTER THAN FARM ANIMALS" SUPPOSED TO BE A COMPLI-MENT?
AH HA HA HA HA!
MUGI-CHAN, I WILL SING FOR YOU.
PON (PAT) PON ぽん ぽん
URRP!
‹Go to sleep, little baby...›
‹The moon up in the sky...›
‹...shines on your cradle.›
A RUS-SIAN LULLA-BY?
YUP.

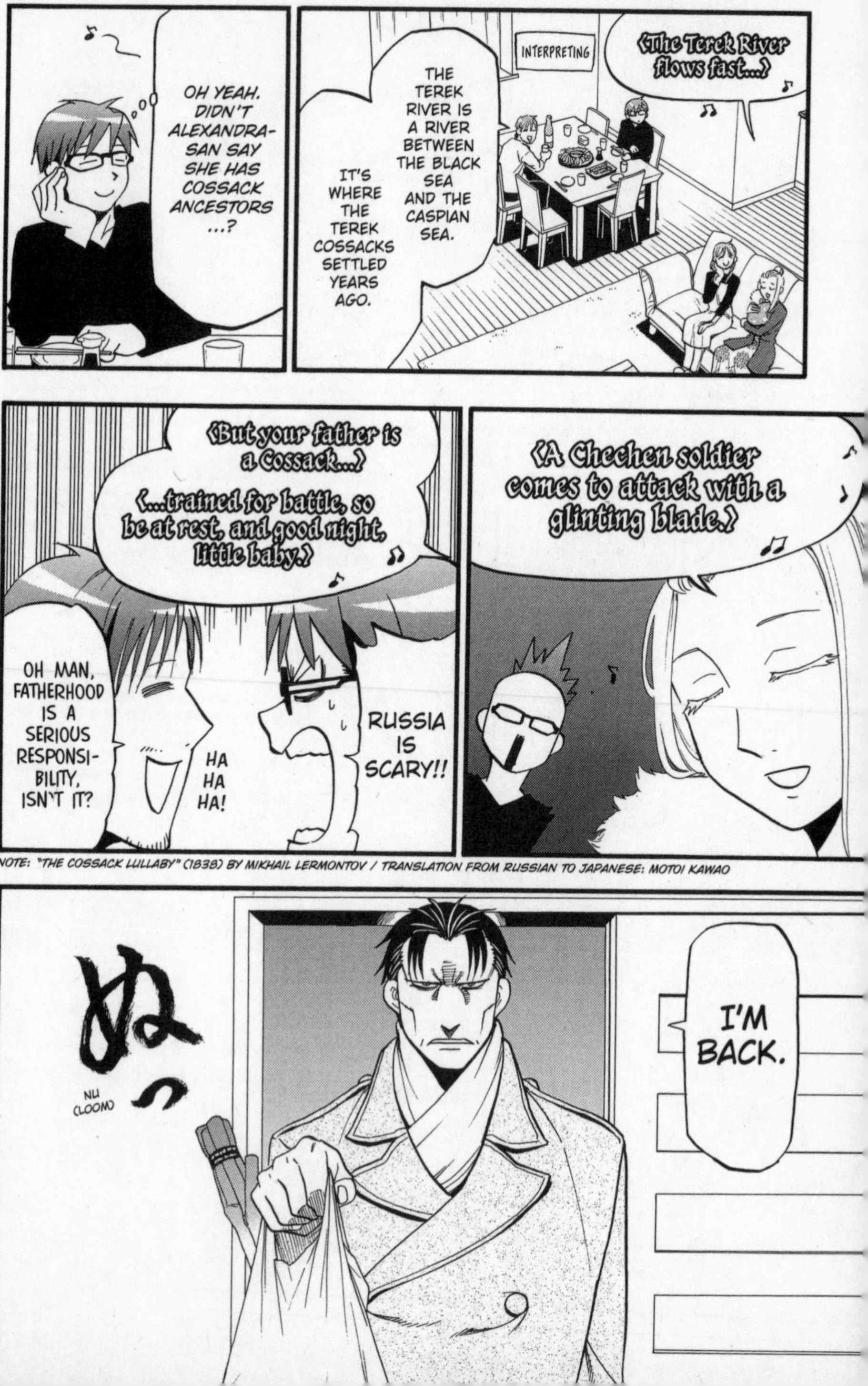
‹The Terek River flows fast...›
INTERPRETING
THE TEREK RIVER IS A RIVER BETWEEN THE BLACK SEA AND THE CASPIAN SEA.
IT'S WHERE THE TEREK COSSACKS SETTLED YEARS AGO.
OH YEAH. DIDN'T ALEXANDRA-SAN SAY SHE HAS COSSACK ANCESTORS ...?
‹A Chechen soldier comes to attack with a glinting blade.›
‹But your father is a Cossack...›
‹...trained for battle, so be at rest, and good night, little baby.›
RUSSIA IS SCARY!!
HA HA HA!
OH MAN, FATHERHOOD IS A SERIOUS RESPONSI-BILITY, ISN'T IT?
I'M BACK.
ぬっ
NU (LOOM)

NOTE: "THE COSSACK LULLABY" (1838) BY MIKHAIL LERMONTOV / TRANSLATION FROM RUSSIAN TO JAPANESE: MOTOI KAWAO

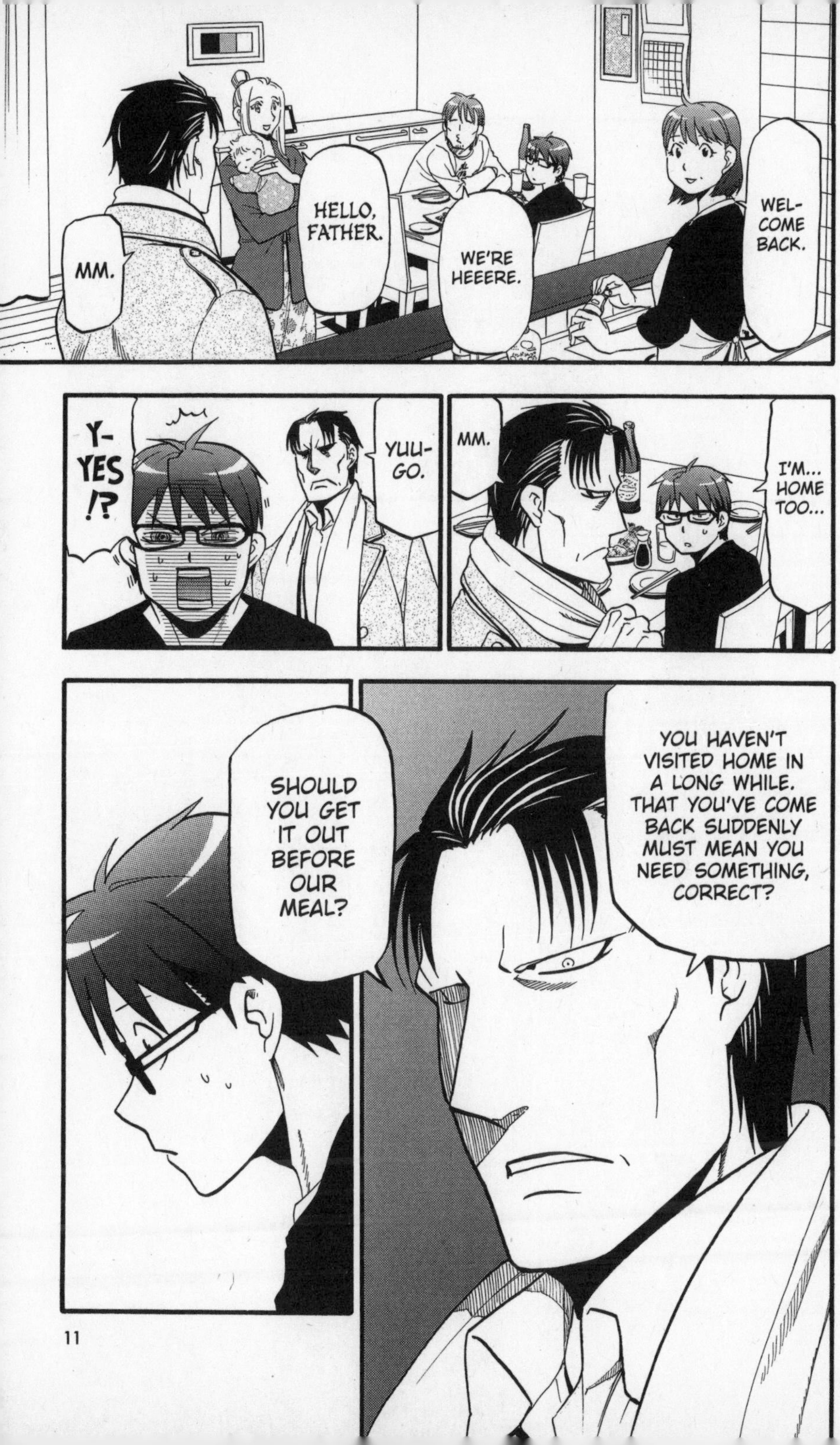
WEL-COME BACK.
WE'RE HEEERE.
HELLO, FATHER.
MM.
I'M... HOME TOO...
MM.
YUU-GO.
Y-YES!?
YOU HAVEN'T VISITED HOME IN A LONG WHILE. THAT YOU'VE COME BACK SUDDENLY MUST MEAN YOU NEED SOMETHING, CORRECT?
SHOULD YOU GET IT OUT BEFORE OUR MEAL?

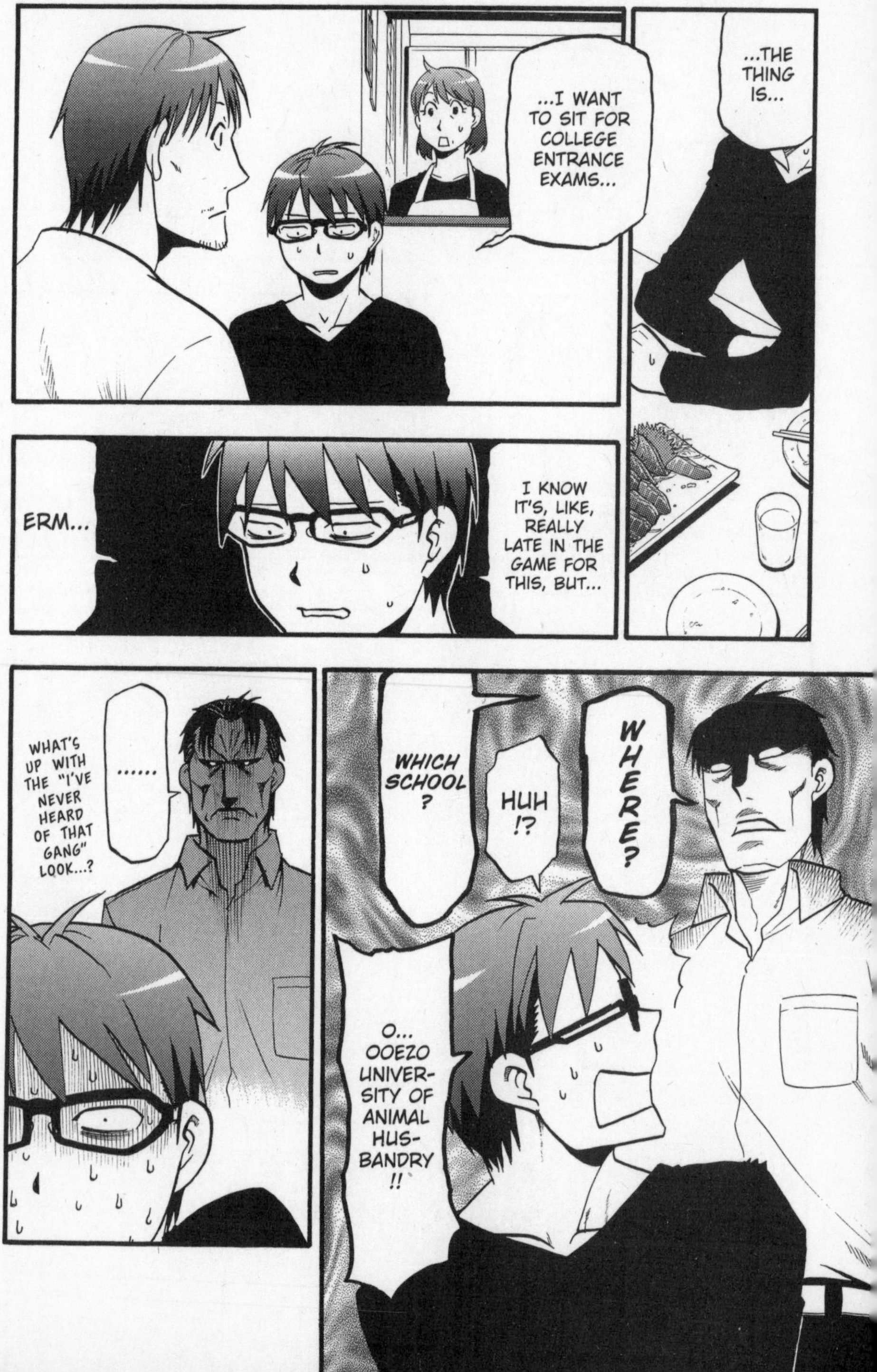
...THE THING IS...
...I WANT TO SIT FOR COLLEGE ENTRANCE EXAMS...
I KNOW IT'S, LIKE, REALLY LATE IN THE GAME FOR THIS, BUT...
ERM...
WHERE?
HUH!?
WHICH SCHOOL?
O... OOEZO UNIVERSITY OF ANIMAL HUS-BANDRY!!
......
WHAT'S UP WITH THE "I'VE NEVER HEARD OF THAT GANG" LOOK...?

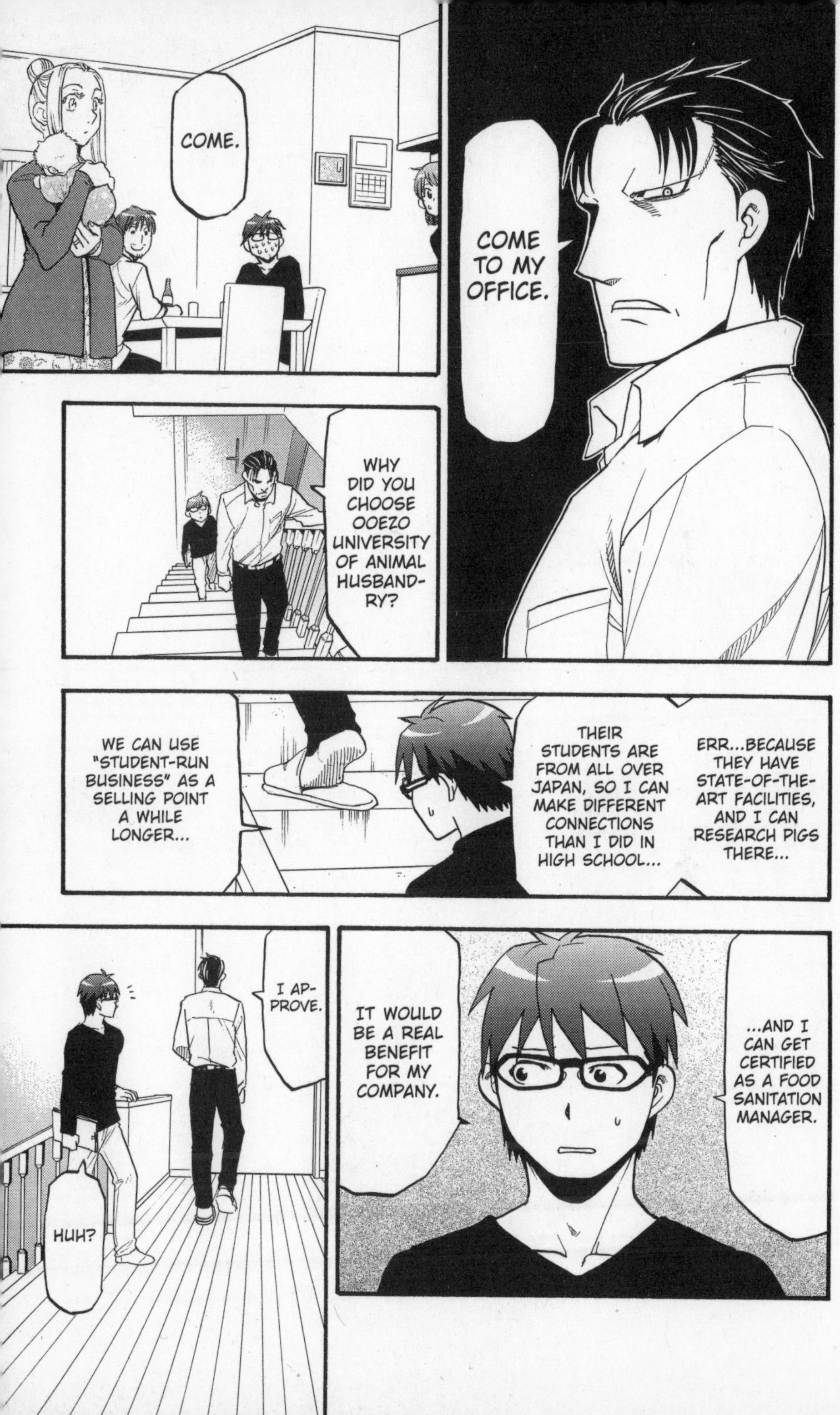
COME TO MY OFFICE.
COME.
WHY DID YOU CHOOSE OOEZO UNIVERSITY OF ANIMAL HUSBANDRY?
ERR...BECAUSE THEY HAVE STATE-OF-THE-ART FACILITIES, AND I CAN RESEARCH PIGS THERE...
THEIR STUDENTS ARE FROM ALL OVER JAPAN, SO I CAN MAKE DIFFERENT CONNECTIONS THAN I DID IN HIGH SCHOOL...
WE CAN USE "STUDENT-RUN BUSINESS" AS A SELLING POINT A WHILE LONGER...
...AND I CAN GET CERTIFIED AS A FOOD SANITATION MANAGER.
IT WOULD BE A REAL BENEFIT FOR MY COMPANY.
I AP-PROVE.
HUH?

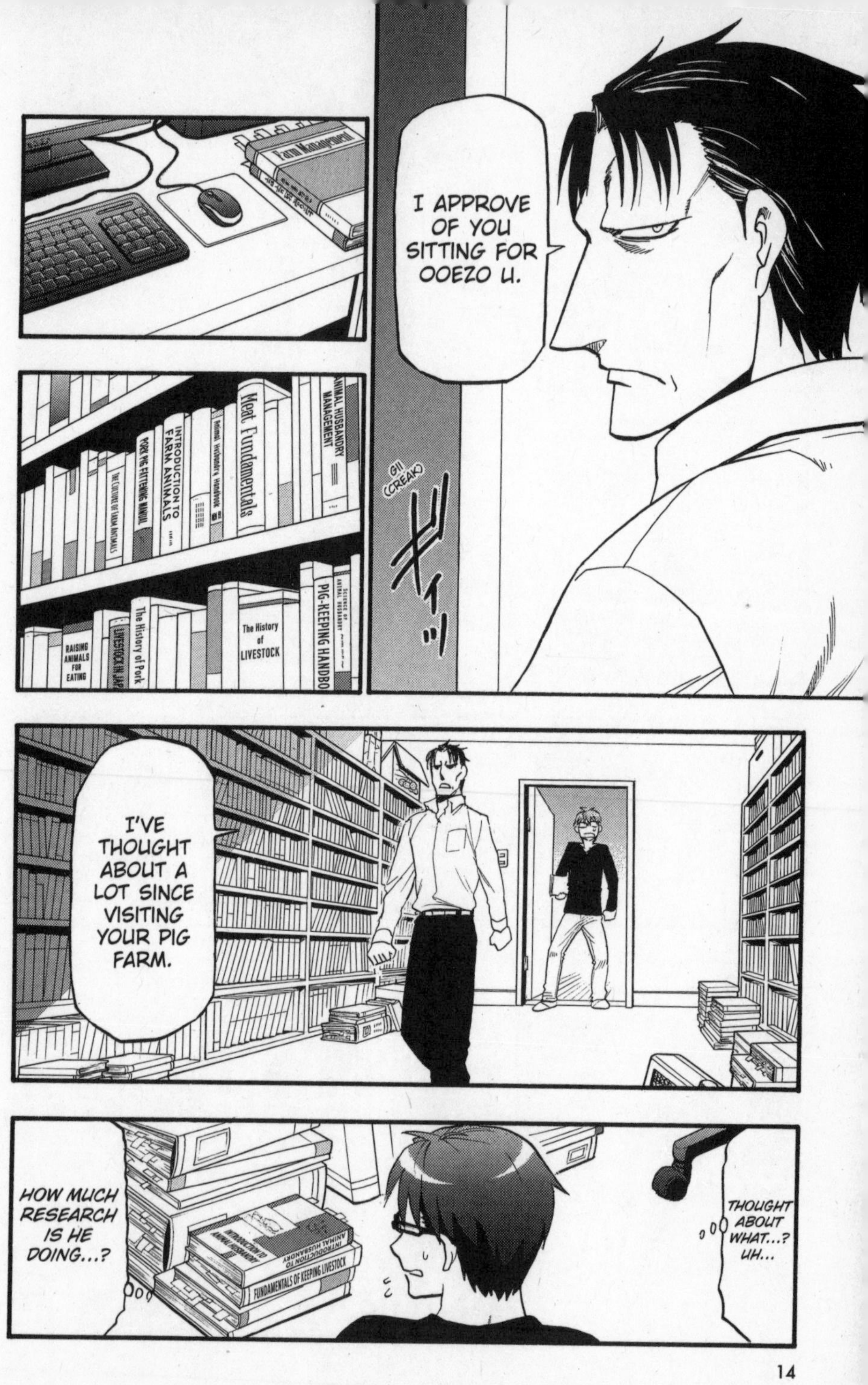
I APPROVE OF YOU SITTING FOR OOEZO U.
GII (CREAK)
Farm Management
ANIMAL HUSBANDRY MANAGEMENT
Meat Fundamentals
Animal Husbandry's Handbook
INTRODUCTION TO FARM ANIMALS
PORK PIG FATTENING MANUAL
THE CULTURE OF FARM ANIMALS
SCIENCE OF ANIMAL HUSBANDRY
PIG-KEEPING HANDBO
The History of LIVESTOCK
The History of Pork
LIVESTOCK IN JAP
RAISING ANIMALS FOR EATING
I'VE THOUGHT ABOUT A LOT SINCE VISITING YOUR PIG FARM.
THOUGHT ABOUT WHAT...? UH...
HOW MUCH RESEARCH IS HE DOING...?
INTRODUCTION TO ANIMAL HUSBANDRY
FUNDAMENTALS OF KEEPING LIVESTOCK

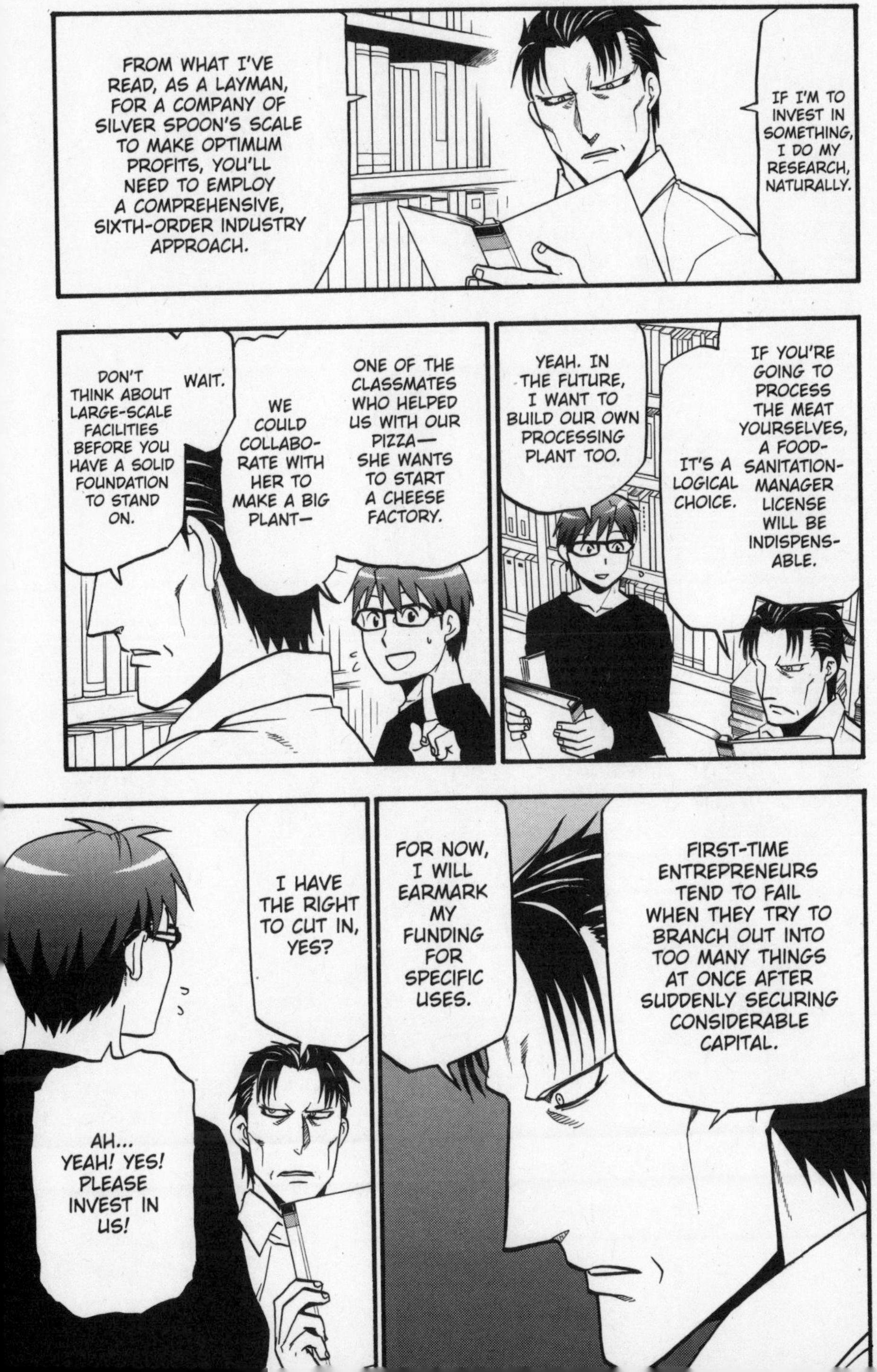
IF I'M TO INVEST IN SOMETHING, I DO MY RESEARCH, NATURALLY.
FROM WHAT I'VE READ, AS A LAYMAN, FOR A COMPANY OF SILVER SPOON'S SCALE TO MAKE OPTIMUM PROFITS, YOU'LL NEED TO EMPLOY A COMPREHENSIVE, SIXTH-ORDER INDUSTRY APPROACH.
IF YOU'RE GOING TO PROCESS THE MEAT YOURSELVES, A FOOD-SANITATION-MANAGER LICENSE WILL BE INDISPENS-ABLE.
IT'S A LOGICAL CHOICE.
YEAH. IN THE FUTURE, I WANT TO BUILD OUR OWN PROCESSING PLANT TOO.
ONE OF THE CLASSMATES WHO HELPED US WITH OUR PIZZA— SHE WANTS TO START A CHEESE FACTORY.
WE COULD COLLABO-RATE WITH HER TO MAKE A BIG PLANT—
WAIT.
DON'T THINK ABOUT LARGE-SCALE FACILITIES BEFORE YOU HAVE A SOLID FOUNDATION TO STAND ON.
FIRST-TIME ENTREPRENEURS TEND TO FAIL WHEN THEY TRY TO BRANCH OUT INTO TOO MANY THINGS AT ONCE AFTER SUDDENLY SECURING CONSIDERABLE CAPITAL.
FOR NOW, I WILL EARMARK MY FUNDING FOR SPECIFIC USES.
I HAVE THE RIGHT TO CUT IN, YES?
AH... YEAH! YES! PLEASE INVEST IN US!

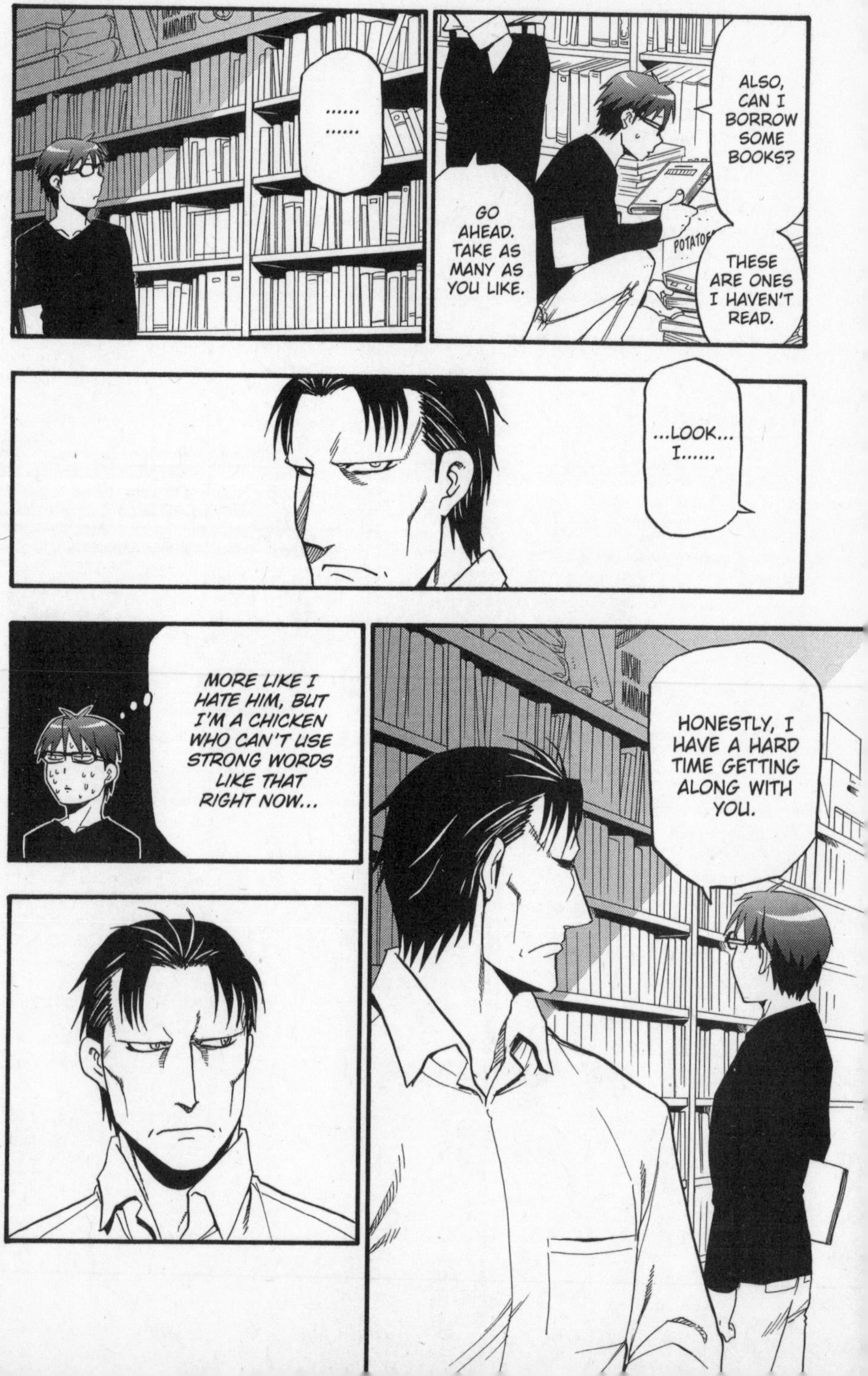
ALSO, CAN I BORROW SOME BOOKS?
THESE ARE ONES I HAVEN'T READ.
GO AHEAD. TAKE AS MANY AS YOU LIKE.
...... ......
...LOOK... I......
HONESTLY, I HAVE A HARD TIME GETTING ALONG WITH YOU.
MORE LIKE I HATE HIM, BUT I'M A CHICKEN WHO CAN'T USE STRONG WORDS LIKE THAT RIGHT NOW...

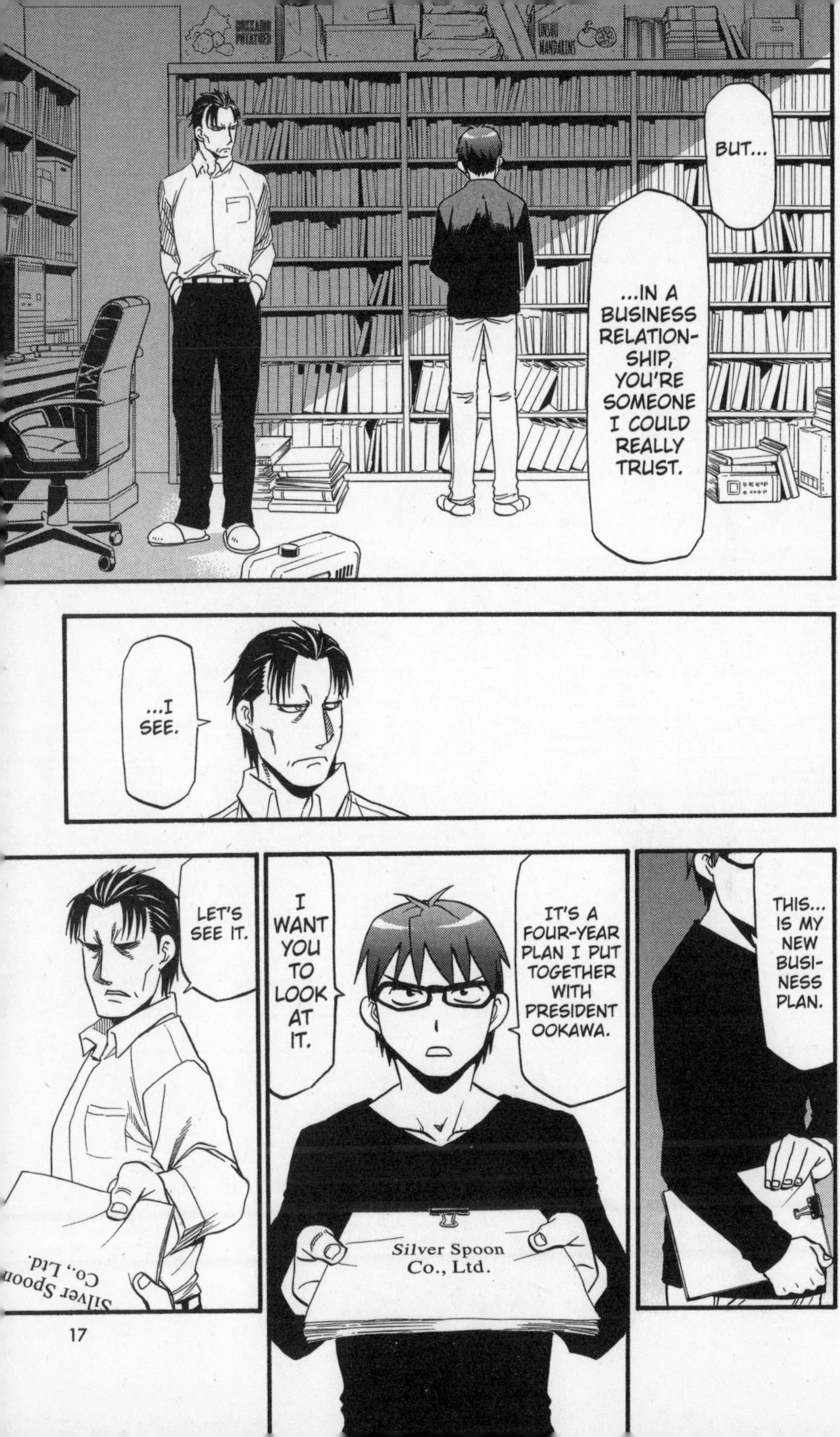
BUT...
...IN A BUSINESS RELATION-SHIP, YOU'RE SOMEONE I COULD REALLY TRUST.
...I SEE.
THIS... IS MY NEW BUSI-NESS PLAN.
IT'S A FOUR-YEAR PLAN I PUT TOGETHER WITH PRESIDENT OOKAWA.
Silver Spoon Co., Ltd.
I WANT YOU TO LOOK AT IT.
LET'S SEE IT.
Silver Spoon Co., Ltd.

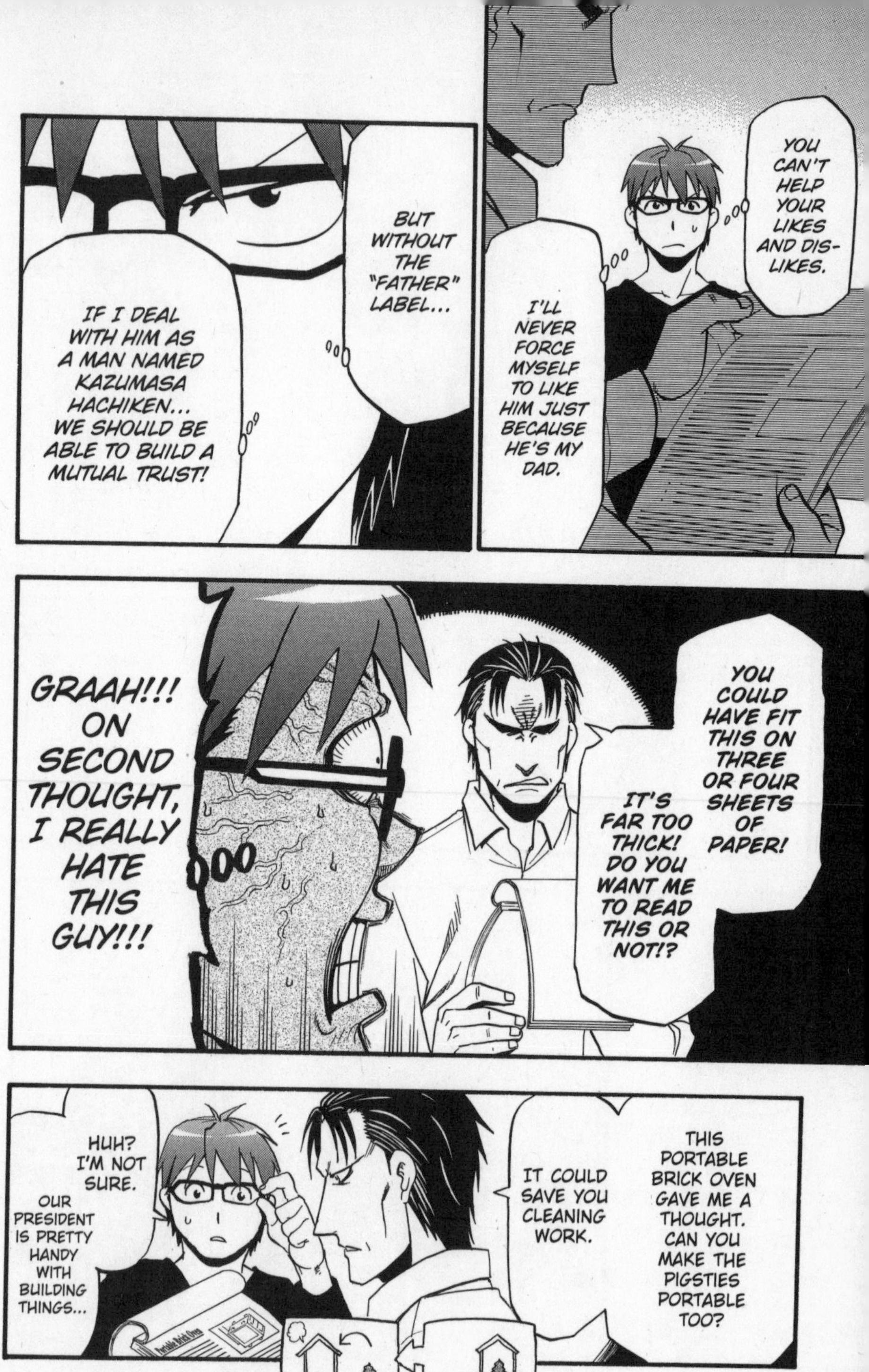
YOU CAN'T HELP YOUR LIKES AND DIS-LIKES.
I'LL NEVER FORCE MYSELF TO LIKE HIM JUST BECAUSE HE'S MY DAD.
BUT WITHOUT THE "FATHER" LABEL...
IF I DEAL WITH HIM AS A MAN NAMED KAZUMASA HACHIKEN... WE SHOULD BE ABLE TO BUILD A MUTUAL TRUST!
YOU COULD HAVE FIT THIS ON THREE OR FOUR SHEETS OF PAPER!
IT'S FAR TOO THICK! DO YOU WANT ME TO READ THIS OR NOT!?
GRAAH!!! ON SECOND THOUGHT, I REALLY HATE THIS GUY!!!
THIS PORTABLE BRICK OVEN GAVE ME A THOUGHT. CAN YOU MAKE THE PIGSTIES PORTABLE TOO?
IT COULD SAVE YOU CLEANING WORK.
HUH? I'M NOT SURE.
OUR PRESIDENT IS PRETTY HANDY WITH BUILDING THINGS...

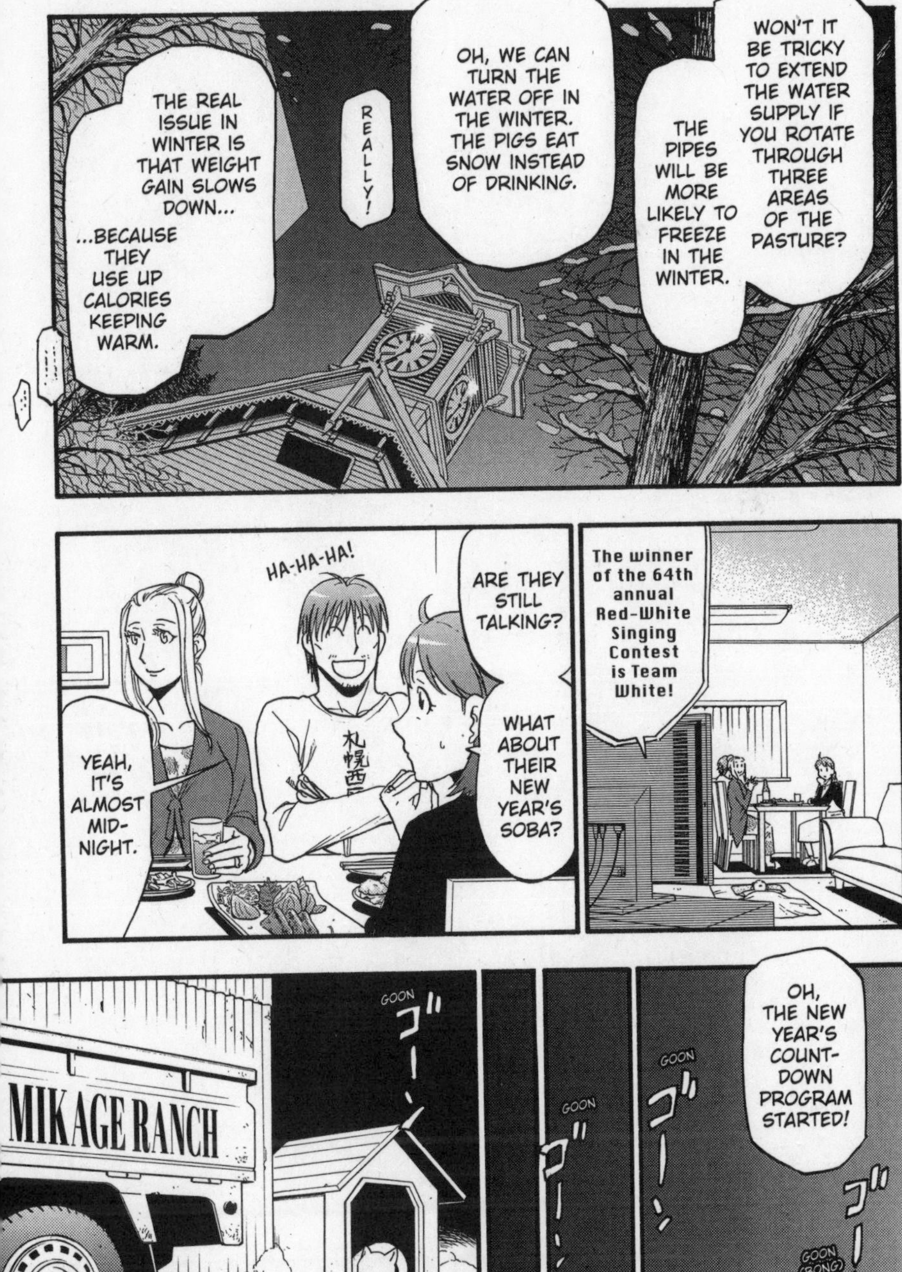
WON'T IT BE TRICKY TO EXTEND THE WATER SUPPLY IF YOU ROTATE THROUGH THREE AREAS OF THE PASTURE?
THE PIPES WILL BE MORE LIKELY TO FREEZE IN THE WINTER.
OH, WE CAN TURN THE WATER OFF IN THE WINTER. THE PIGS EAT SNOW INSTEAD OF DRINKING.
REALLY!
THE REAL ISSUE IN WINTER IS THAT WEIGHT GAIN SLOWS DOWN...
...BECAUSE THEY USE UP CALORIES KEEPING WARM.
The winner of the 64th annual Red-White Singing Contest is Team White!
ARE THEY STILL TALKING?
HA-HA-HA!
WHAT ABOUT THEIR NEW YEAR'S SOBA?
YEAH, IT'S ALMOST MID-NIGHT.
OH, THE NEW YEAR'S COUNT-DOWN PROGRAM STARTED!
GOON (BONG)
GOON
GOON
GOON
MIKAGE RANCH

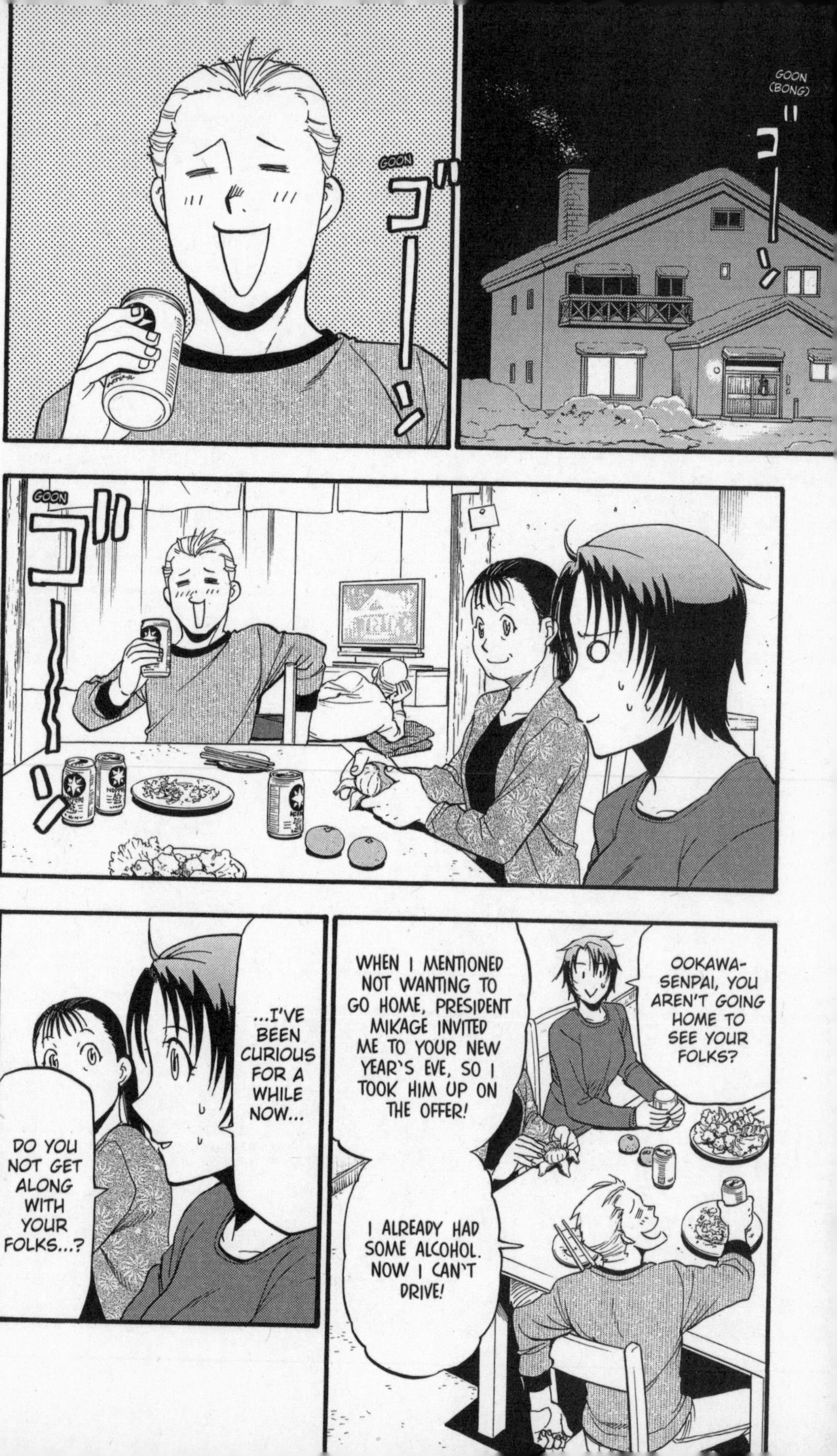
GOON (BONG)
GOON
GOON
OOKAWA-SENPAI, YOU AREN'T GOING HOME TO SEE YOUR FOLKS?
WHEN I MENTIONED NOT WANTING TO GO HOME, PRESIDENT MIKAGE INVITED ME TO YOUR NEW YEAR'S EVE, SO I TOOK HIM UP ON THE OFFER!
I ALREADY HAD SOME ALCOHOL. NOW I CAN'T DRIVE!
...I'VE BEEN CURIOUS FOR A WHILE NOW...
DO YOU NOT GET ALONG WITH YOUR FOLKS...?

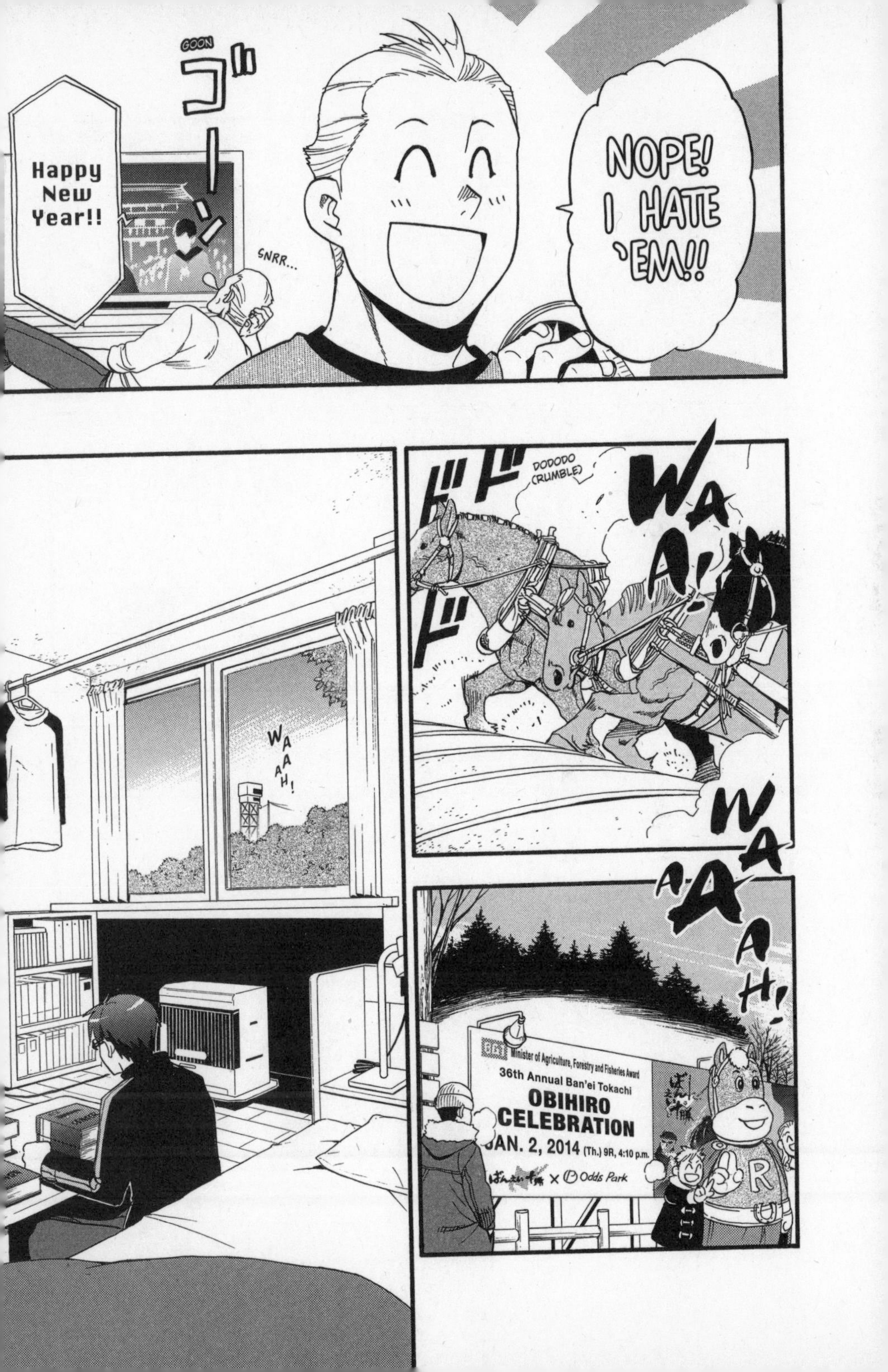
NOPE! I HATE 'EM!!
GOON
ゴーン
SNRR...
Happy New Year!!
DODODO (RUMBLE)
ドドド
WAA!
WAAAAAH!
Minister of Agriculture, Forestry and Fisheries Award
36th Annual Ban'ei Tokachi
OBIHIRO CELEBRATION
JAN. 2, 2014 (Th.) 9R, 4:10 p.m.
Odds Park
WAAAH!

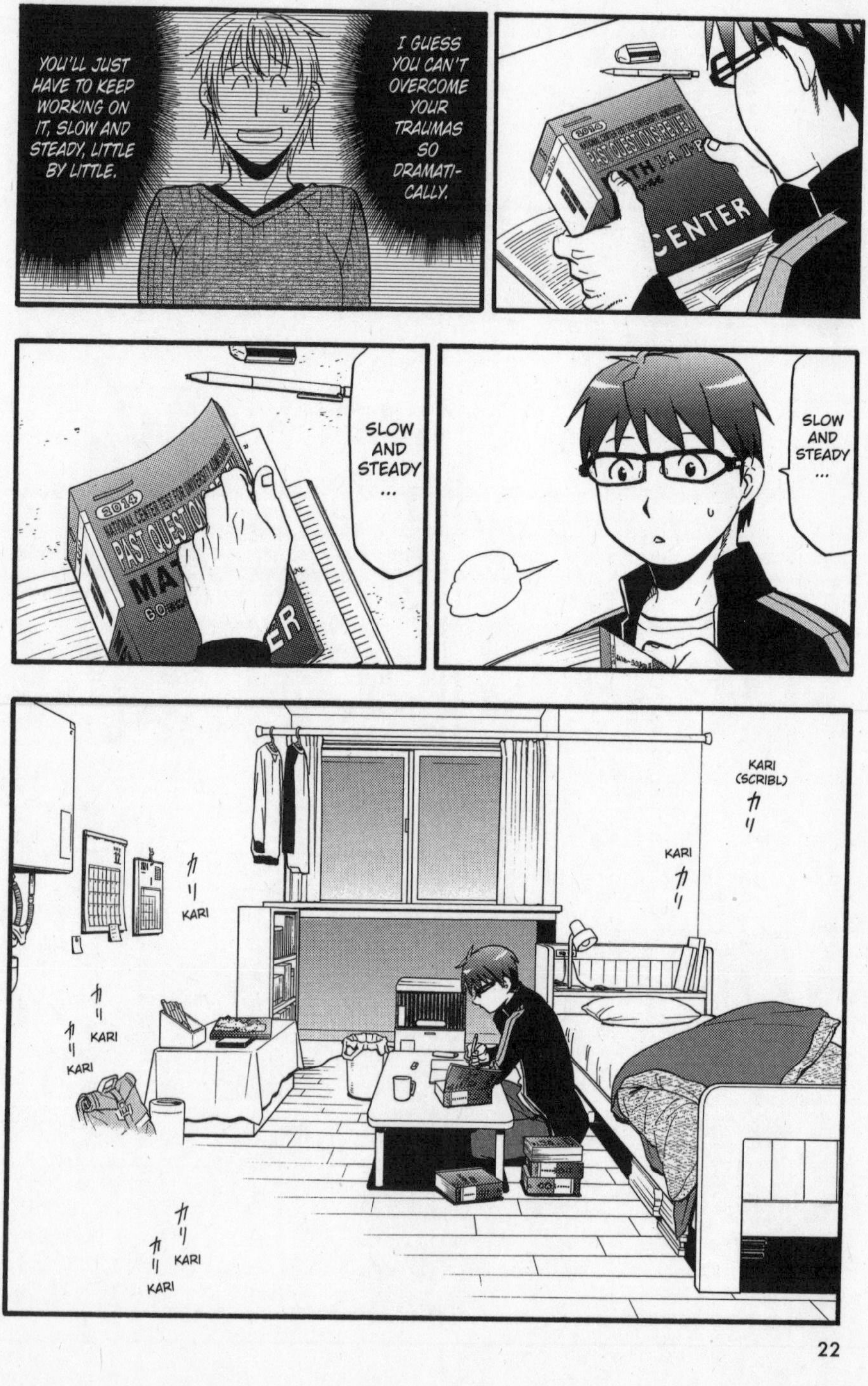
2014
CENTER
I GUESS YOU CAN'T OVERCOME YOUR TRAUMAS SO DRAMATICALLY.
YOU'LL JUST HAVE TO KEEP WORKING ON IT, SLOW AND STEADY, LITTLE BY LITTLE.
SLOW AND STEADY ...
2014
SLOW AND STEADY ...
カリ KARI (SCRIBL)
カリ KARI
カリ KARI
カリ KARI
カリ KARI
カリ KARI
カリ KARI

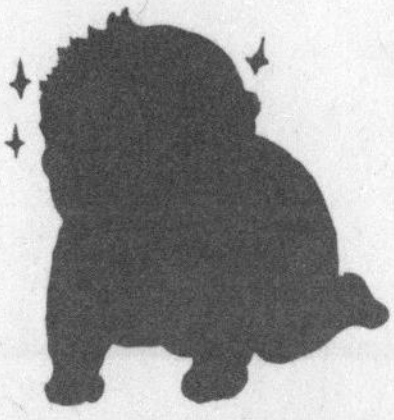

Silver Spoon

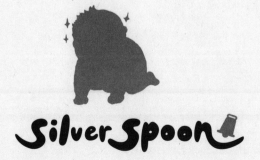

## THE EQUESTRIAN CLUB UNDERCLASSMAN

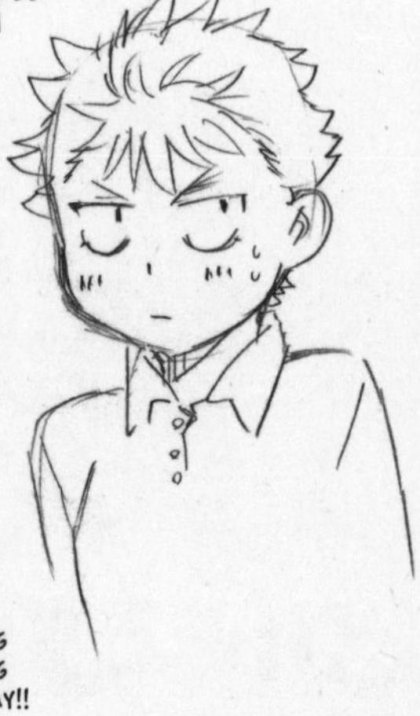

WHEN I WAS THINKING ABOUT WHAT TO NAME THIS CHARACTER, I GOT A LOT OF READER LETTERS SAYING, "ME TOO! I WAS ALSO A SHEEP WHO ENROLLED IN FARM SCHOOL AFTER READING THIS MANGA! I ALSO WENT THE EQUESTRIAN CLUB WAY, AND PEOPLE WARNED ME I DIDN'T KNOW WHAT I WAS GETTING INTO... BUT I'M DOING MY BEST!!"

AND I THOUGHT, "AH, I'M NOT GOING TO NAME HER."

THIS CHARACTER IS YOU, DOING YOUR BEST, WITHOUT WORRYING ABOUT WHAT OTHER PEOPLE SAY!!

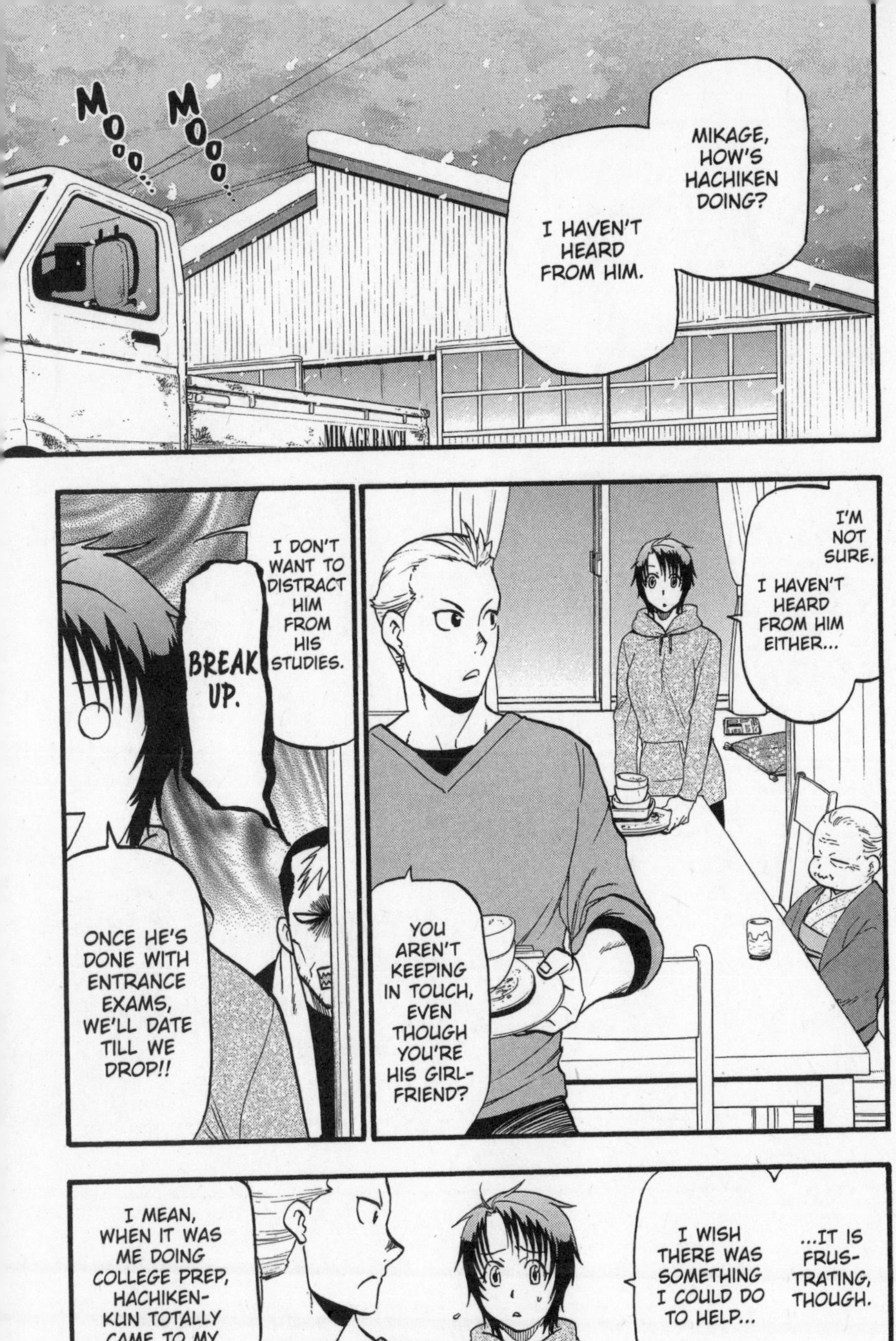
MOO...
MOO...
MIKAGE, HOW'S HACHIKEN DOING?
I HAVEN'T HEARD FROM HIM.
MIKAGE RANCH
I'M NOT SURE. I HAVEN'T HEARD FROM HIM EITHER...
YOU AREN'T KEEPING IN TOUCH, EVEN THOUGH YOU'RE HIS GIRL-FRIEND?
I DON'T WANT TO DISTRACT HIM FROM HIS STUDIES.
BREAK UP.
ONCE HE'S DONE WITH ENTRANCE EXAMS, WE'LL DATE TILL WE DROP!!
...IT IS FRUS-TRATING, THOUGH.
I WISH THERE WAS SOMETHING I COULD DO TO HELP...
I MEAN, WHEN IT WAS ME DOING COLLEGE PREP, HACHIKEN-KUN TOTALLY CAME TO MY RESCUE...

## Chapter 124:
## Tale of Four Seasons ㉗

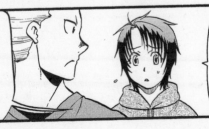

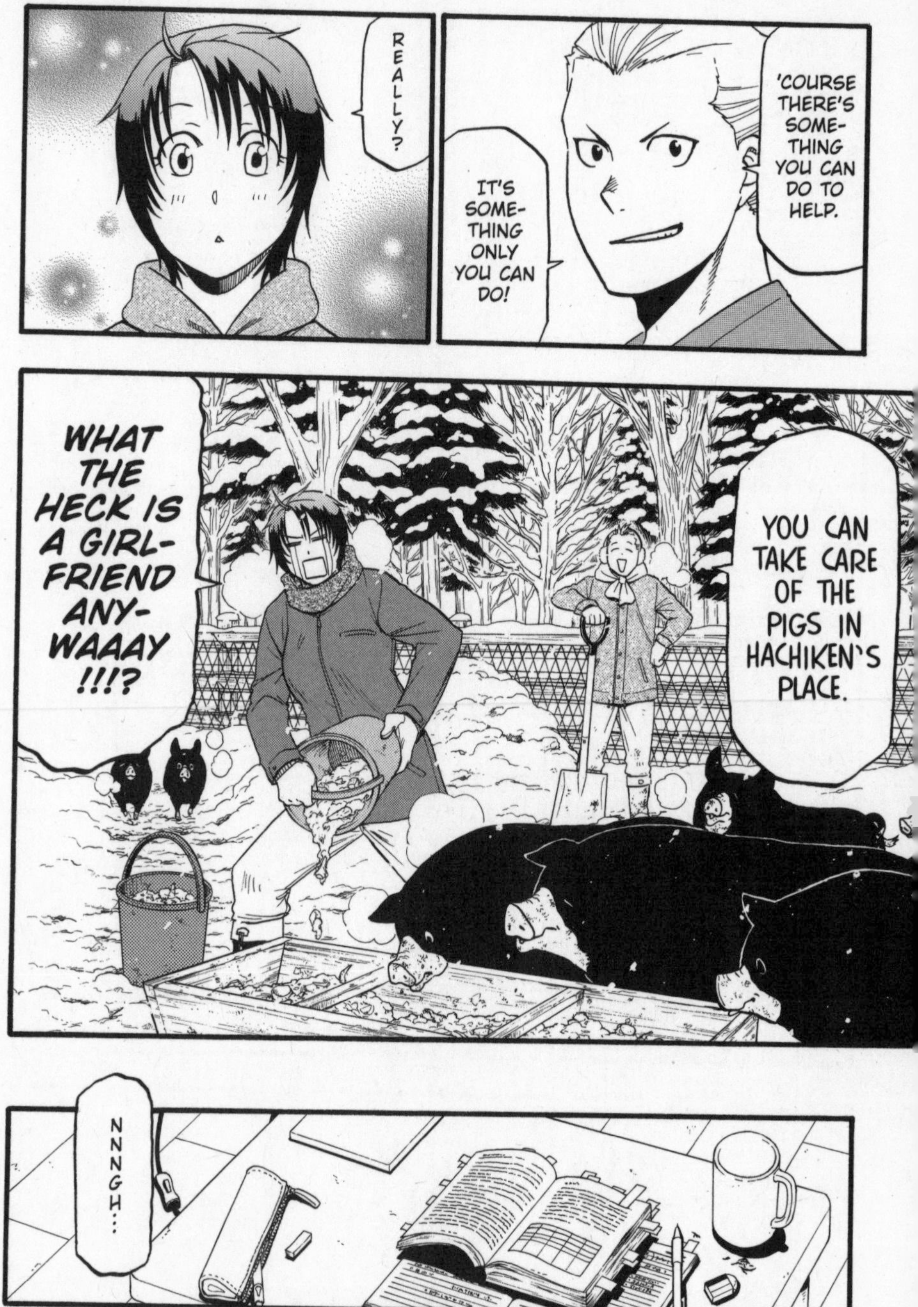
'COURSE THERE'S SOMETHING YOU CAN DO TO HELP.
IT'S SOMETHING ONLY YOU CAN DO!
REALLY?
YOU CAN TAKE CARE OF THE PIGS IN HACHIKEN'S PLACE.
WHAT THE HECK IS A GIRLFRIEND ANYWAAAY!!!?
NNNGH...

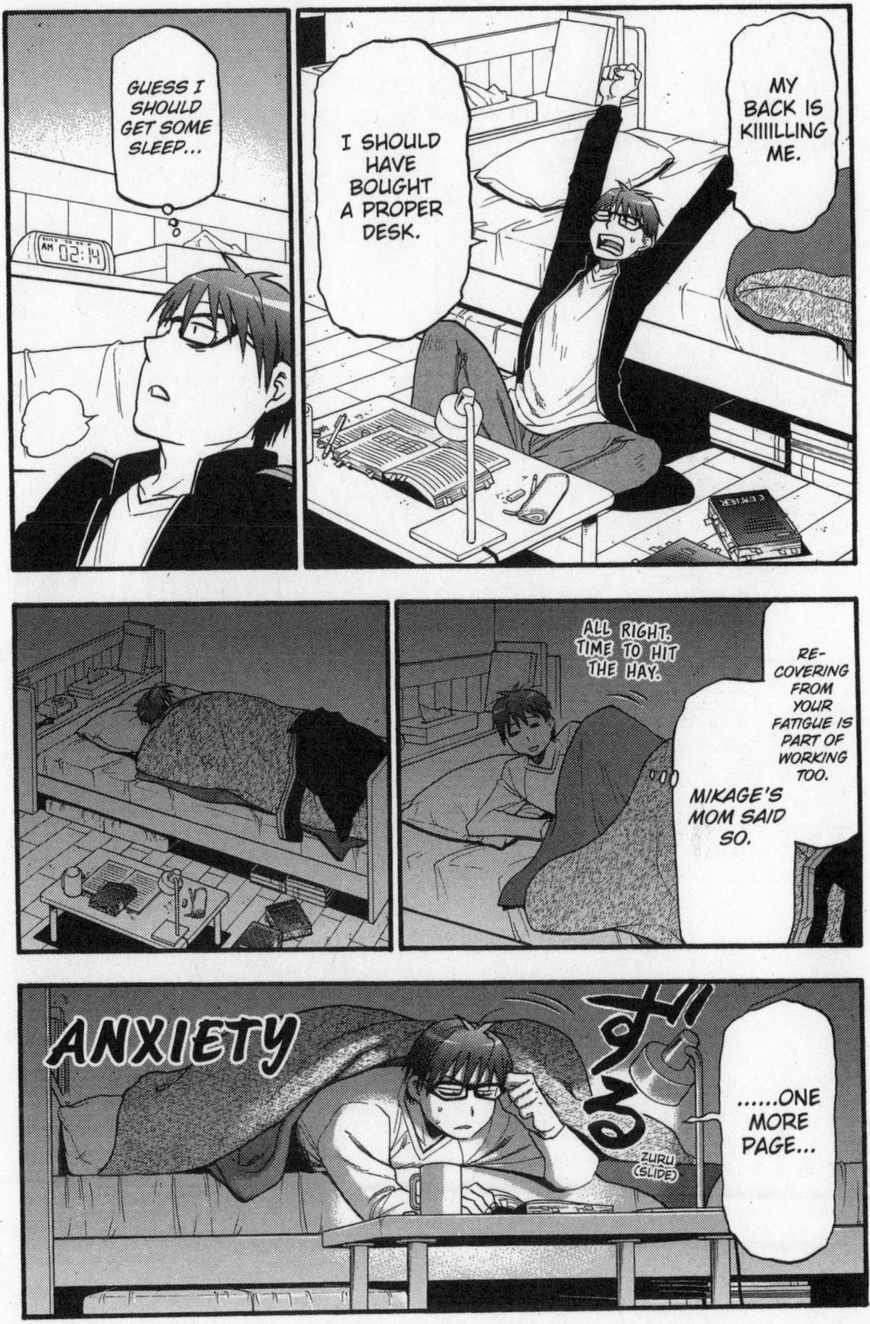
MY BACK IS KIIIILLING ME.
I SHOULD HAVE BOUGHT A PROPER DESK.
GUESS I SHOULD GET SOME SLEEP...
AM 02:14
ALL RIGHT. TIME TO HIT THE HAY.
RE-COVERING FROM YOUR FATIGUE IS PART OF WORKING TOO.
MIKAGE'S MOM SAID SO.
......ONE MORE PAGE...
ZURU (SLIDE)
ANXIETY

# Chapter 124: Tale of Four Seasons ㉗

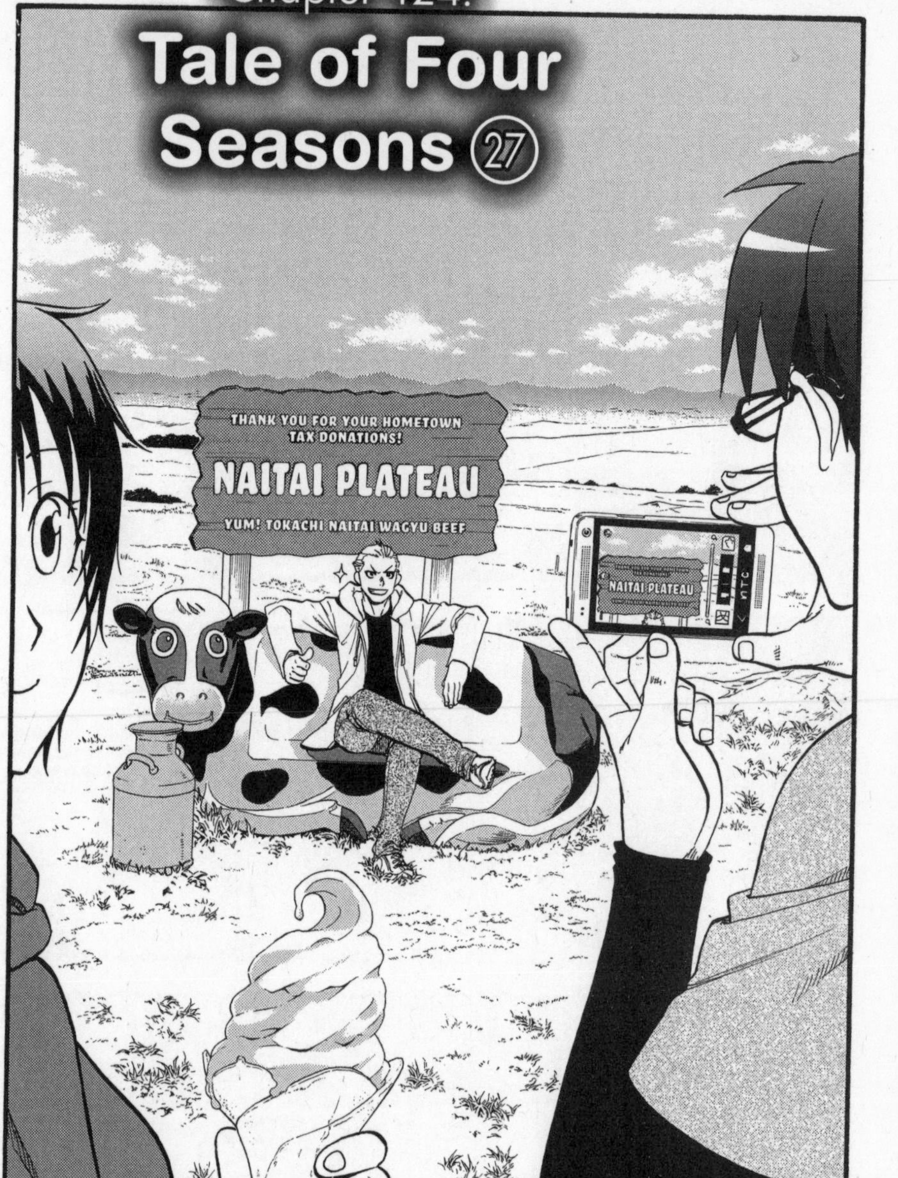
THANK YOU FOR YOUR HOMETOWN TAX DONATIONS!
NAITAI PLATEAU
YUM! TOKACHI NAITAI WAGYU BEEF
NAITAI PLATEAU
Ice Cream

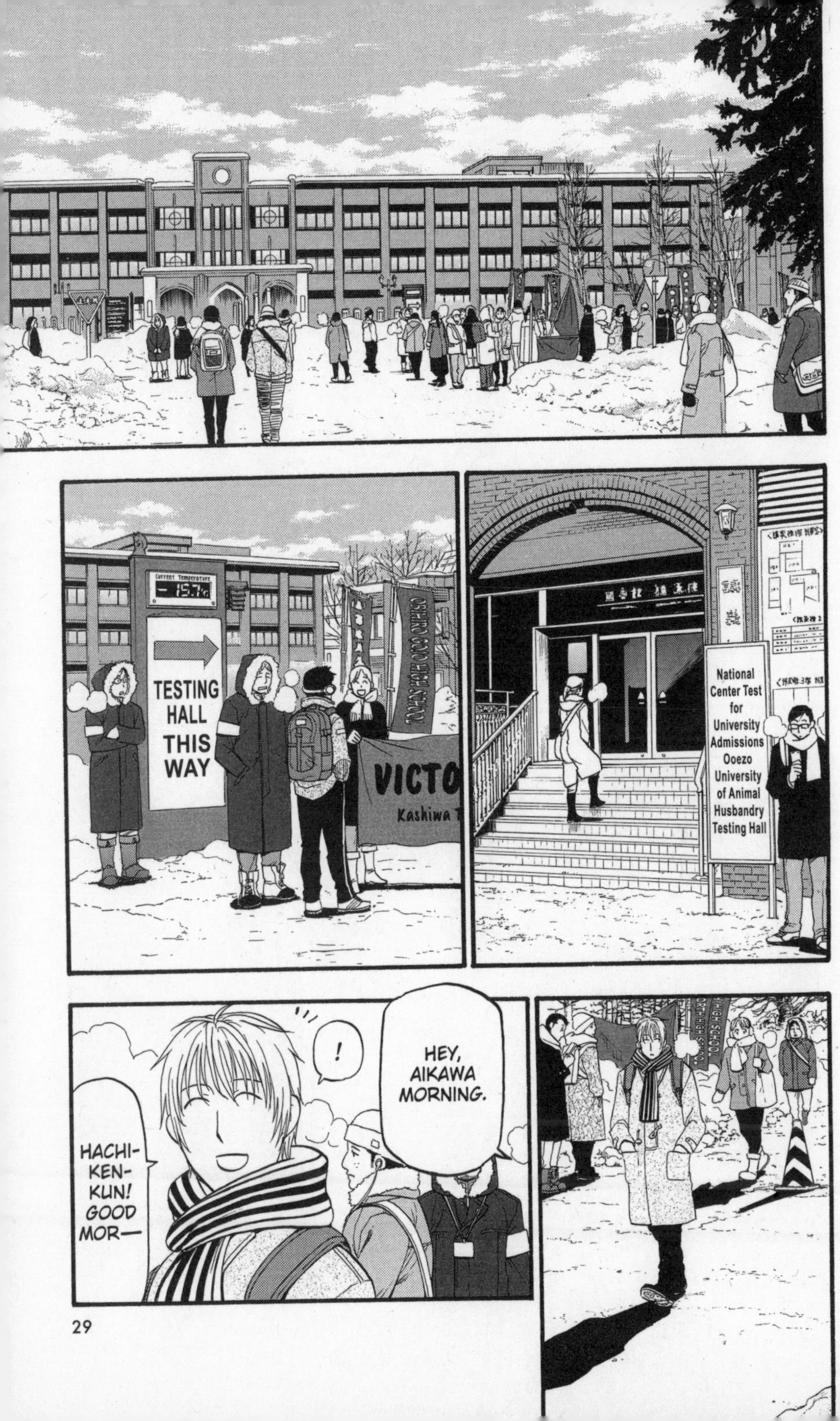
National
Center Test
for
University
Admissions
Ooezo
University
of Animal
Husbandry
Testing Hall
Current Temperature
-19.7°C
TESTING HALL THIS WAY
OSHIRO GOJO HIGH SCHOOL
VICTO
Kashiwa
HIGH SCHOOL
HEY, AIKAWA MORNING.
!
HACHI-KEN-KUN! GOOD MOR—

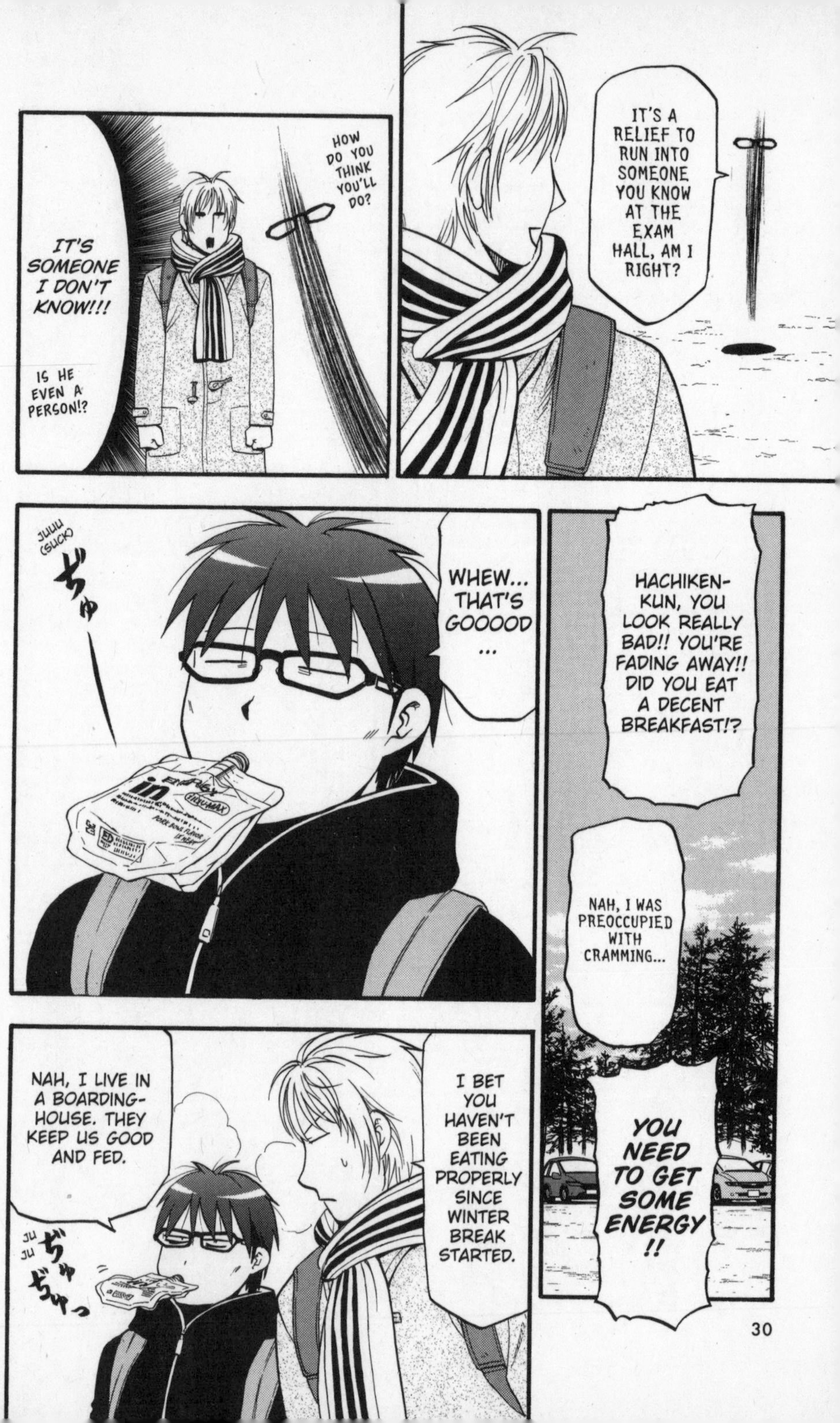
IT'S A RELIEF TO RUN INTO SOMEONE YOU KNOW AT THE EXAM HALL, AM I RIGHT?
HOW DO YOU THINK YOU'LL DO?
IT'S SOMEONE I DON'T KNOW!!!
IS HE EVEN A PERSON!?
HACHIKEN-KUN, YOU LOOK REALLY BAD!! YOU'RE FADING AWAY!! DID YOU EAT A DECENT BREAKFAST!?
NAH, I WAS PREOCCUPIED WITH CRAMMING...
YOU NEED TO GET SOME ENERGY!!
JUUU (SUCK)
WHEW... THAT'S GOOOOD...
I BET YOU HAVEN'T BEEN EATING PROPERLY SINCE WINTER BREAK STARTED.
NAH, I LIVE IN A BOARDING-HOUSE. THEY KEEP US GOOD AND FED.
JU JU

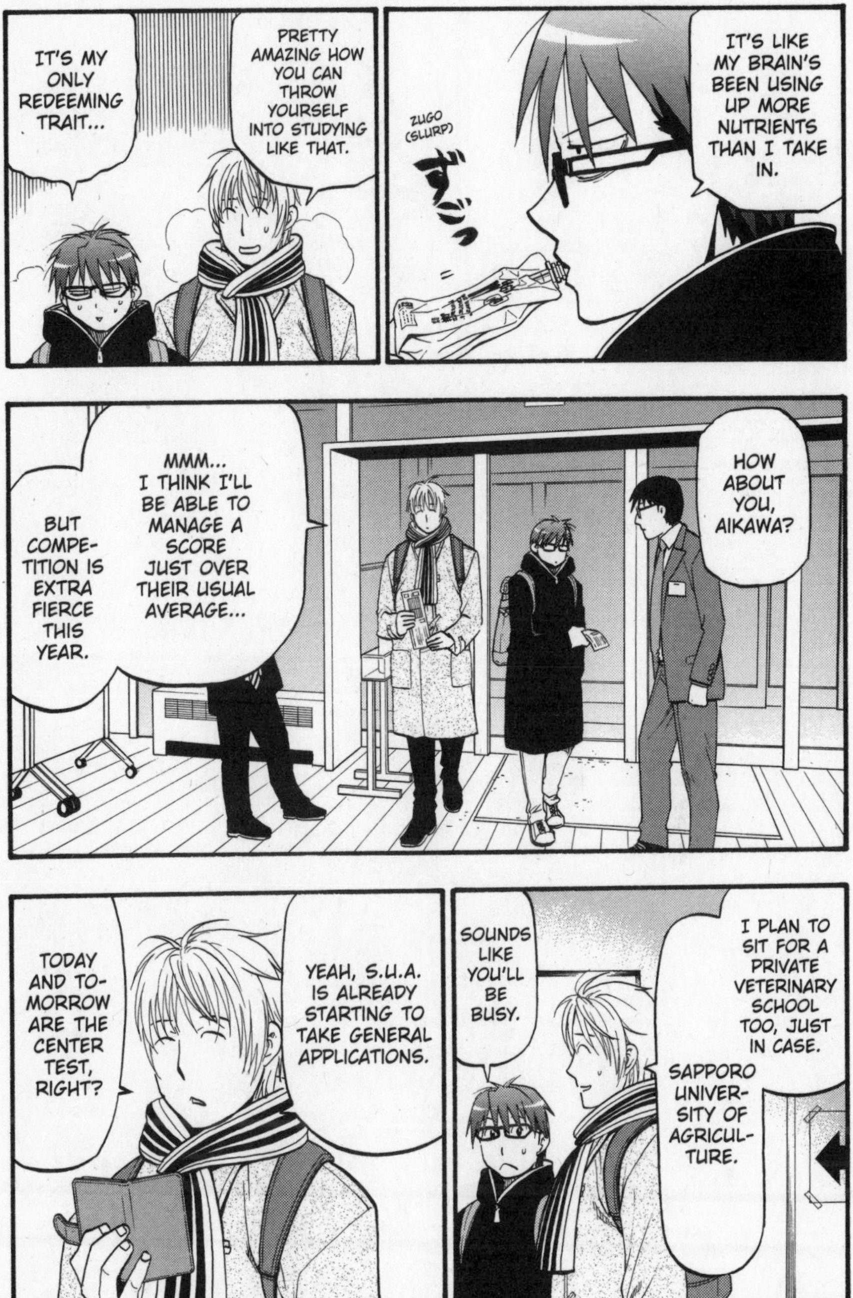
IT'S LIKE MY BRAIN'S BEEN USING UP MORE NUTRIENTS THAN I TAKE IN.
ZUGO (SLURP)
PRETTY AMAZING HOW YOU CAN THROW YOURSELF INTO STUDYING LIKE THAT.
IT'S MY ONLY REDEEMING TRAIT...
HOW ABOUT YOU, AIKAWA?
MMM... I THINK I'LL BE ABLE TO MANAGE A SCORE JUST OVER THEIR USUAL AVERAGE...
BUT COMPETITION IS EXTRA FIERCE THIS YEAR.
I PLAN TO SIT FOR A PRIVATE VETERINARY SCHOOL TOO, JUST IN CASE.
SAPPORO UNIVERSITY OF AGRICULTURE.
SOUNDS LIKE YOU'LL BE BUSY.
YEAH, S.U.A. IS ALREADY STARTING TO TAKE GENERAL APPLICATIONS.
TODAY AND TO-MORROW ARE THE CENTER TEST, RIGHT?

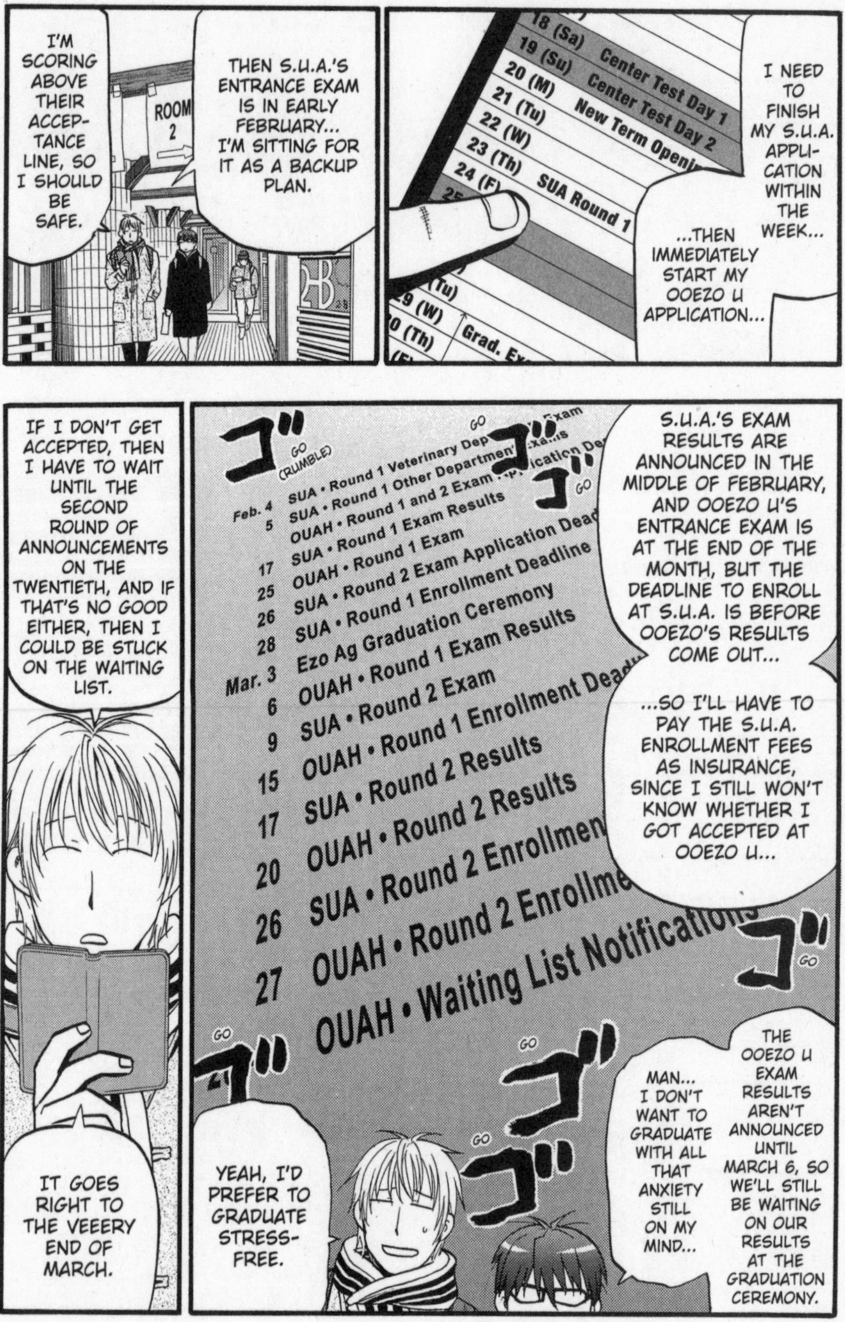
18 (Sa)
19 (Su) Center Test Day 1
20 (M) Center Test Day 2
21 (Tu) New Term Openi
22 (W)
23 (Th)
24 (F) SUA Round 1
(Tu)
(W)
(Th) Grad. Ex
I NEED TO FINISH MY S.U.A. APPLICATION WITHIN THE WEEK...
...THEN IMMEDIATELY START MY OOEZO U APPLICATION...
ROOM 2
THEN S.U.A.'S ENTRANCE EXAM IS IN EARLY FEBRUARY... I'M SITTING FOR IT AS A BACKUP PLAN.
I'M SCORING ABOVE THEIR ACCEPTANCE LINE, SO I SHOULD BE SAFE.
S.U.A.'S EXAM RESULTS ARE ANNOUNCED IN THE MIDDLE OF FEBRUARY, AND OOEZO U'S ENTRANCE EXAM IS AT THE END OF THE MONTH, BUT THE DEADLINE TO ENROLL AT S.U.A. IS BEFORE OOEZO'S RESULTS COME OUT...
...SO I'LL HAVE TO PAY THE S.U.A. ENROLLMENT FEES AS INSURANCE, SINCE I STILL WON'T KNOW WHETHER I GOT ACCEPTED AT OOEZO U...
GO (RUMBLE)
GO
GO
Feb. 4 SUA • Round 1 Veterinary Dep
5 SUA • Round 1 Other Departmen
OUAH • Round 1 and 2 Exam
SUA • Round 1 Exam Results
17 OUAH • Round 1 Exam
25 SUA • Round 2 Exam Application Dead
26 SUA • Round 1 Enrollment Deadline
28 Ezo Ag Graduation Ceremony
Mar. 3 OUAH • Round 1 Exam Results
6 SUA • Round 2 Exam
9 OUAH • Round 1 Enrollment Dead
15 SUA • Round 2 Results
17 OUAH • Round 2 Results
20 SUA • Round 2 Enrollmen
26 OUAH • Round 2 Enrollme
27 OUAH • Waiting List Notifications
GO
GO
GO
GO
THE OOEZO U EXAM RESULTS AREN'T ANNOUNCED UNTIL MARCH 6, SO WE'LL STILL BE WAITING ON OUR RESULTS AT THE GRADUATION CEREMONY.
MAN... I DON'T WANT TO GRADUATE WITH ALL THAT ANXIETY STILL ON MY MIND...
YEAH, I'D PREFER TO GRADUATE STRESS-FREE.
IF I DON'T GET ACCEPTED, THEN I HAVE TO WAIT UNTIL THE SECOND ROUND OF ANNOUNCEMENTS ON THE TWENTIETH, AND IF THAT'S NO GOOD EITHER, THEN I COULD BE STUCK ON THE WAITING LIST.
IT GOES RIGHT TO THE VEEERY END OF MARCH.

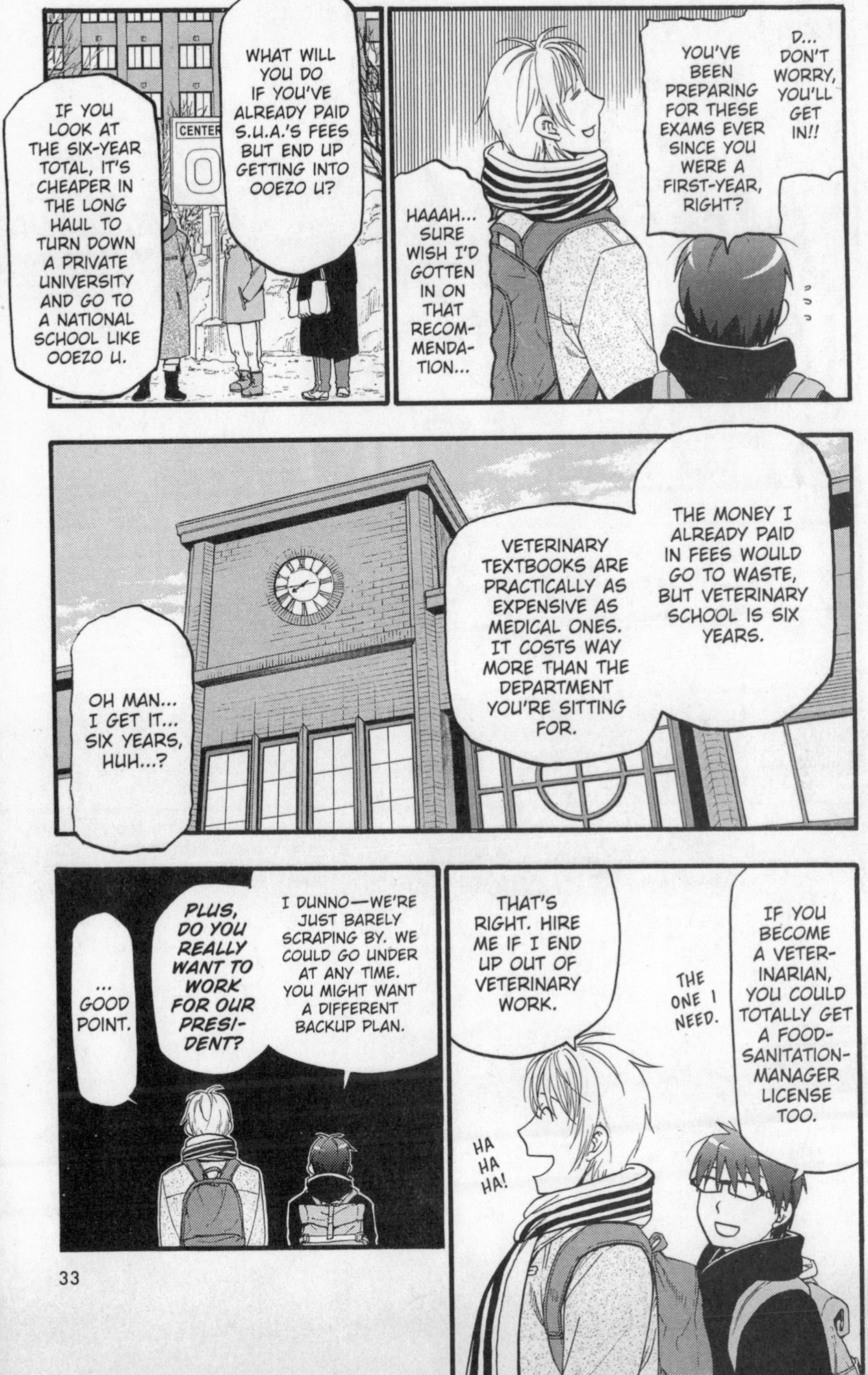
D... DON'T WORRY, YOU'LL GET IN!!
YOU'VE BEEN PREPARING FOR THESE EXAMS EVER SINCE YOU WERE A FIRST-YEAR, RIGHT?
HAAAH... SURE WISH I'D GOTTEN IN ON THAT RECOMMENDATION...
WHAT WILL YOU DO IF YOU'VE ALREADY PAID S.U.A.'S FEES BUT END UP GETTING INTO OOEZO U?
IF YOU LOOK AT THE SIX-YEAR TOTAL, IT'S CHEAPER IN THE LONG HAUL TO TURN DOWN A PRIVATE UNIVERSITY AND GO TO A NATIONAL SCHOOL LIKE OOEZO U.
CENTER
THE MONEY I ALREADY PAID IN FEES WOULD GO TO WASTE, BUT VETERINARY SCHOOL IS SIX YEARS.
VETERINARY TEXTBOOKS ARE PRACTICALLY AS EXPENSIVE AS MEDICAL ONES. IT COSTS WAY MORE THAN THE DEPARTMENT YOU'RE SITTING FOR.
OH MAN... I GET IT... SIX YEARS, HUH...?
IF YOU BECOME A VETERINARIAN, YOU COULD TOTALLY GET A FOOD-SANITATION-MANAGER LICENSE TOO.
THE ONE I NEED.
THAT'S RIGHT. HIRE ME IF I END UP OUT OF VETERINARY WORK.
HA HA HA!
I DUNNO—WE'RE JUST BARELY SCRAPING BY. WE COULD GO UNDER AT ANY TIME. YOU MIGHT WANT A DIFFERENT BACKUP PLAN.
PLUS, DO YOU REALLY WANT TO WORK FOR OUR PRESIDENT?
... GOOD POINT.

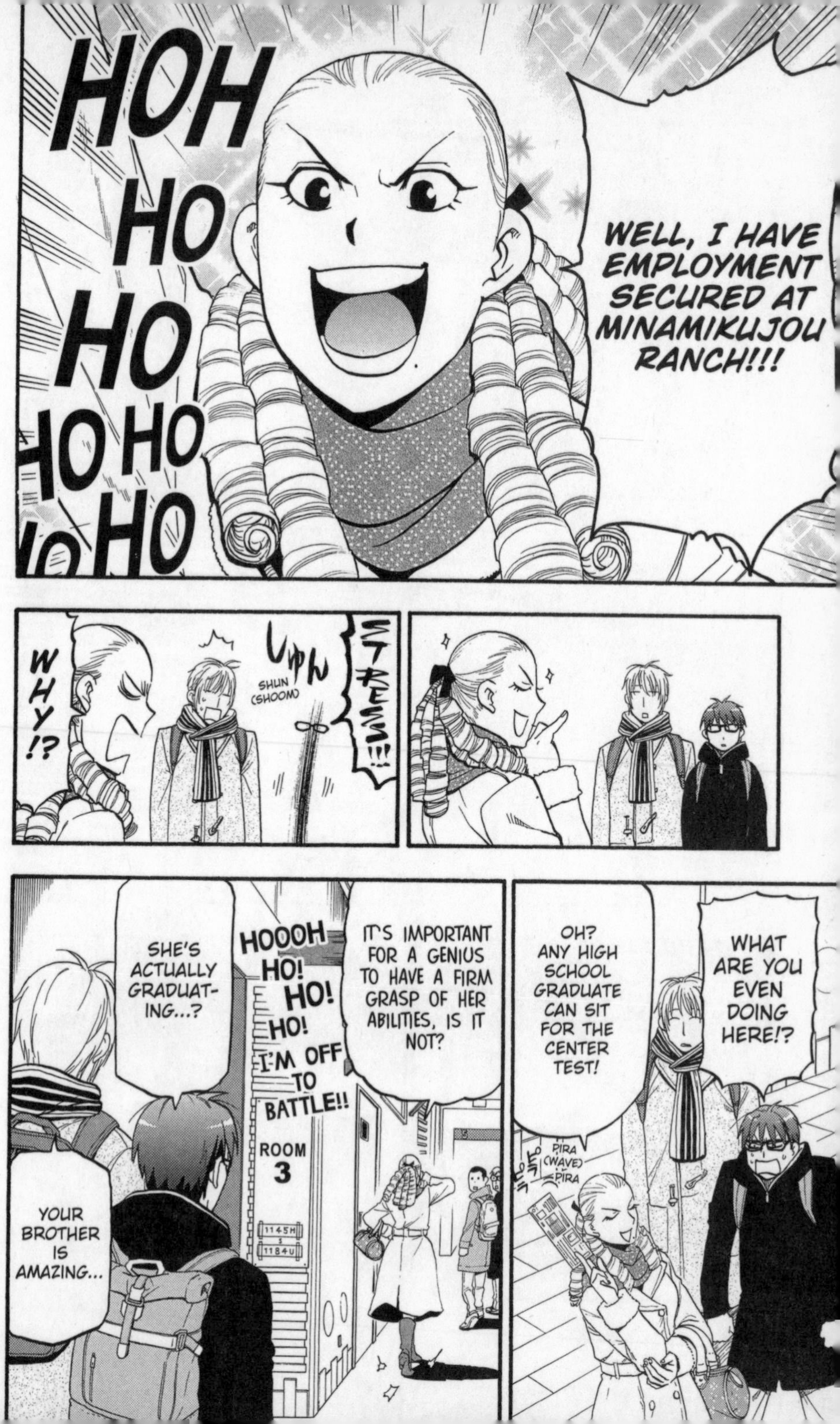
WELL, I HAVE EMPLOYMENT SECURED AT MINAMIKUJOU RANCH!!!
HOH HO HO HO HO HO HO
STRESS!!!
しゅん
SHUN (SHOOM)
WHY!?
WHAT ARE YOU EVEN DOING HERE!?
OH? ANY HIGH SCHOOL GRADUATE CAN SIT FOR THE CENTER TEST!
PIRA (WAVE) PIRA
IT'S IMPORTANT FOR A GENIUS TO HAVE A FIRM GRASP OF HER ABILITIES, IS IT NOT?
HOOOH HO! HO! HO! I'M OFF TO BATTLE!!
ROOM 3
1145H
1184U
SHE'S ACTUALLY GRADUAT-ING...?
YOUR BROTHER IS AMAZING...

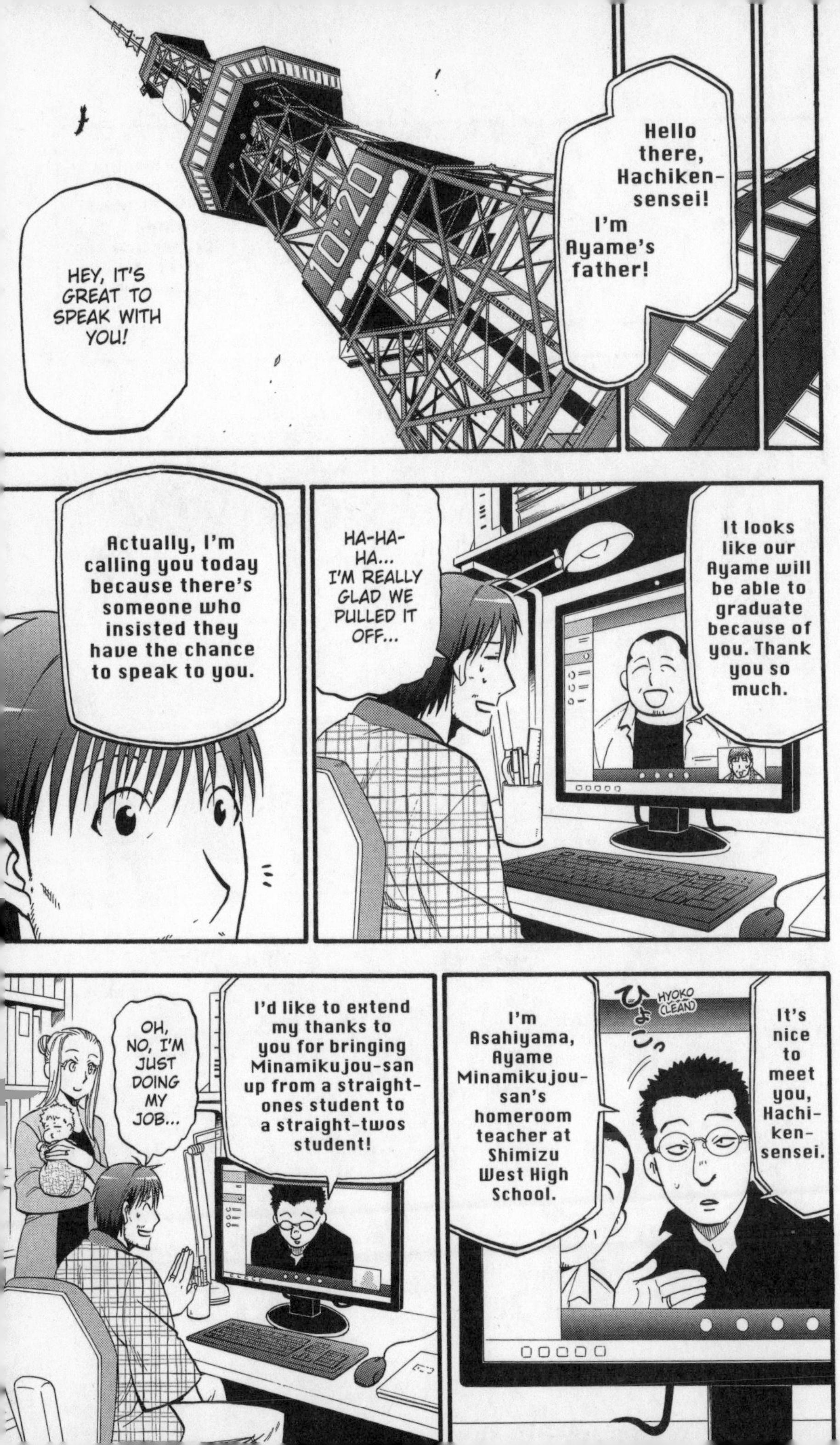
Hello there, Hachiken-sensei! I'm Ayame's father!
HEY, IT'S GREAT TO SPEAK WITH YOU!
It looks like our Ayame will be able to graduate because of you. Thank you so much.
HA-HA-HA... I'M REALLY GLAD WE PULLED IT OFF...
Actually, I'm calling you today because there's someone who insisted they have the chance to speak to you.
It's nice to meet you, Hachi-ken-sensei.
HYOKO (LEAN)
I'm Asahiyama, Ayame Minamikujou-san's homeroom teacher at Shimizu West High School.
I'd like to extend my thanks to you for bringing Minamikujou-san up from a straight-ones student to a straight-twos student!
OH, NO, I'M JUST DOING MY JOB...

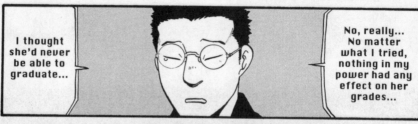

No, really... No matter what I tried, nothing in my power had any effect on her grades...
I thought she'd never be able to graduate...
.....Nh!!!
ZABA (BLOOSH)
Thank you! Thank you! Thank you so much!! Thank you sooooo much!!
THAT IS WONDERFUL!
NO... ERR...I'M SURE YOU WORKED HARD. SOOOOO HARD.
Hello, Hachiken-san.
I'm Ayame's mother!
NH! UU!
I really can't thank you enough for what you've done!
All our relatives are overjoyed that she's graduating on time!
Over here, Grandma! You say thanks too!
HA HA HA!

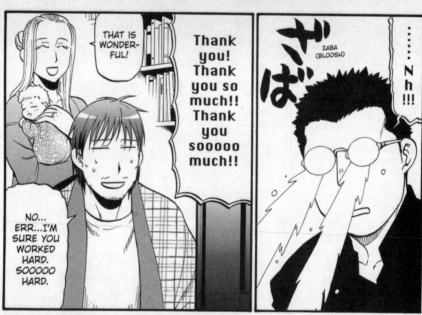

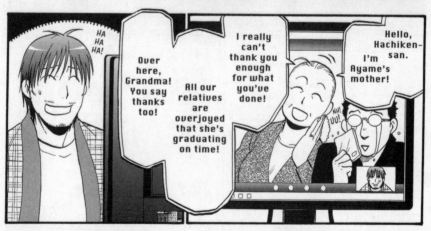

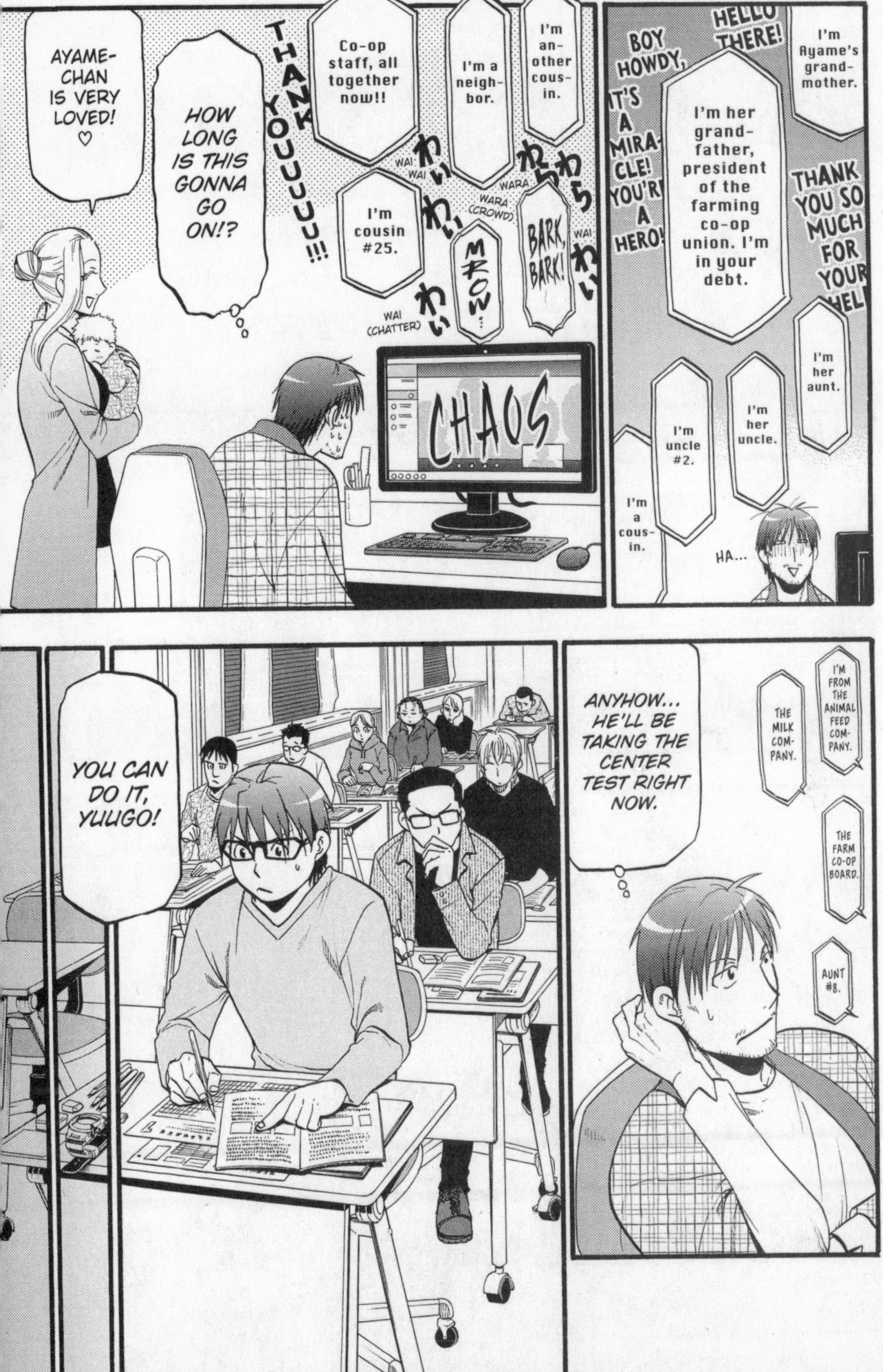
I'm Ayame's grand-mother.
HELLO THERE!
BOY HOWDY, IT'S A MIRA-CLE! YOU'R A HERO!
I'm her grand-father, president of the farming co-op union. I'm in your debt.
THANK YOU SO MUCH FOR YOUR HEL
I'm her aunt.
I'm her uncle.
I'm uncle #2.
I'm a cous-in.
HA...
I'm an-other cous-in.
I'm a neigh-bor.
Co-op staff, all together now!!
THANK YOUUUUUU!!!
WAI WAI
WARA WARA (CROWD)
BARK, BARK!
WAI
MROW...
I'm cousin #25.
WAI (CHATTER)
CHAOS
HOW LONG IS THIS GONNA GO ON!?
AYAME-CHAN IS VERY LOVED! ♡
I'M FROM THE ANIMAL FEED COM-PANY.
THE MILK COM-PANY.
THE FARM CO-OP BOARD.
AUNT #8.
ANYHOW... HE'LL BE TAKING THE CENTER TEST RIGHT NOW.
YOU CAN DO IT, YUUGO!

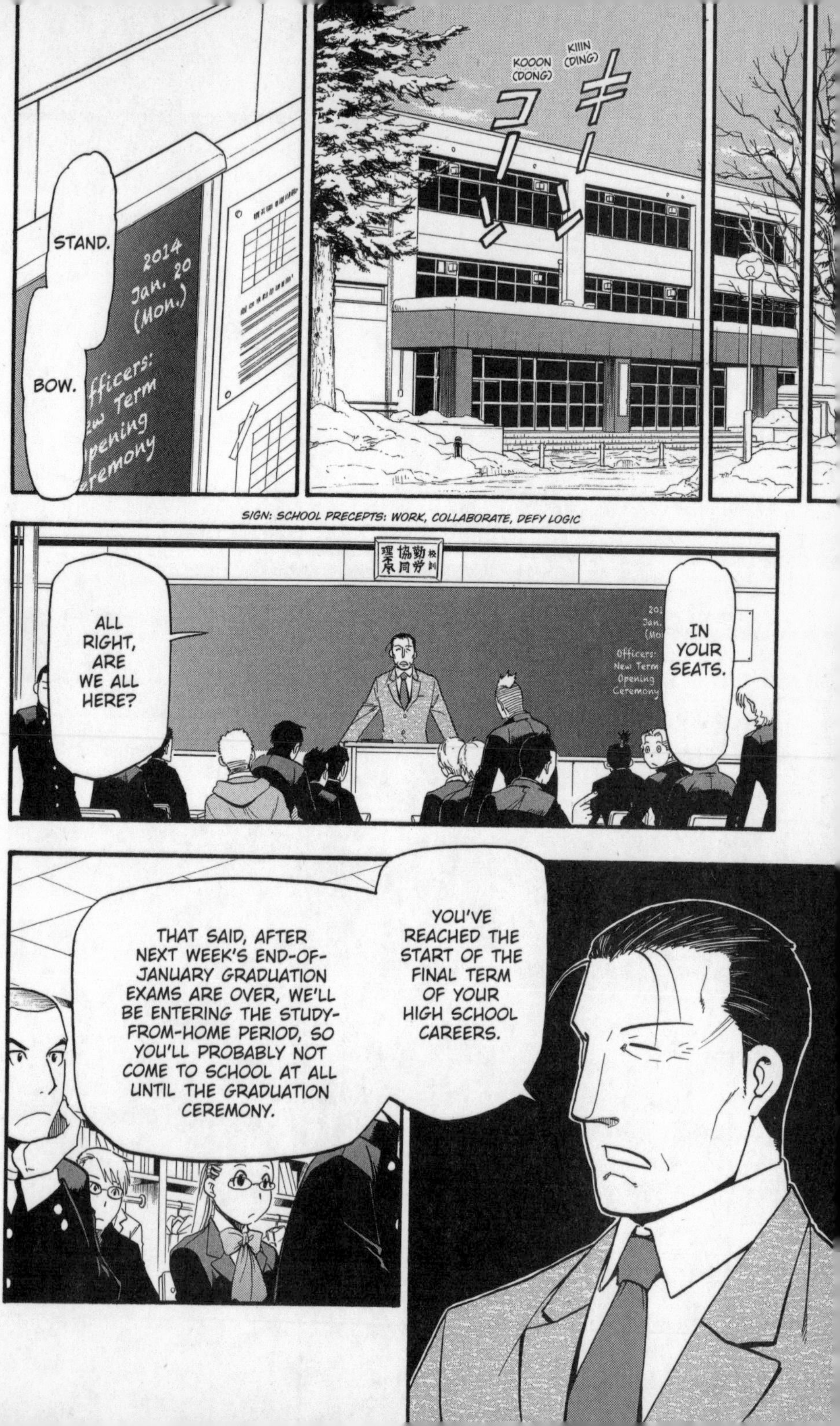
KIIIN (DING)
KOOON (DONG)
STAND.
BOW.
2014 Jan. 20 (Mon.)
fficers: ew Term pening eremony
SIGN: SCHOOL PRECEPTS: WORK, COLLABORATE, DEFY LOGIC
IN YOUR SEATS.
ALL RIGHT, ARE WE ALL HERE?
Officers: New Term Opening Ceremony
YOU'VE REACHED THE START OF THE FINAL TERM OF YOUR HIGH SCHOOL CAREERS.
THAT SAID, AFTER NEXT WEEK'S END-OF-JANUARY GRADUATION EXAMS ARE OVER, WE'LL BE ENTERING THE STUDY-FROM-HOME PERIOD, SO YOU'LL PROBABLY NOT COME TO SCHOOL AT ALL UNTIL THE GRADUATION CEREMONY.

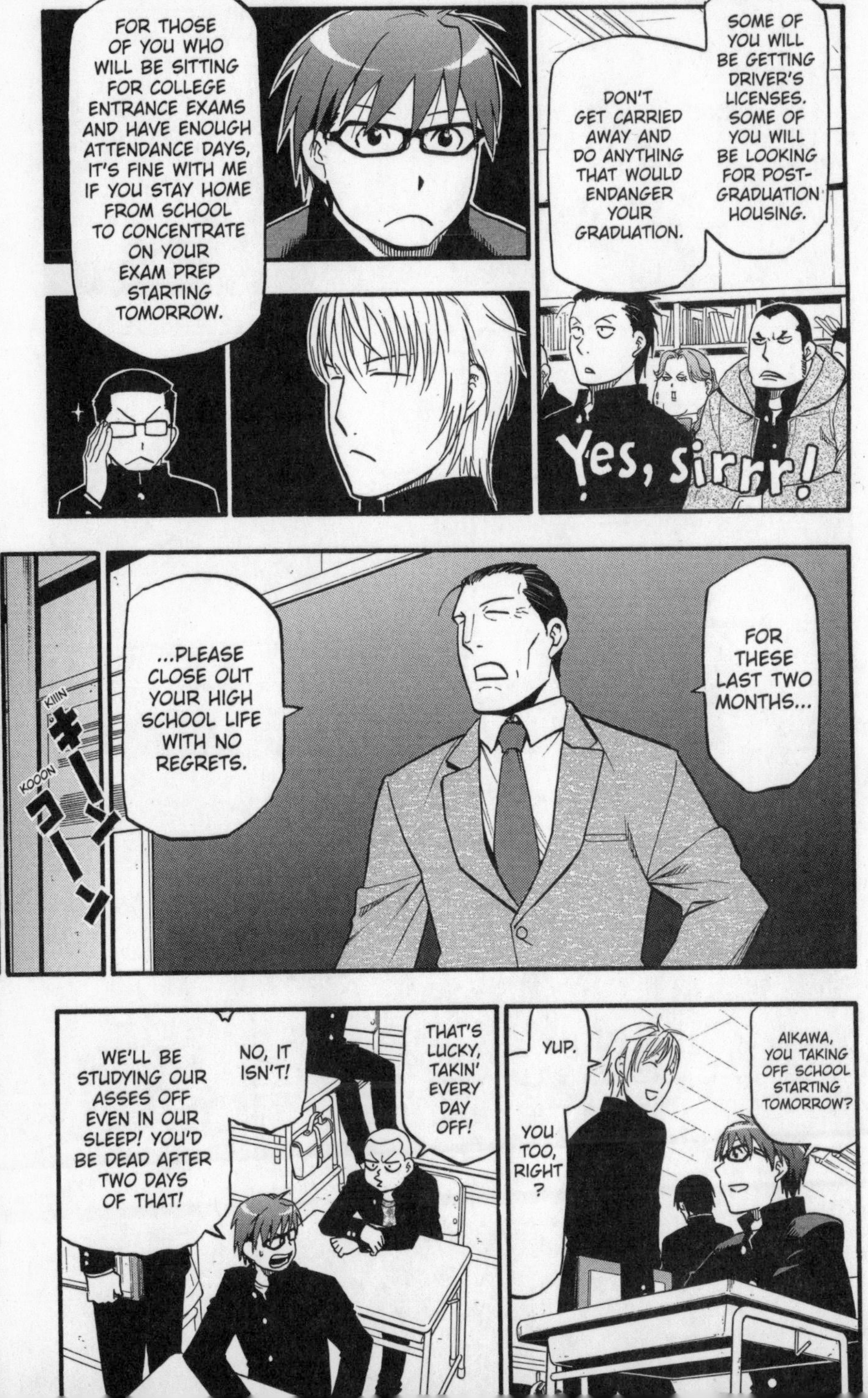
SOME OF YOU WILL BE GETTING DRIVER'S LICENSES. SOME OF YOU WILL BE LOOKING FOR POST-GRADUATION HOUSING.
DON'T GET CARRIED AWAY AND DO ANYTHING THAT WOULD ENDANGER YOUR GRADUATION.
Yes, sirrr!
FOR THOSE OF YOU WHO WILL BE SITTING FOR COLLEGE ENTRANCE EXAMS AND HAVE ENOUGH ATTENDANCE DAYS, IT'S FINE WITH ME IF YOU STAY HOME FROM SCHOOL TO CONCENTRATE ON YOUR EXAM PREP STARTING TOMORROW.
FOR THESE LAST TWO MONTHS...
...PLEASE CLOSE OUT YOUR HIGH SCHOOL LIFE WITH NO REGRETS.
KIIIN
KOOON
AIKAWA, YOU TAKING OFF SCHOOL STARTING TOMORROW?
YUP.
YOU TOO, RIGHT?
THAT'S LUCKY, TAKIN' EVERY DAY OFF!
NO, IT ISN'T!
WE'LL BE STUDYING OUR ASSES OFF EVEN IN OUR SLEEP! YOU'D BE DEAD AFTER TWO DAYS OF THAT!

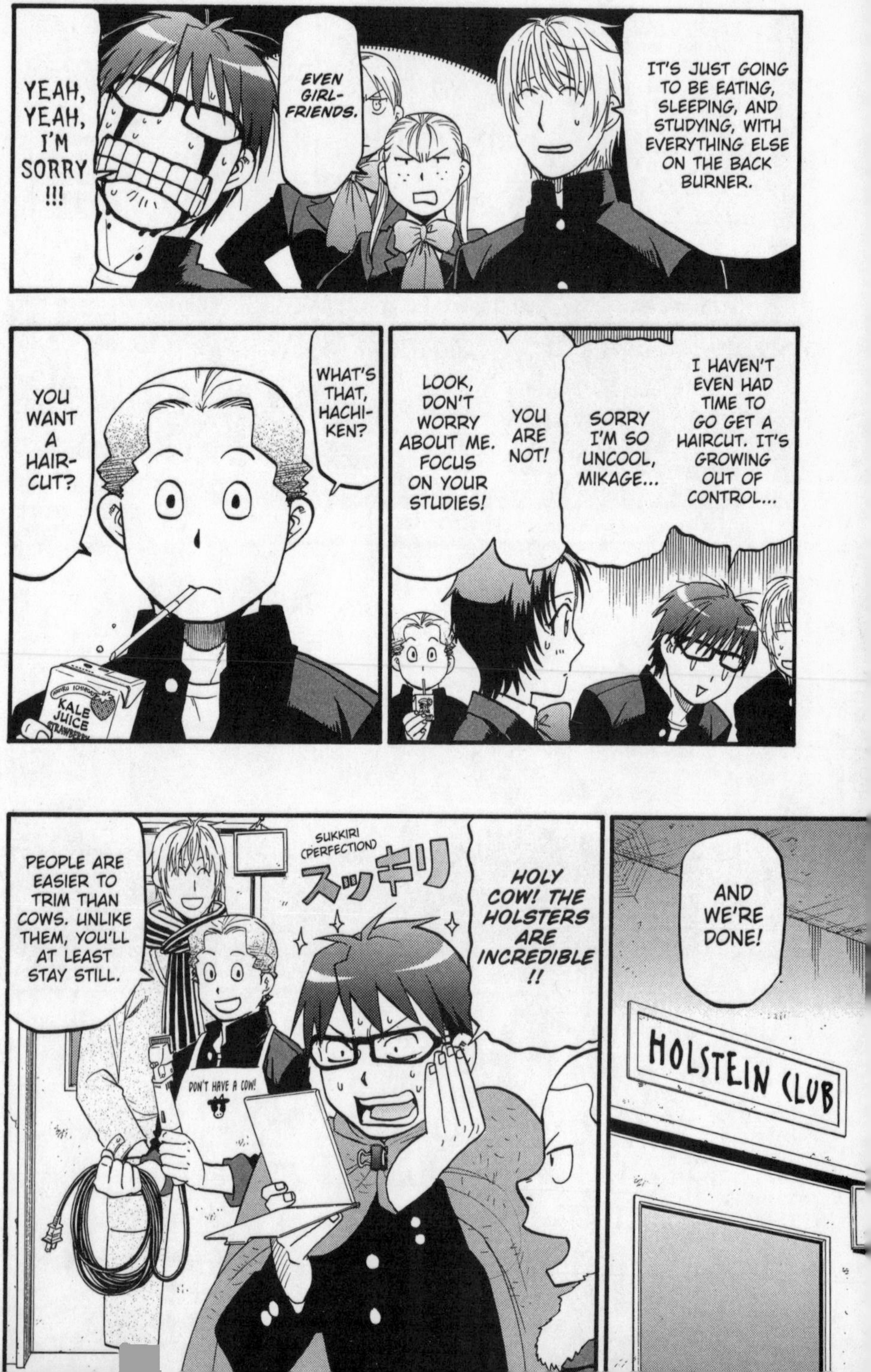
IT'S JUST GOING TO BE EATING, SLEEPING, AND STUDYING, WITH EVERYTHING ELSE ON THE BACK BURNER.
EVEN GIRL-FRIENDS.
YEAH, YEAH, I'M SORRY!!!
I HAVEN'T EVEN HAD TIME TO GO GET A HAIRCUT. IT'S GROWING OUT OF CONTROL...
SORRY I'M SO UNCOOL, MIKAGE...
YOU ARE NOT!
LOOK, DON'T WORRY ABOUT ME. FOCUS ON YOUR STUDIES!
WHAT'S THAT, HACHI-KEN?
YOU WANT A HAIR-CUT?
KALE JUICE
AND WE'RE DONE!
HOLSTEIN CLUB
HOLY COW! THE HOLSTERS ARE INCREDIBLE!!
SUKKIRI (PERFECTION)
スッキリ
PEOPLE ARE EASIER TO TRIM THAN COWS. UNLIKE THEM, YOU'LL AT LEAST STAY STILL.
DON'T HAVE A COW!

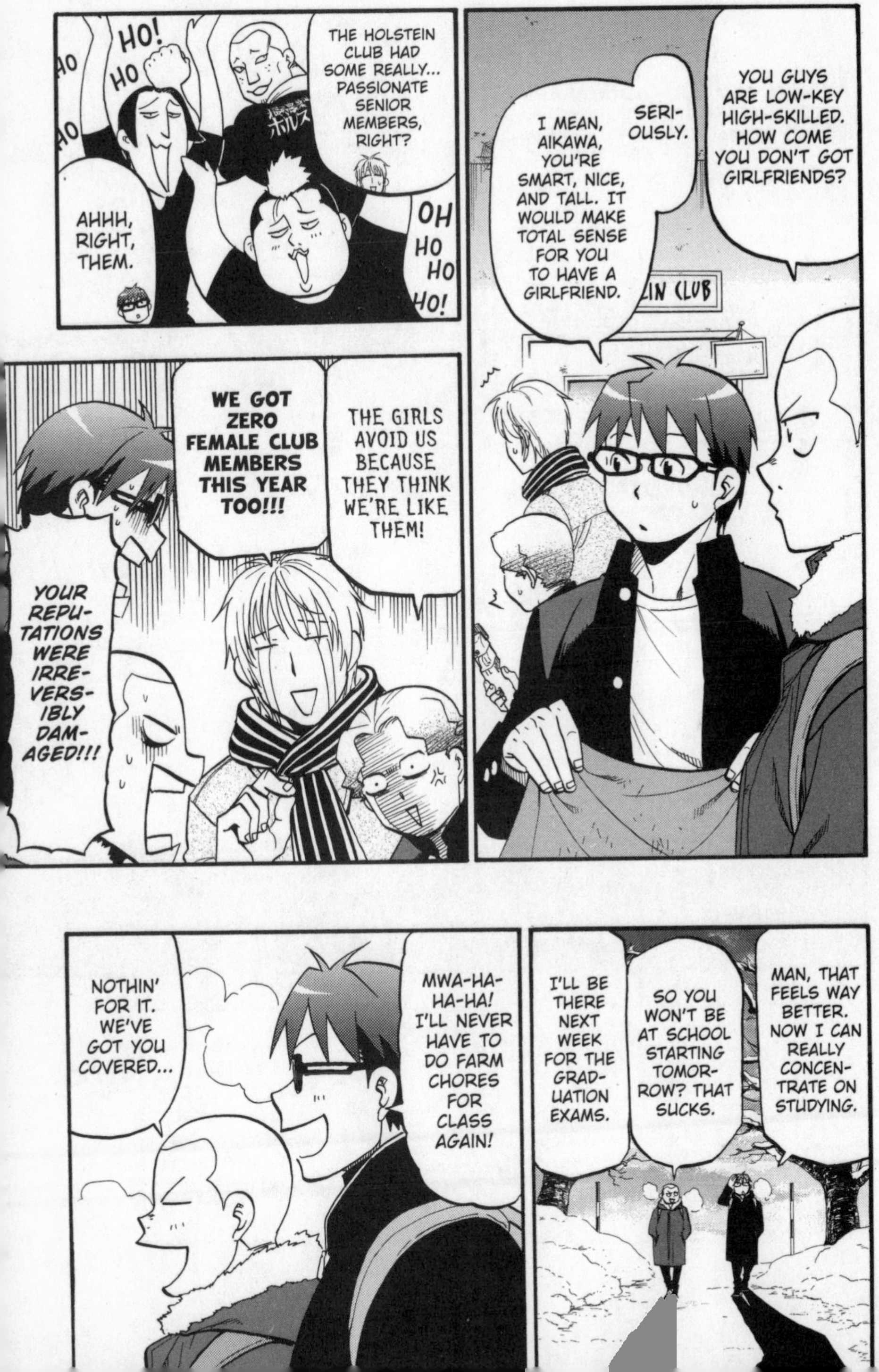
YOU GUYS ARE LOW-KEY HIGH-SKILLED. HOW COME YOU DON'T GOT GIRLFRIENDS?
SERI-OUSLY.
I MEAN, AIKAWA, YOU'RE SMART, NICE, AND TALL. IT WOULD MAKE TOTAL SENSE FOR YOU TO HAVE A GIRLFRIEND.
LIN CLUB
THE HOLSTEIN CLUB HAD SOME REALLY... PASSIONATE SENIOR MEMBERS, RIGHT?
HO! HO
HO
HO
OH HO HO HO!
AHHH, RIGHT, THEM.
WE GOT ZERO FEMALE CLUB MEMBERS THIS YEAR TOO!!!
THE GIRLS AVOID US BECAUSE THEY THINK WE'RE LIKE THEM!
YOUR REPU-TATIONS WERE IRRE-VERS-IBLY DAM-AGED!!!
MAN, THAT FEELS WAY BETTER. NOW I CAN REALLY CONCEN-TRATE ON STUDYING.
SO YOU WON'T BE AT SCHOOL STARTING TOMOR-ROW? THAT SUCKS.
I'LL BE THERE NEXT WEEK FOR THE GRAD-UATION EXAMS.
MWA-HA-HA-HA! I'LL NEVER HAVE TO DO FARM CHORES FOR CLASS AGAIN!
NOTHIN' FOR IT. WE'VE GOT YOU COVERED...

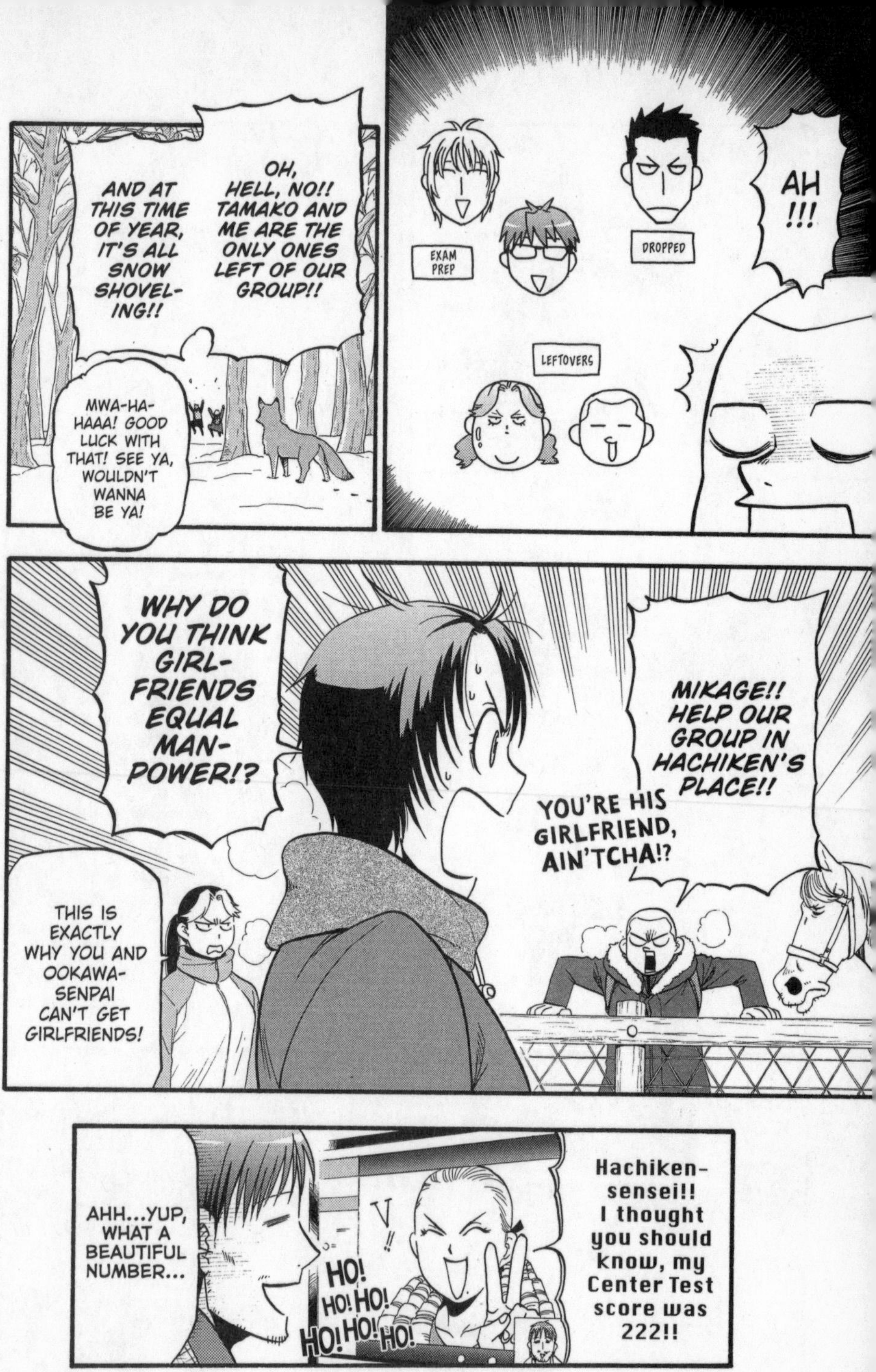
AH!!!
DROPPED
EXAM PREP
LEFTOVERS
OH, HELL, NO!! TAMAKO AND ME ARE THE ONLY ONES LEFT OF OUR GROUP!!
AND AT THIS TIME OF YEAR, IT'S ALL SNOW SHOVELING!!
MWA-HA-HAAA! GOOD LUCK WITH THAT! SEE YA, WOULDN'T WANNA BE YA!
MIKAGE!! HELP OUR GROUP IN HACHIKEN'S PLACE!!
YOU'RE HIS GIRLFRIEND, AIN'TCHA!?
WHY DO YOU THINK GIRLFRIENDS EQUAL MANPOWER!?
THIS IS EXACTLY WHY YOU AND OOKAWA-SENPAI CAN'T GET GIRLFRIENDS!
Hachiken-sensei!! I thought you should know, my Center Test score was 222!!
V!!
HO! HO! HO! HO! HO! HO!
AHH...YUP, WHAT A BEAUTIFUL NUMBER...

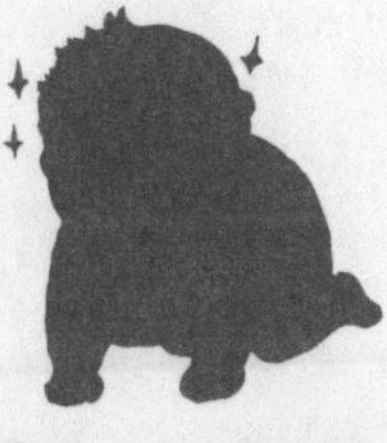

Silver Spoon

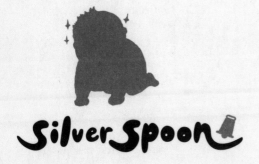

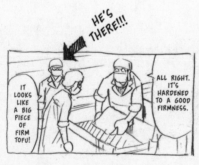

HE'S THERE!!!
ALL RIGHT. IT'S HARDENED TO A GOOD FIRMNESS.
IT LOOKS LIKE A BIG PIECE OF FIRM TOFU!

EVEN THOUGH THE MANGA PAGES ARE CHECKED OVER SEVERAL TIMES BY SEVERAL PEOPLE AT SEVERAL MOMENTS THROUGHOUT THE PROCESS, OCCASIONALLY, MISTAKES IN THE ART WILL SLIP PAST ALL OF THOSE NUMEROUS DEFENSES AND FIND THEIR WAY INTO THE READERS' HANDS.

IN THE FIRST PANEL OF PAGE 19 OF VOLUME 8, TOKIWA IS SOMEHOW BACK IN THE CHEESE LAB AFTER HE WAS KICKED OUT OF IT!!!
(A VENGEFUL SPIRIT!?)

I THOUGHT ABOUT CORRECTING IT FOR SUBSEQUENT PRINTINGS OF THE BOOK, BUT IT WAS FUNNY, SO I ENDED UP LEAVING IT LIKE THAT. SORRY.

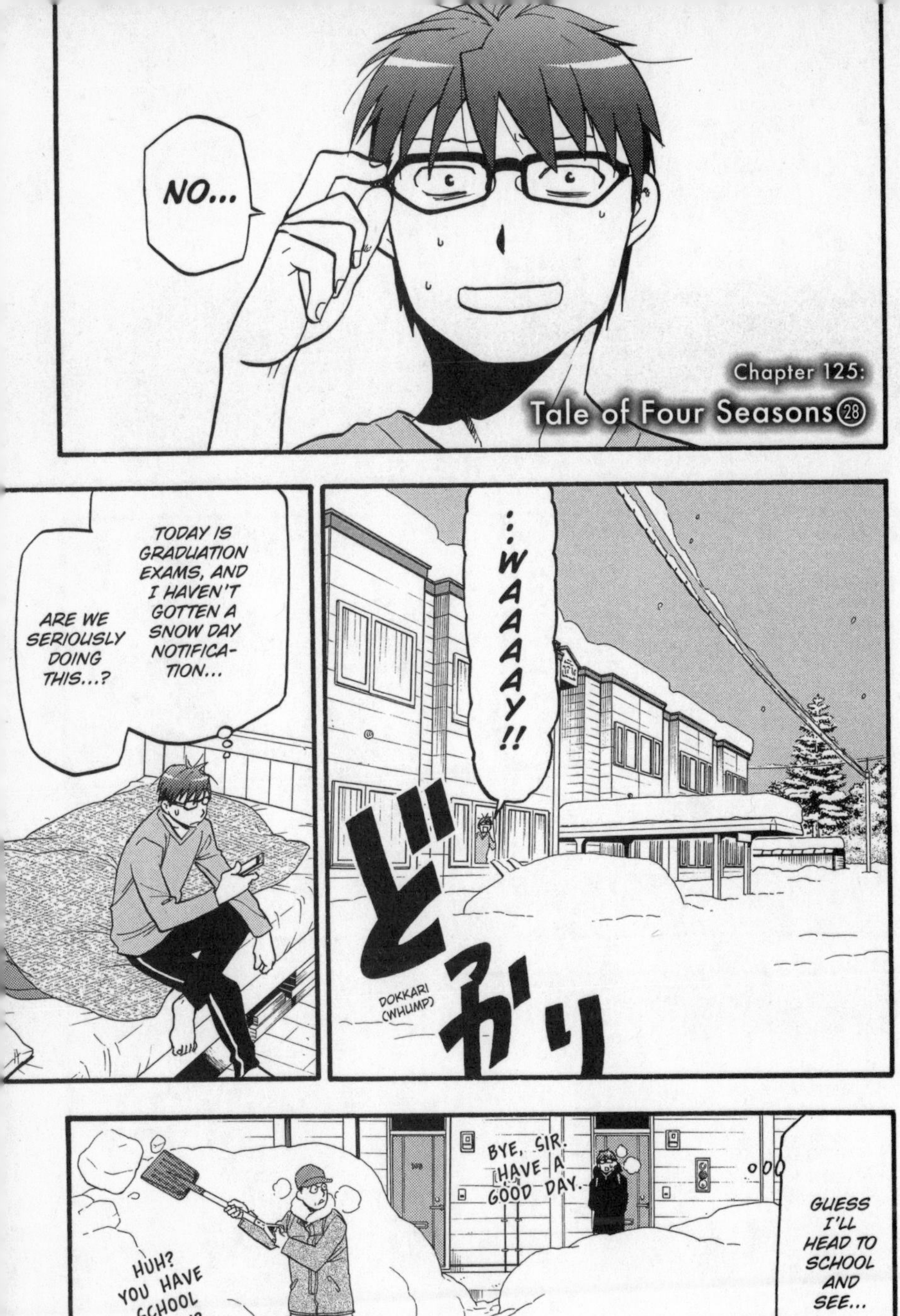
NO...
Chapter 125:
Tale of Four Seasons㉘
...WAAAAAY!!
どっかり
DOKKARI (WHUMP)
TODAY IS GRADUATION EXAMS, AND I HAVEN'T GOTTEN A SNOW DAY NOTIFICATION...
ARE WE SERIOUSLY DOING THIS...?
GUESS I'LL HEAD TO SCHOOL AND SEE...
BYE, SIR. HAVE A GOOD DAY.
HUH? YOU HAVE SCHOOL TODAY?

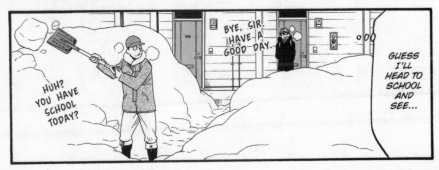

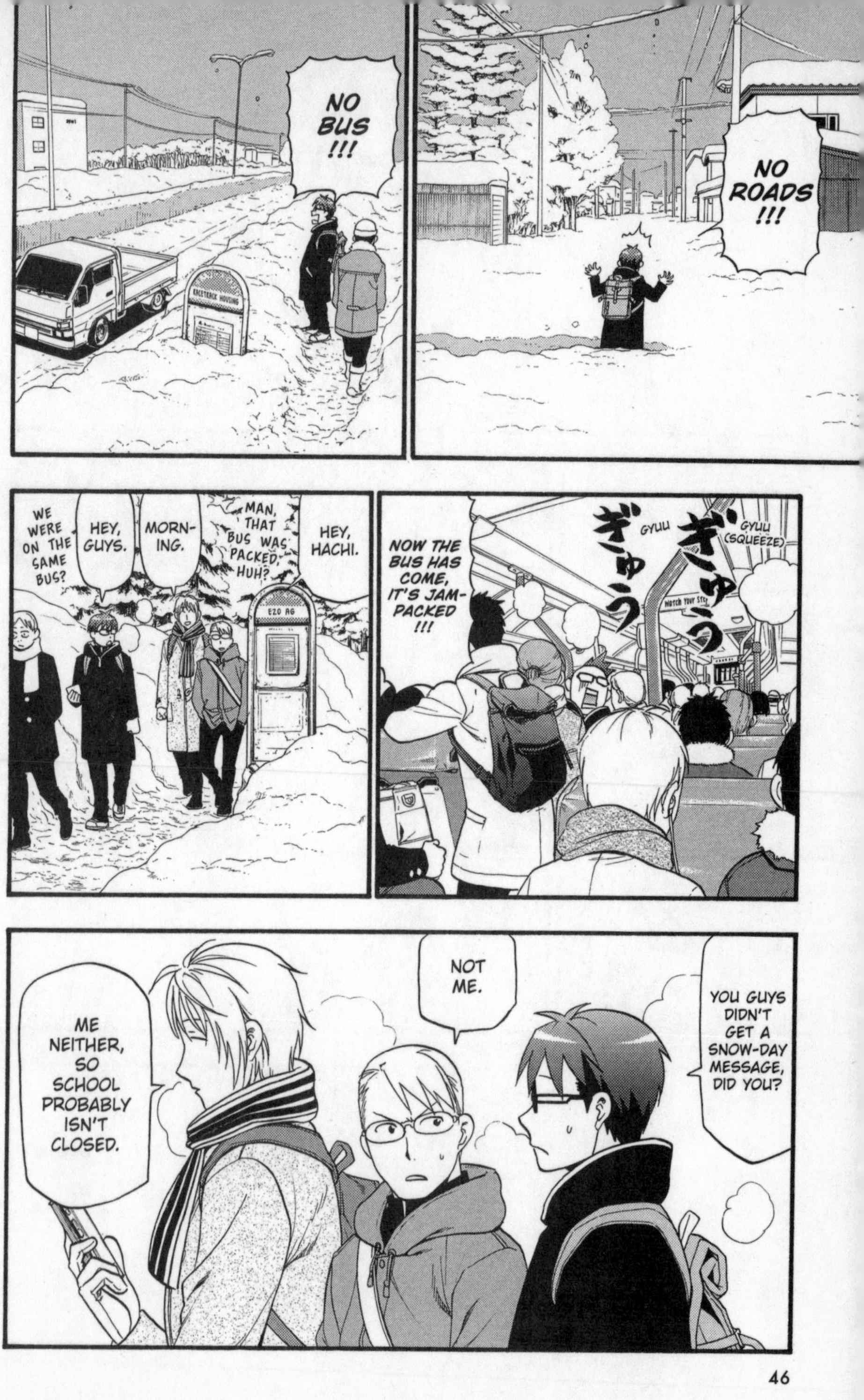
NO ROADS!!!
NO BUS!!!
NOW THE BUS HAS COME, IT'S JAM-PACKED!!!
ぎゅう
GYUU (SQUEEZE)
ぎゅう
GYUU
HEY, HACHI.
MAN, THAT BUS WAS PACKED, HUH?
MORNING.
HEY, GUYS.
WE WERE ON THE SAME BUS?
EZO AG
YOU GUYS DIDN'T GET A SNOW-DAY MESSAGE, DID YOU?
NOT ME.
ME NEITHER, SO SCHOOL PROBABLY ISN'T CLOSED.

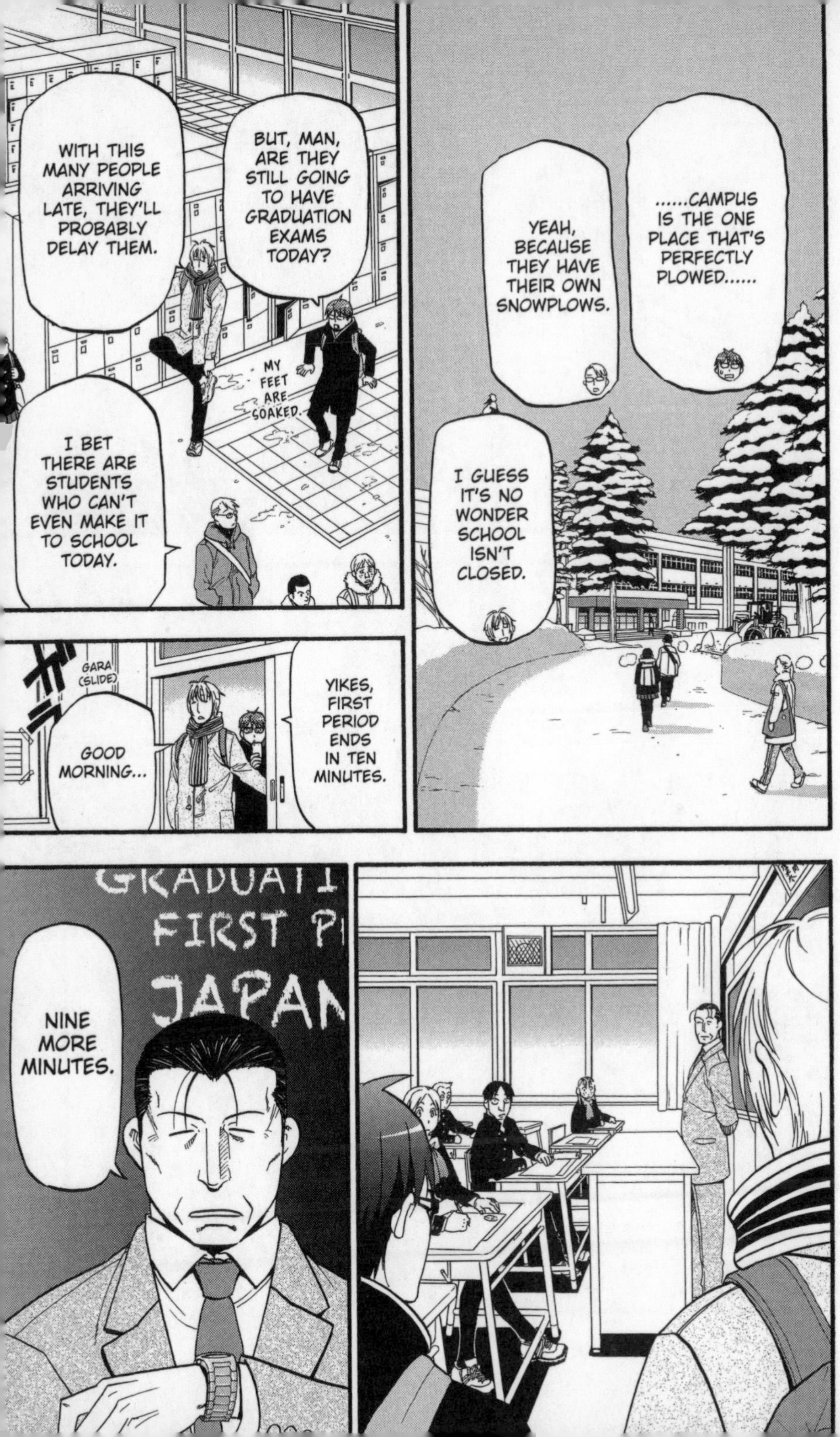
......CAMPUS IS THE ONE PLACE THAT'S PERFECTLY PLOWED......
YEAH, BECAUSE THEY HAVE THEIR OWN SNOWPLOWS.
I GUESS IT'S NO WONDER SCHOOL ISN'T CLOSED.
BUT, MAN, ARE THEY STILL GOING TO HAVE GRADUATION EXAMS TODAY?
WITH THIS MANY PEOPLE ARRIVING LATE, THEY'LL PROBABLY DELAY THEM.
MY FEET ARE SOAKED.
I BET THERE ARE STUDENTS WHO CAN'T EVEN MAKE IT TO SCHOOL TODAY.
YIKES, FIRST PERIOD ENDS IN TEN MINUTES.
GARA (SLIDE)
GOOD MORNING...
GRADUATI
FIRST P
JAPAN
NINE MORE MINUTES.

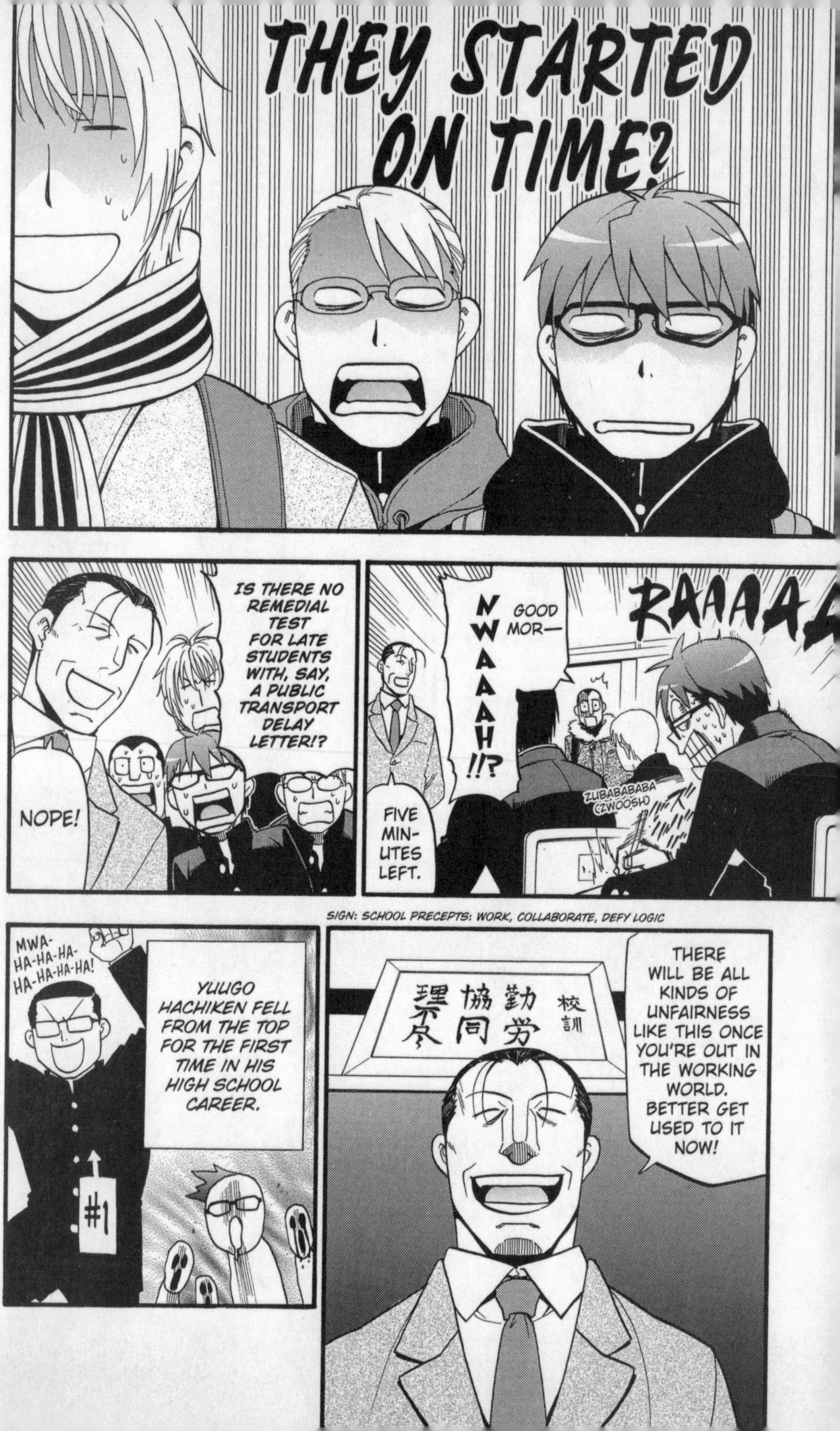
THEY STARTED ON TIME?
RAAAAA
GOOD MOR—
NWAAAAH!!?
ZUBABABABA (ZWOOSH)
FIVE MINUTES LEFT.
IS THERE NO REMEDIAL TEST FOR LATE STUDENTS WITH, SAY, A PUBLIC TRANSPORT DELAY LETTER!?
NOPE!
SIGN: SCHOOL PRECEPTS: WORK, COLLABORATE, DEFY LOGIC
校訓
勤労
協同
THERE WILL BE ALL KINDS OF UNFAIRNESS LIKE THIS ONCE YOU'RE OUT IN THE WORKING WORLD. BETTER GET USED TO IT NOW!
YUUGO HACHIKEN FELL FROM THE TOP FOR THE FIRST TIME IN HIS HIGH SCHOOL CAREER.
MWA-HA-HA-HA-HA-HA-HA!
#1

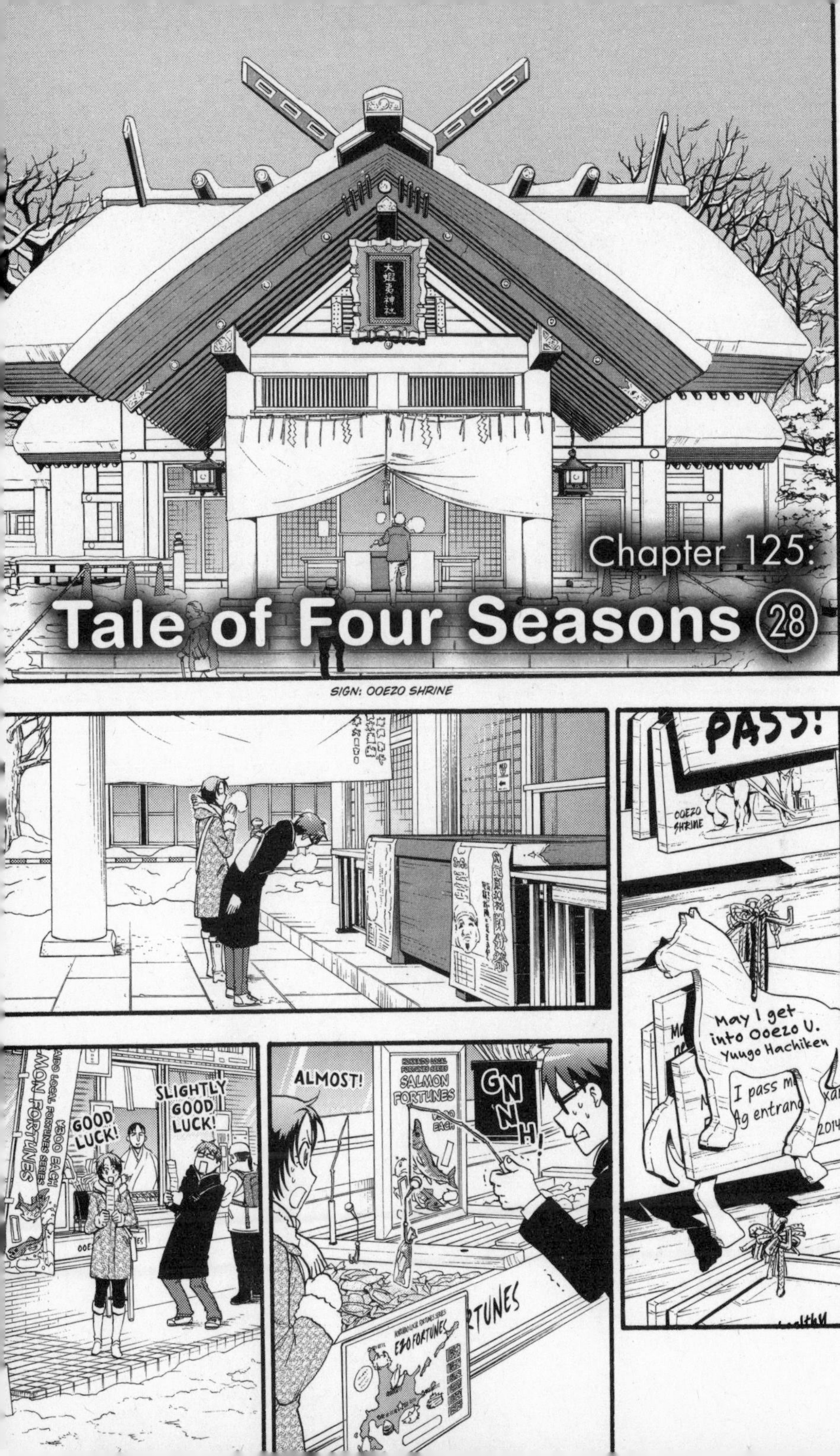
Chapter 125:
Tale of Four Seasons ㉘
PASS!
OOEZO SHRINE
May I get into Ooezo U.
Yuugo Hachiken
ALMOST!
HOKKAIDO LOCAL FORTUNES SERIES
SALMON FORTUNES
¥300 EACH
GNNH!
FORTUNES
EZO FORTUNES
GOOD LUCK!
SLIGHTLY GOOD LUCK!
¥300 EACH
SIGN: OOEZO SHRINE

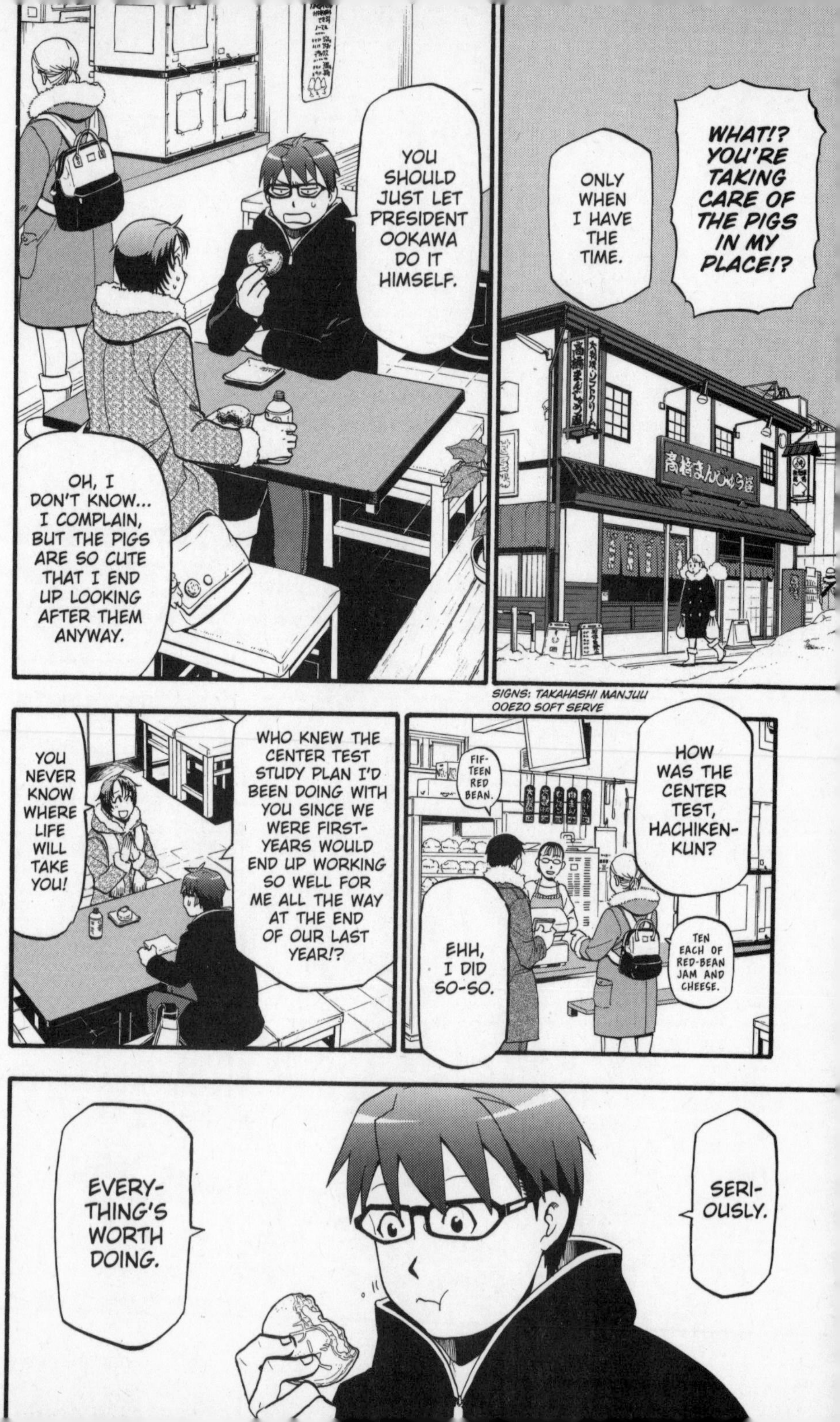
WHAT!? YOU'RE TAKING CARE OF THE PIGS IN MY PLACE!?
ONLY WHEN I HAVE THE TIME.
SIGNS: TAKAHASHI MANJUU OOEZO SOFT SERVE
YOU SHOULD JUST LET PRESIDENT OOKAWA DO IT HIMSELF.
OH, I DON'T KNOW... I COMPLAIN, BUT THE PIGS ARE SO CUTE THAT I END UP LOOKING AFTER THEM ANYWAY.
HOW WAS THE CENTER TEST, HACHIKEN-KUN?
FIFTEEN RED BEAN.
TEN EACH OF RED-BEAN JAM AND CHEESE.
EHH, I DID SO-SO.
WHO KNEW THE CENTER TEST STUDY PLAN I'D BEEN DOING WITH YOU SINCE WE WERE FIRST-YEARS WOULD END UP WORKING SO WELL FOR ME ALL THE WAY AT THE END OF OUR LAST YEAR!?
YOU NEVER KNOW WHERE LIFE WILL TAKE YOU!
SERIOUSLY.
EVERYTHING'S WORTH DOING.

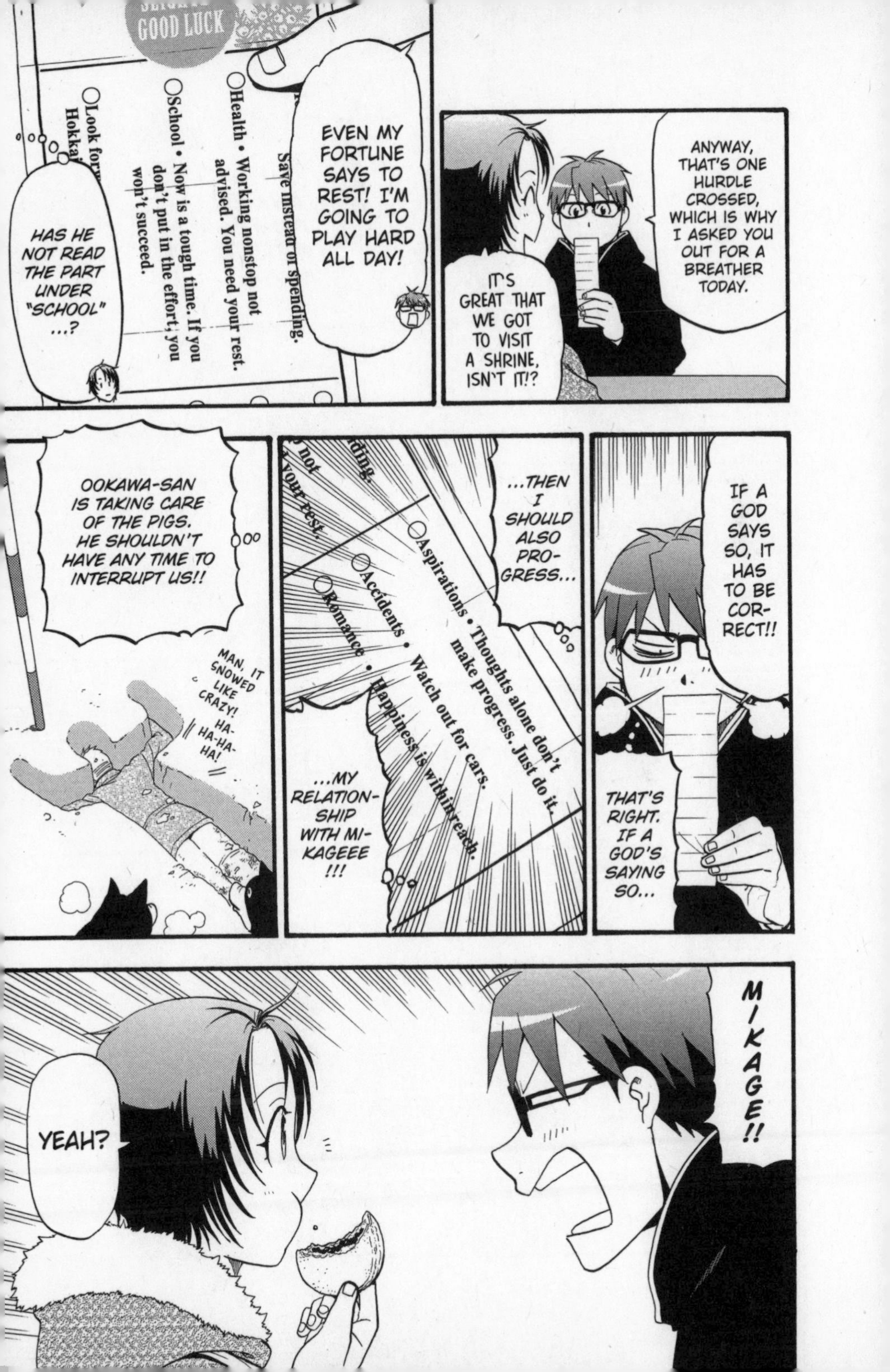
ANYWAY, THAT'S ONE HURDLE CROSSED, WHICH IS WHY I ASKED YOU OUT FOR A BREATHER TODAY.
IT'S GREAT THAT WE GOT TO VISIT A SHRINE, ISN'T IT!?
GOOD LUCK
Save instead of spending.
Health • Working nonstop not advised. You need your rest.
School • Now is a tough time. If you don't put in the effort, you won't succeed.
EVEN MY FORTUNE SAYS TO REST! I'M GOING TO PLAY HARD ALL DAY!
HAS HE NOT READ THE PART UNDER "SCHOOL" ...?
IF A GOD SAYS SO, IT HAS TO BE COR-RECT!!
THAT'S RIGHT. IF A GOD'S SAYING SO...
...THEN I SHOULD ALSO PRO-GRESS...
Aspirations • Thoughts alone don't make progress. Just do it.
Accidents • Watch out for cars.
Romance • Happiness is within reach.
...MY RELATION-SHIP WITH MI-KAGEEE !!!
OOKAWA-SAN IS TAKING CARE OF THE PIGS. HE SHOULDN'T HAVE ANY TIME TO INTERRUPT US!!
MAN, IT SNOWED LIKE CRAZY! HA-HA-HA-HA!
MIKAGE!!
YEAH?

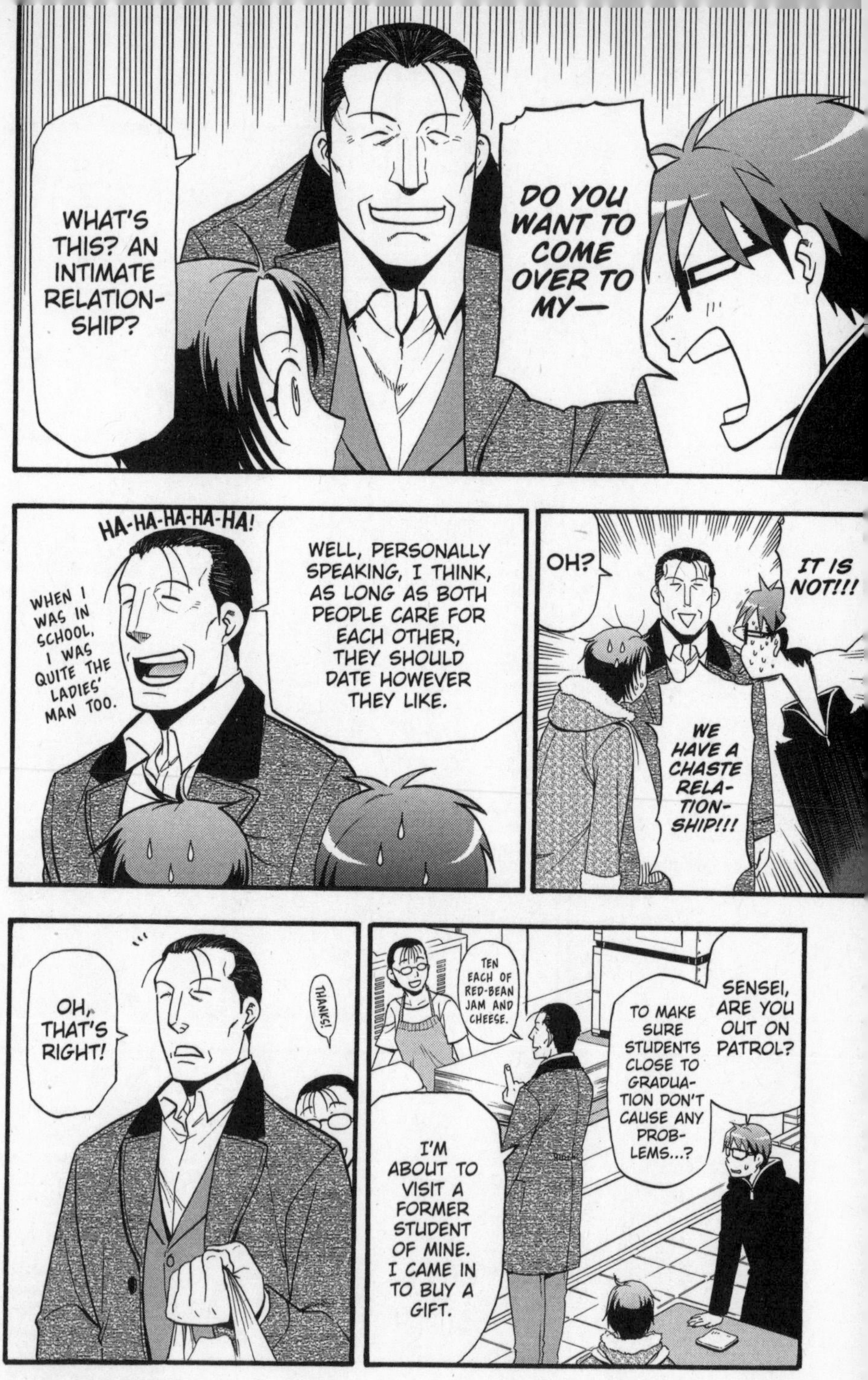

DO YOU WANT TO COME OVER TO MY—
WHAT'S THIS? AN INTIMATE RELATIONSHIP?
IT IS NOT!!!
OH?
WE HAVE A CHASTE RELATIONSHIP!!!
HA-HA-HA-HA-HA!
WELL, PERSONALLY SPEAKING, I THINK, AS LONG AS BOTH PEOPLE CARE FOR EACH OTHER, THEY SHOULD DATE HOWEVER THEY LIKE.
WHEN I WAS IN SCHOOL, I WAS QUITE THE LADIES' MAN TOO.
SENSEI, ARE YOU OUT ON PATROL?
TO MAKE SURE STUDENTS CLOSE TO GRADUATION DON'T CAUSE ANY PROBLEMS...?
TEN EACH OF RED-BEAN JAM AND CHEESE.
I'M ABOUT TO VISIT A FORMER STUDENT OF MINE. I CAME IN TO BUY A GIFT.
THANKS!
OH, THAT'S RIGHT!

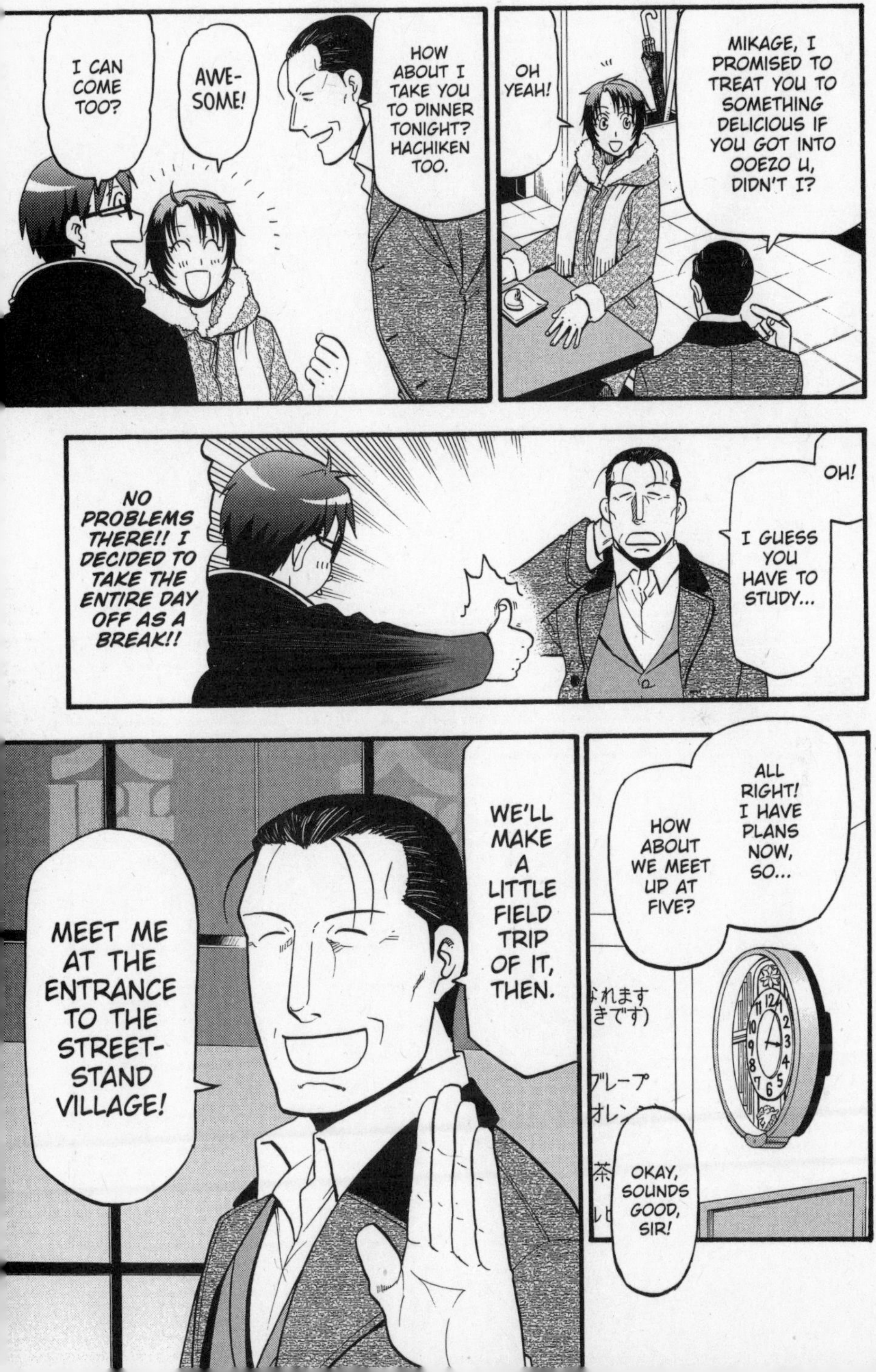
MIKAGE, I PROMISED TO TREAT YOU TO SOMETHING DELICIOUS IF YOU GOT INTO OOEZO U, DIDN'T I?
OH YEAH!
HOW ABOUT I TAKE YOU TO DINNER TONIGHT? HACHIKEN TOO.
AWE-SOME!
I CAN COME TOO?
OH!
I GUESS YOU HAVE TO STUDY...
NO PROBLEMS THERE!! I DECIDED TO TAKE THE ENTIRE DAY OFF AS A BREAK!!
ALL RIGHT! I HAVE PLANS NOW, SO...
HOW ABOUT WE MEET UP AT FIVE?
OKAY, SOUNDS GOOD, SIR!
WE'LL MAKE A LITTLE FIELD TRIP OF IT, THEN.
MEET ME AT THE ENTRANCE TO THE STREET-STAND VILLAGE!

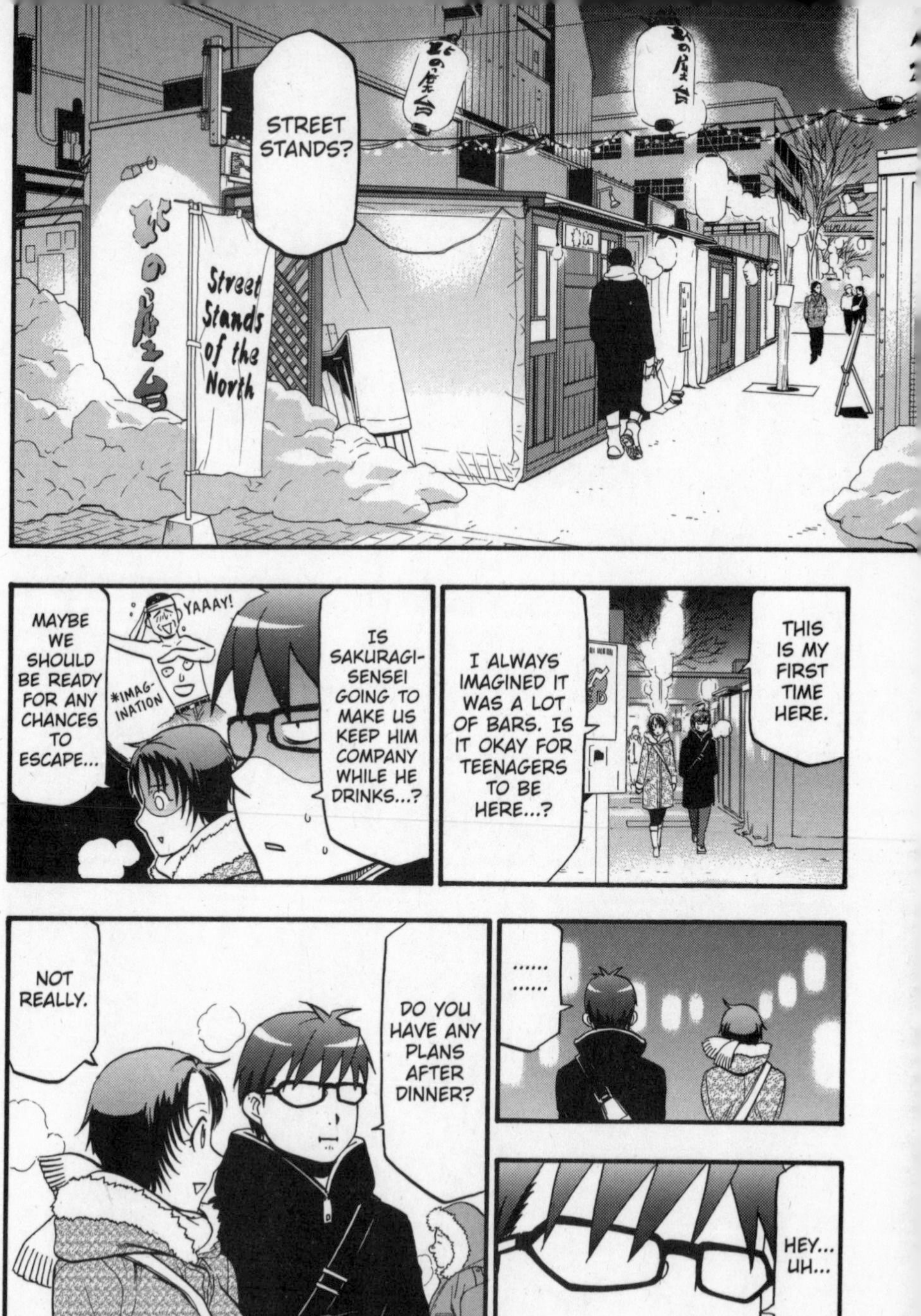

STREET STANDS?
Street Stands of the North
THIS IS MY FIRST TIME HERE.
I ALWAYS IMAGINED IT WAS A LOT OF BARS. IS IT OKAY FOR TEENAGERS TO BE HERE...?
IS SAKURAGI-SENSEI GOING TO MAKE US KEEP HIM COMPANY WHILE HE DRINKS...?
YAAAY!
*IMAGINATION
MAYBE WE SHOULD BE READY FOR ANY CHANCES TO ESCAPE...
......
......
HEY... UH...
DO YOU HAVE ANY PLANS AFTER DINNER?
NOT REALLY.

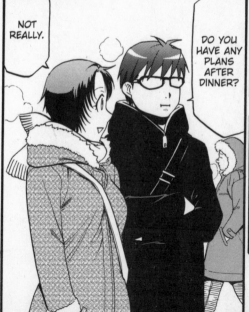

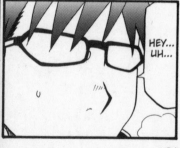

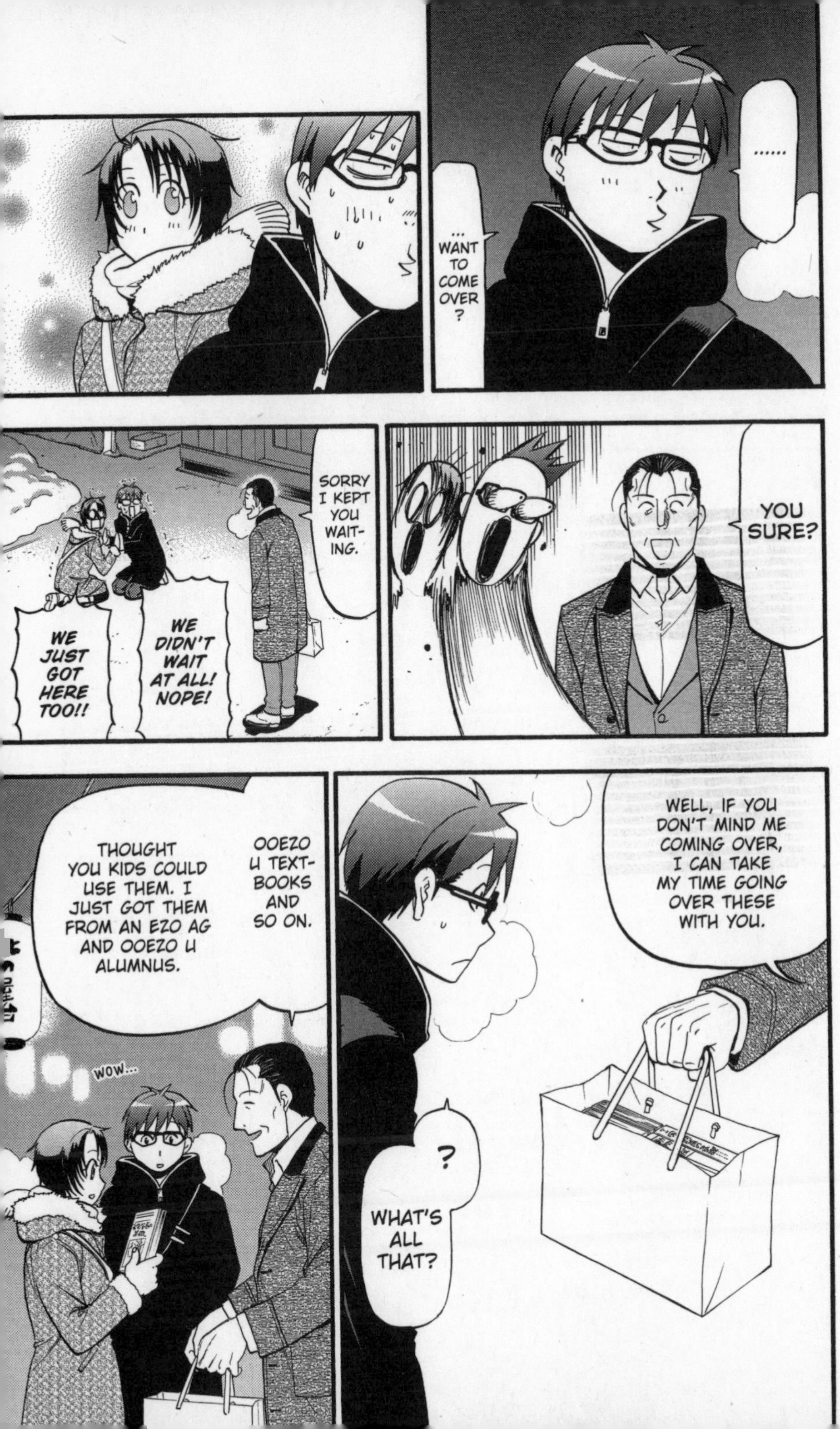
......
... WANT TO COME OVER ?
YOU SURE?
SORRY I KEPT YOU WAITING.
WE DIDN'T WAIT AT ALL! NOPE!
WE JUST GOT HERE TOO!!
WELL, IF YOU DON'T MIND ME COMING OVER, I CAN TAKE MY TIME GOING OVER THESE WITH YOU.
?
WHAT'S ALL THAT?
OOEZO U TEXT-BOOKS AND SO ON.
THOUGHT YOU KIDS COULD USE THEM. I JUST GOT THEM FROM AN EZO AG AND OOEZO U ALUMNUS.
WOW...

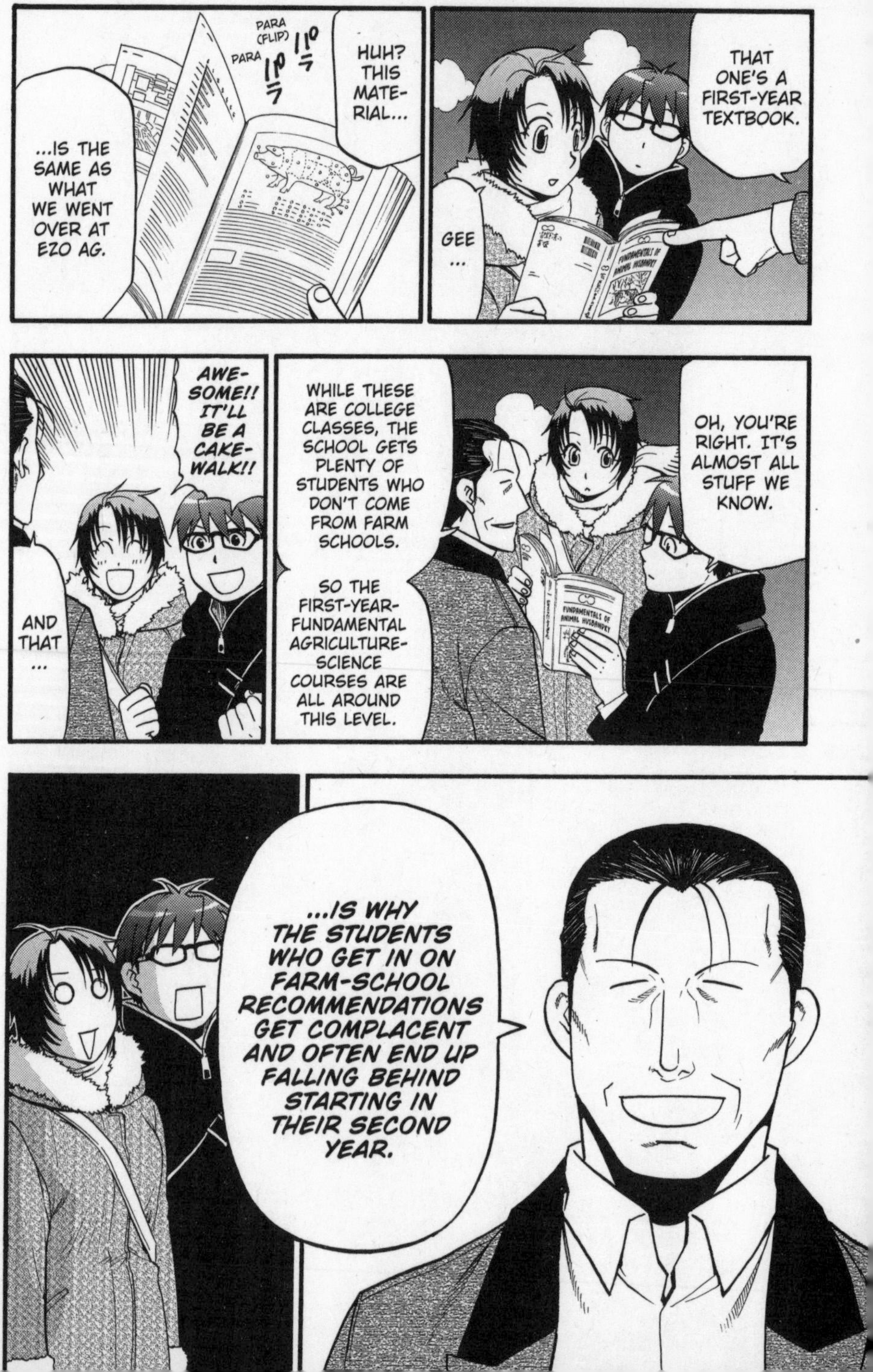
THAT ONE'S A FIRST-YEAR TEXTBOOK.
GEE...
HUH? THIS MATERIAL...
PARA (FLIP) PARA
...IS THE SAME AS WHAT WE WENT OVER AT EZO AG.
OH, YOU'RE RIGHT. IT'S ALMOST ALL STUFF WE KNOW.
WHILE THESE ARE COLLEGE CLASSES, THE SCHOOL GETS PLENTY OF STUDENTS WHO DON'T COME FROM FARM SCHOOLS.
SO THE FIRST-YEAR-FUNDAMENTAL AGRICULTURE-SCIENCE COURSES ARE ALL AROUND THIS LEVEL.
FUNDAMENTALS OF ANIMAL HUSBANDRY
AWESOME!! IT'LL BE A CAKEWALK!!
AND THAT...
...IS WHY THE STUDENTS WHO GET IN ON FARM-SCHOOL RECOMMENDATIONS GET COMPLACENT AND OFTEN END UP FALLING BEHIND STARTING IN THEIR SECOND YEAR.

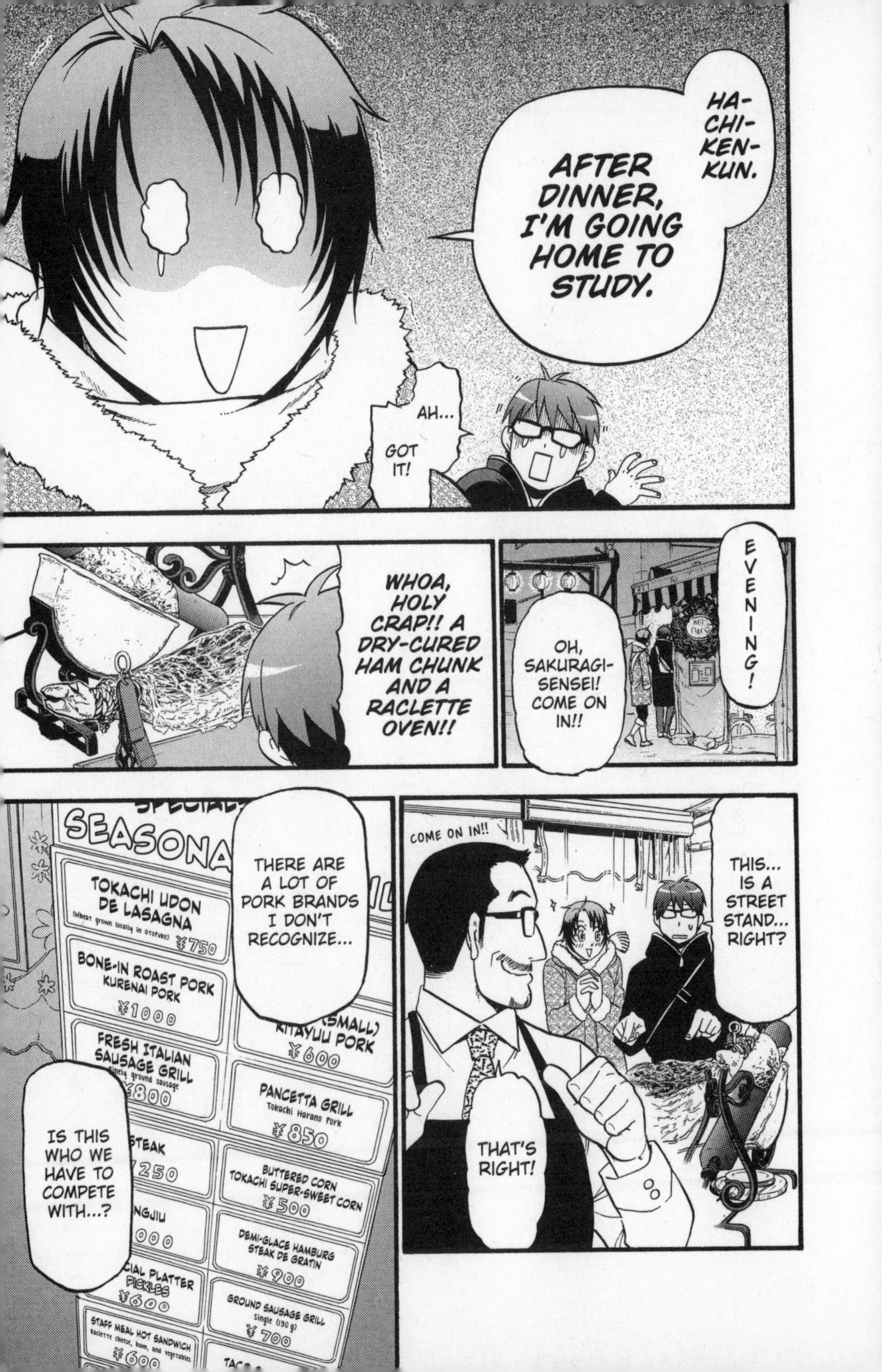
HA-CHI-KEN-KUN.
AFTER DINNER, I'M GOING HOME TO STUDY.
AH...
GOT IT!
EVENING!
OH, SAKURAGI-SENSEI! COME ON IN!!
WHOA, HOLY CRAP!! A DRY-CURED HAM CHUNK AND A RACLETTE OVEN!!
COME ON IN!!
THIS... IS A STREET STAND... RIGHT?
THAT'S RIGHT!
THERE ARE A LOT OF PORK BRANDS I DON'T RECOGNIZE...
SEASONA
TOKACHI UDON DE LASAGNA
(Wheat grown locally in Otofuke) ¥750
BONE-IN ROAST PORK
KURENAI PORK
¥1000
FRESH ITALIAN SAUSAGE GRILL
¥800
STEAK
250
NGJIU
000
PICKLES
¥600
STAFF MEAL HOT SANDWICH
Raclette cheese, ham, and vegetables
¥600
(SMALL)
KITAYUU PORK
¥600
PANCETTA GRILL
Tokachi Harano Pork
¥850
BUTTERED CORN
TOKACHI SUPER-SWEET CORN
¥500
DEMI-GLACE HAMBURG STEAK DE GRATIN
¥900
GROUND SAUSAGE GRILL
Single (130 g)
¥700
IS THIS WHO WE HAVE TO COMPETE WITH...?

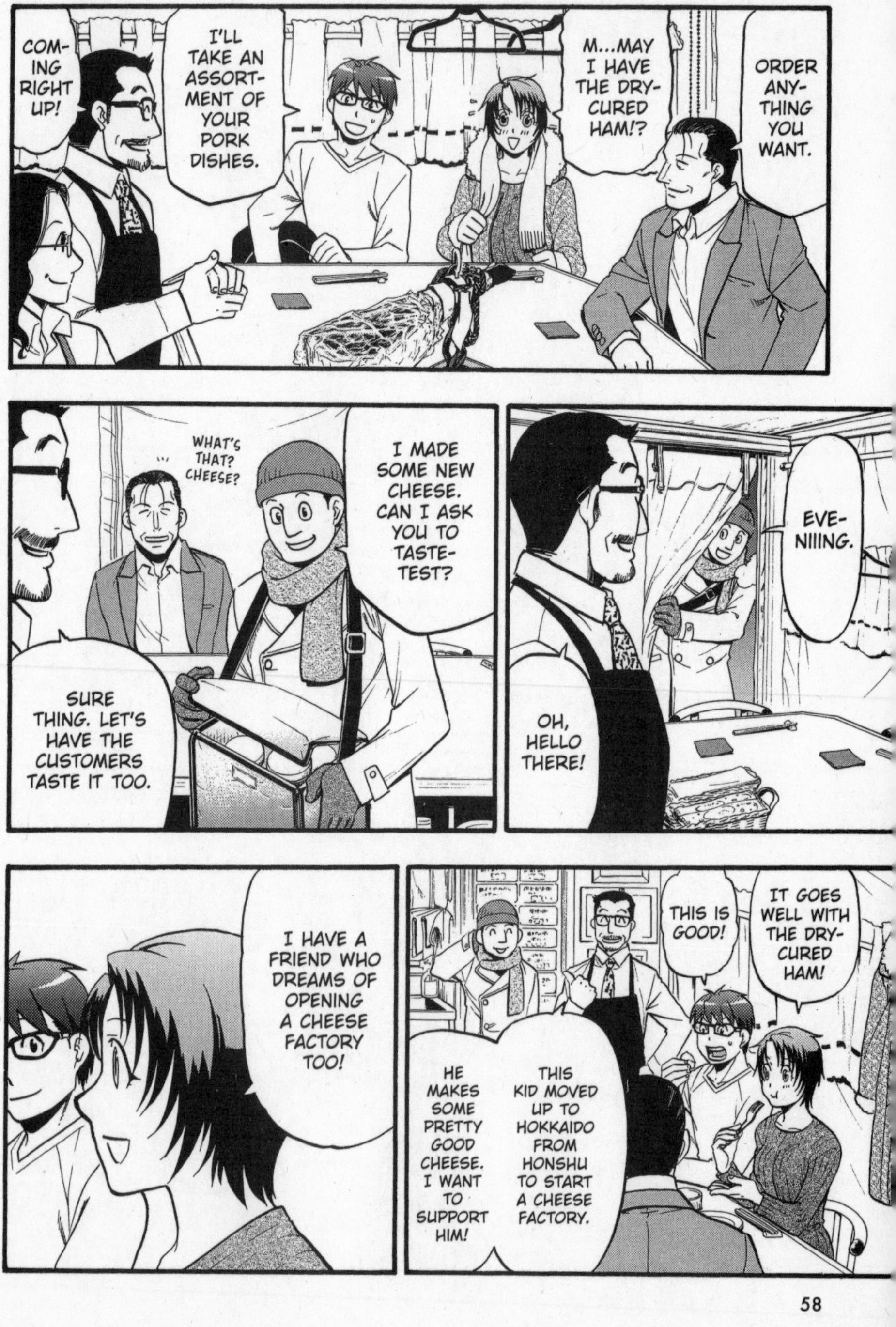
ORDER ANYTHING YOU WANT.
M...MAY I HAVE THE DRY-CURED HAM!?
I'LL TAKE AN ASSORTMENT OF YOUR PORK DISHES.
COMING RIGHT UP!
EVENIIING.
OH, HELLO THERE!
I MADE SOME NEW CHEESE. CAN I ASK YOU TO TASTE-TEST?
WHAT'S THAT? CHEESE?
SURE THING. LET'S HAVE THE CUSTOMERS TASTE IT TOO.
IT GOES WELL WITH THE DRY-CURED HAM!
THIS IS GOOD!
THIS KID MOVED UP TO HOKKAIDO FROM HONSHU TO START A CHEESE FACTORY.
HE MAKES SOME PRETTY GOOD CHEESE. I WANT TO SUPPORT HIM!
I HAVE A FRIEND WHO DREAMS OF OPENING A CHEESE FACTORY TOO!

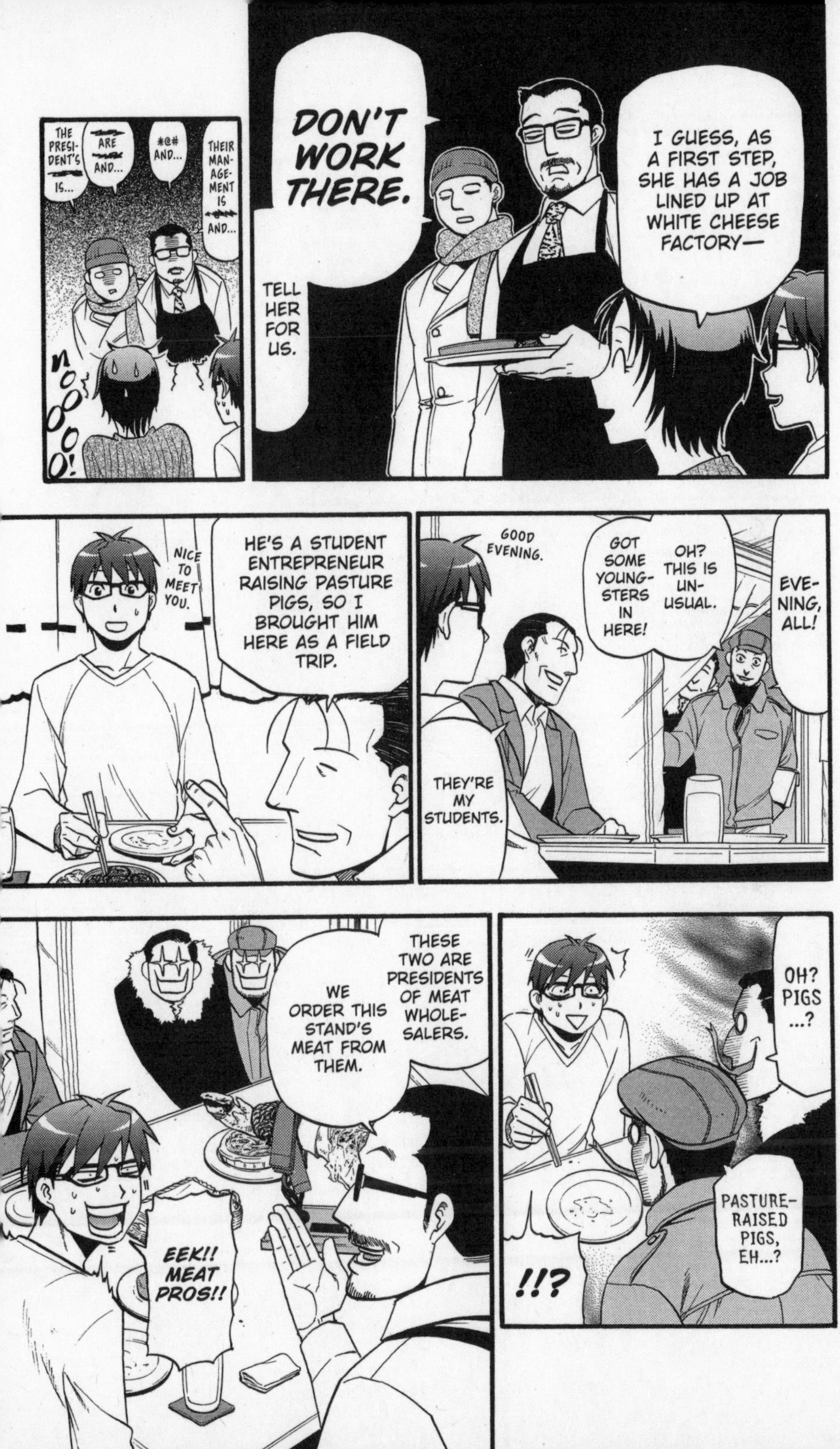
I GUESS, AS A FIRST STEP, SHE HAS A JOB LINED UP AT WHITE CHEESE FACTORY—
DON'T WORK THERE.
TELL HER FOR US.
THEIR MAN-AGE-MENT IS AND...
*@# AND...
ARE AND...
THE PRESI-DENT'S IS...
NOOOOOO!
EVE-NING, ALL!
OH? THIS IS UN-USUAL.
GOT SOME YOUNG-STERS IN HERE!
GOOD EVENING.
THEY'RE MY STUDENTS.
HE'S A STUDENT ENTREPRENEUR RAISING PASTURE PIGS, SO I BROUGHT HIM HERE AS A FIELD TRIP.
NICE TO MEET YOU.
OH? PIGS ...?
PASTURE-RAISED PIGS, EH...?
!!?
THESE TWO ARE PRESIDENTS OF MEAT WHOLE-SALERS.
WE ORDER THIS STAND'S MEAT FROM THEM.
EEK!! MEAT PROS!!

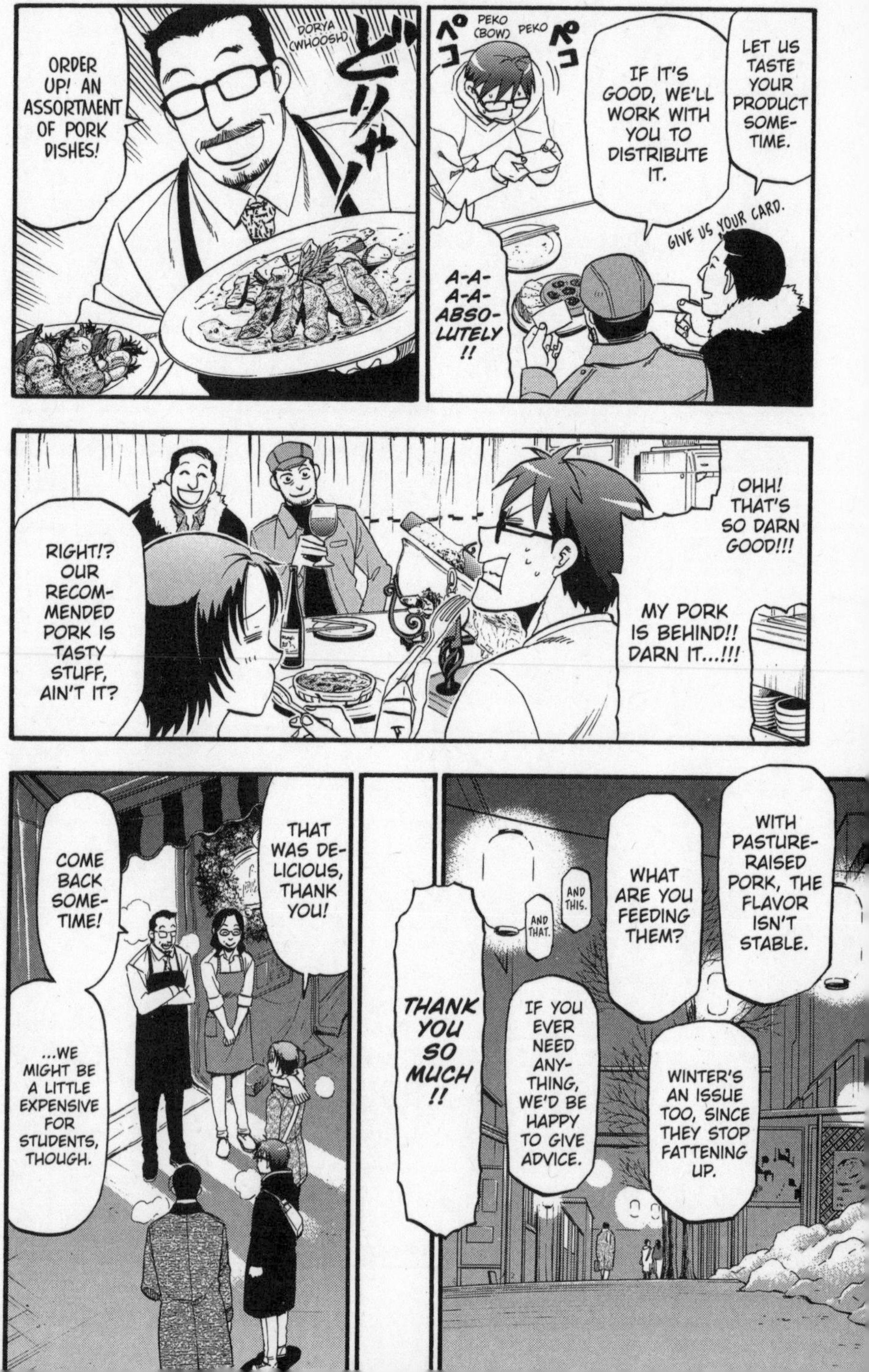
LET US TASTE YOUR PRODUCT SOMETIME.
IF IT'S GOOD, WE'LL WORK WITH YOU TO DISTRIBUTE IT.
PEKO (BOW) PEKO
GIVE US YOUR CARD.
A-A-A-A-ABSOLUTELY!!
DORYA (WHOOSH)
ORDER UP! AN ASSORTMENT OF PORK DISHES!
OHH! THAT'S SO DARN GOOD!!!
MY PORK IS BEHIND!! DARN IT...!!!
RIGHT!? OUR RECOMMENDED PORK IS TASTY STUFF, AIN'T IT?
WITH PASTURE-RAISED PORK, THE FLAVOR ISN'T STABLE.
WHAT ARE YOU FEEDING THEM?
AND THIS.
AND THAT.
WINTER'S AN ISSUE TOO, SINCE THEY STOP FATTENING UP.
IF YOU EVER NEED ANYTHING, WE'D BE HAPPY TO GIVE ADVICE.
THANK YOU SO MUCH!!
THAT WAS DELICIOUS, THANK YOU!
COME BACK SOMETIME!
...WE MIGHT BE A LITTLE EXPENSIVE FOR STUDENTS, THOUGH.

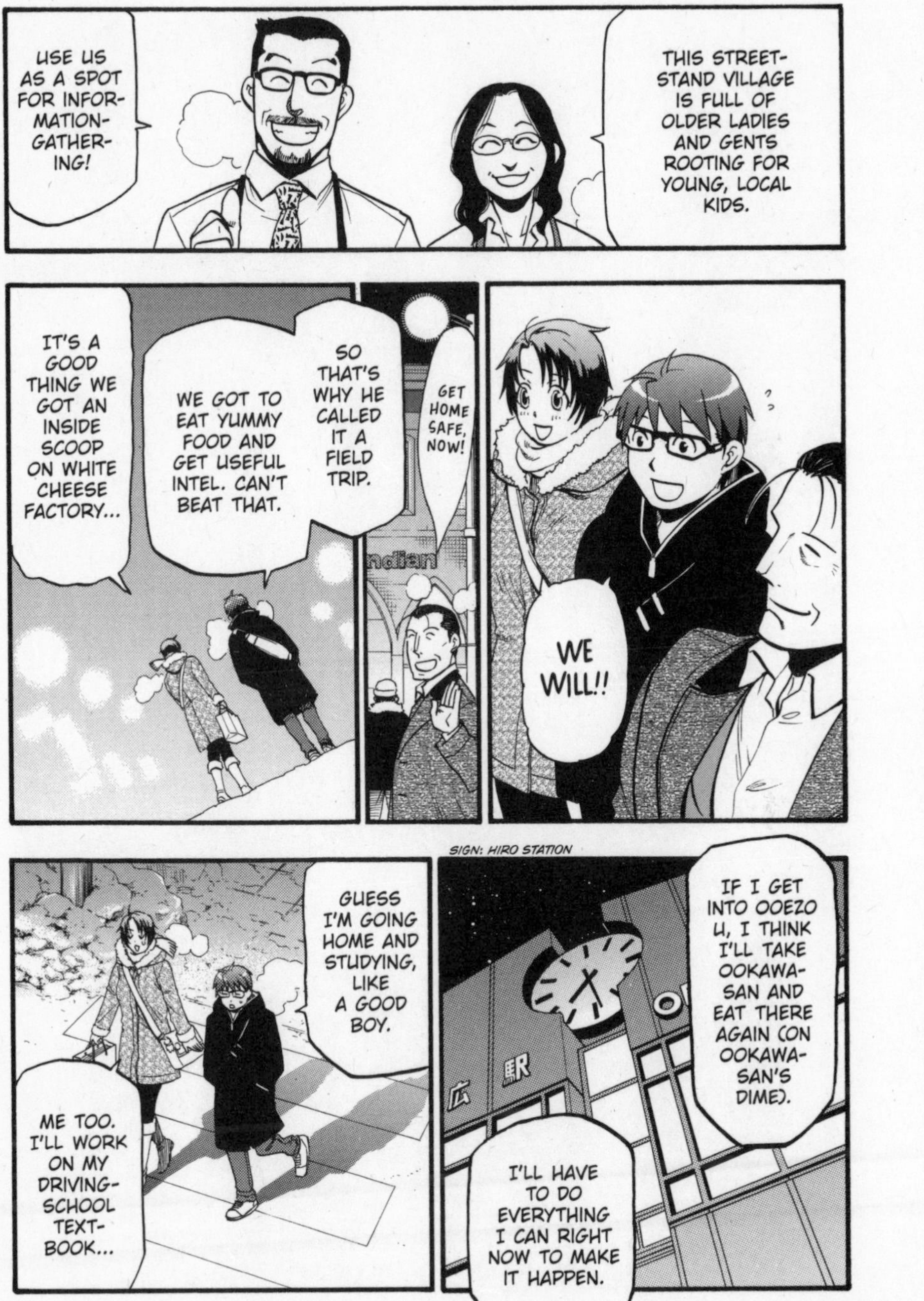
THIS STREET-STAND VILLAGE IS FULL OF OLDER LADIES AND GENTS ROOTING FOR YOUNG, LOCAL KIDS.
USE US AS A SPOT FOR INFORMATION-GATHERING!
WE WILL!!
GET HOME SAFE, NOW!
SO THAT'S WHY HE CALLED IT A FIELD TRIP.
WE GOT TO EAT YUMMY FOOD AND GET USEFUL INTEL. CAN'T BEAT THAT.
IT'S A GOOD THING WE GOT AN INSIDE SCOOP ON WHITE CHEESE FACTORY...
SIGN: HIRO STATION
広駅
IF I GET INTO OOEZO U, I THINK I'LL TAKE OOKAWA-SAN AND EAT THERE AGAIN (ON OOKAWA-SAN'S DIME).
I'LL HAVE TO DO EVERYTHING I CAN RIGHT NOW TO MAKE IT HAPPEN.
GUESS I'M GOING HOME AND STUDYING, LIKE A GOOD BOY.
ME TOO. I'LL WORK ON MY DRIVING-SCHOOL TEXTBOOK...

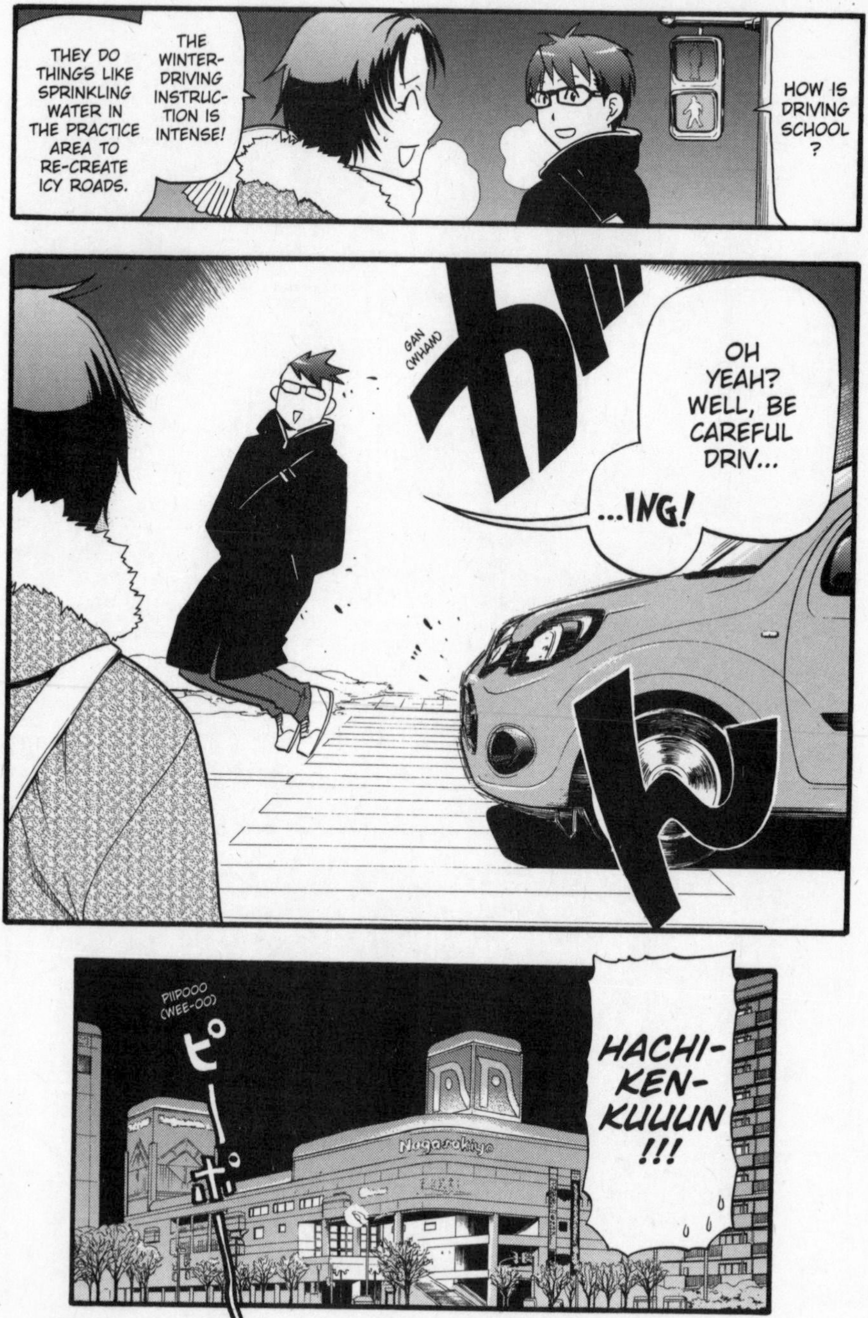
HOW IS DRIVING SCHOOL?
THE WINTER-DRIVING INSTRUCTION IS INTENSE!
THEY DO THINGS LIKE SPRINKLING WATER IN THE PRACTICE AREA TO RE-CREATE ICY ROADS.
OH YEAH? WELL, BE CAREFUL DRIV... ...ING!
GAN (WHAM)
HACHI-KEN-KUUUN!!!
PIIPOOO (WEE-OO)
Nagasakiya

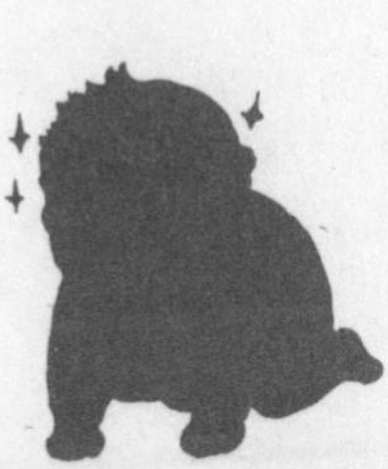

Silver Spoon

### THE PRINCIPAL

WHEN IT CAME TIME TO
MAKE THE BONUSES FOR
VOLUME 15'S SPECIAL
EDITION, I REALIZED I
NEVER GAVE HIM A NAME.

## KOREMICHI KITAKA...

...IS THE NAME I
DECIDED ON.

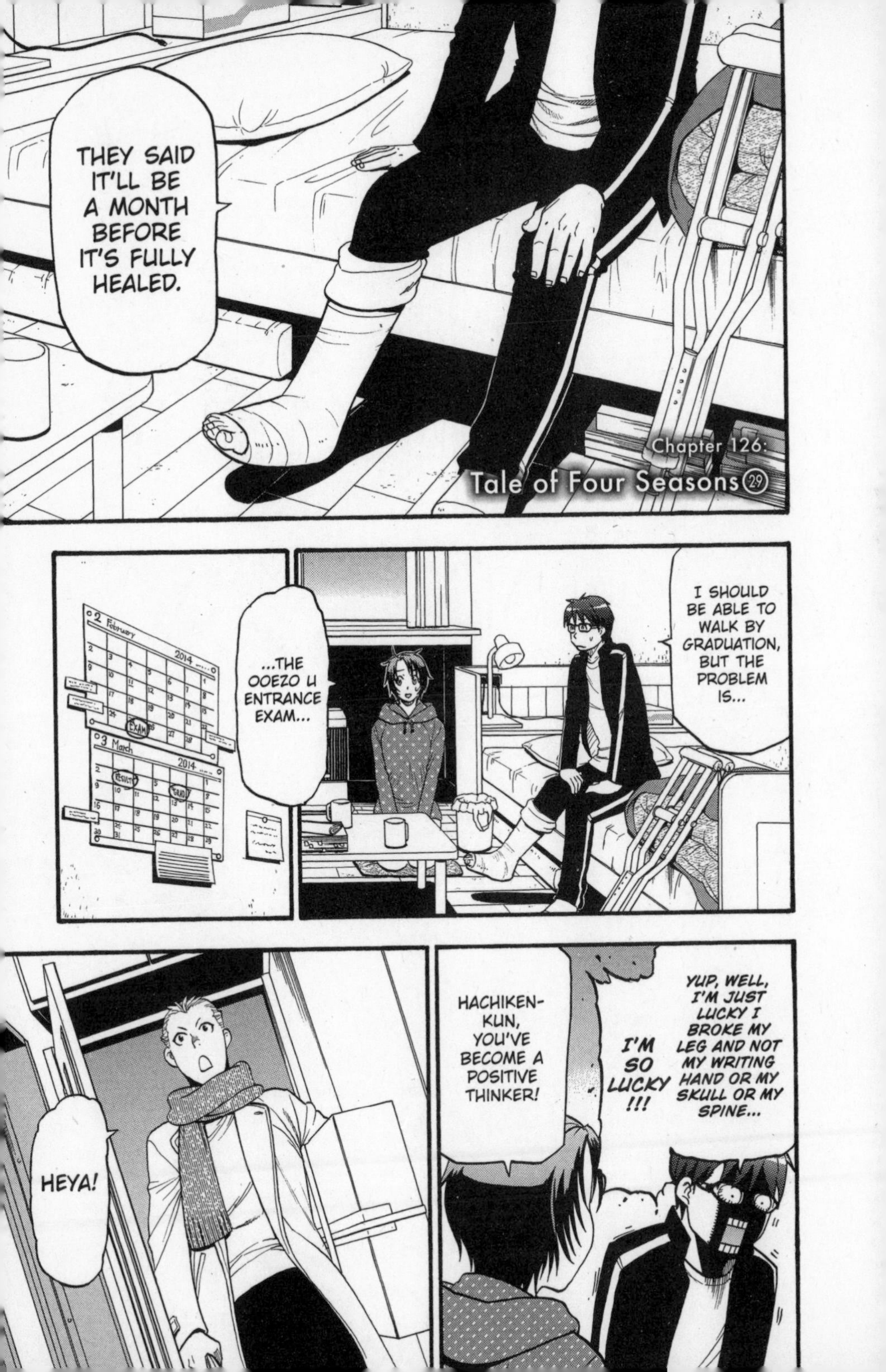
THEY SAID IT'LL BE A MONTH BEFORE IT'S FULLY HEALED.
Chapter 126:
Tale of Four Seasons ㉙
I SHOULD BE ABLE TO WALK BY GRADUATION, BUT THE PROBLEM IS...
...THE OOEZO U ENTRANCE EXAM...
YUP, WELL, I'M JUST LUCKY I BROKE MY LEG AND NOT MY WRITING HAND OR MY SKULL OR MY SPINE...
I'M SO LUCKY!!!
HACHIKEN-KUN, YOU'VE BECOME A POSITIVE THINKER!
HEYA!

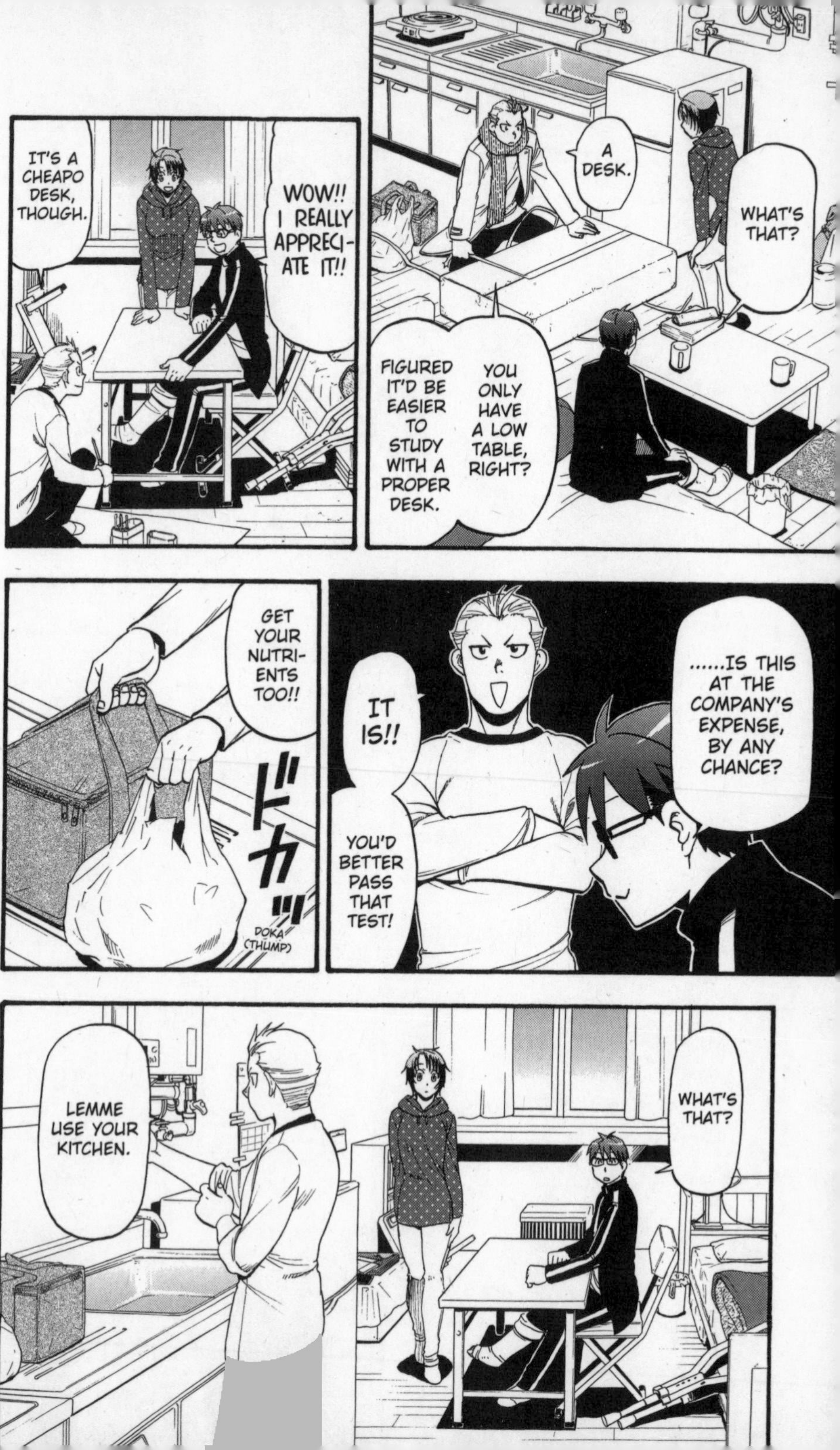
WHAT'S THAT?
A DESK.
YOU ONLY HAVE A LOW TABLE, RIGHT?
FIGURED IT'D BE EASIER TO STUDY WITH A PROPER DESK.
WOW!! I REALLY APPRECIATE IT!!
IT'S A CHEAPO DESK, THOUGH.
......IS THIS AT THE COMPANY'S EXPENSE, BY ANY CHANCE?
IT IS!!
YOU'D BETTER PASS THAT TEST!
GET YOUR NUTRIENTS TOO!!
ドカッ
DOKA (THUMP)
WHAT'S THAT?
LEMME USE YOUR KITCHEN.

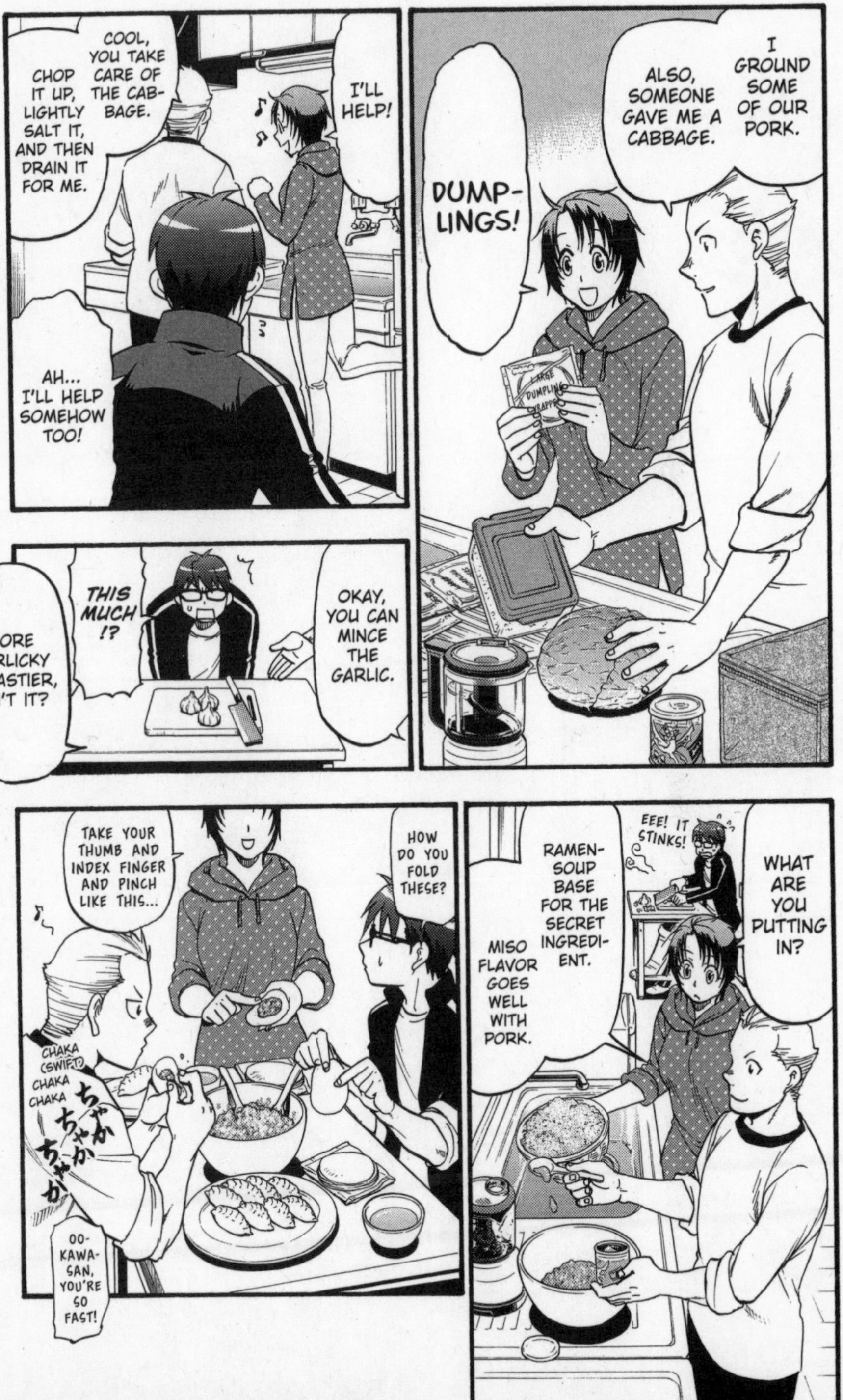
I GROUND SOME OF OUR PORK.
ALSO, SOMEONE GAVE ME A CABBAGE.
DUMPLINGS!
I'LL HELP!
COOL, YOU TAKE CARE OF THE CABBAGE.
CHOP IT UP, LIGHTLY SALT IT, AND THEN DRAIN IT FOR ME.
AH... I'LL HELP SOMEHOW TOO!
OKAY, YOU CAN MINCE THE GARLIC.
THIS MUCH!?
MORE GARLICKY IS TASTIER, ISN'T IT?
WHAT ARE YOU PUTTING IN?
EEE! IT STINKS!
RAMEN-SOUP BASE FOR THE SECRET INGREDIENT.
MISO FLAVOR GOES WELL WITH PORK.
HOW DO YOU FOLD THESE?
TAKE YOUR THUMB AND INDEX FINGER AND PINCH LIKE THIS...
CHAKA (SWIFT) CHAKA CHAKA
ちゃかちゃかちゃか
OO-KAWA-SAN, YOU'RE SO FAST!

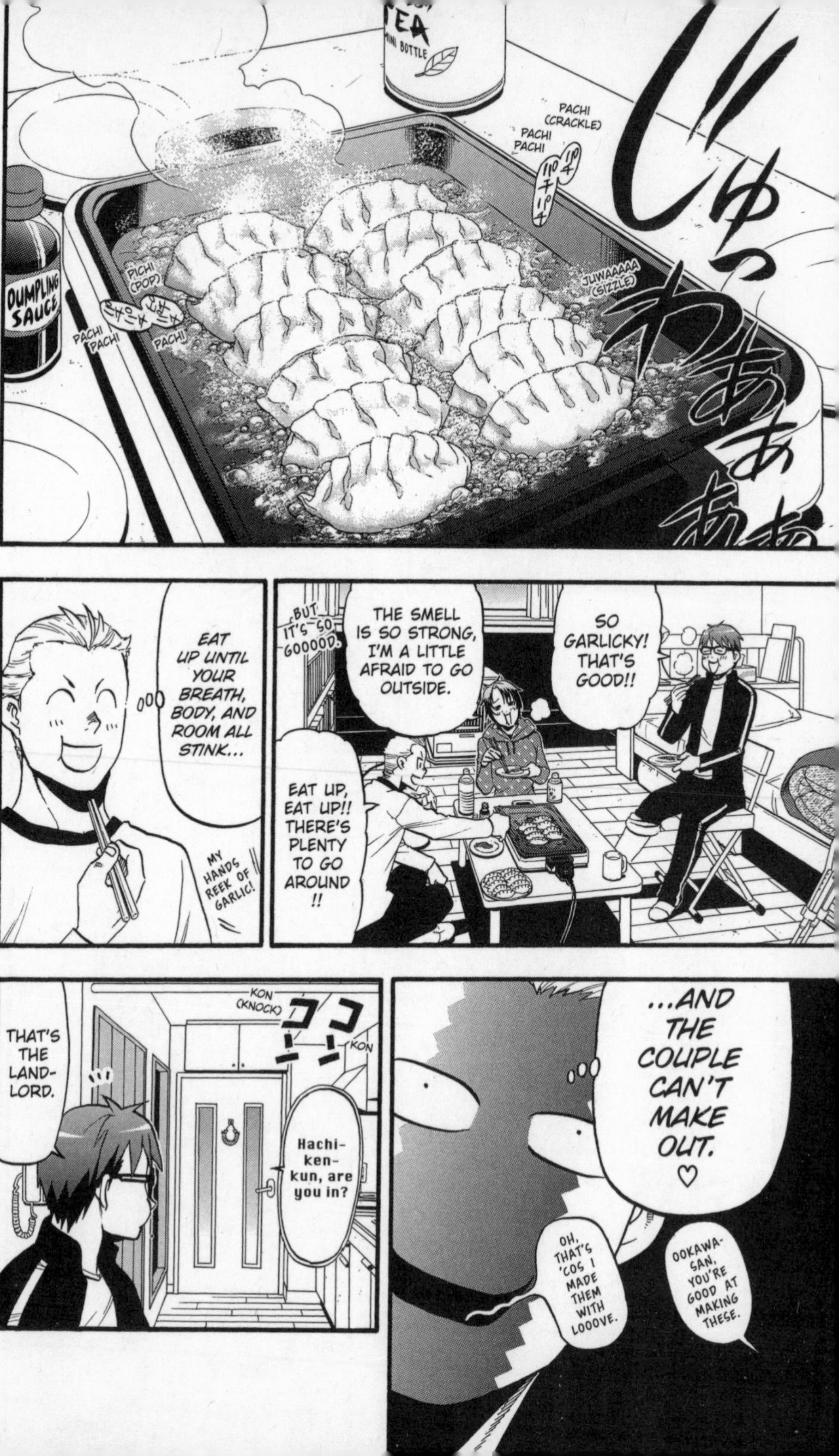
TEA
MINI BOTTLE
JUWAAAAA (SIZZLE)
PACHI (CRACKLE) PACHI PACHI
DUMPLING SAUCE
PICHI (POP)
PACHI PACHI PACHI
SO GARLICKY! THAT'S GOOD!!
THE SMELL IS SO STRONG, I'M A LITTLE AFRAID TO GO OUTSIDE.
BUT IT'S SO GOOOOD.
EAT UP, EAT UP!! THERE'S PLENTY TO GO AROUND !!
MY HANDS REEK OF GARLIC!
EAT UP UNTIL YOUR BREATH, BODY, AND ROOM ALL STINK...
...AND THE COUPLE CAN'T MAKE OUT. ♡
OOKAWA-SAN, YOU'RE GOOD AT MAKING THESE.
OH, THAT'S 'COS I MADE THEM WITH LOOOVE.
KON (KNOCK)
KON
Hachi-ken-kun, are you in?
THAT'S THE LAND-LORD.

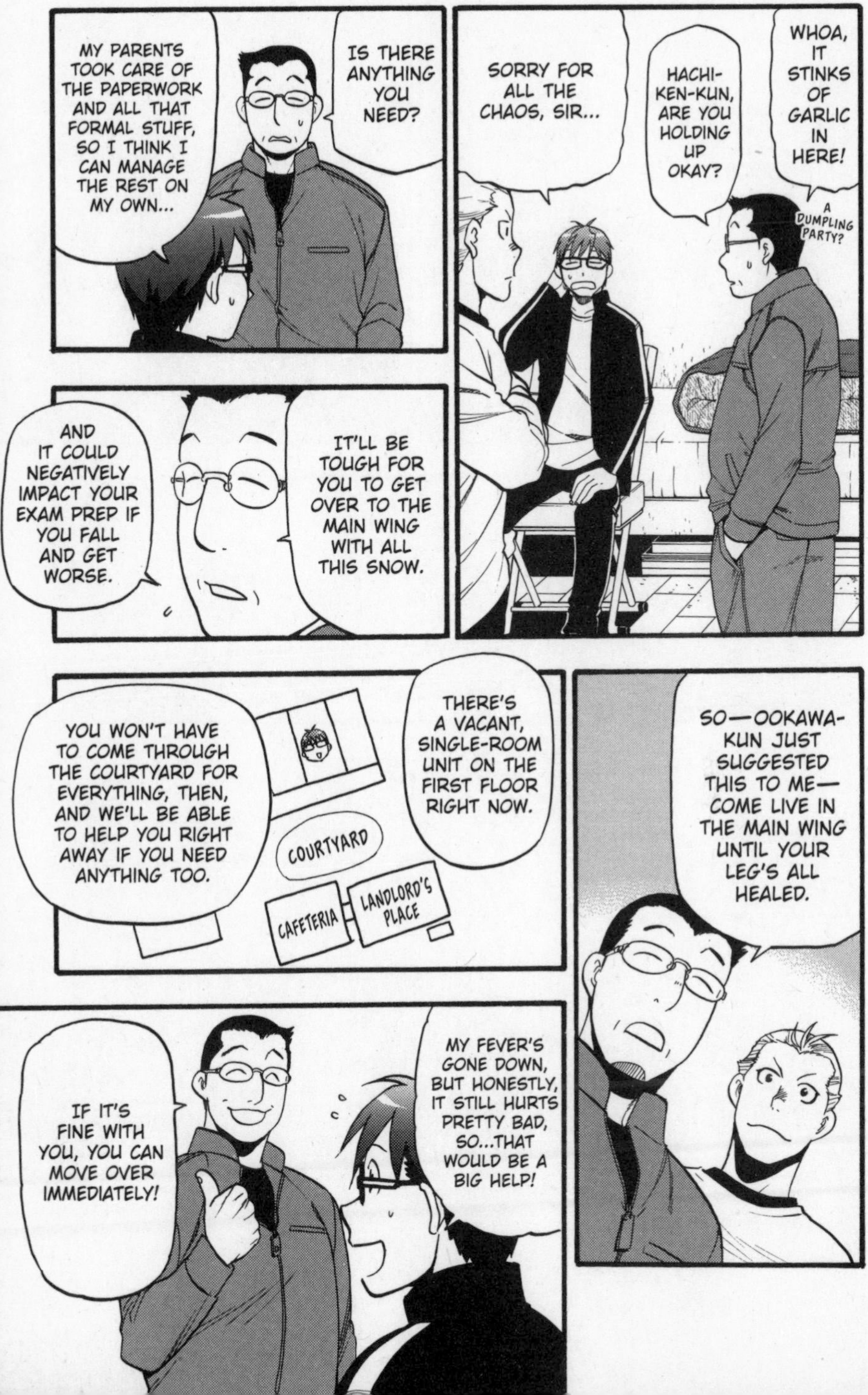
WHOA, IT STINKS OF GARLIC IN HERE!
A DUMPLING PARTY?
HACHI-KEN-KUN, ARE YOU HOLDING UP OKAY?
SORRY FOR ALL THE CHAOS, SIR...
IS THERE ANYTHING YOU NEED?
MY PARENTS TOOK CARE OF THE PAPERWORK AND ALL THAT FORMAL STUFF, SO I THINK I CAN MANAGE THE REST ON MY OWN...
IT'LL BE TOUGH FOR YOU TO GET OVER TO THE MAIN WING WITH ALL THIS SNOW.
AND IT COULD NEGATIVELY IMPACT YOUR EXAM PREP IF YOU FALL AND GET WORSE.
SO—OOKAWA-KUN JUST SUGGESTED THIS TO ME—COME LIVE IN THE MAIN WING UNTIL YOUR LEG'S ALL HEALED.
THERE'S A VACANT, SINGLE-ROOM UNIT ON THE FIRST FLOOR RIGHT NOW.
YOU WON'T HAVE TO COME THROUGH THE COURTYARD FOR EVERYTHING, THEN, AND WE'LL BE ABLE TO HELP YOU RIGHT AWAY IF YOU NEED ANYTHING TOO.
COURTYARD
LANDLORD'S PLACE
CAFETERIA
MY FEVER'S GONE DOWN, BUT HONESTLY, IT STILL HURTS PRETTY BAD, SO...THAT WOULD BE A BIG HELP!
IF IT'S FINE WITH YOU, YOU CAN MOVE OVER IMMEDIATELY!

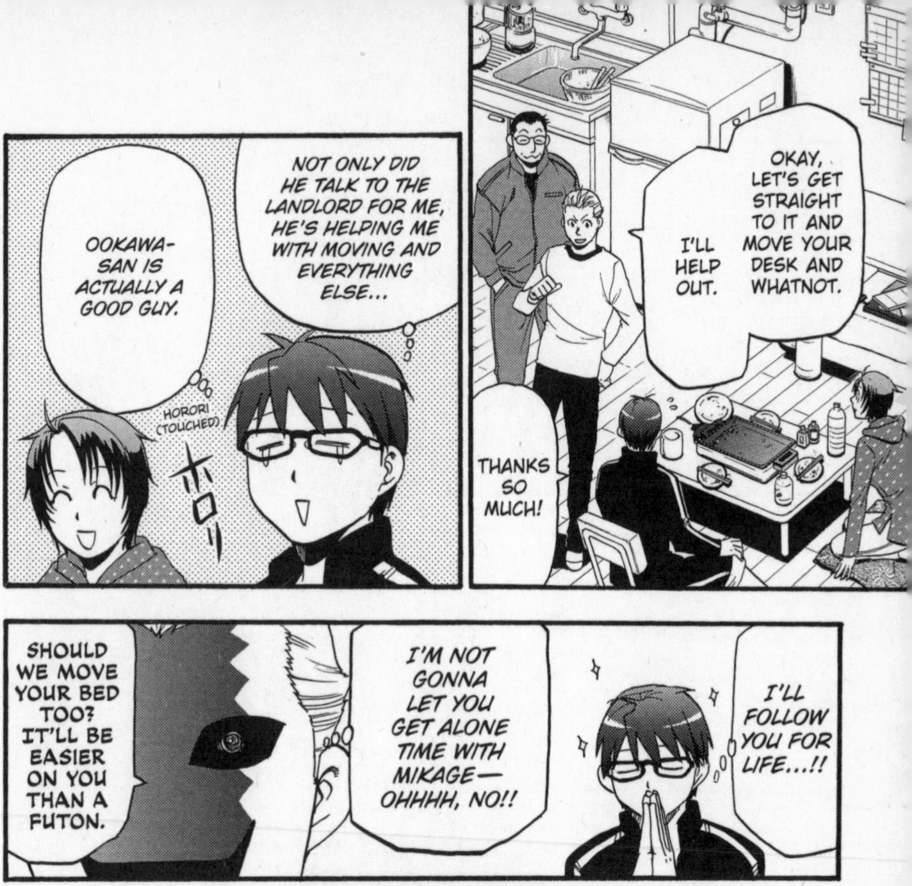
OKAY, LET'S GET STRAIGHT TO IT AND MOVE YOUR DESK AND WHATNOT.
I'LL HELP OUT.
THANKS SO MUCH!
NOT ONLY DID HE TALK TO THE LANDLORD FOR ME, HE'S HELPING ME WITH MOVING AND EVERYTHING ELSE...
OOKAWA-SAN IS ACTUALLY A GOOD GUY.
HORORI (TOUCHED)
I'LL FOLLOW YOU FOR LIFE...!!
I'M NOT GONNA LET YOU GET ALONE TIME WITH MIKAGE—OHHHH, NO!!
SHOULD WE MOVE YOUR BED TOO? IT'LL BE EASIER ON YOU THAN A FUTON.

## Chapter 126:

# Tale of Four Seasons ㉙

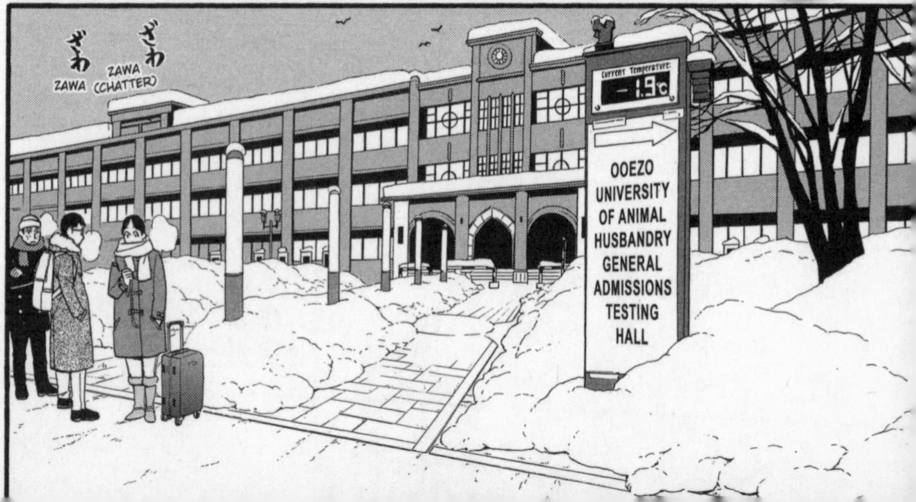
Current Temperature:
-1.9°C
OOEZO UNIVERSITY OF ANIMAL HUSBANDRY GENERAL ADMISSIONS TESTING HALL
ZAWA (CHATTER)
ZAWA

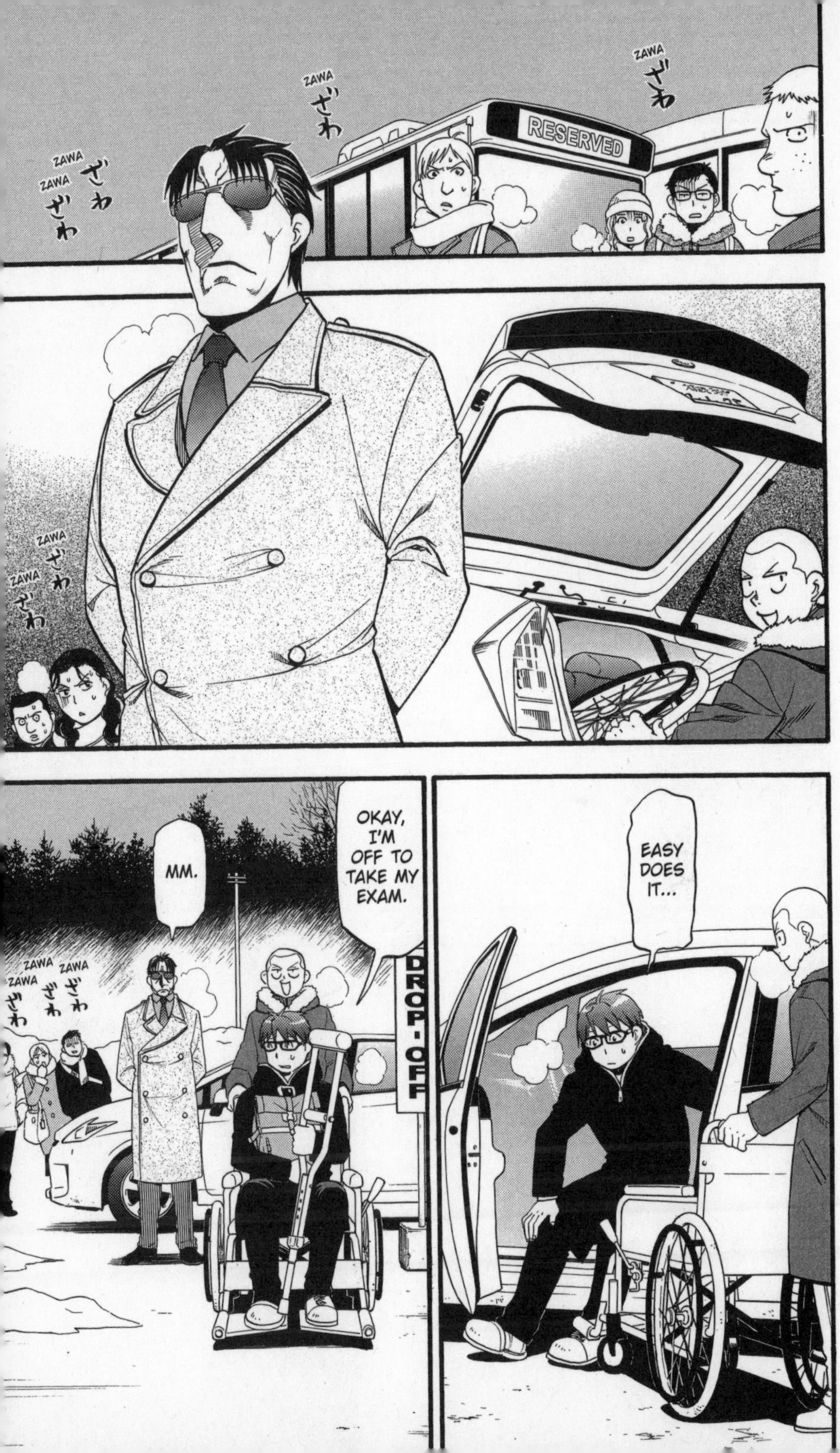
ZAWA ざわ
RESERVED
ZAWA ざわ
ZAWA ざわ
ZAWA ざわ
ZAWA ざわ
ZAWA ざわ
EASY DOES IT...
OKAY, I'M OFF TO TAKE MY EXAM.
MM.
DROP-OFF
ZAWA ざわ
ZAWA ざわ
ZAWA ざわ

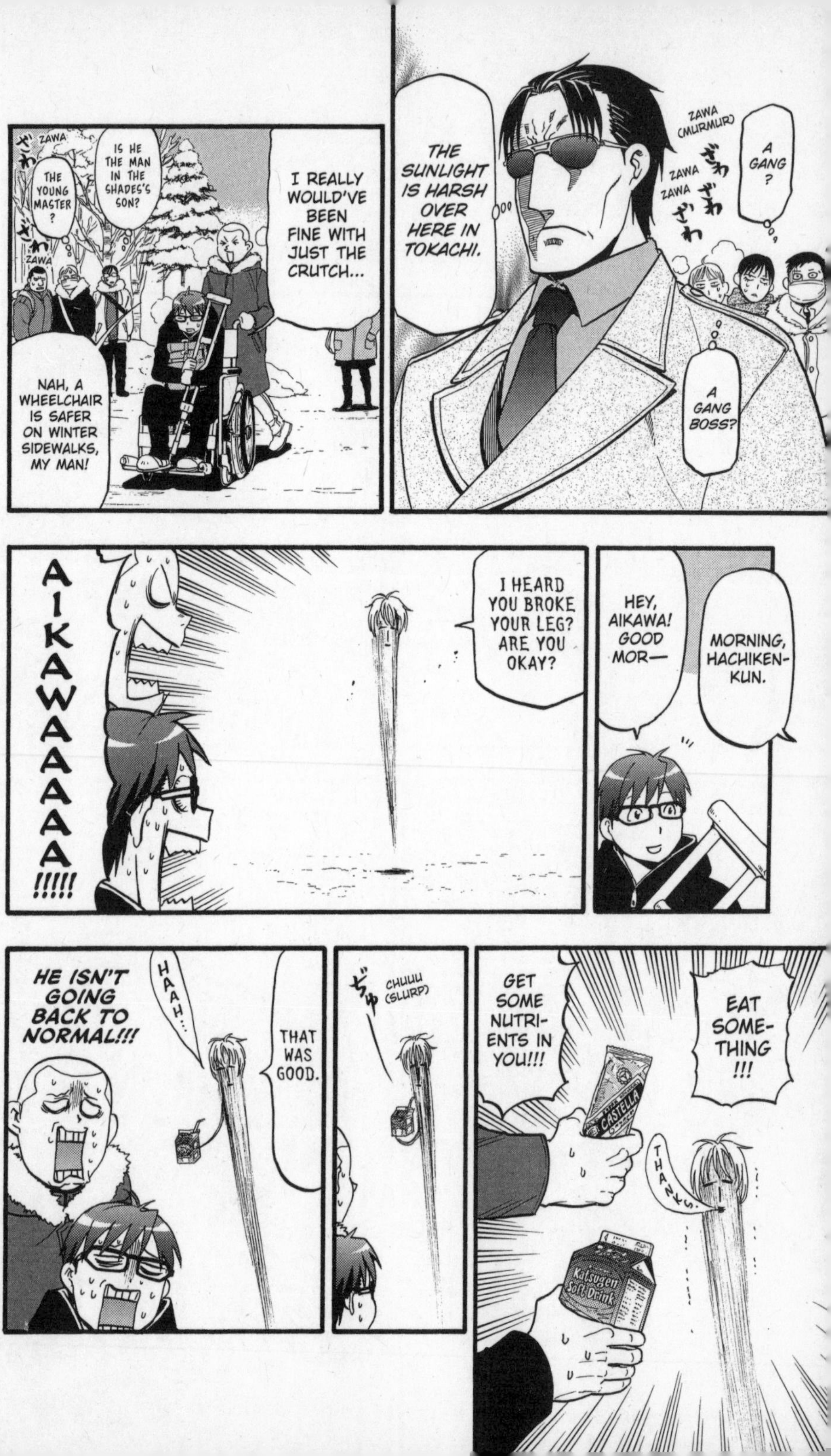
ZAWA (MURMUR)
A GANG?
ZAWA ZAWA
THE SUNLIGHT IS HARSH OVER HERE IN TOKACHI.
A GANG BOSS?
I REALLY WOULD'VE BEEN FINE WITH JUST THE CRUTCH...
IS HE THE MAN IN THE SHADES'S SON?
ZAWA
THE YOUNG MASTER?
ZAWA
NAH, A WHEELCHAIR IS SAFER ON WINTER SIDEWALKS, MY MAN!
MORNING, HACHIKEN-KUN.
HEY, AIKAWA! GOOD MOR—
I HEARD YOU BROKE YOUR LEG? ARE YOU OKAY?
AIKAWAAAAAAA!!!!!
EAT SOMETHING!!!
GET SOME NUTRIENTS IN YOU!!!
CASTELLA
THANKS.
Katsugen Soft Drink
CHUUU (SLURP)
THAT WAS GOOD.
HAAH...
HE ISN'T GOING BACK TO NORMAL!!!

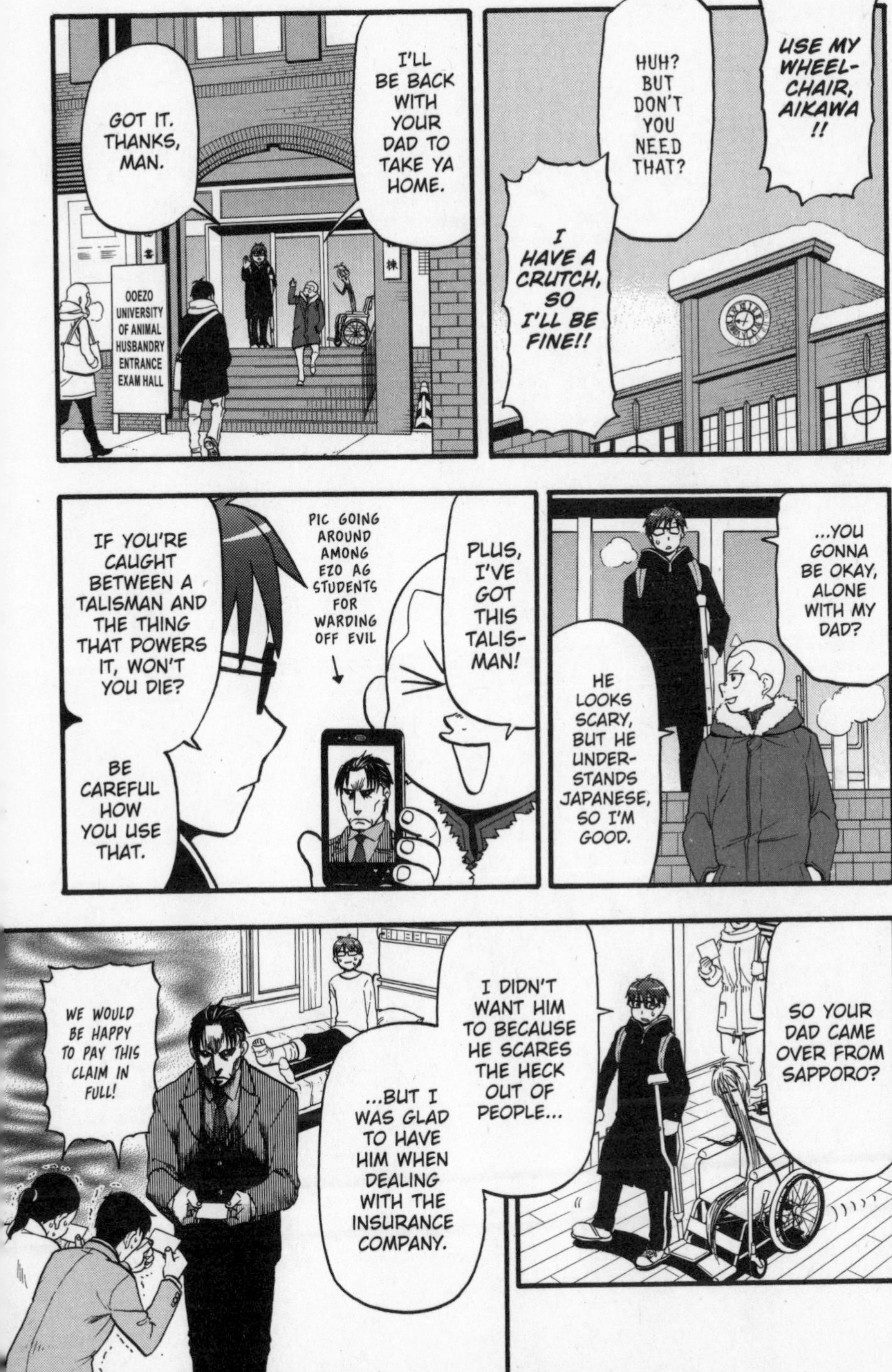
USE MY WHEEL-CHAIR, AIKAWA!!
HUH? BUT DON'T YOU NEED THAT?
I HAVE A CRUTCH, SO I'LL BE FINE!!
I'LL BE BACK WITH YOUR DAD TO TAKE YA HOME.
GOT IT. THANKS, MAN.
OOEZO UNIVERSITY OF ANIMAL HUSBANDRY ENTRANCE EXAM HALL
...YOU GONNA BE OKAY, ALONE WITH MY DAD?
HE LOOKS SCARY, BUT HE UNDER-STANDS JAPANESE, SO I'M GOOD.
PLUS, I'VE GOT THIS TALIS-MAN!
PIC GOING AROUND AMONG EZO AG STUDENTS FOR WARDING OFF EVIL
IF YOU'RE CAUGHT BETWEEN A TALISMAN AND THE THING THAT POWERS IT, WON'T YOU DIE?
BE CAREFUL HOW YOU USE THAT.
SO YOUR DAD CAME OVER FROM SAPPORO?
I DIDN'T WANT HIM TO BECAUSE HE SCARES THE HECK OUT OF PEOPLE...
...BUT I WAS GLAD TO HAVE HIM WHEN DEALING WITH THE INSURANCE COMPANY.
WE WOULD BE HAPPY TO PAY THIS CLAIM IN FULL!

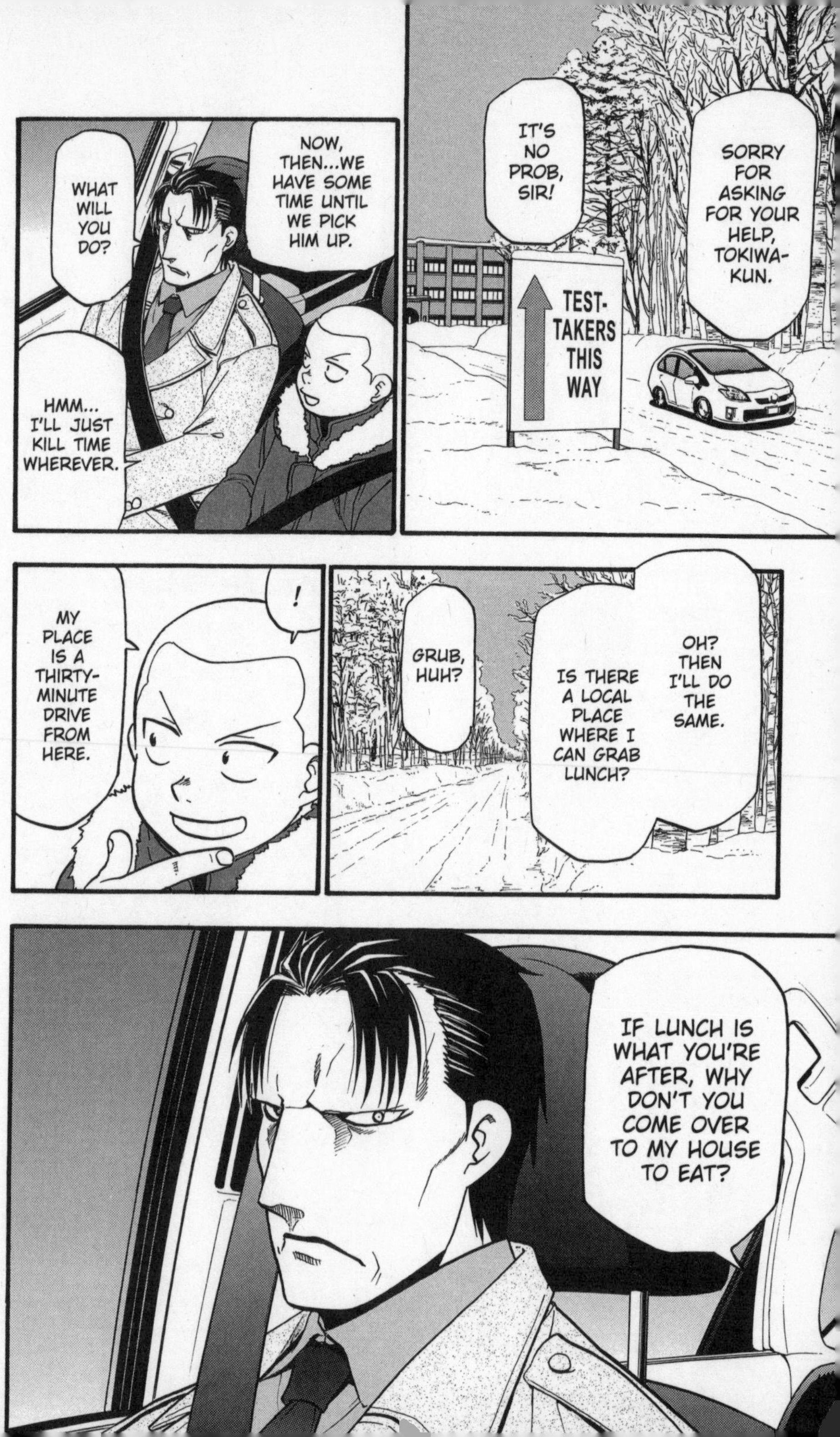
SORRY FOR ASKING FOR YOUR HELP, TOKIWA-KUN.
IT'S NO PROB, SIR!
TEST-TAKERS THIS WAY
NOW, THEN...WE HAVE SOME TIME UNTIL WE PICK HIM UP.
WHAT WILL YOU DO?
HMM... I'LL JUST KILL TIME WHEREVER.
OH? THEN I'LL DO THE SAME.
IS THERE A LOCAL PLACE WHERE I CAN GRAB LUNCH?
GRUB, HUH?
!
MY PLACE IS A THIRTY-MINUTE DRIVE FROM HERE.
IF LUNCH IS WHAT YOU'RE AFTER, WHY DON'T YOU COME OVER TO MY HOUSE TO EAT?

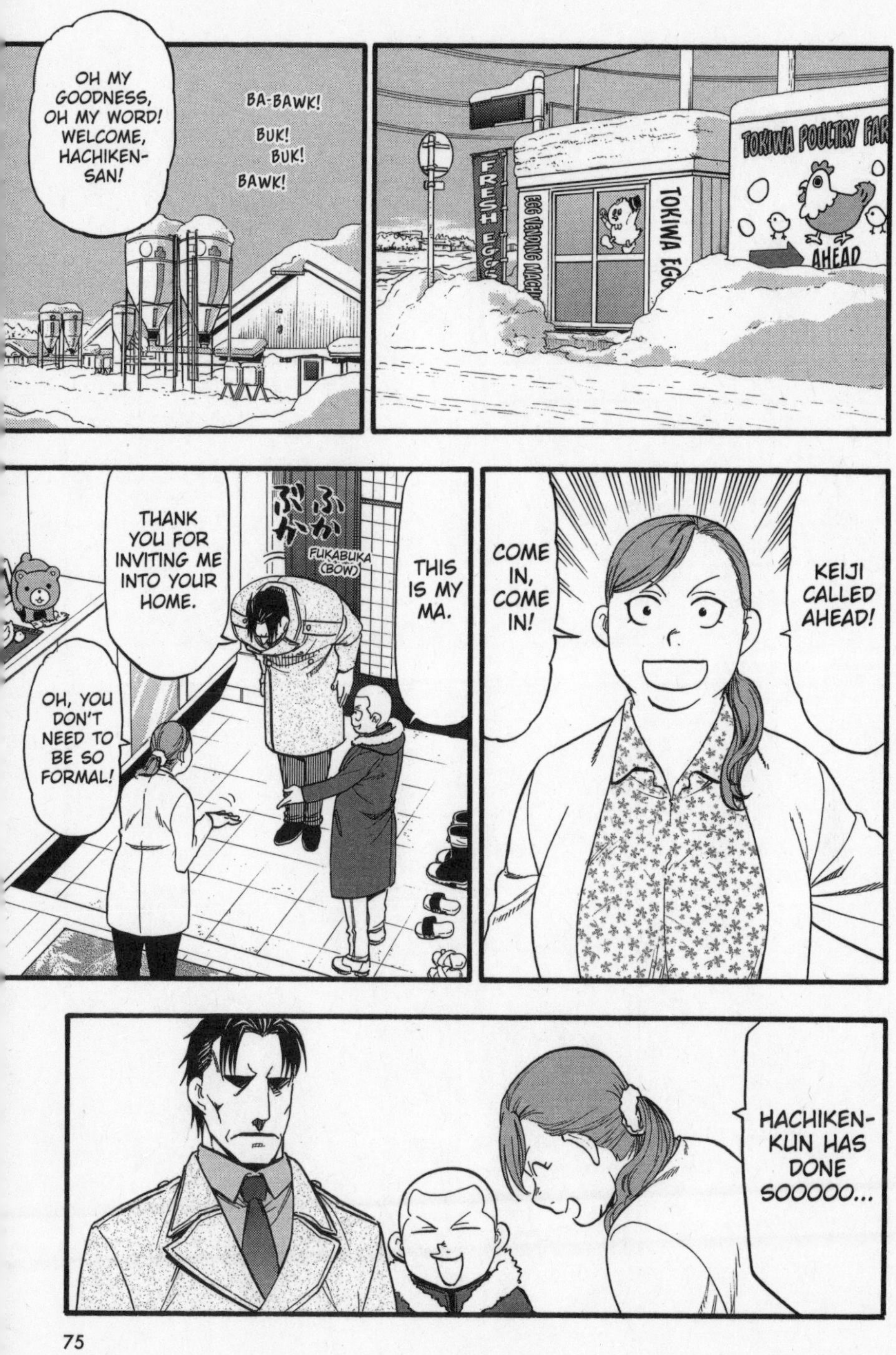

TOKIWA POULTRY FAR
AHEAD
TOKIWA EGG
EGG VENDING MACH
FRESH EGG
OH MY GOODNESS, OH MY WORD! WELCOME, HACHIKEN-SAN!
BA-BAWK!
BUK! BUK!
BAWK!
KEIJI CALLED AHEAD!
COME IN, COME IN!
THIS IS MY MA.
ふかぶか
FUKABUKA (BOW)
THANK YOU FOR INVITING ME INTO YOUR HOME.
OH, YOU DON'T NEED TO BE SO FORMAL!
HACHIKEN-KUN HAS DONE SOOOOO...

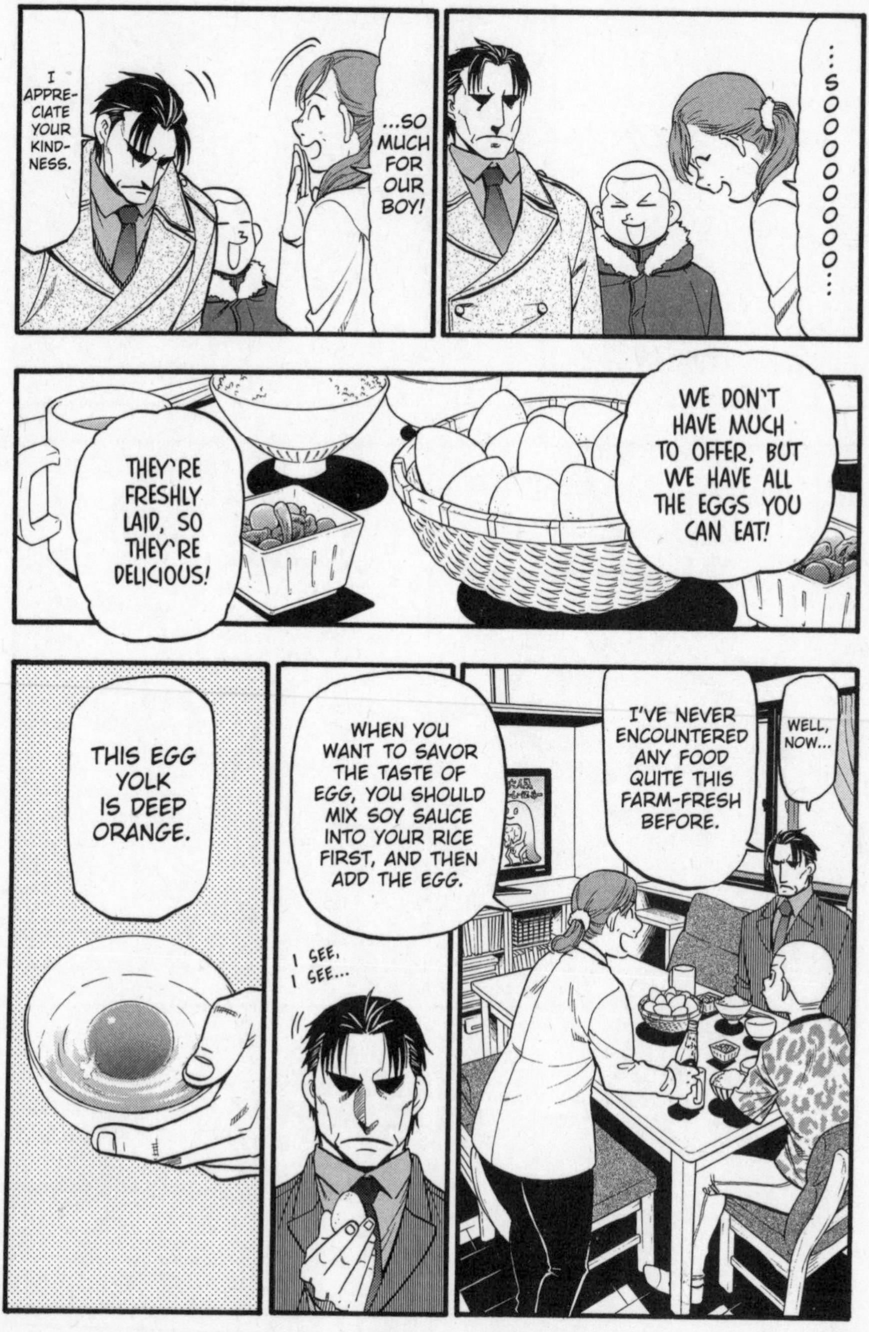
...SOOOOOOOOO...
...SO MUCH FOR OUR BOY!
I APPRECIATE YOUR KINDNESS.
WE DON'T HAVE MUCH TO OFFER, BUT WE HAVE ALL THE EGGS YOU CAN EAT!
THEY'RE FRESHLY LAID, SO THEY'RE DELICIOUS!
WELL, NOW...
I'VE NEVER ENCOUNTERED ANY FOOD QUITE THIS FARM-FRESH BEFORE.
WHEN YOU WANT TO SAVOR THE TASTE OF EGG, YOU SHOULD MIX SOY SAUCE INTO YOUR RICE FIRST, AND THEN ADD THE EGG.
I SEE, I SEE...
THIS EGG YOLK IS DEEP ORANGE.

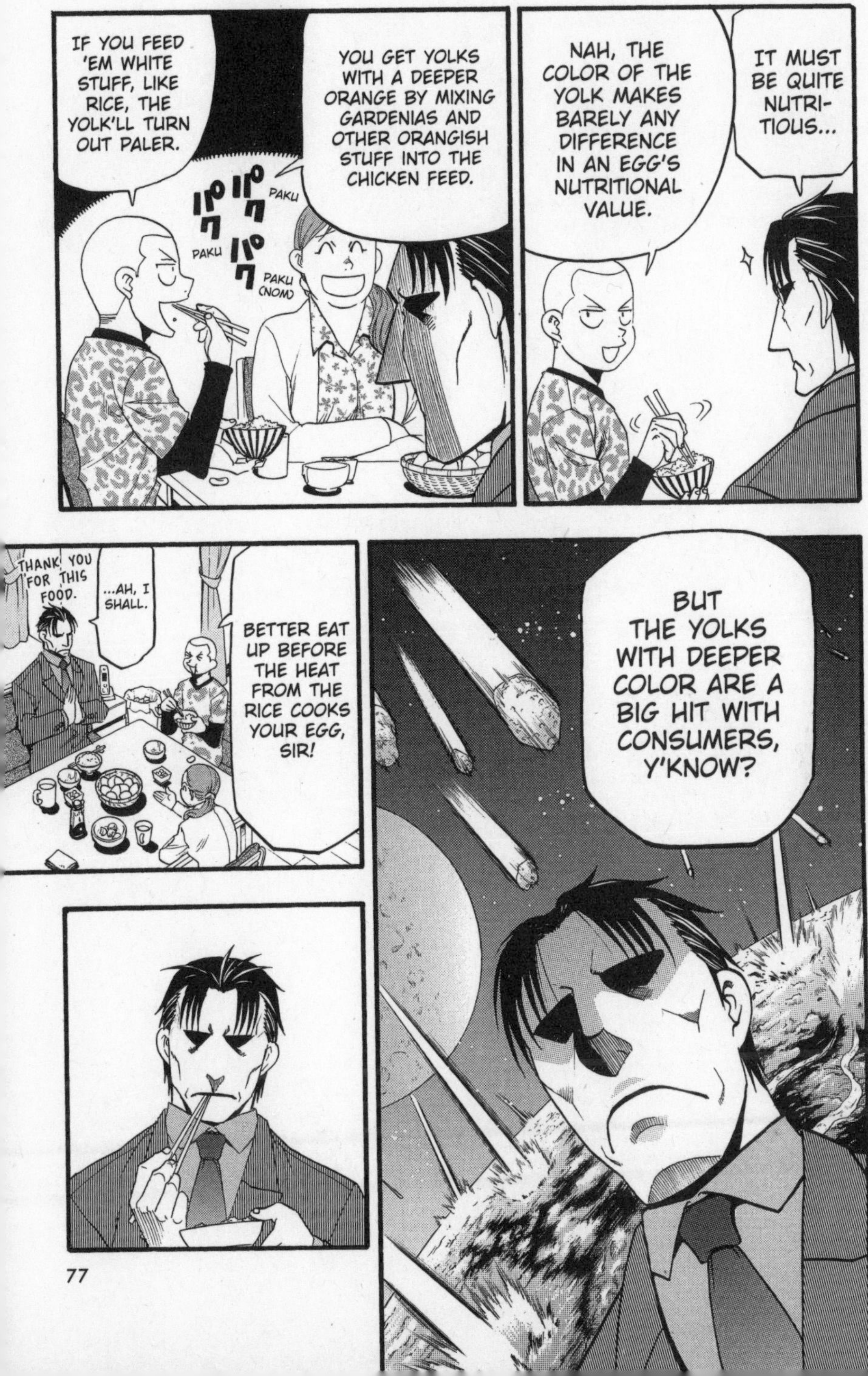
IT MUST BE QUITE NUTRITIOUS...
NAH, THE COLOR OF THE YOLK MAKES BARELY ANY DIFFERENCE IN AN EGG'S NUTRITIONAL VALUE.
YOU GET YOLKS WITH A DEEPER ORANGE BY MIXING GARDENIAS AND OTHER ORANGISH STUFF INTO THE CHICKEN FEED.
PAKU
PAKU
PAKU (NOM)
IF YOU FEED 'EM WHITE STUFF, LIKE RICE, THE YOLK'LL TURN OUT PALER.
BUT THE YOLKS WITH DEEPER COLOR ARE A BIG HIT WITH CONSUMERS, Y'KNOW?
BETTER EAT UP BEFORE THE HEAT FROM THE RICE COOKS YOUR EGG, SIR!
...AH, I SHALL.
THANK YOU FOR THIS FOOD.

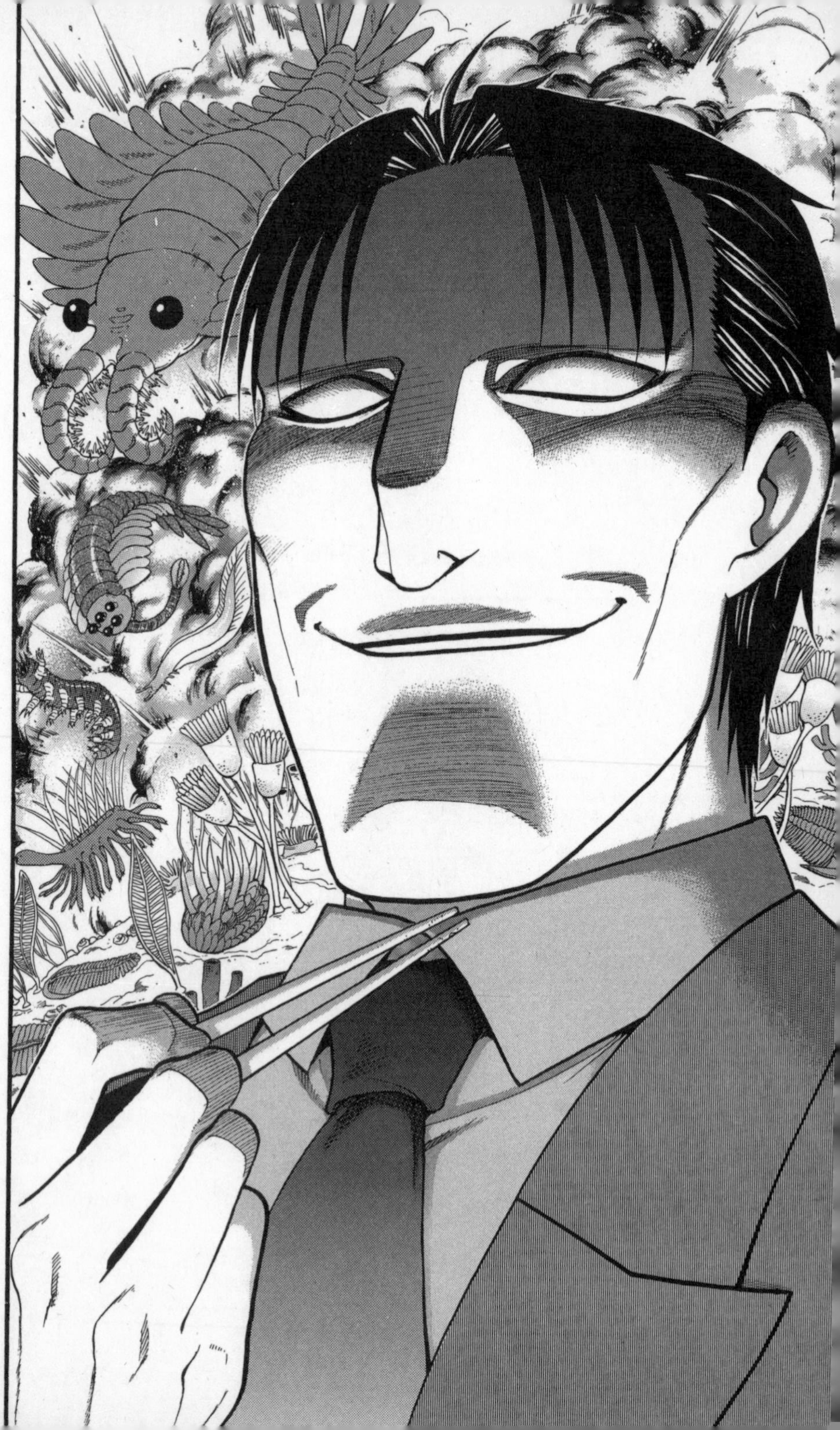

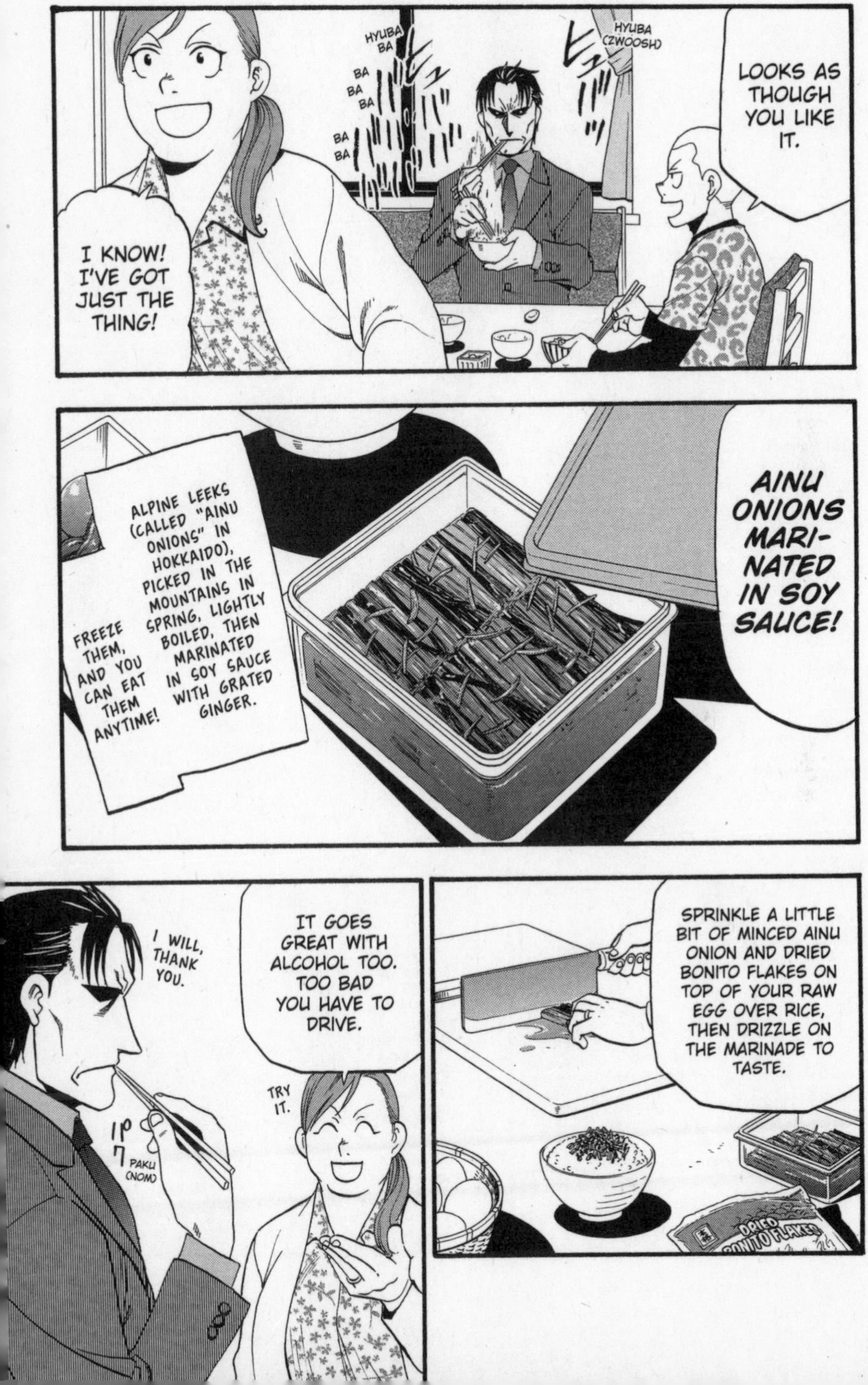
LOOKS AS THOUGH YOU LIKE IT.
HYUBA (ZWOOSH)
HYUBA BA
BA BA BA
BA BA
I KNOW! I'VE GOT JUST THE THING!
AINU ONIONS MARI-NATED IN SOY SAUCE!
ALPINE LEEKS (CALLED "AINU ONIONS" IN HOKKAIDO), PICKED IN THE MOUNTAINS IN SPRING, LIGHTLY BOILED, THEN MARINATED IN SOY SAUCE WITH GRATED GINGER.
FREEZE THEM, AND YOU CAN EAT THEM ANYTIME!
SPRINKLE A LITTLE BIT OF MINCED AINU ONION AND DRIED BONITO FLAKES ON TOP OF YOUR RAW EGG OVER RICE, THEN DRIZZLE ON THE MARINADE TO TASTE.
DRIED BONITO FLAKES
IT GOES GREAT WITH ALCOHOL TOO. TOO BAD YOU HAVE TO DRIVE.
I WILL, THANK YOU.
TRY IT.
PAKU (NOM)

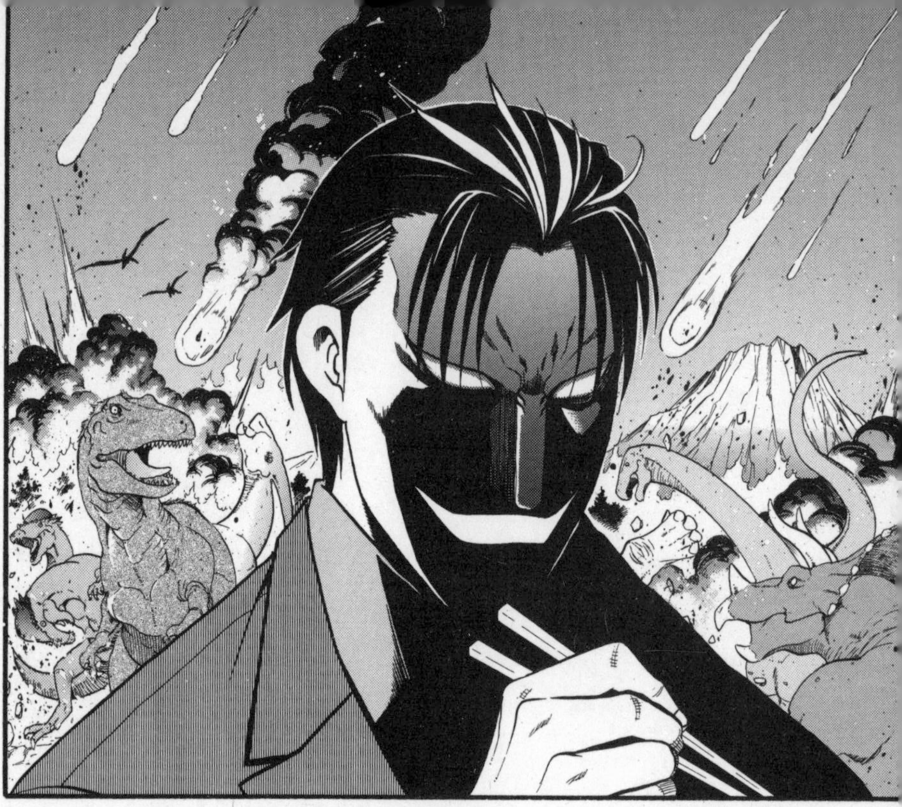

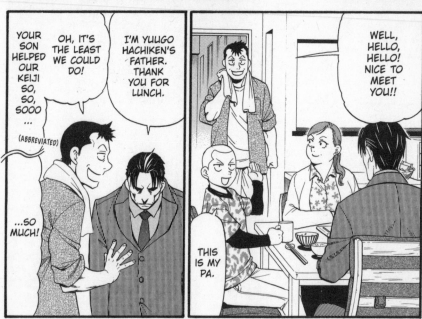

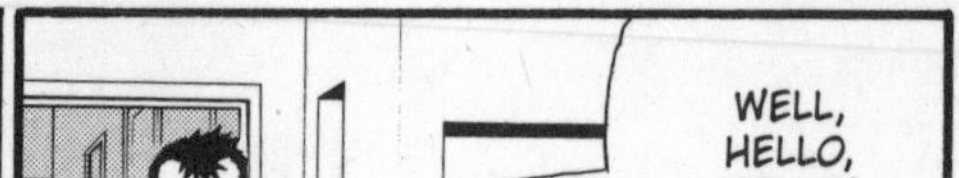
WELL, HELLO, HELLO! NICE TO MEET YOU!!
THIS IS MY PA.

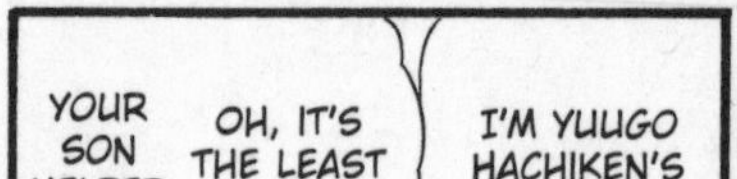
I'M YUUGO HACHIKEN'S FATHER. THANK YOU FOR LUNCH.
OH, IT'S THE LEAST WE COULD DO!
YOUR SON HELPED OUR KEIJI SO, SO, SOOO ...
(ABBREVIATED)
...SO MUCH!

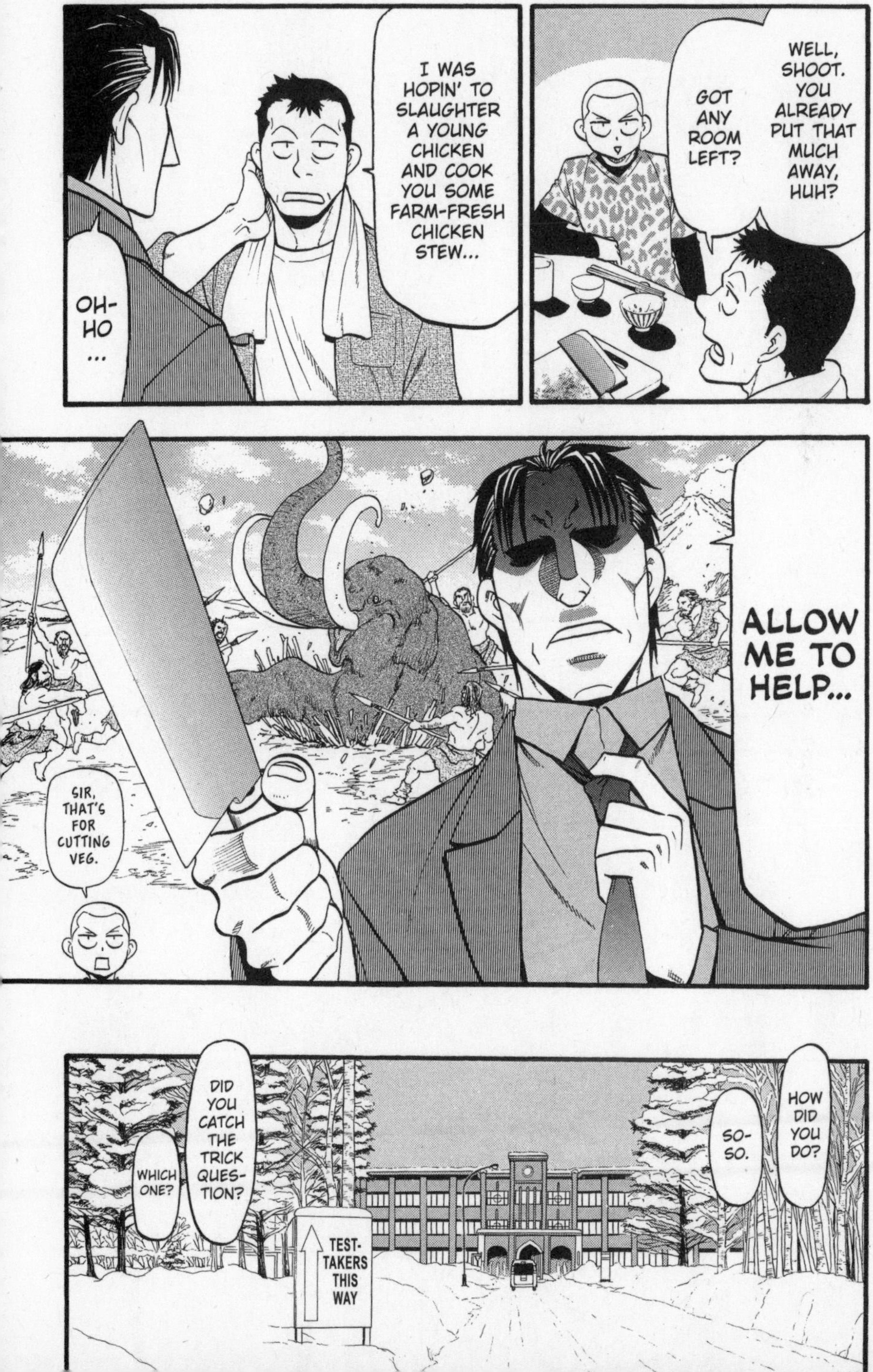
WELL, SHOOT. YOU ALREADY PUT THAT MUCH AWAY, HUH?
GOT ANY ROOM LEFT?
I WAS HOPIN' TO SLAUGHTER A YOUNG CHICKEN AND COOK YOU SOME FARM-FRESH CHICKEN STEW...
OH-HO...
ALLOW ME TO HELP...
SIR, THAT'S FOR CUTTING VEG.
HOW DID YOU DO?
SO-SO.
DID YOU CATCH THE TRICK QUES-TION?
WHICH ONE?
TEST-TAKERS THIS WAY

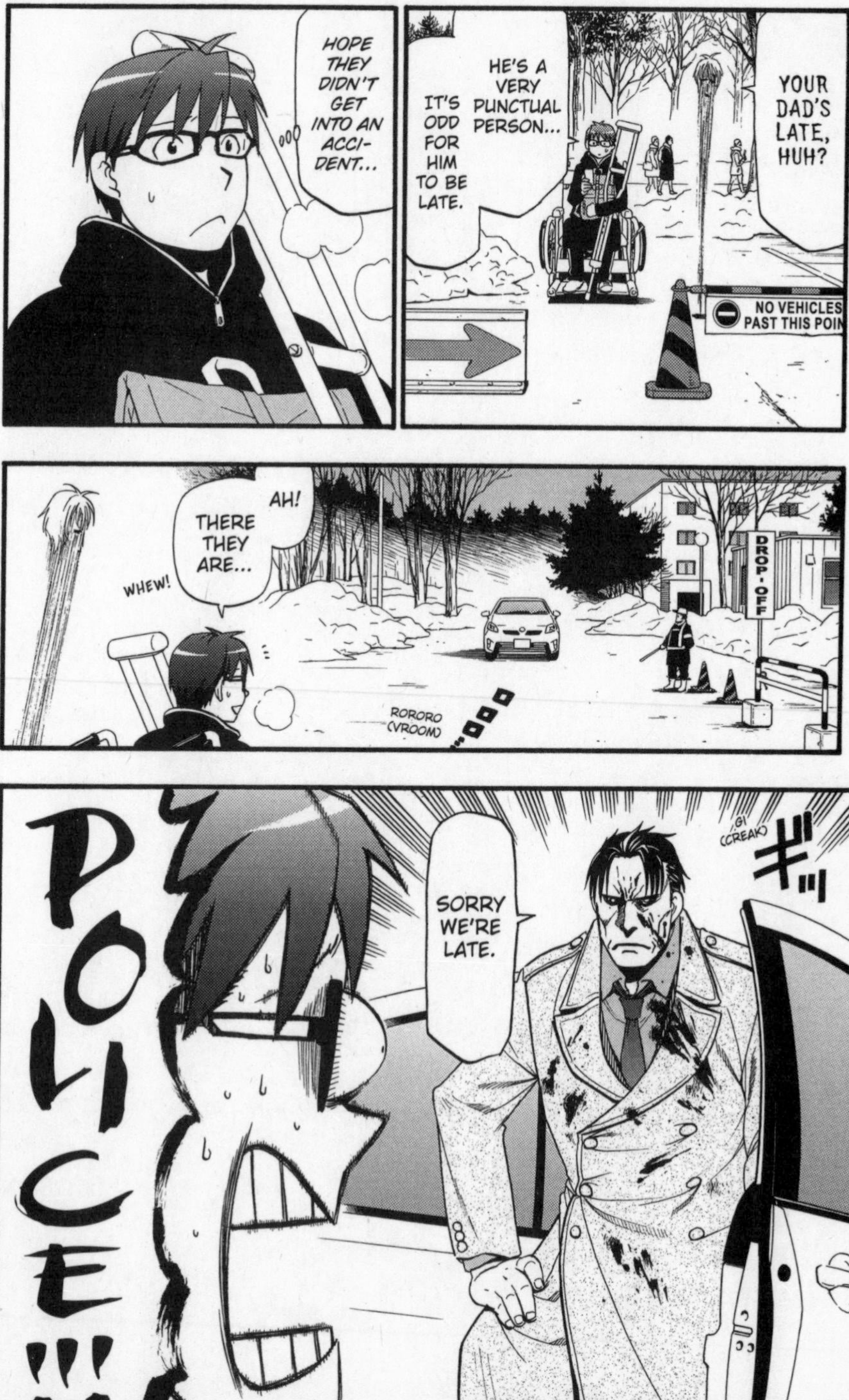
YOUR DAD'S LATE, HUH?
HE'S A VERY PUNCTUAL PERSON...
IT'S ODD FOR HIM TO BE LATE.
NO VEHICLES PAST THIS POIN
HOPE THEY DIDN'T GET INTO AN ACCI-DENT...
AH! THERE THEY ARE...
WHEW!
DROP-OFF
RORORO (VROOM)
GI (CREAK)
SORRY WE'RE LATE.
POLICE!!!

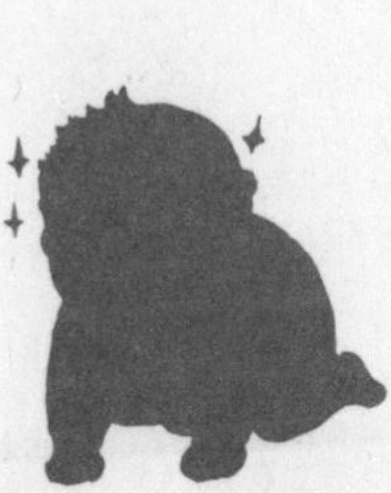

Silver Spoon

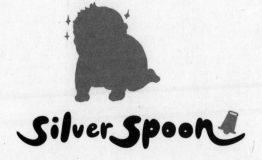

HELLO,
WE'RE THE
HAGGARDS.

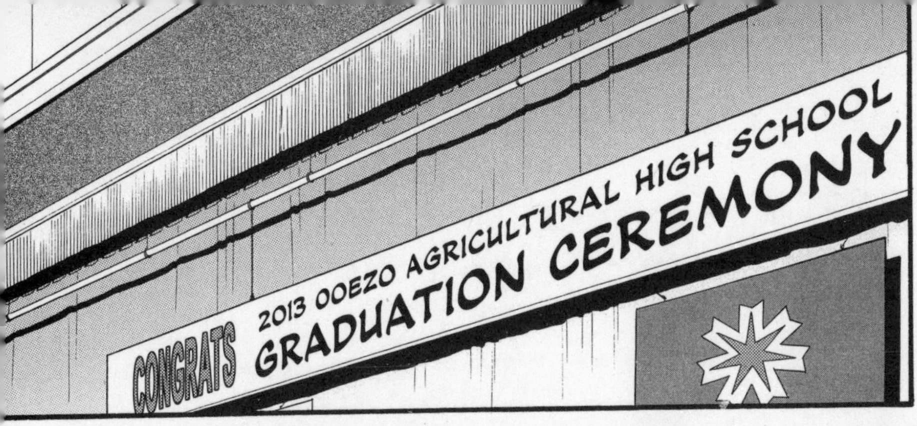
CONGRATS
2013 OOEZO AGRICULTURAL HIGH SCHOOL
GRADUATION CEREMONY

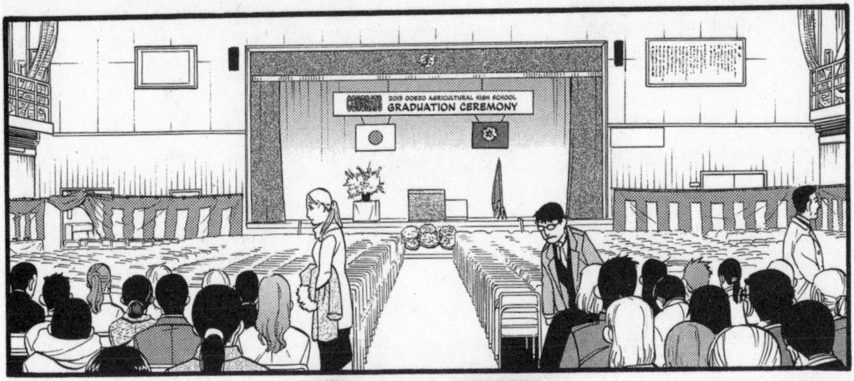
CONGRATS
2013 OOEZO AGRICULTURAL HIGH SCHOOL
GRADUATION CEREMONY

# Chapter 127: Tale of Four Seasons ㉚

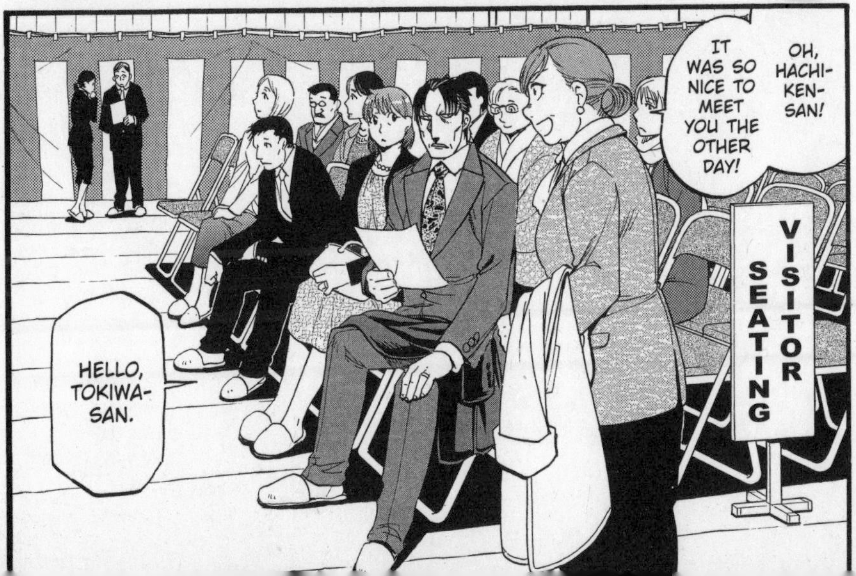
OH, HACHI-KEN-SAN!
IT WAS SO NICE TO MEET YOU THE OTHER DAY!
VISITOR SEATING
HELLO, TOKIWA-SAN.

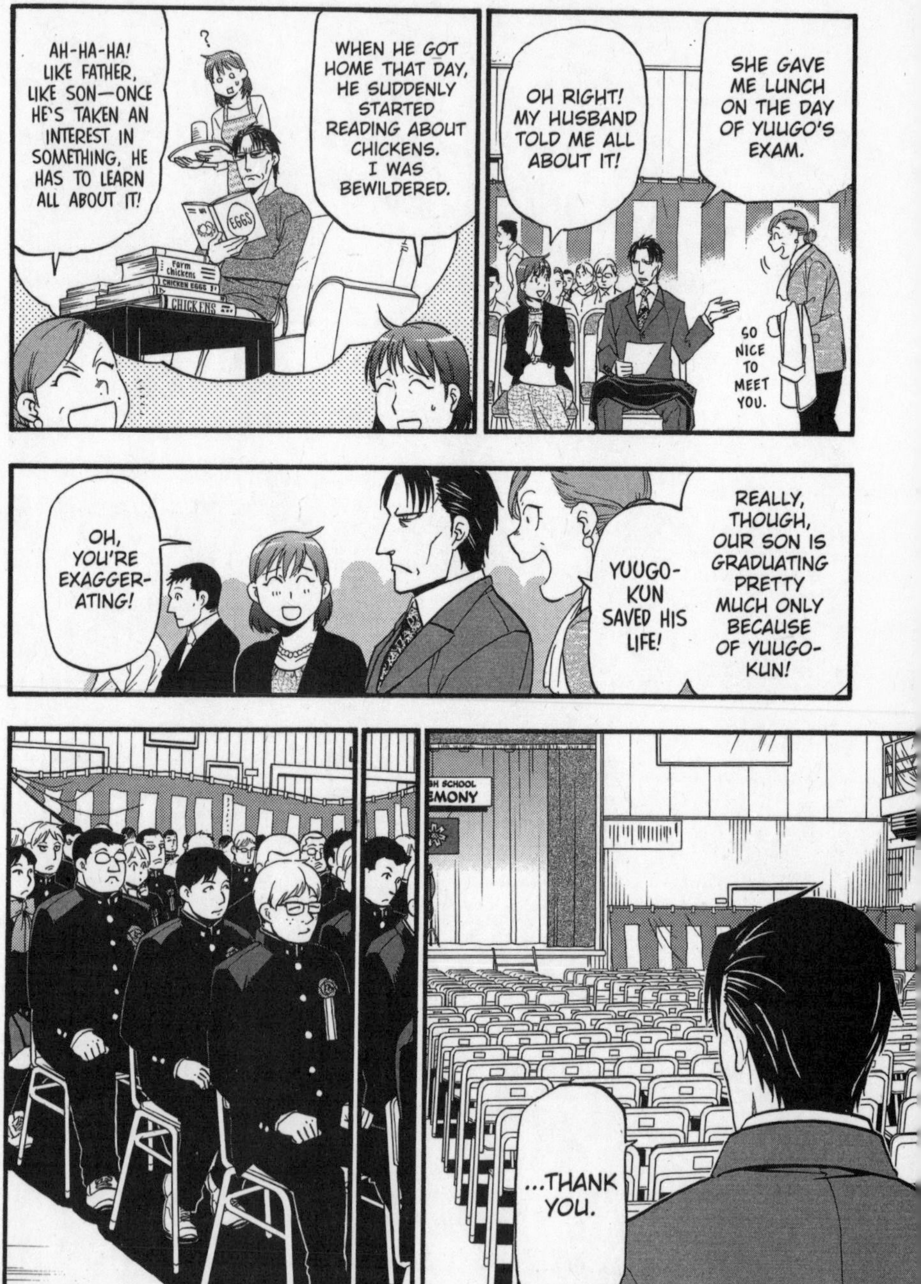
SHE GAVE ME LUNCH ON THE DAY OF YUUGO'S EXAM.
SO NICE TO MEET YOU.
OH RIGHT! MY HUSBAND TOLD ME ALL ABOUT IT!
WHEN HE GOT HOME THAT DAY, HE SUDDENLY STARTED READING ABOUT CHICKENS. I WAS BEWILDERED.
AH-HA-HA! LIKE FATHER, LIKE SON—ONCE HE'S TAKEN AN INTEREST IN SOMETHING, HE HAS TO LEARN ALL ABOUT IT!
EGGS
Farm Chickens
CHICKEN EGGS
CHICKENS
REALLY, THOUGH, OUR SON IS GRADUATING PRETTY MUCH ONLY BECAUSE OF YUUGO-KUN!
YUUGO-KUN SAVED HIS LIFE!
OH, YOU'RE EXAGGER-ATING!
...THANK YOU.

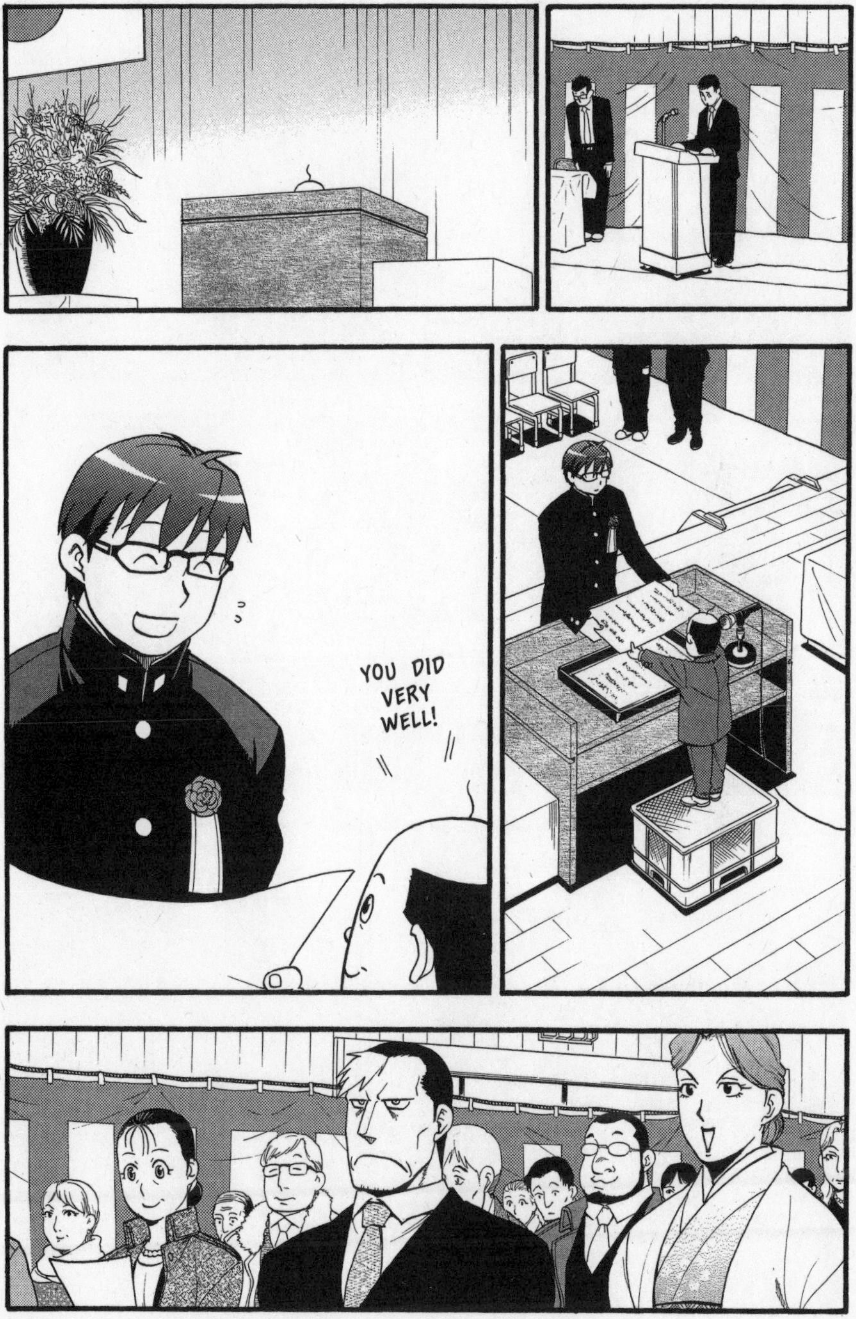
YOU DID VERY WELL!

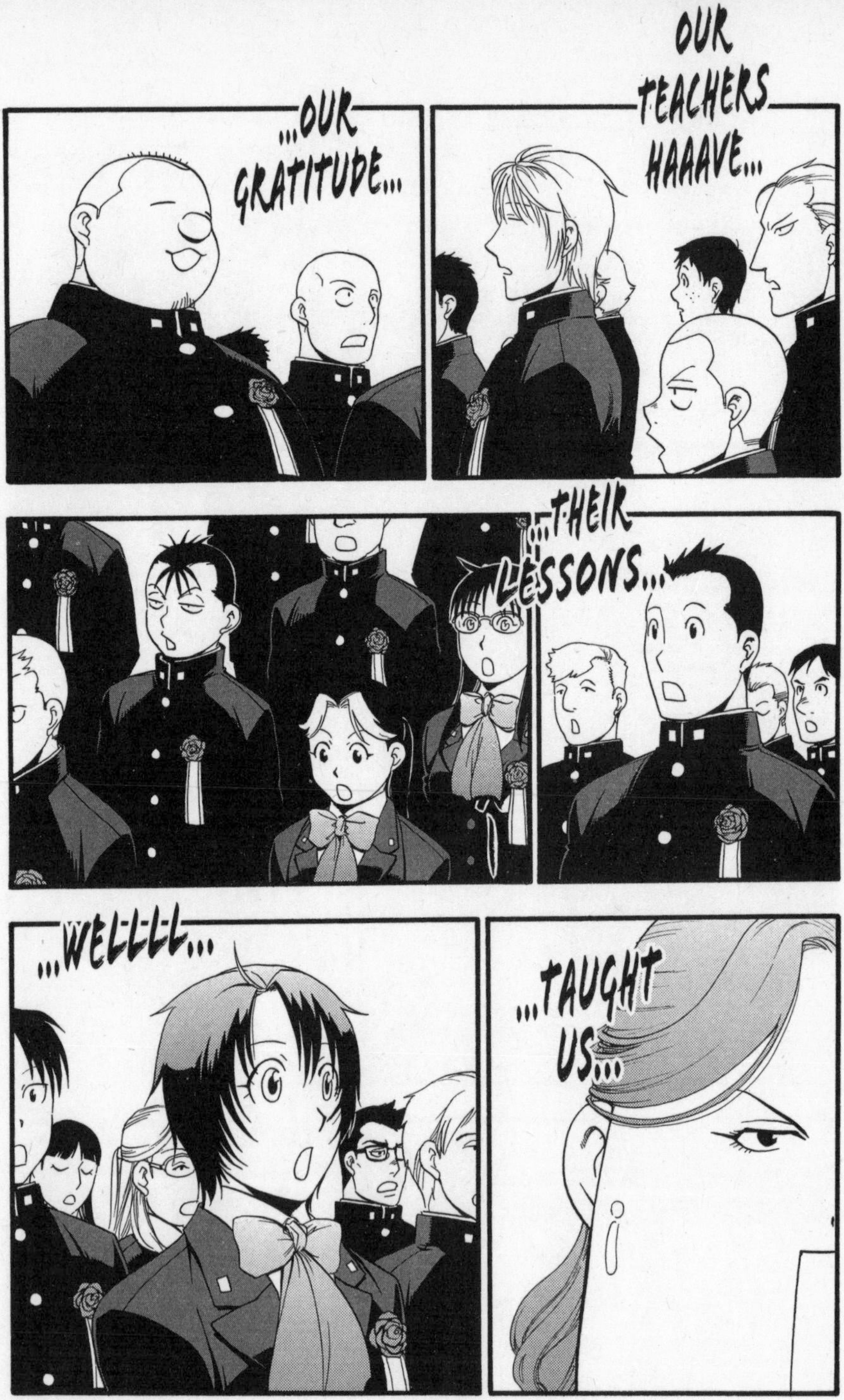
OUR TEACHERS HAAAVE...
...OUR GRATITUDE...
...THEIR LESSONS...
...TAUGHT US...
...WELLLL...

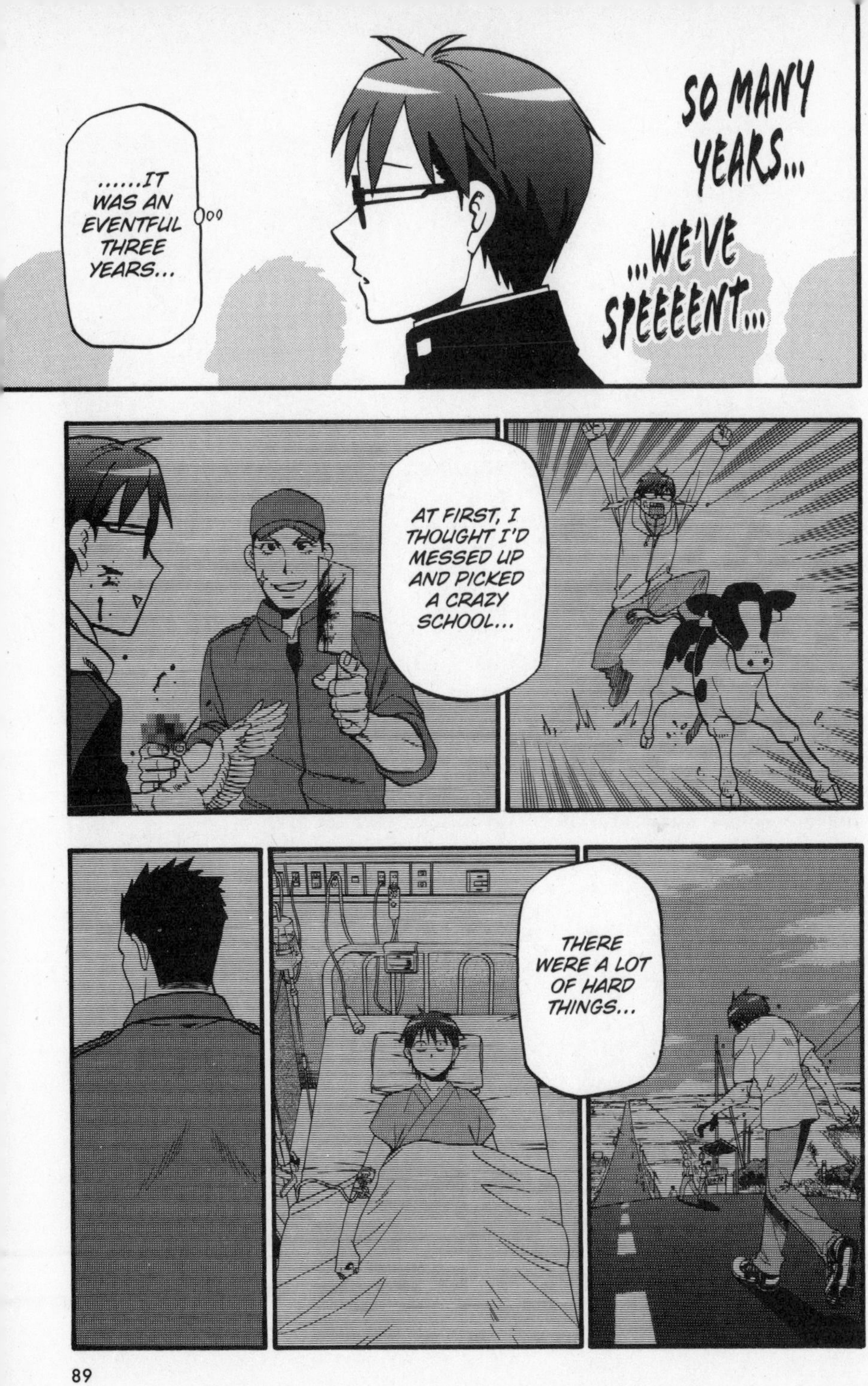
SO MANY YEARS...
...WE'VE SPEEEENT...
......IT WAS AN EVENTFUL THREE YEARS...
AT FIRST, I THOUGHT I'D MESSED UP AND PICKED A CRAZY SCHOOL...
THERE WERE A LOT OF HARD THINGS...

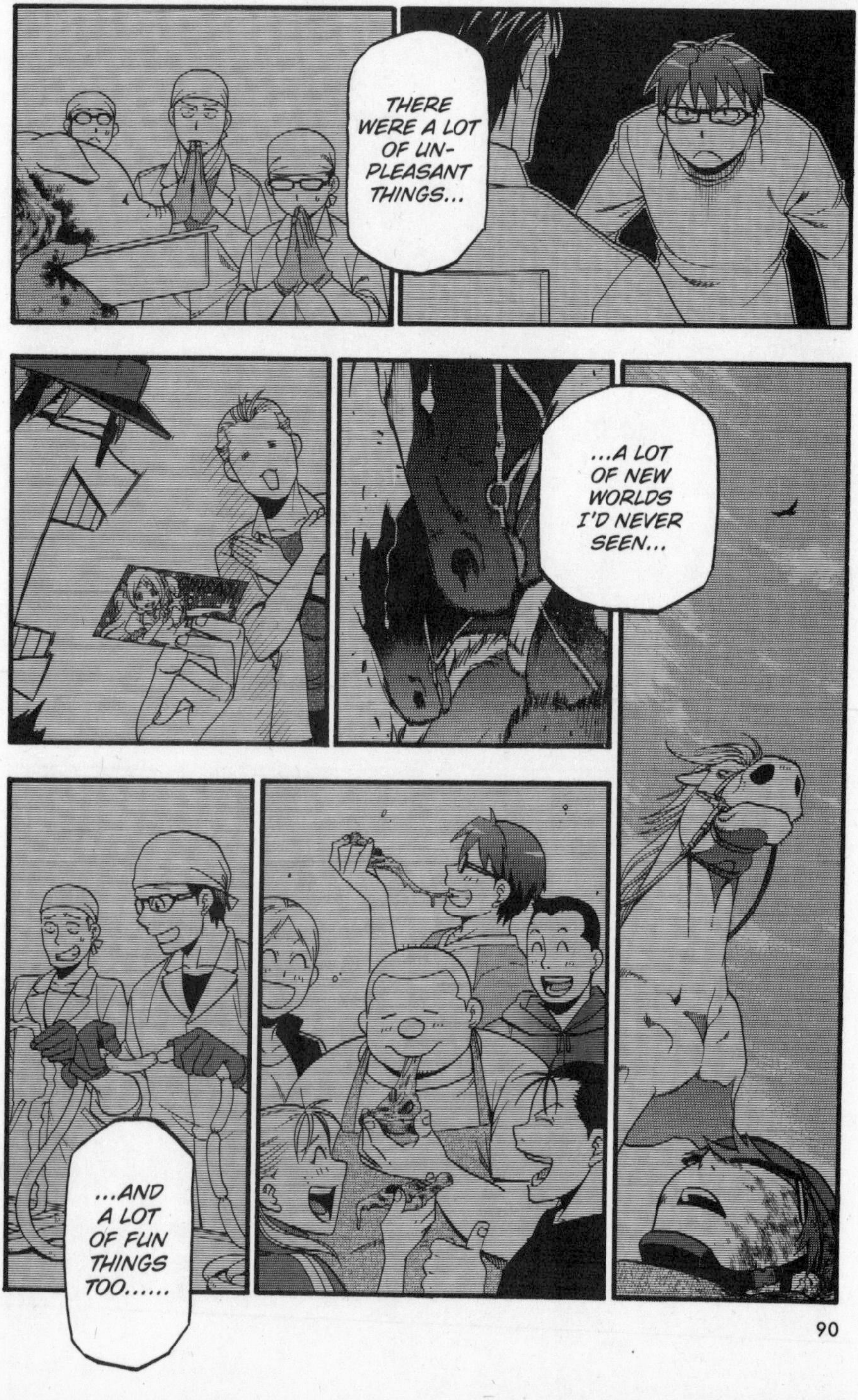
THERE WERE A LOT OF UN-PLEASANT THINGS...
...A LOT OF NEW WORLDS I'D NEVER SEEN...
...AND A LOT OF FUN THINGS TOO......

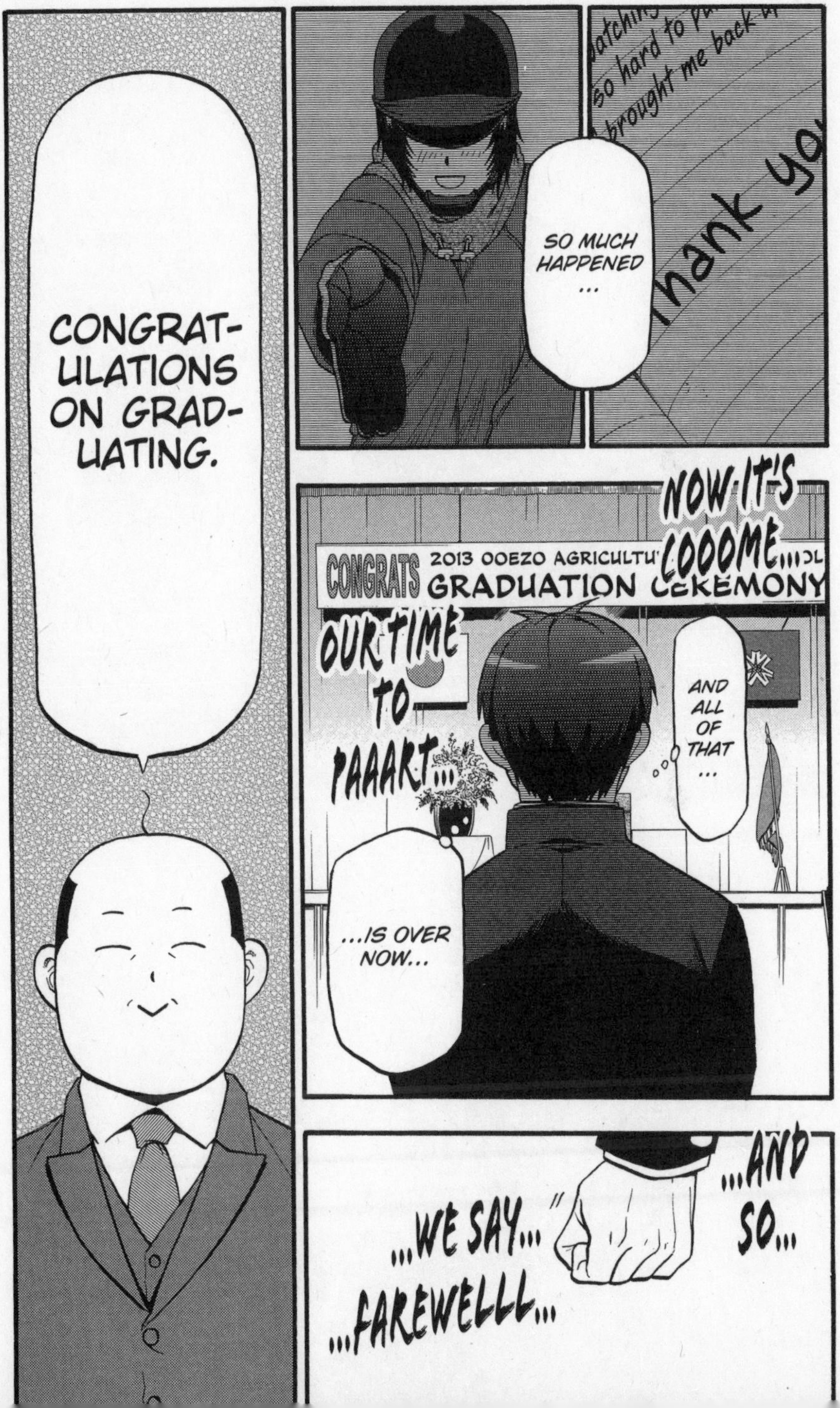
so hard to
brought me back
SO MUCH HAPPENED...
CONGRATS
GRADUATION
NOW IT'S COOOME...
AND ALL OF THAT...
OUR TIME TO PAAART...
...IS OVER NOW...
...AND SO...
...WE SAY...
...FAREWELLL...
CONGRATULATIONS ON GRADUATING.

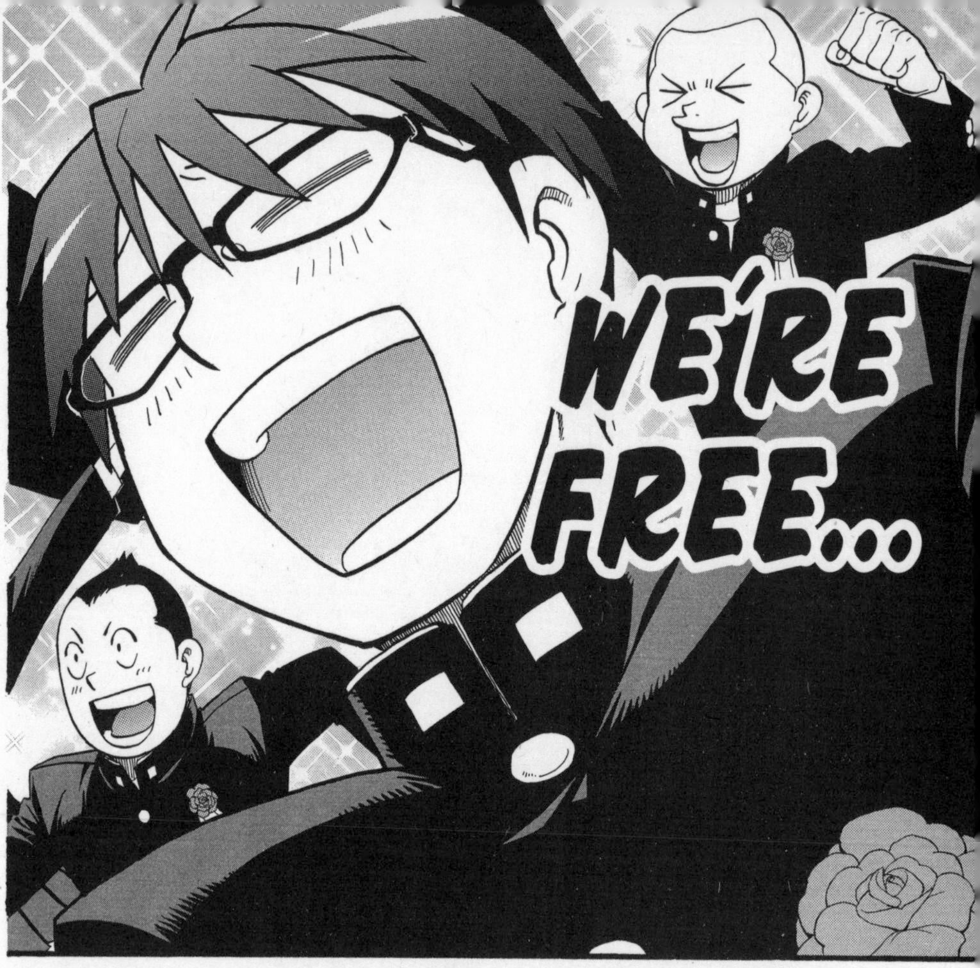
WE'RE FREE...

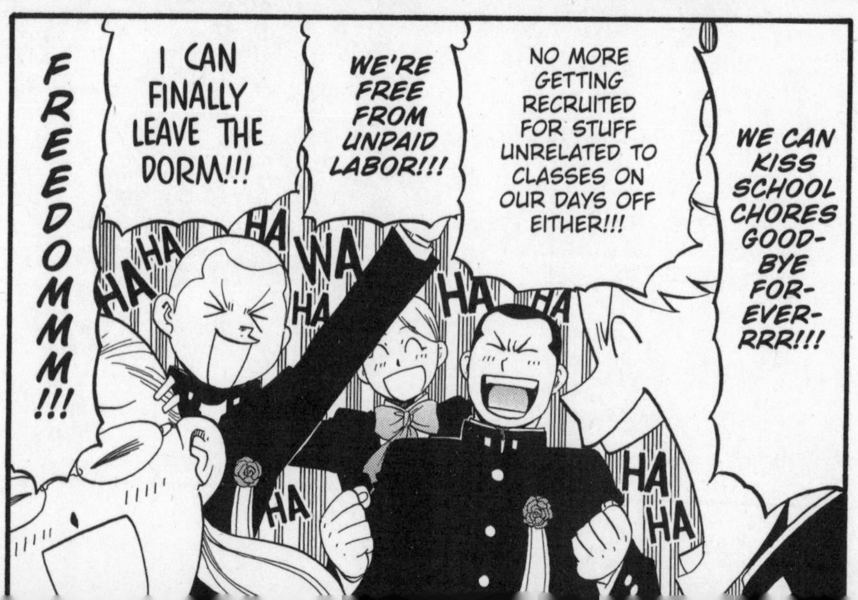
WE CAN KISS SCHOOL CHORES GOOD-BYE FOR-EVER-RRR!!!
NO MORE GETTING RECRUITED FOR STUFF UNRELATED TO CLASSES ON OUR DAYS OFF EITHER!!!
WE'RE FREE FROM UNPAID LABOR!!!
I CAN FINALLY LEAVE THE DORM!!!
FREEDOMMMM!!!
HA HA HA HA
WA HA HA
HA HA
HA HA HA HA

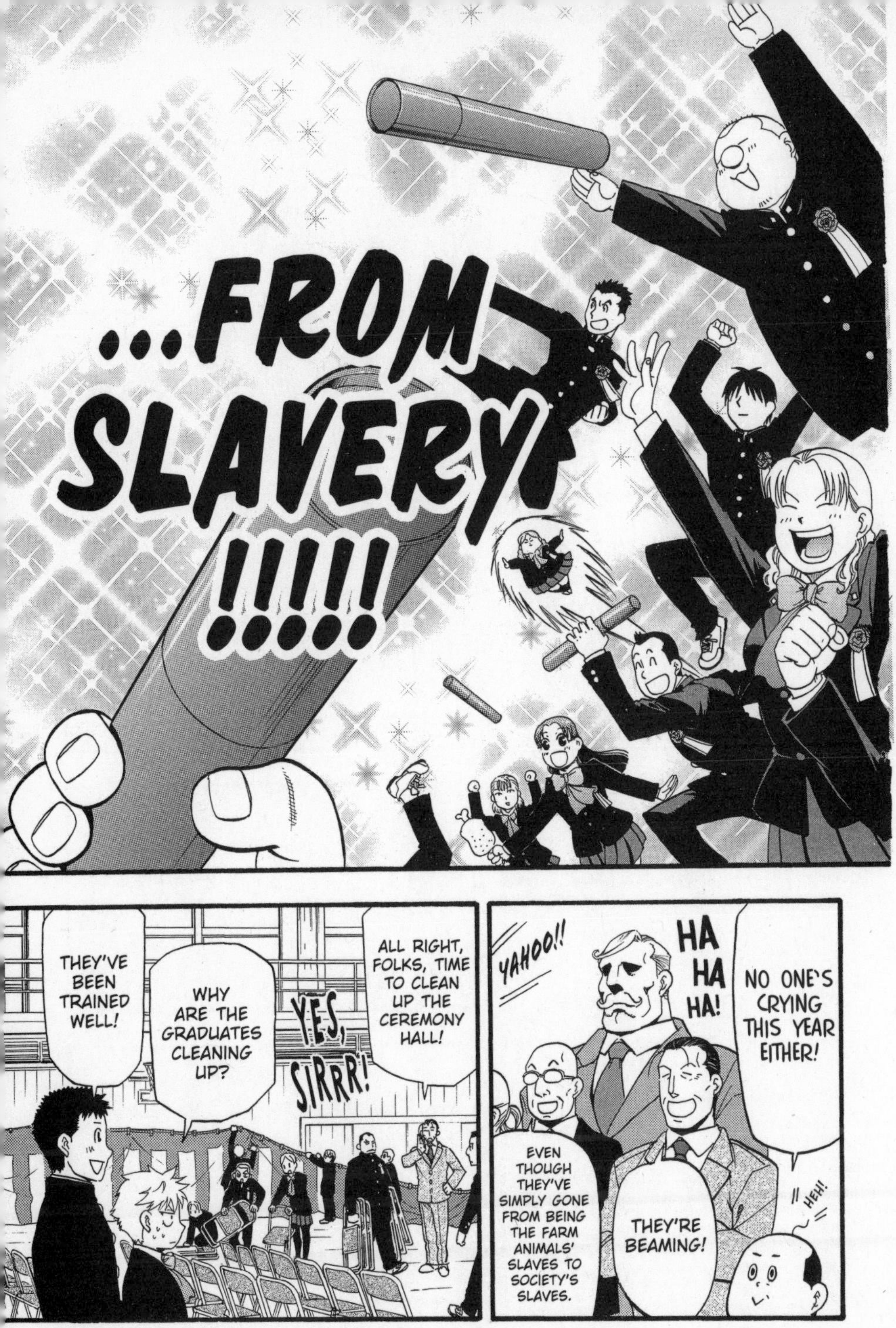
...FROM SLAVERY!!!!!!
NO ONE'S CRYING THIS YEAR EITHER!
HA HA HA!
YAHOO!!
HEH!
THEY'RE BEAMING!
EVEN THOUGH THEY'VE SIMPLY GONE FROM BEING THE FARM ANIMALS' SLAVES TO SOCIETY'S SLAVES.
ALL RIGHT, FOLKS, TIME TO CLEAN UP THE CEREMONY HALL!
YES, SIRRR!
WHY ARE THE GRADUATES CLEANING UP?
THEY'VE BEEN TRAINED WELL!

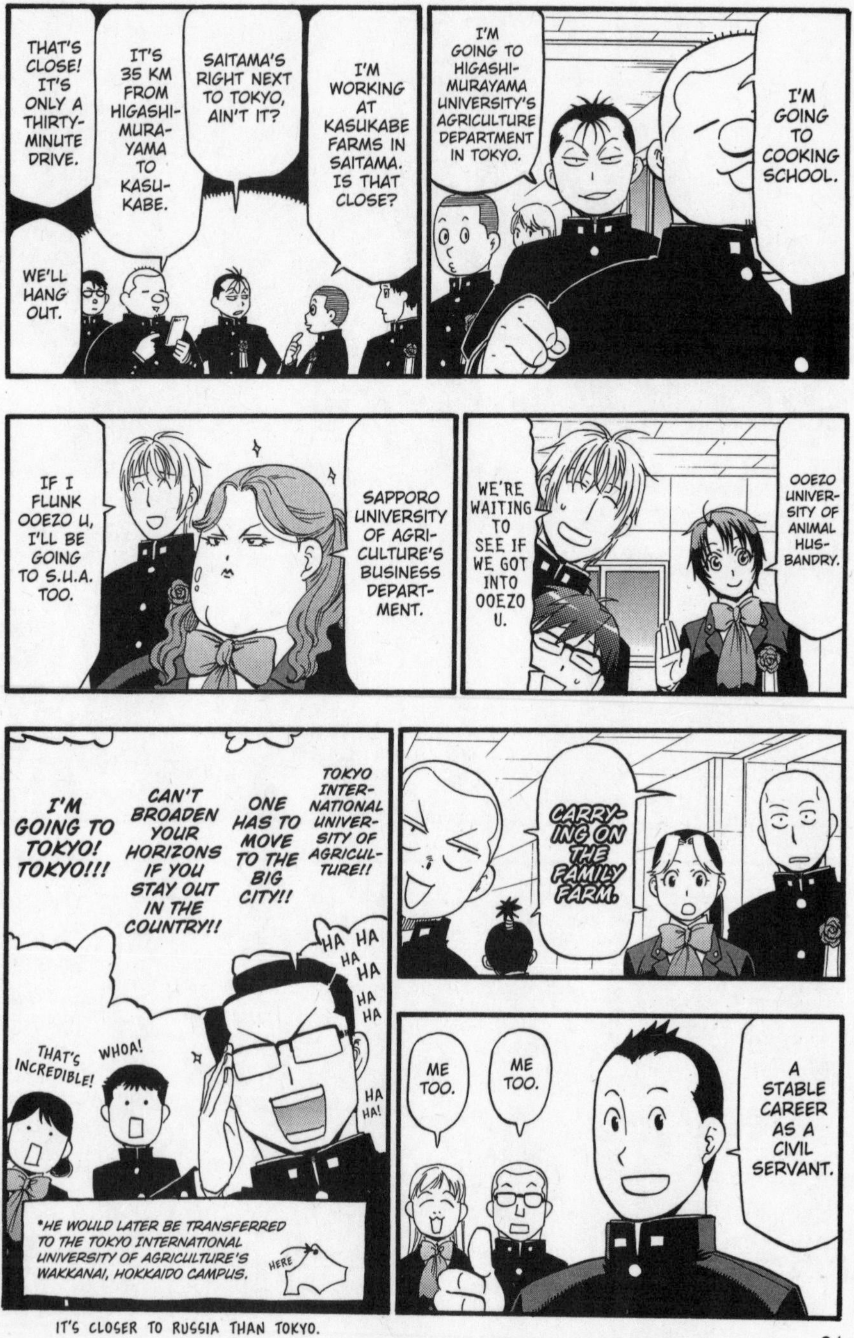
I'M GOING TO COOKING SCHOOL.
I'M GOING TO HIGASHI-MURAYAMA UNIVERSITY'S AGRICULTURE DEPARTMENT IN TOKYO.
I'M WORKING AT KASUKABE FARMS IN SAITAMA. IS THAT CLOSE?
SAITAMA'S RIGHT NEXT TO TOKYO, AIN'T IT?
IT'S 35 KM FROM HIGASHI-MURAYAMA TO KASUKABE.
THAT'S CLOSE! IT'S ONLY A THIRTY-MINUTE DRIVE.
WE'LL HANG OUT.
OOEZO UNIVERSITY OF ANIMAL HUSBANDRY.
WE'RE WAITING TO SEE IF WE GOT INTO OOEZO U.
SAPPORO UNIVERSITY OF AGRICULTURE'S BUSINESS DEPARTMENT.
IF I FLUNK OOEZO U, I'LL BE GOING TO S.U.A. TOO.
CARRYING ON THE FAMILY FARM.
A STABLE CAREER AS A CIVIL SERVANT.
ME TOO.
ME TOO.
TOKYO INTERNATIONAL UNIVERSITY OF AGRICULTURE!!
ONE HAS TO MOVE TO THE BIG CITY!!
CAN'T BROADEN YOUR HORIZONS IF YOU STAY OUT IN THE COUNTRY!!
I'M GOING TO TOKYO! TOKYO!!!
HA HA HA HA HA HA HA
HA HA!
WHOA!
THAT'S INCREDIBLE!
*HE WOULD LATER BE TRANSFERRED TO THE TOKYO INTERNATIONAL UNIVERSITY OF AGRICULTURE'S WAKKANAI, HOKKAIDO CAMPUS.
HERE

IT'S CLOSER TO RUSSIA THAN TOKYO.

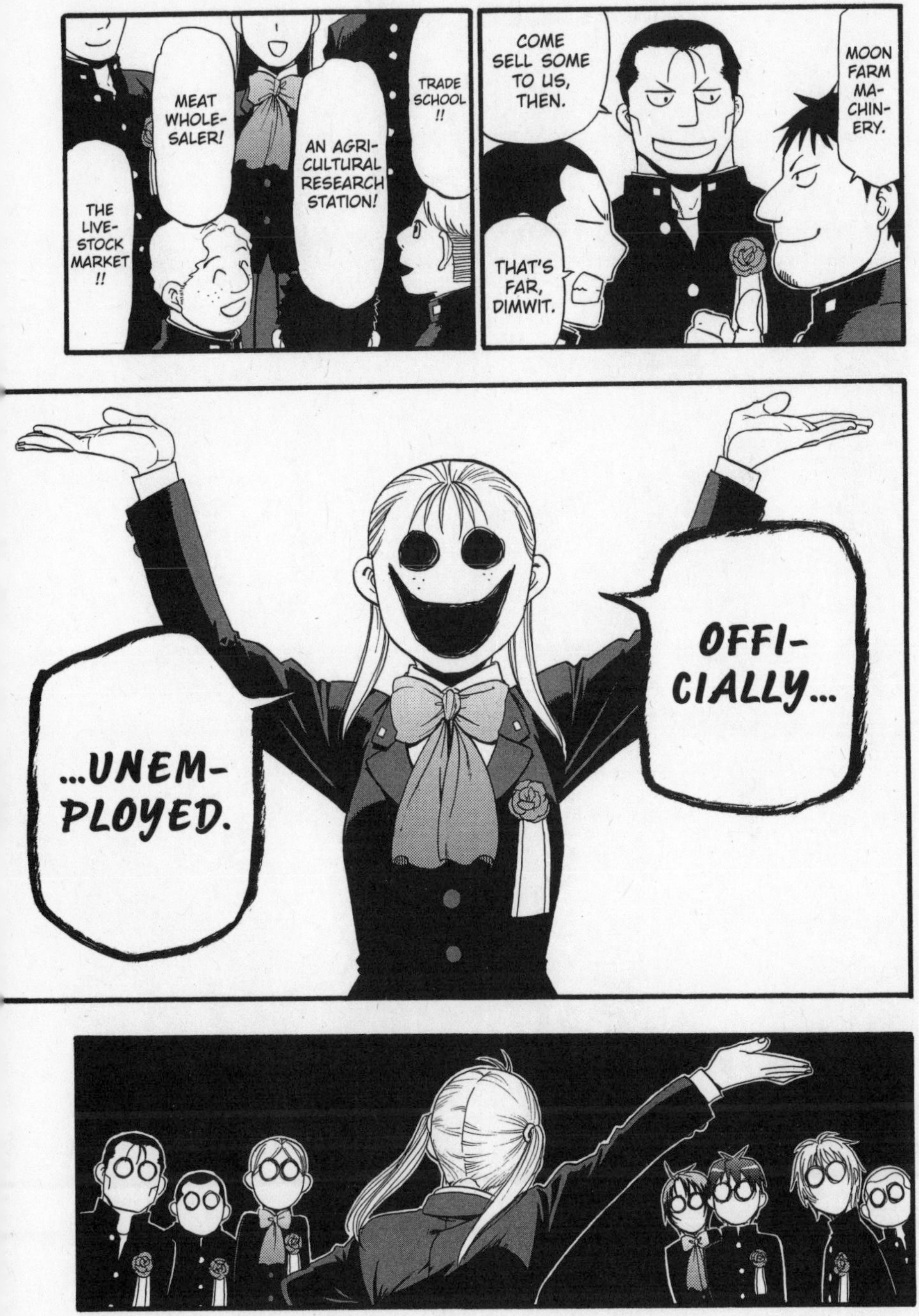
MOON FARM MACHINERY.
COME SELL SOME TO US, THEN.
THAT'S FAR, DIMWIT.
TRADE SCHOOL!!
AN AGRICULTURAL RESEARCH STATION!
MEAT WHOLESALER!
THE LIVESTOCK MARKET!!
OFFICIALLY...
...UNEMPLOYED.

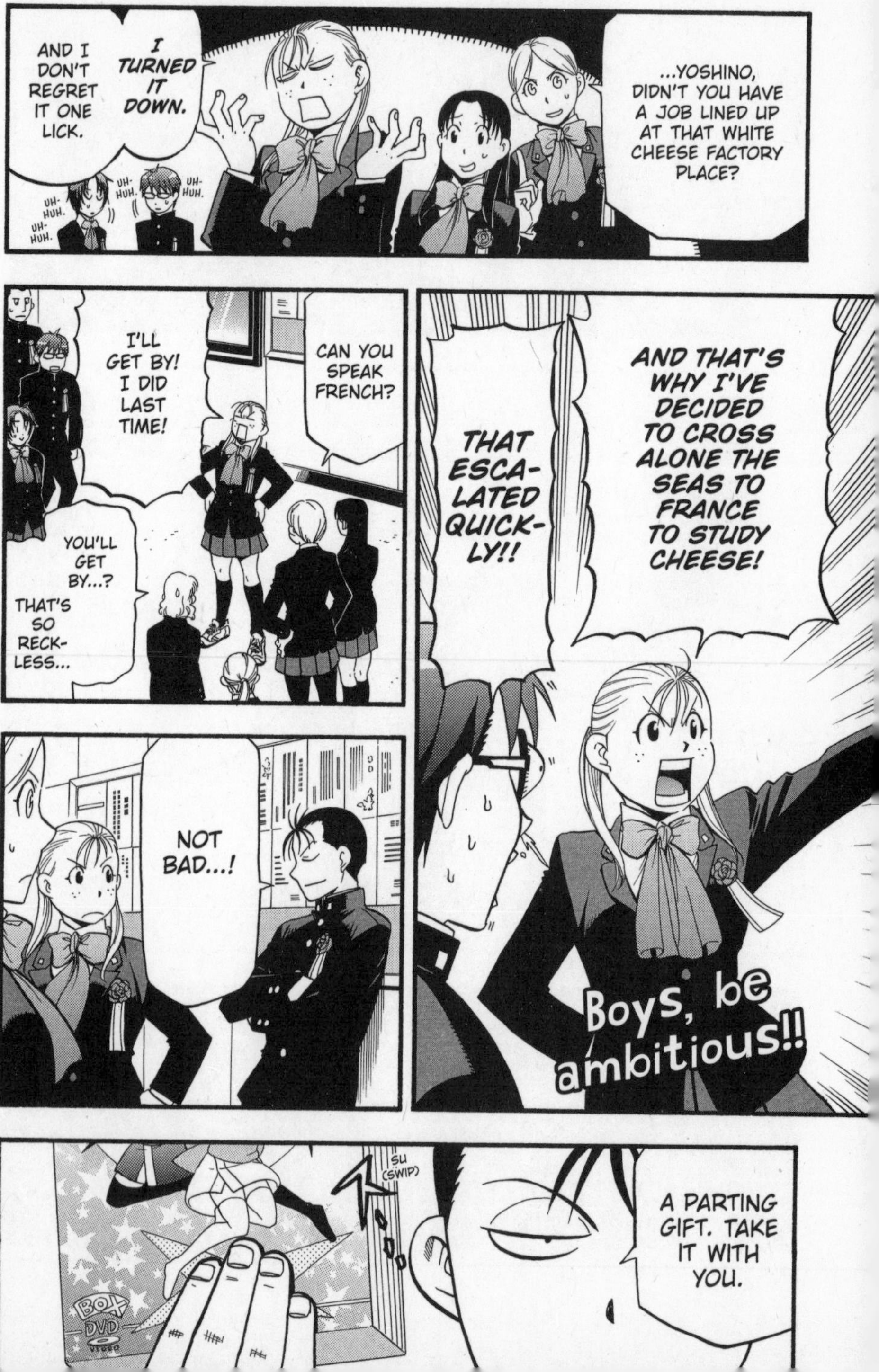
...YOSHINO, DIDN'T YOU HAVE A JOB LINED UP AT THAT WHITE CHEESE FACTORY PLACE?
I TURNED IT DOWN.
AND I DON'T REGRET IT ONE LICK.
UH-HUH. UH-HUH.
UH-HUH. UH-HUH.
AND THAT'S WHY I'VE DECIDED TO CROSS ALONE THE SEAS TO FRANCE TO STUDY CHEESE!
THAT ESCA-LATED QUICK-LY!!
Boys, be ambitious!!
CAN YOU SPEAK FRENCH?
I'LL GET BY! I DID LAST TIME!
YOU'LL GET BY...? THAT'S SO RECK-LESS...
NOT BAD...!
A PARTING GIFT. TAKE IT WITH YOU.
SU (SWIP)
BOX DVD

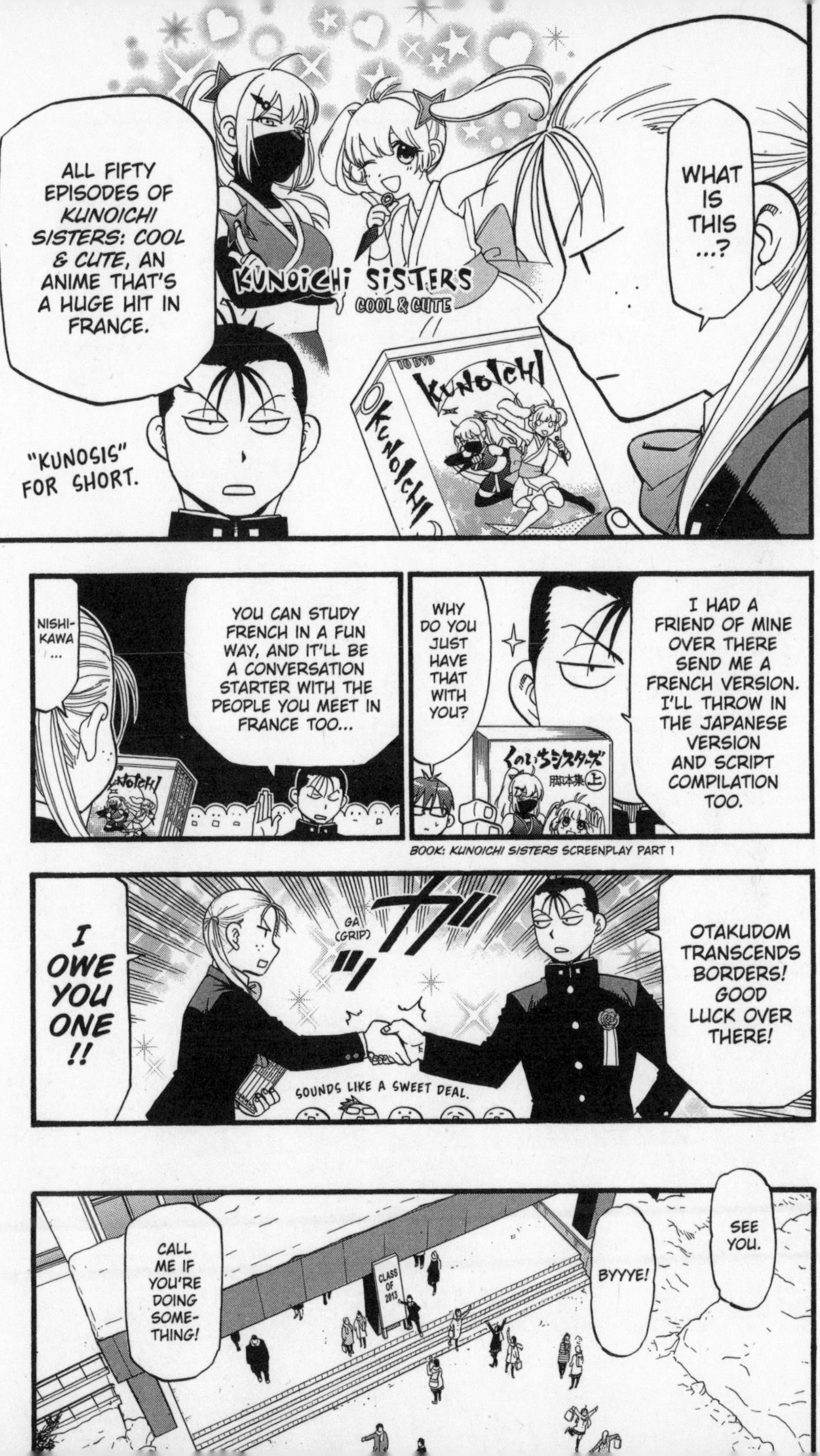
WHAT IS THIS ...?
ALL FIFTY EPISODES OF KUNOICHI SISTERS: COOL & CUTE, AN ANIME THAT'S A HUGE HIT IN FRANCE.
KUNOICHI SISTERS
COOL & CUTE
10 DVD
KUNOICHI
KUNOICHI
"KUNOSIS" FOR SHORT.
I HAD A FRIEND OF MINE OVER THERE SEND ME A FRENCH VERSION. I'LL THROW IN THE JAPANESE VERSION AND SCRIPT COMPILATION TOO.
WHY DO YOU JUST HAVE THAT WITH YOU?
くのいちシスターズ
脚本集上
BOOK: KUNOICHI SISTERS SCREENPLAY PART 1
YOU CAN STUDY FRENCH IN A FUN WAY, AND IT'LL BE A CONVERSATION STARTER WITH THE PEOPLE YOU MEET IN FRANCE TOO...
NISHI-KAWA ...
KUNOICHI
OTAKUDOM TRANSCENDS BORDERS! GOOD LUCK OVER THERE!
GA (GRIP)
I OWE YOU ONE!!
SOUNDS LIKE A SWEET DEAL.
SEE YOU.
BYYYE!
CALL ME IF YOU'RE DOING SOME-THING!
CLASS OF 2013

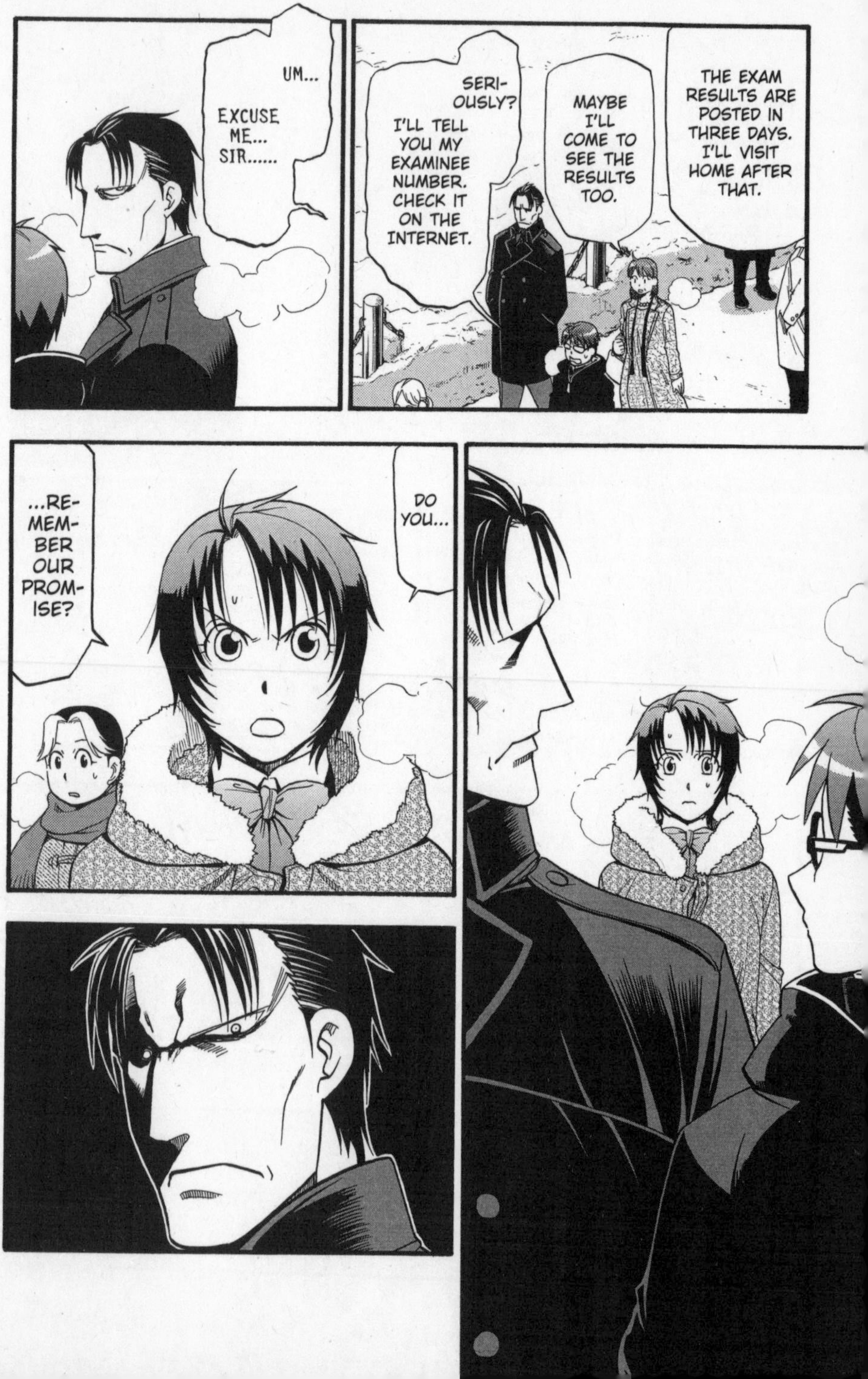
THE EXAM RESULTS ARE POSTED IN THREE DAYS. I'LL VISIT HOME AFTER THAT.
MAYBE I'LL COME TO SEE THE RESULTS TOO.
SERI-OUSLY? I'LL TELL YOU MY EXAMINEE NUMBER. CHECK IT ON THE INTERNET.
UM...
EXCUSE ME... SIR......
DO YOU...
...RE-MEM-BER OUR PROM-ISE?

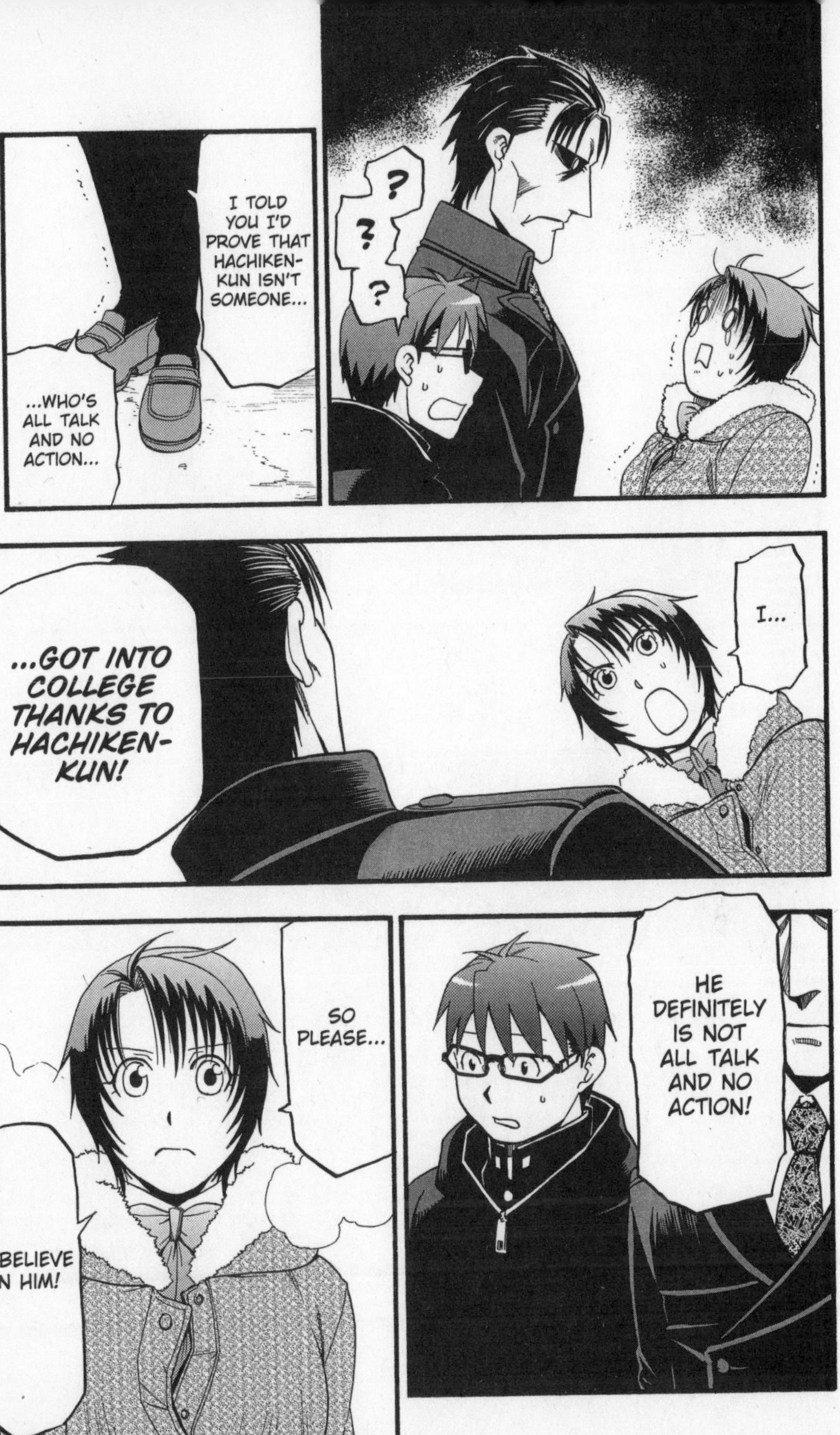
?
?
?
I TOLD YOU I'D PROVE THAT HACHIKEN-KUN ISN'T SOMEONE...
...WHO'S ALL TALK AND NO ACTION...
I...
...GOT INTO COLLEGE THANKS TO HACHIKEN-KUN!
HE DEFINITELY IS NOT ALL TALK AND NO ACTION!
SO PLEASE...
...BELIEVE IN HIM!

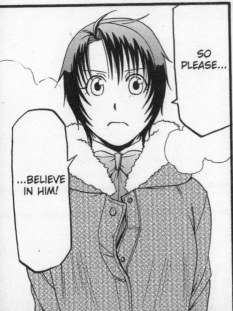

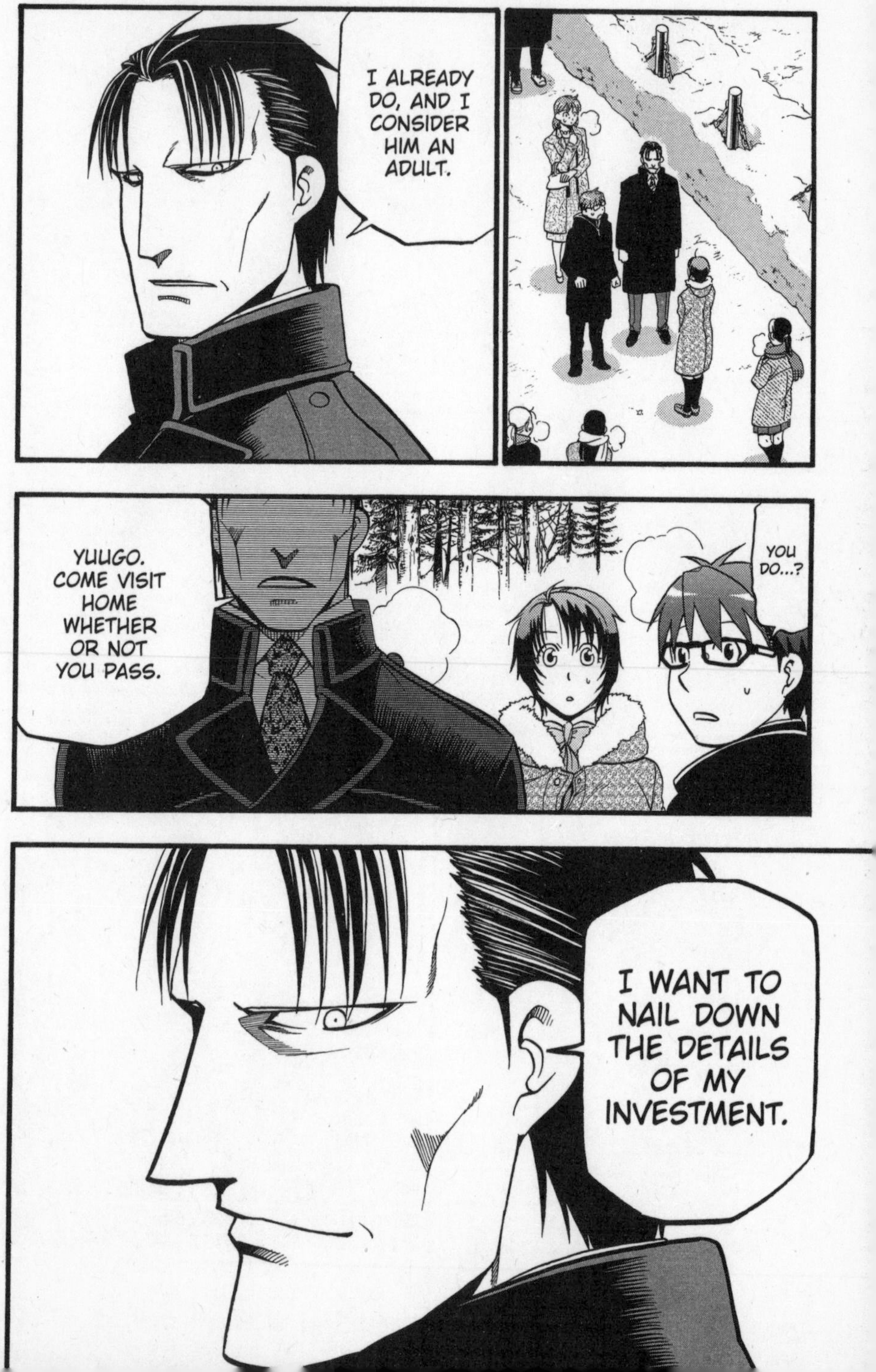
I ALREADY DO, AND I CONSIDER HIM AN ADULT.
YOU DO...?
YUUGO. COME VISIT HOME WHETHER OR NOT YOU PASS.
I WANT TO NAIL DOWN THE DETAILS OF MY INVESTMENT.

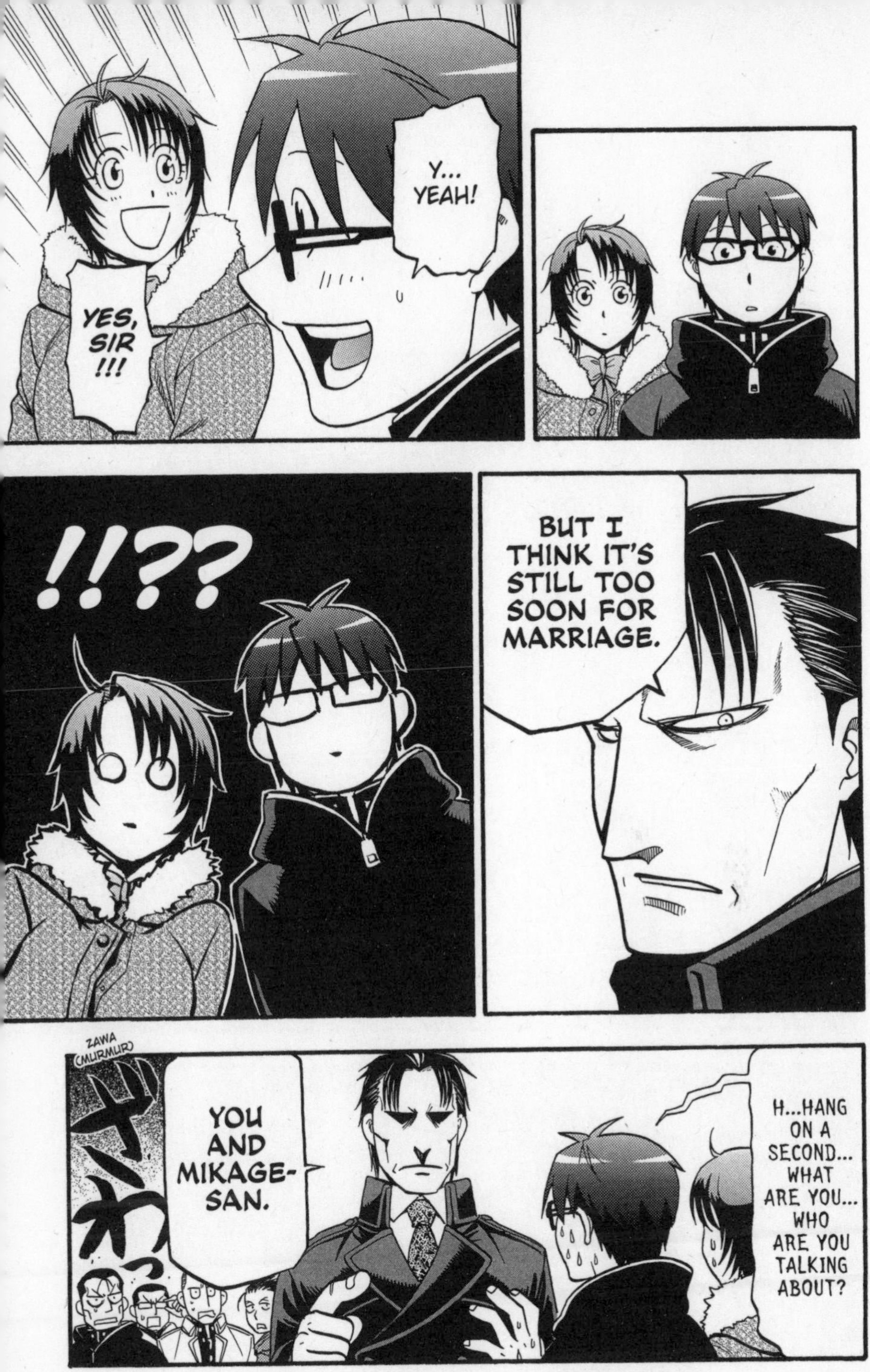
Y... YEAH!
YES, SIR!!!
BUT I THINK IT'S STILL TOO SOON FOR MARRIAGE.
!!??
H...HANG ON A SECOND... WHAT ARE YOU... WHO ARE YOU TALKING ABOUT?
YOU AND MIKAGE-SAN.
ZAWA (MURMUR)

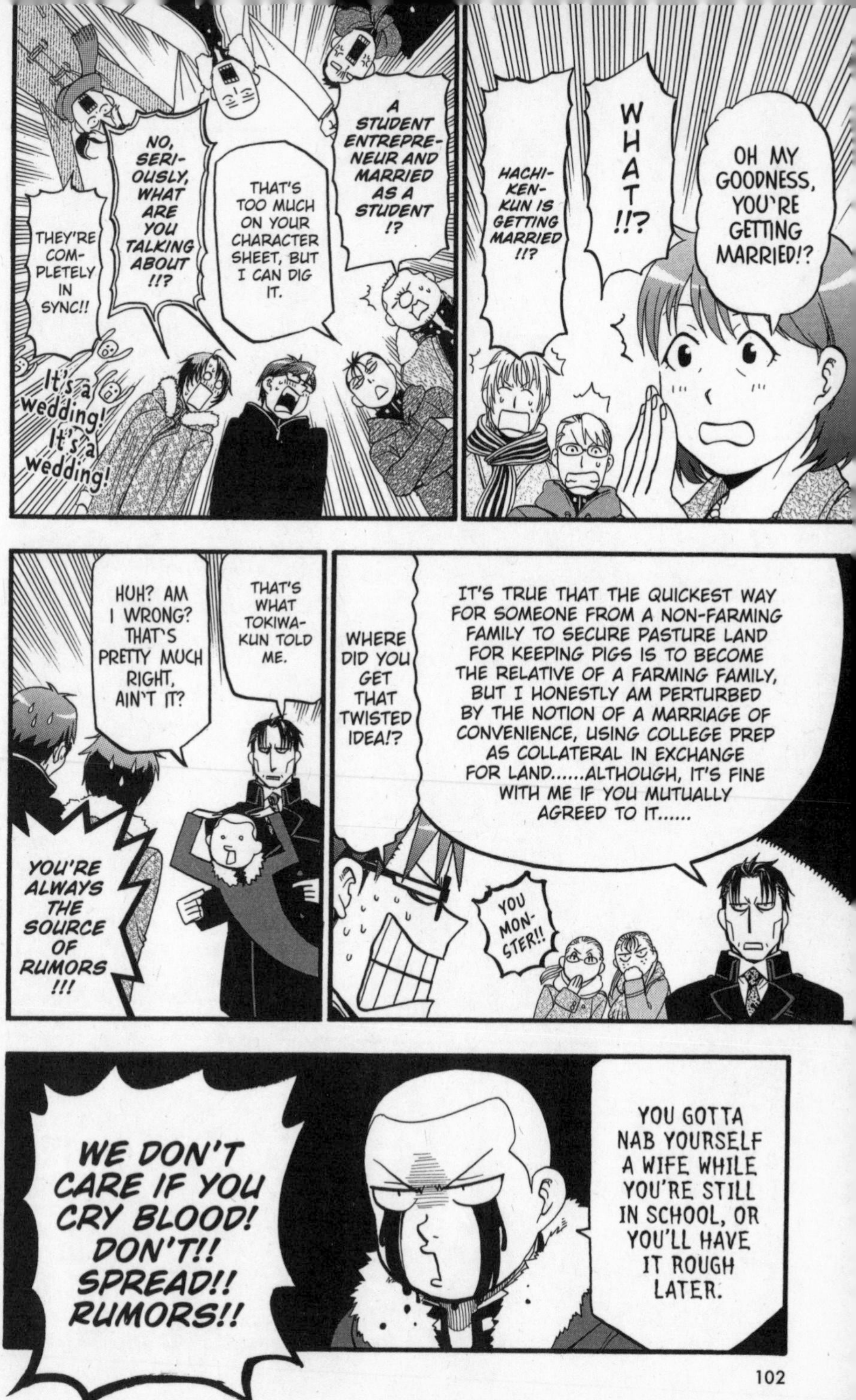
OH MY GOODNESS, YOU'RE GETTING MARRIED!?
WHAT!!?
HACHIKEN-KUN IS GETTING MARRIED!!?
A STUDENT ENTREPRENEUR AND MARRIED AS A STUDENT!?
THAT'S TOO MUCH ON YOUR CHARACTER SHEET, BUT I CAN DIG IT.
NO, SERIOUSLY, WHAT ARE YOU TALKING ABOUT!!?
THEY'RE COMPLETELY IN SYNC!!
It's a wedding! It's a wedding!
IT'S TRUE THAT THE QUICKEST WAY FOR SOMEONE FROM A NON-FARMING FAMILY TO SECURE PASTURE LAND FOR KEEPING PIGS IS TO BECOME THE RELATIVE OF A FARMING FAMILY, BUT I HONESTLY AM PERTURBED BY THE NOTION OF A MARRIAGE OF CONVENIENCE, USING COLLEGE PREP AS COLLATERAL IN EXCHANGE FOR LAND......ALTHOUGH, IT'S FINE WITH ME IF YOU MUTUALLY AGREED TO IT......
YOU MONSTER!!
WHERE DID YOU GET THAT TWISTED IDEA!?
THAT'S WHAT TOKIWA-KUN TOLD ME.
HUH? AM I WRONG? THAT'S PRETTY MUCH RIGHT, AIN'T IT?
YOU'RE ALWAYS THE SOURCE OF RUMORS!!!
YOU GOTTA NAB YOURSELF A WIFE WHILE YOU'RE STILL IN SCHOOL, OR YOU'LL HAVE IT ROUGH LATER.
WE DON'T CARE IF YOU CRY BLOOD! DON'T!! SPREAD!! RUMORS!!

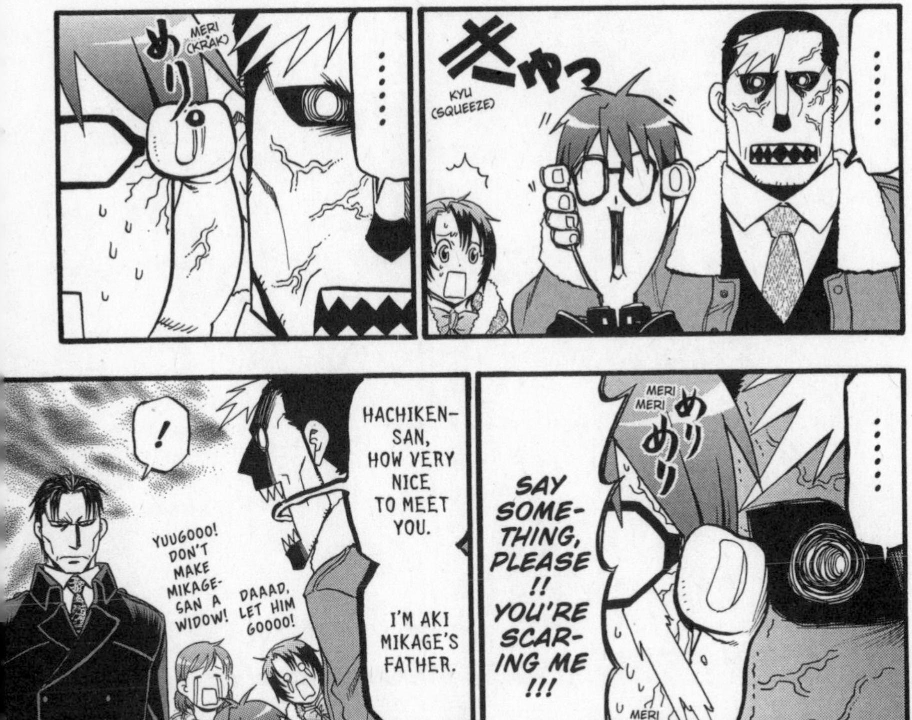
きゅっ
KYU (SQUEEZE)
......
めり
MERI (KRAK)
......
MERI MERI
めり
めり
......
SAY SOMETHING, PLEASE!! YOU'RE SCARING ME!!!
MERI
めり
HACHIKEN-SAN, HOW VERY NICE TO MEET YOU.
I'M AKI MIKAGE'S FATHER.
!
DAAAD, LET HIM GOOOO!
YUUGOOO! DON'T MAKE MIKAGE-SAN A WIDOW!

SIGNS, L-R: SWEETS FAIR, MEGA-DINO STORE, HUGE SALE, KARAOKE LOVE, MOE & KENTA VIDEO

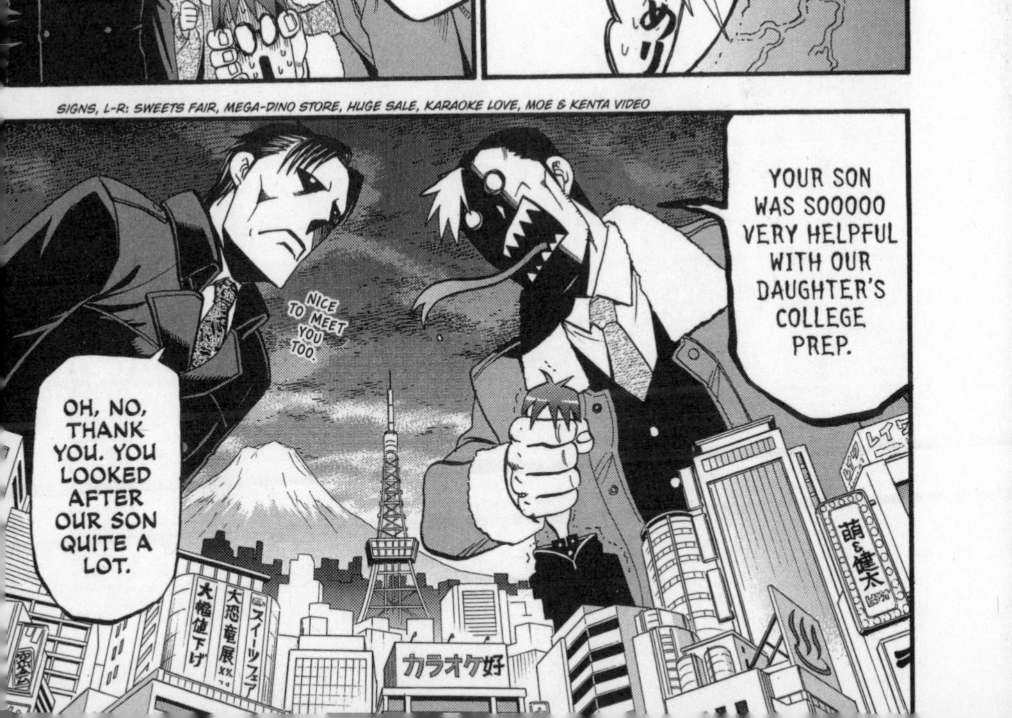
YOUR SON WAS SOOOOO VERY HELPFUL WITH OUR DAUGHTER'S COLLEGE PREP.
NICE TO MEET YOU TOO.
OH, NO, THANK YOU. YOU LOOKED AFTER OUR SON QUITE A LOT.
萌&健太
カラオケ好
スイーツフェア
大恐竜展
大幅値下げ

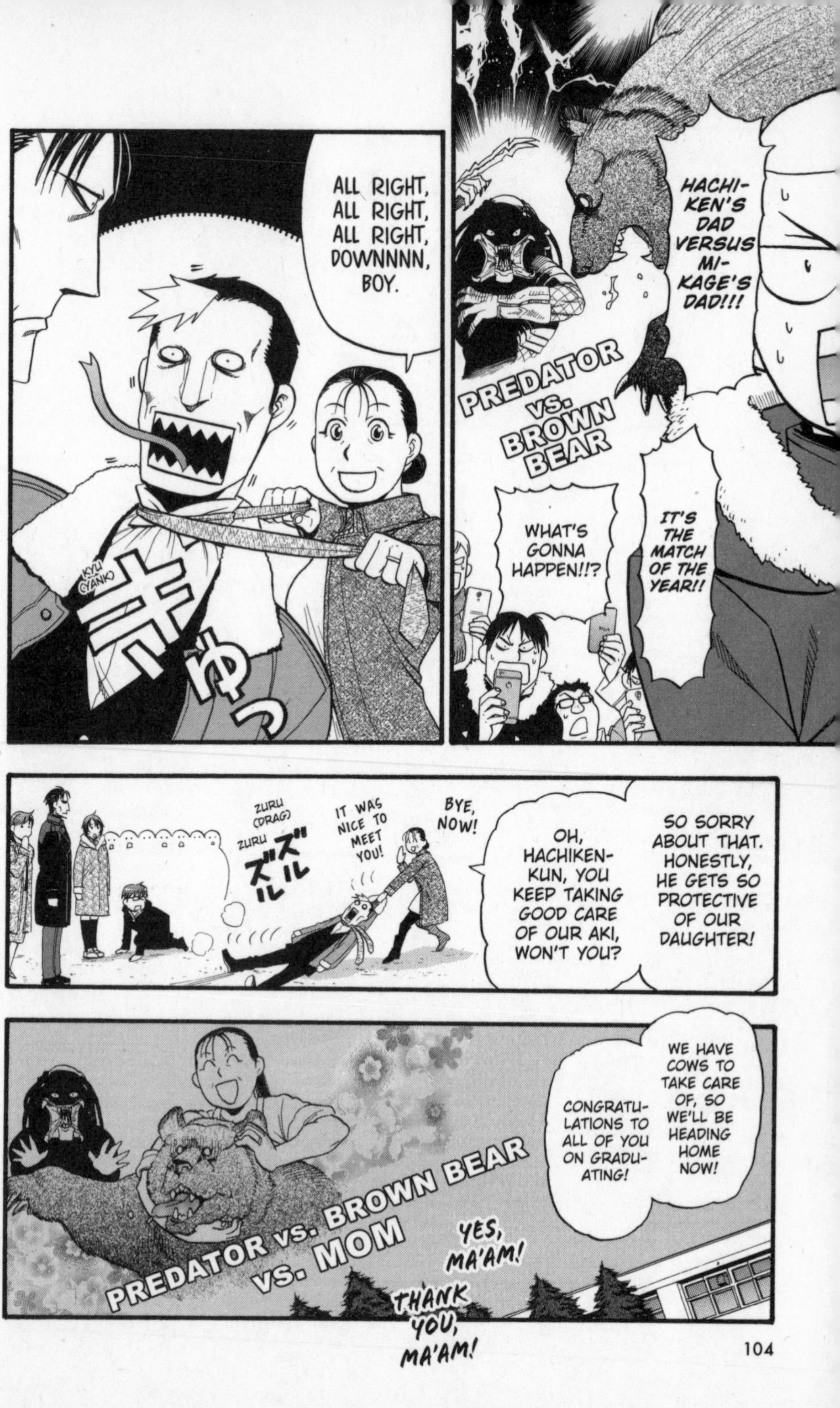
HACHIKEN'S DAD VERSUS MIKAGE'S DAD!!!
PREDATOR vs. BROWN BEAR
IT'S THE MATCH OF THE YEAR!!
WHAT'S GONNA HAPPEN!!?
ALL RIGHT, ALL RIGHT, ALL RIGHT, DOWNNNN, BOY.
KYU (YANK)
きゅっ
SO SORRY ABOUT THAT. HONESTLY, HE GETS SO PROTECTIVE OF OUR DAUGHTER!
OH, HACHIKEN-KUN, YOU KEEP TAKING GOOD CARE OF OUR AKI, WON'T YOU?
BYE, NOW!
IT WAS NICE TO MEET YOU!
ZURU (DRAG) ZURU
ズルズル
WE HAVE COWS TO TAKE CARE OF, SO WE'LL BE HEADING HOME NOW!
CONGRATULATIONS TO ALL OF YOU ON GRADUATING!
PREDATOR vs. BROWN BEAR vs. MOM
YES, MA'AM!
THANK YOU, MA'AM!

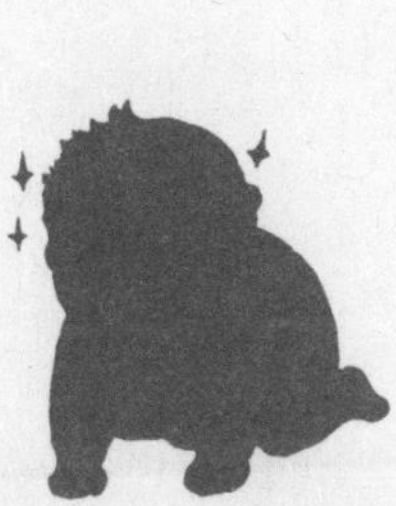

Silver Spoon

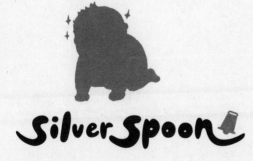

"VS. BROWN BEAR" FILMS

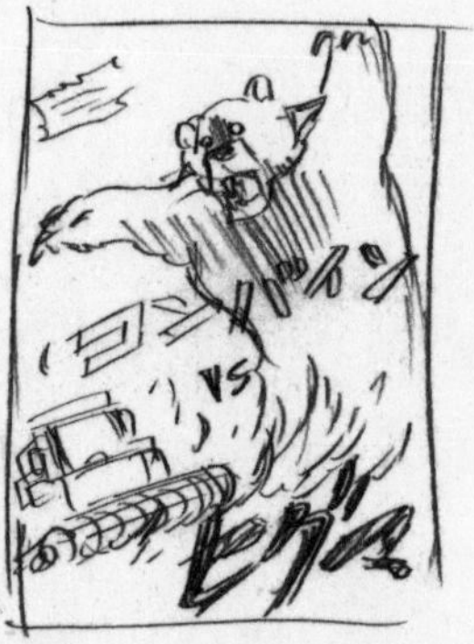
VS
ヒグマ
COMBINE VS. BROWN BEAR

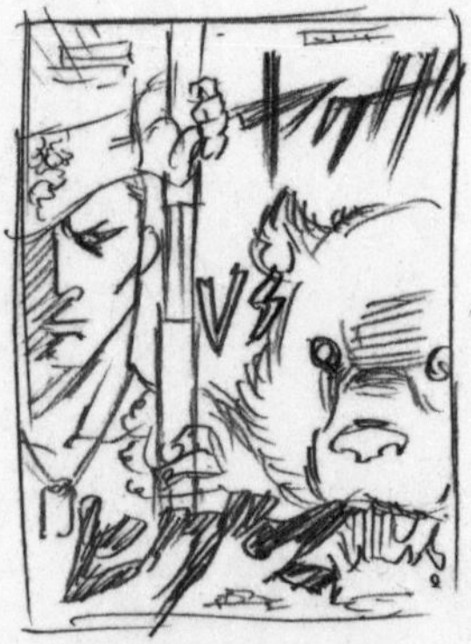
VS
ヒグマ
YAKUZA VS. BROWN BEAR

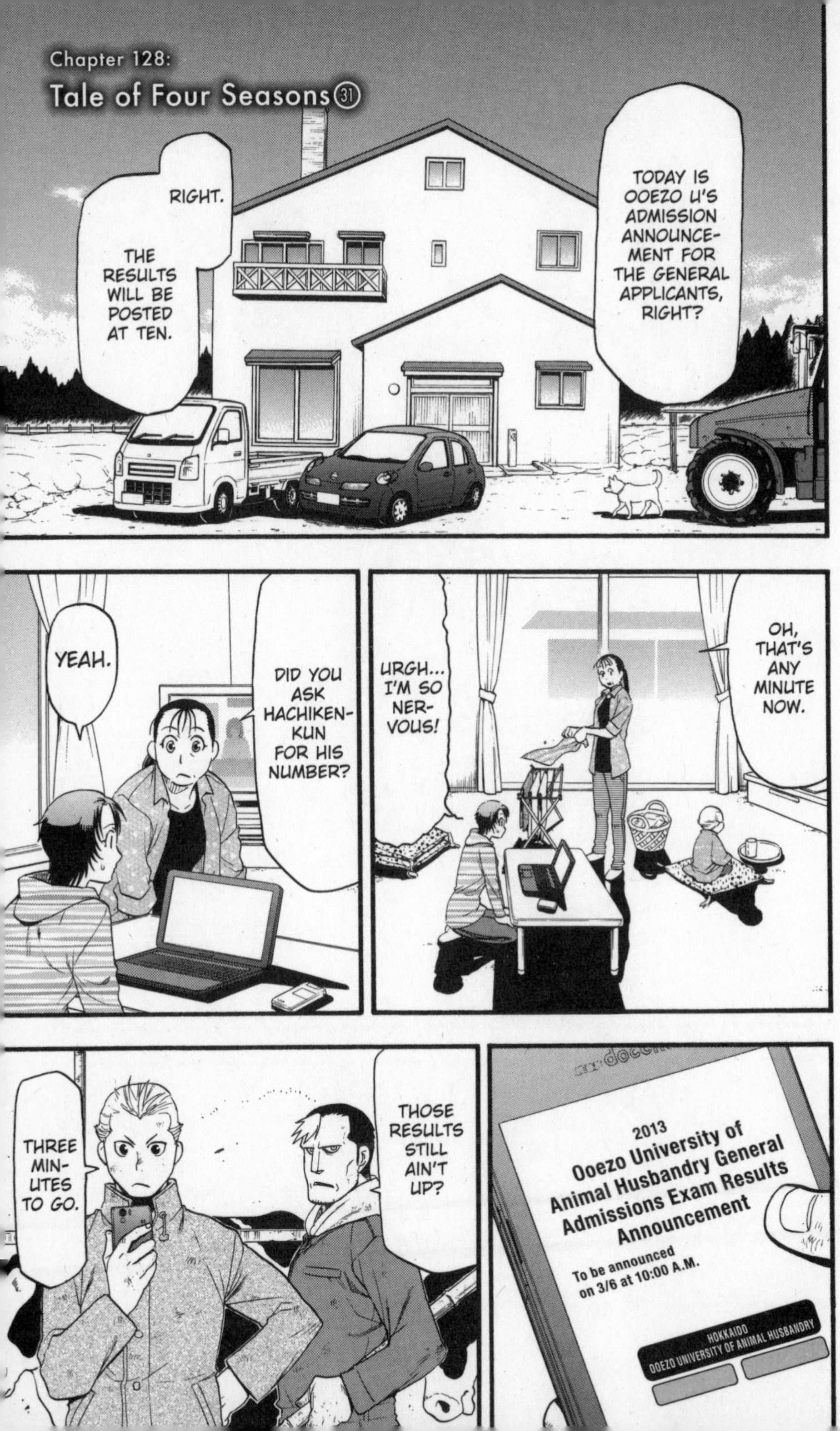
Chapter 128:
Tale of Four Seasons ㉛
TODAY IS OOEZO U'S ADMISSION ANNOUNCEMENT FOR THE GENERAL APPLICANTS, RIGHT?
RIGHT.
THE RESULTS WILL BE POSTED AT TEN.
OH, THAT'S ANY MINUTE NOW.
URGH... I'M SO NERVOUS!
DID YOU ASK HACHIKEN-KUN FOR HIS NUMBER?
YEAH.
2013
Ooezo University of Animal Husbandry General Admissions Exam Results Announcement
To be announced on 3/6 at 10:00 A.M.
HOKKAIDO
OOEZO UNIVERSITY OF ANIMAL HUSBANDRY
THOSE RESULTS STILL AIN'T UP?
THREE MINUTES TO GO.

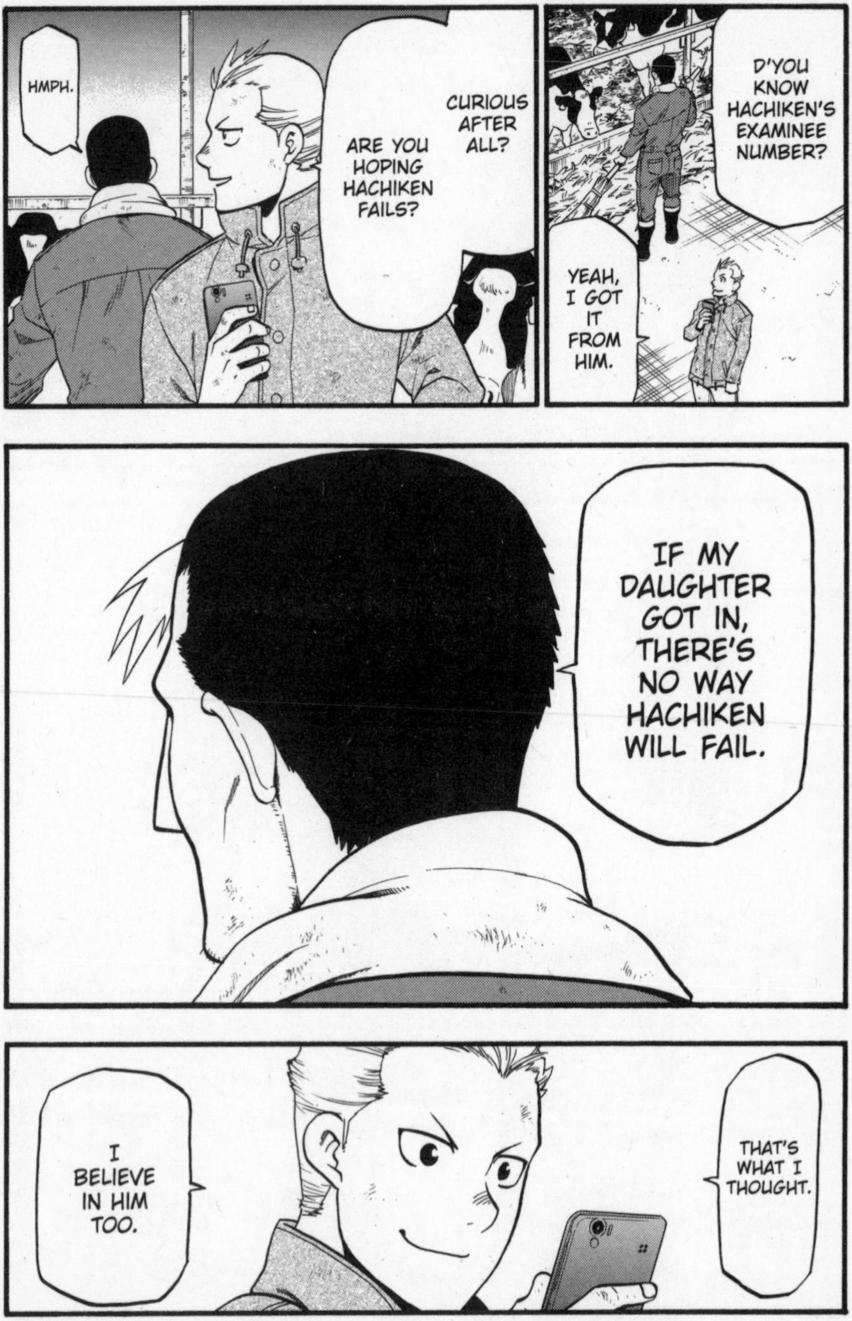
D'YOU KNOW HACHIKEN'S EXAMINEE NUMBER?
YEAH, I GOT IT FROM HIM.
CURIOUS AFTER ALL?
ARE YOU HOPING HACHIKEN FAILS?
HMPH.
IF MY DAUGHTER GOT IN, THERE'S NO WAY HACHIKEN WILL FAIL.
THAT'S WHAT I THOUGHT.
I BELIEVE IN HIM TOO.

# Chapter 128:
# Tale of Four Seasons ㉛

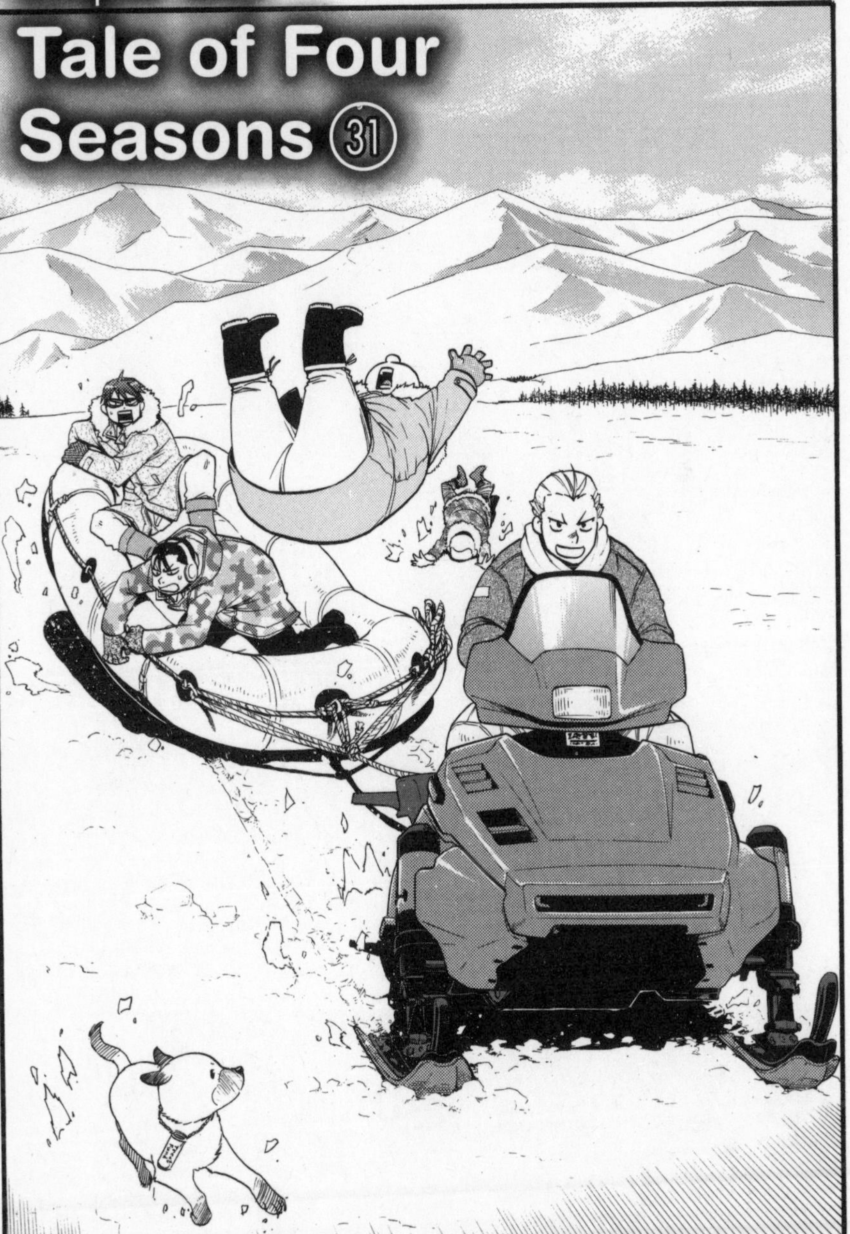

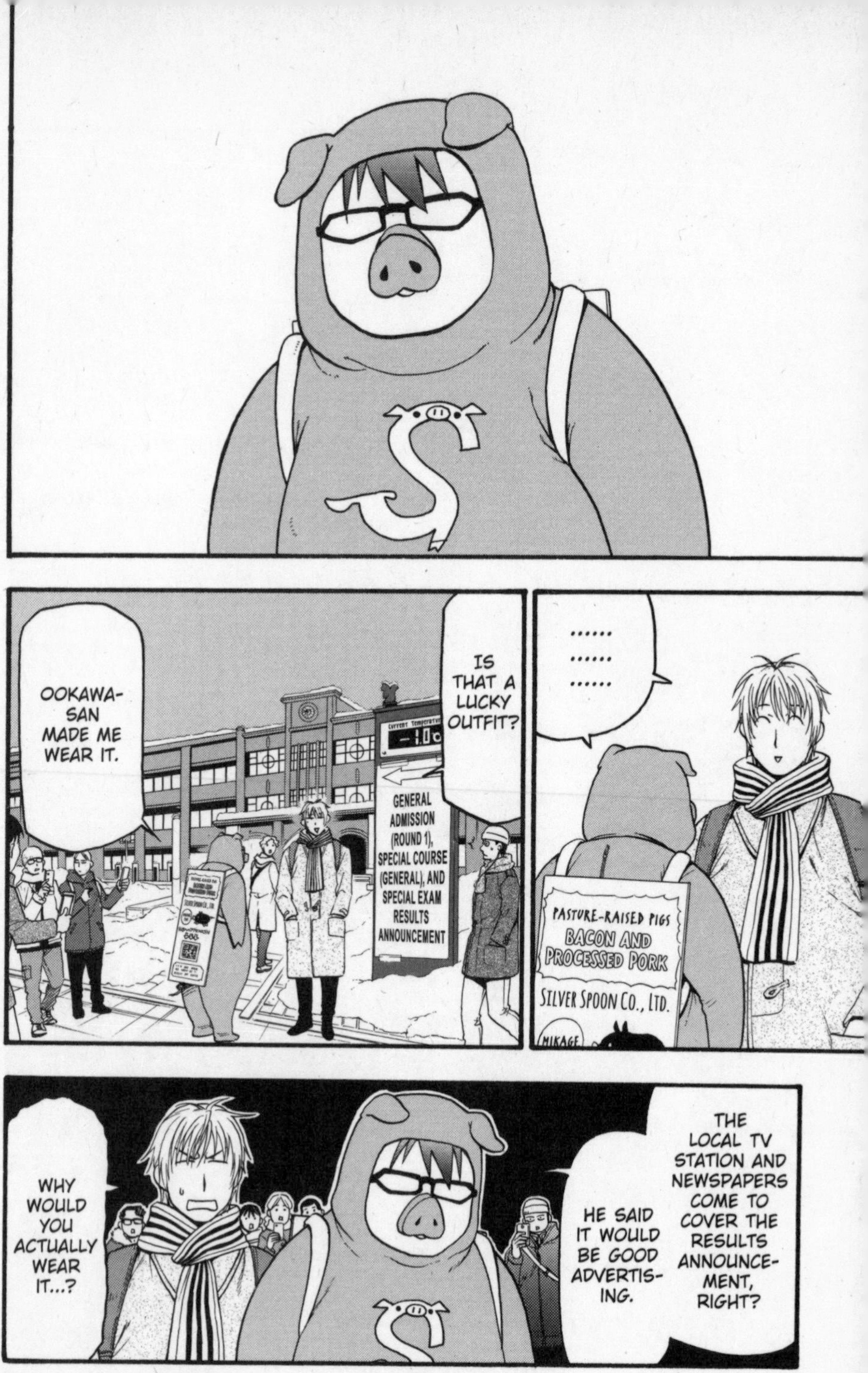
......
......
......
PASTURE-RAISED PIGS
BACON AND PROCESSED PORK
SILVER SPOON CO., LTD.
MIKAGE
IS THAT A LUCKY OUTFIT?
Current Temperature
-1.0°C
GENERAL ADMISSION (ROUND 1), SPECIAL COURSE (GENERAL), AND SPECIAL EXAM RESULTS ANNOUNCEMENT
OOKAWA-SAN MADE ME WEAR IT.
THE LOCAL TV STATION AND NEWSPAPERS COME TO COVER THE RESULTS ANNOUNCEMENT, RIGHT?
HE SAID IT WOULD BE GOOD ADVERTISING.
WHY WOULD YOU ACTUALLY WEAR IT...?

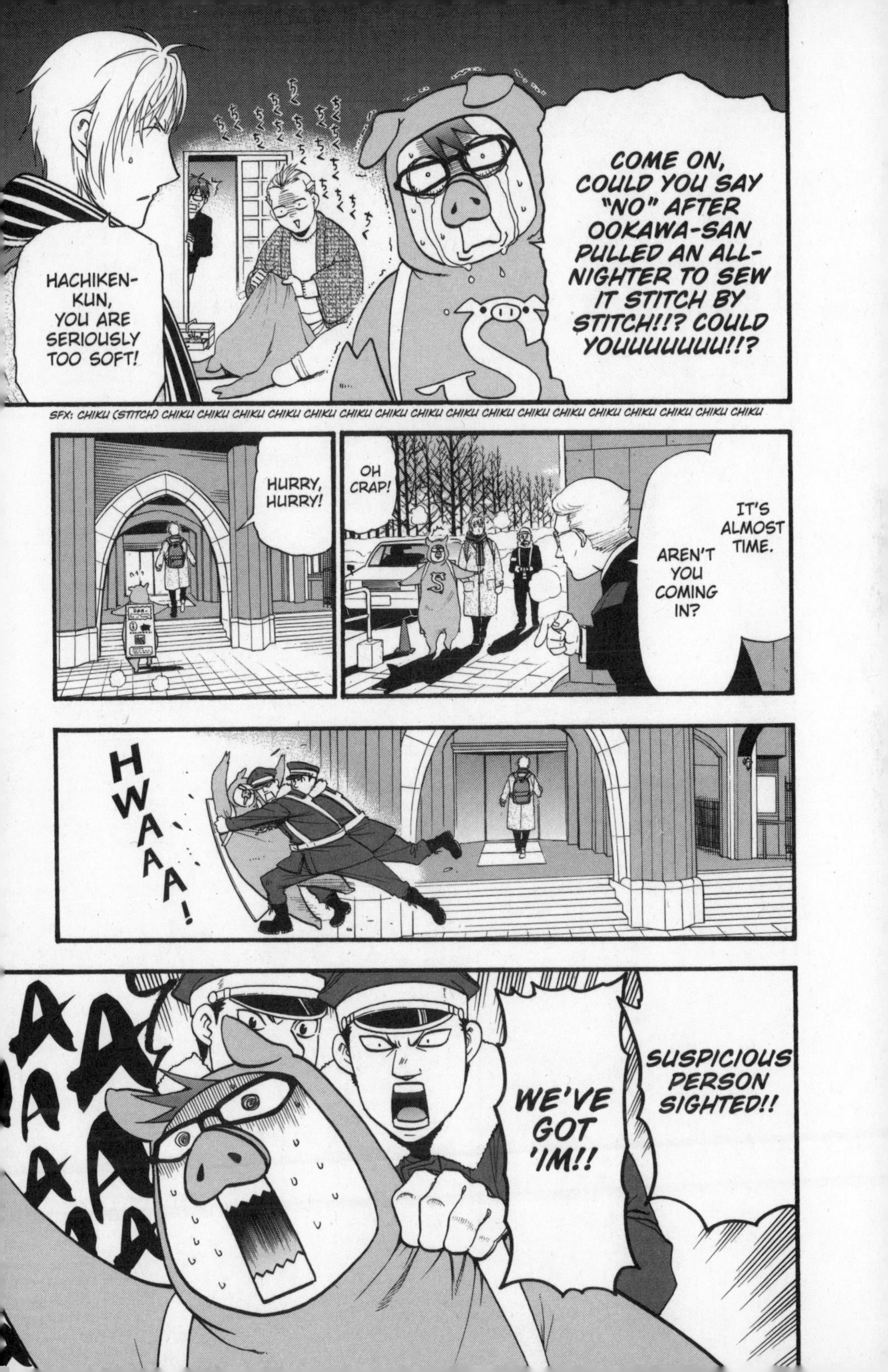
COME ON, COULD YOU SAY "NO" AFTER OOKAWA-SAN PULLED AN ALL-NIGHTER TO SEW IT STITCH BY STITCH!!? COULD YOUUUUUUU!!?
HACHIKEN-KUN, YOU ARE SERIOUSLY TOO SOFT!
SFX: CHIKU (STITCH) CHIKU CHIKU CHIKU CHIKU CHIKU CHIKU CHIKU CHIKU CHIKU CHIKU CHIKU CHIKU CHIKU CHIKU CHIKU CHIKU CHIKU
IT'S ALMOST TIME.
AREN'T YOU COMING IN?
OH CRAP!
HURRY, HURRY!
HWAAAA!
SUSPICIOUS PERSON SIGHTED!!
WE'VE GOT 'IM!!
AAAAAAA

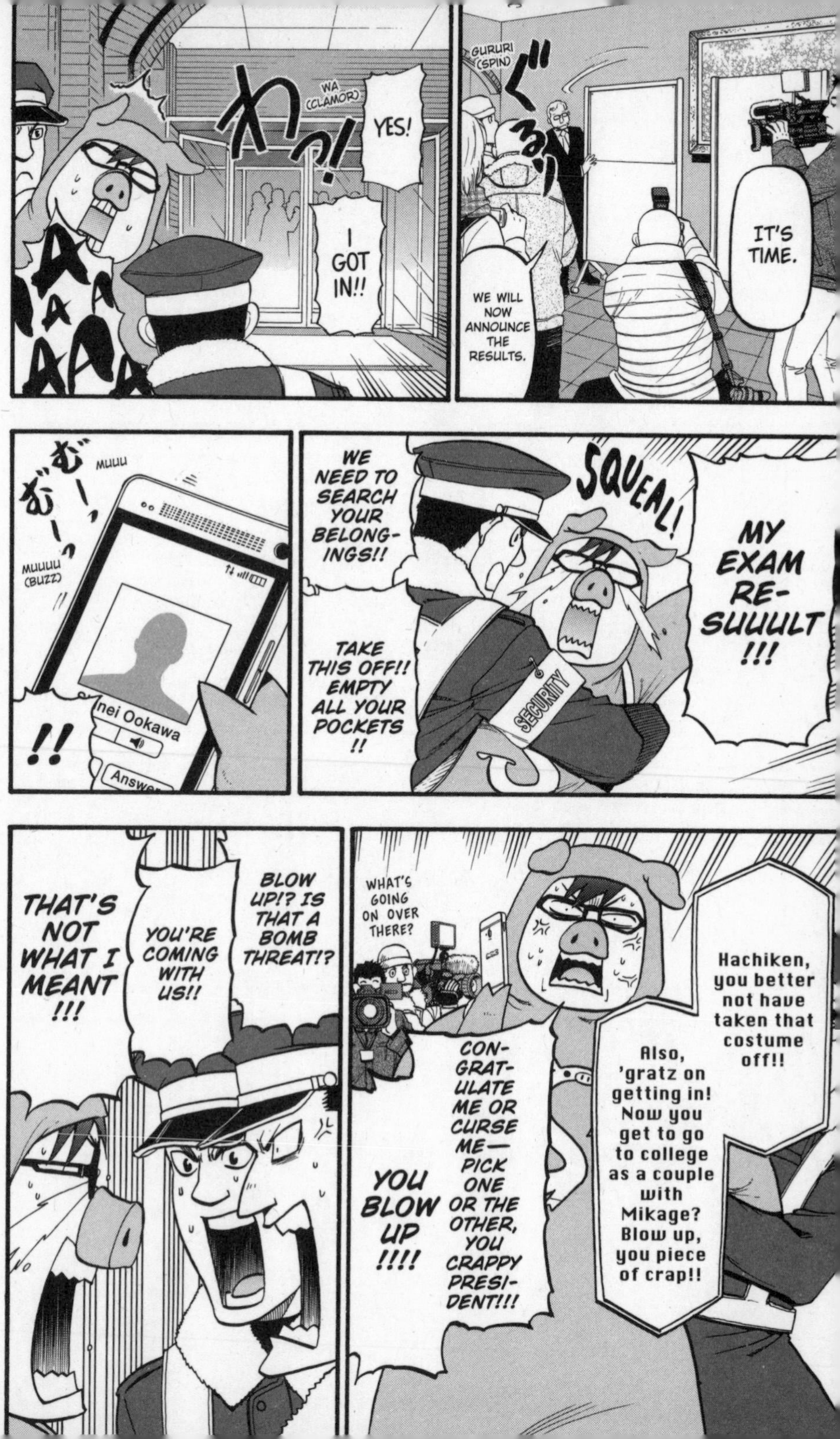
GURURI (SPIN)
IT'S TIME.
WE WILL NOW ANNOUNCE THE RESULTS.
WA (CLAMOR)
YES!
I GOT IN!!
AAAAA
SQUEAL!
MY EXAM RE-SUUULT!!!
WE NEED TO SEARCH YOUR BELONG-INGS!!
TAKE THIS OFF!! EMPTY ALL YOUR POCKETS!!
SECURITY
MUUU
MUUUU (BUZZ)
nei Ookawa
Answer
!!
Hachiken, you better not have taken that costume off!!
Also, 'gratz on getting in! Now you get to go to college as a couple with Mikage? Blow up, you piece of crap!!
WHAT'S GOING ON OVER THERE?
CON-GRAT-ULATE ME OR CURSE ME—PICK ONE OR THE OTHER, YOU CRAPPY PRESI-DENT!!!
YOU BLOW UP!!!!
BLOW UP!? IS THAT A BOMB THREAT!?
YOU'RE COMING WITH US!!
THAT'S NOT WHAT I MEANT!!!

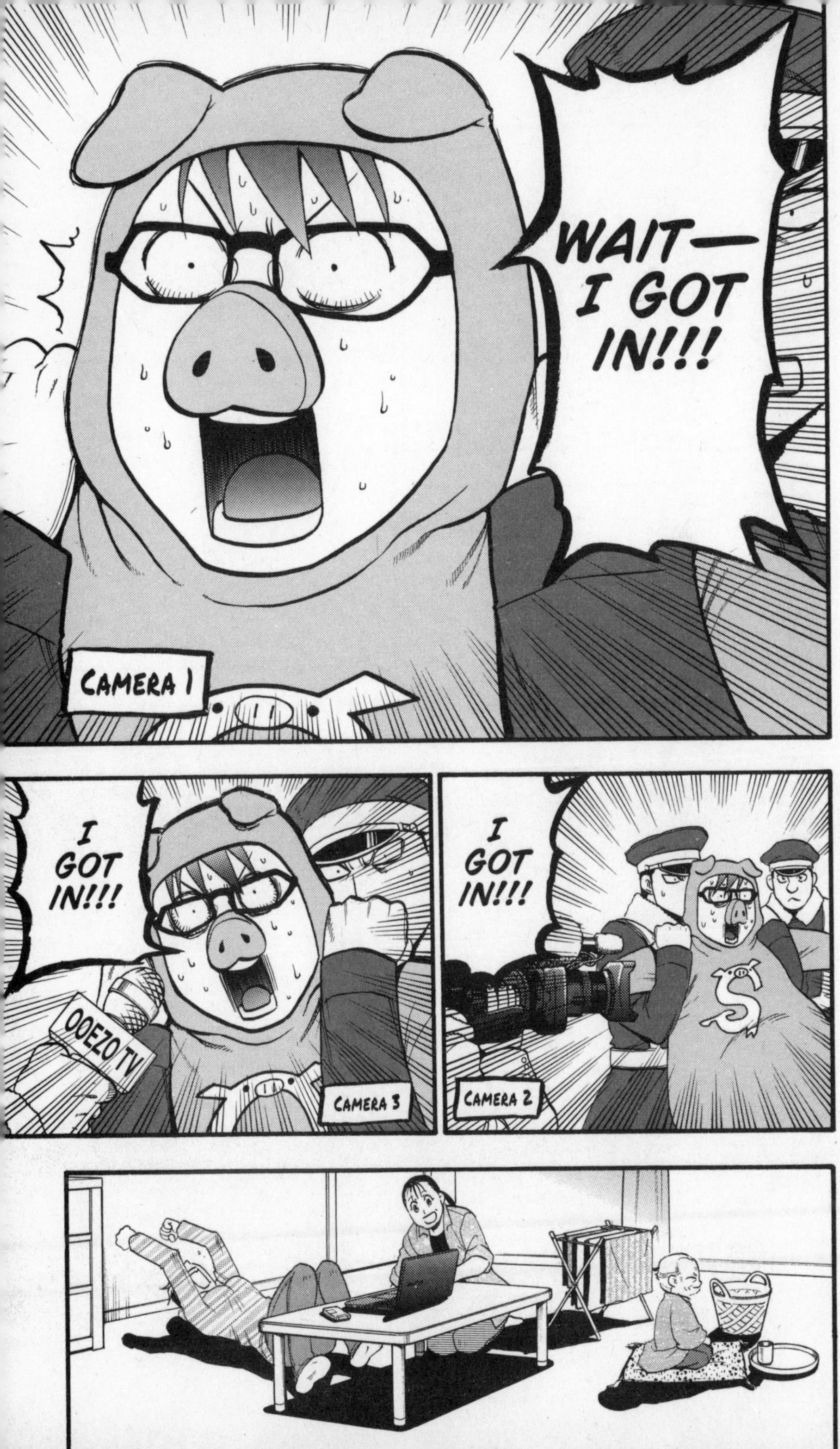
WAIT— I GOT IN!!!
CAMERA 1
I GOT IN!!!
CAMERA 2
I GOT IN!!!
OOEZO TV
CAMERA 3

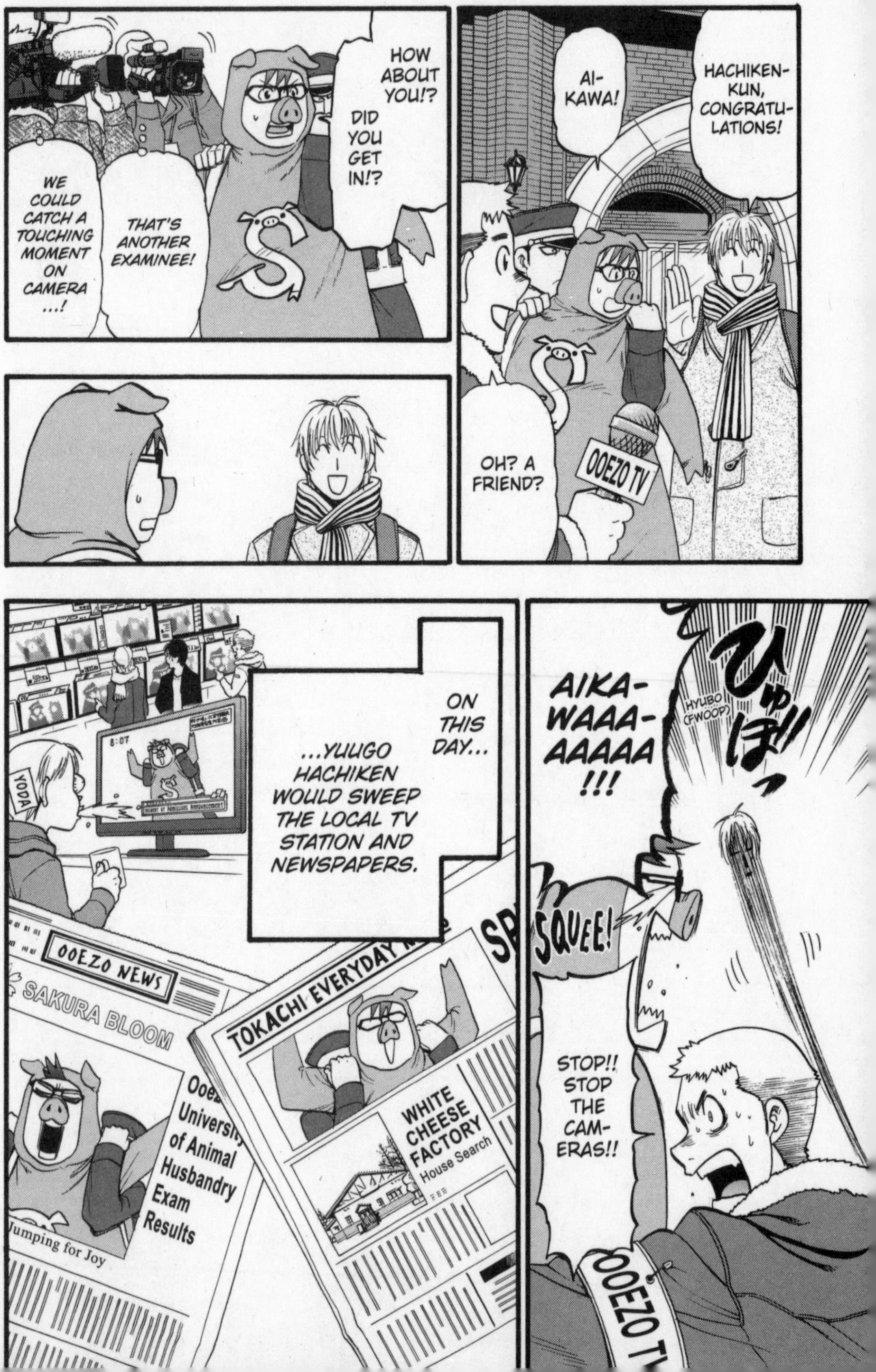
HACHIKEN-KUN, CONGRATULATIONS!
AI-KAWA!
OOEZO TV
OH? A FRIEND?
HOW ABOUT YOU!?
DID YOU GET IN!?
THAT'S ANOTHER EXAMINEE!
WE COULD CATCH A TOUCHING MOMENT ON CAMERA ...!
AIKA-WAAA-AAAAA!!!
ひゅぼっ!!
HYUBO (FWOOP)
SQUEE!
STOP!! STOP THE CAM-ERAS!!
OOEZO TV
ON THIS DAY...
...YUUGO HACHIKEN WOULD SWEEP THE LOCAL TV STATION AND NEWSPAPERS.
YODA
OOEZO NEWS
SAKURA BLOOM
University of Animal Husbandry Exam Results
Jumping for Joy
TOKACHI EVERYDAY
WHITE CHEESE FACTORY
House Search

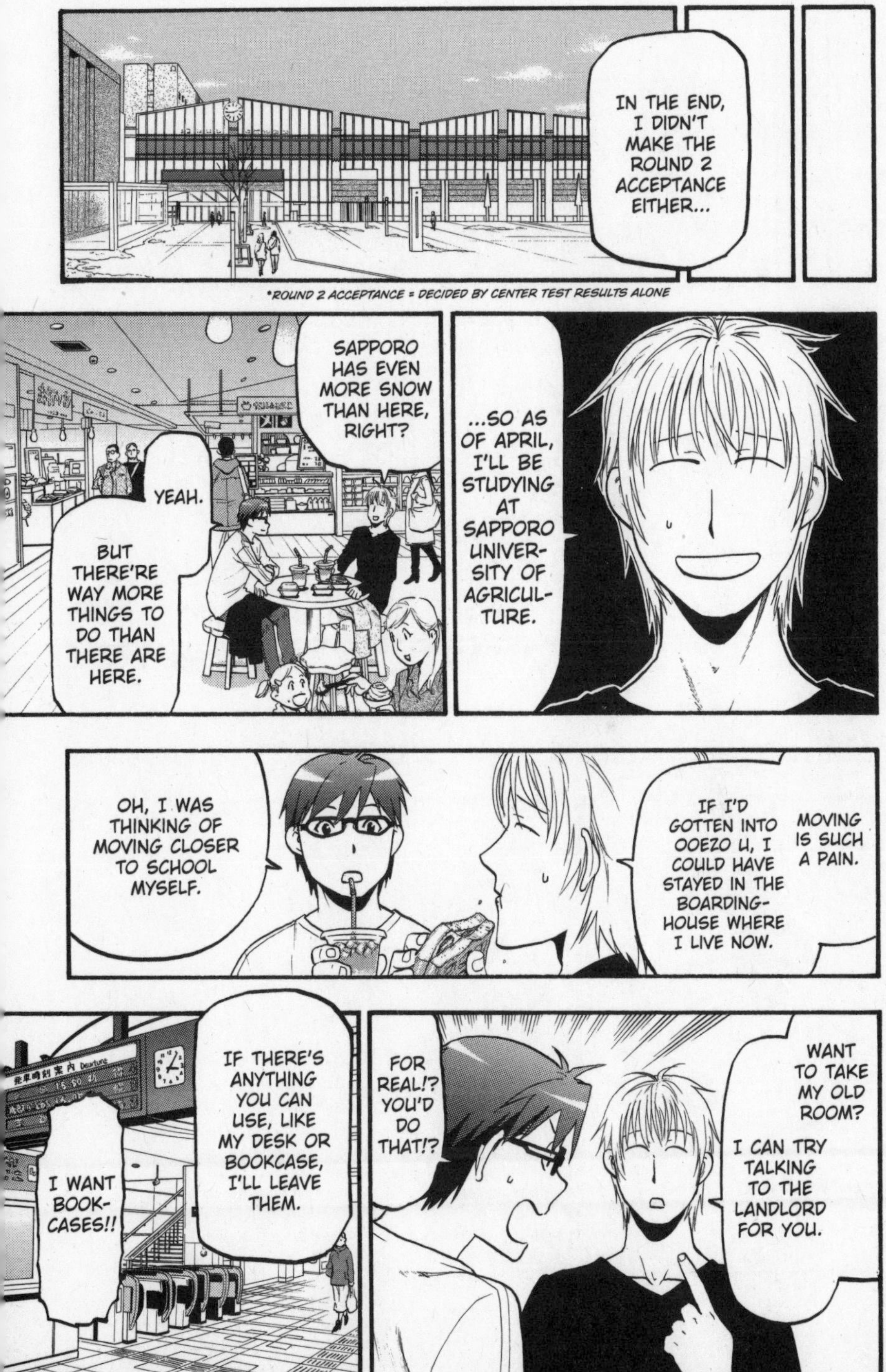
IN THE END, I DIDN'T MAKE THE ROUND 2 ACCEPTANCE EITHER...
*ROUND 2 ACCEPTANCE = DECIDED BY CENTER TEST RESULTS ALONE
...SO AS OF APRIL, I'LL BE STUDYING AT SAPPORO UNIVERSITY OF AGRICULTURE.
SAPPORO HAS EVEN MORE SNOW THAN HERE, RIGHT?
YEAH.
BUT THERE'RE WAY MORE THINGS TO DO THAN THERE ARE HERE.
MOVING IS SUCH A PAIN.
IF I'D GOTTEN INTO OOEZO U, I COULD HAVE STAYED IN THE BOARDING-HOUSE WHERE I LIVE NOW.
OH, I WAS THINKING OF MOVING CLOSER TO SCHOOL MYSELF.
WANT TO TAKE MY OLD ROOM?
I CAN TRY TALKING TO THE LANDLORD FOR YOU.
FOR REAL!? YOU'D DO THAT!?
IF THERE'S ANYTHING YOU CAN USE, LIKE MY DESK OR BOOKCASE, I'LL LEAVE THEM.
I WANT BOOK-CASES!!

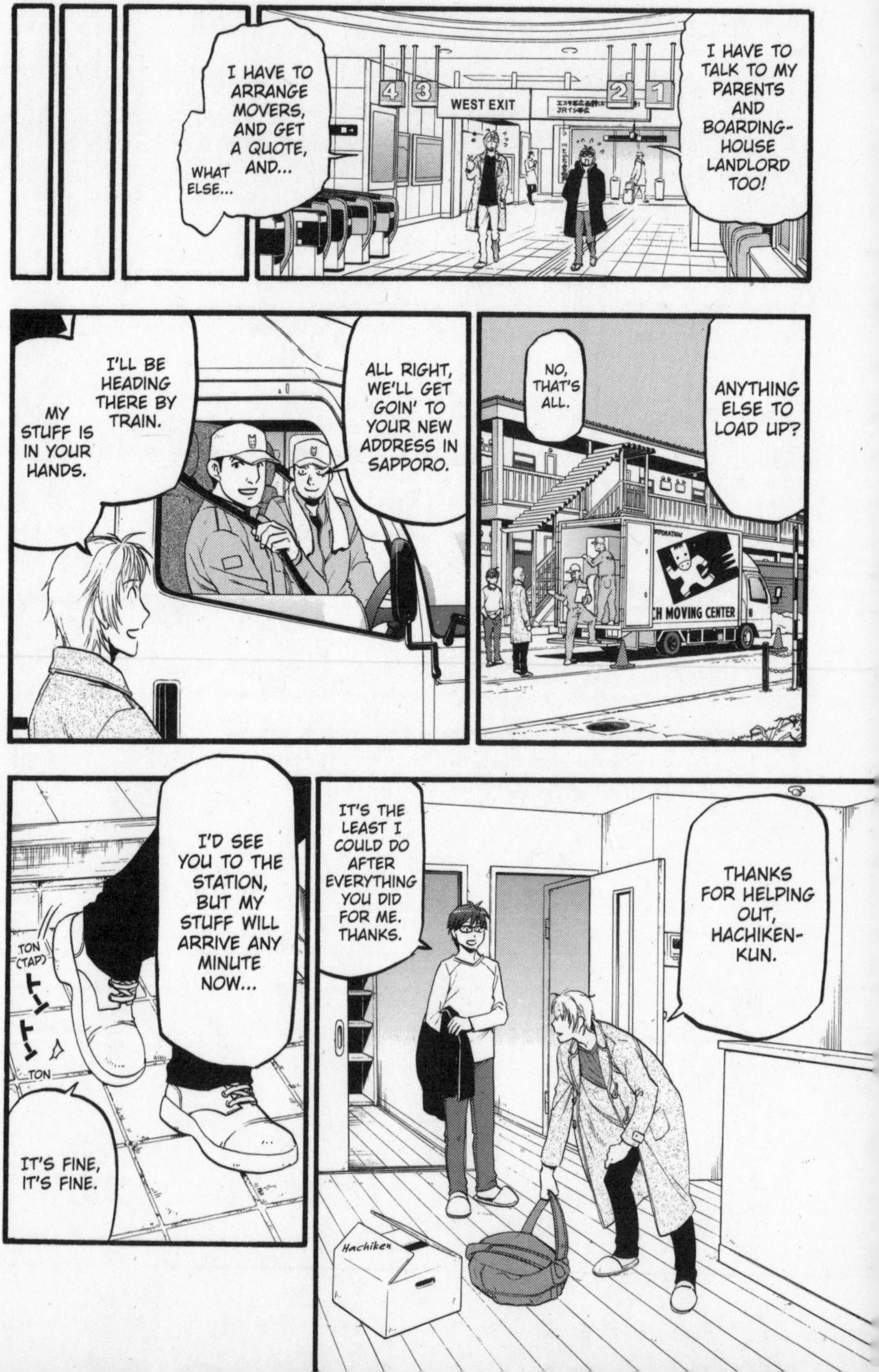
I HAVE TO TALK TO MY PARENTS AND BOARDING-HOUSE LANDLORD TOO!
WEST EXIT
4
3
2
1
I HAVE TO ARRANGE MOVERS, AND GET A QUOTE, AND...
WHAT ELSE...
ANYTHING ELSE TO LOAD UP?
NO, THAT'S ALL.
ORPORATION
CH MOVING CENTER
ALL RIGHT, WE'LL GET GOIN' TO YOUR NEW ADDRESS IN SAPPORO.
I'LL BE HEADING THERE BY TRAIN.
MY STUFF IS IN YOUR HANDS.
THANKS FOR HELPING OUT, HACHIKEN-KUN.
IT'S THE LEAST I COULD DO AFTER EVERYTHING YOU DID FOR ME. THANKS.
Hachiken
I'D SEE YOU TO THE STATION, BUT MY STUFF WILL ARRIVE ANY MINUTE NOW...
TON (TAP)
トン
トン
TON
IT'S FINE, IT'S FINE.

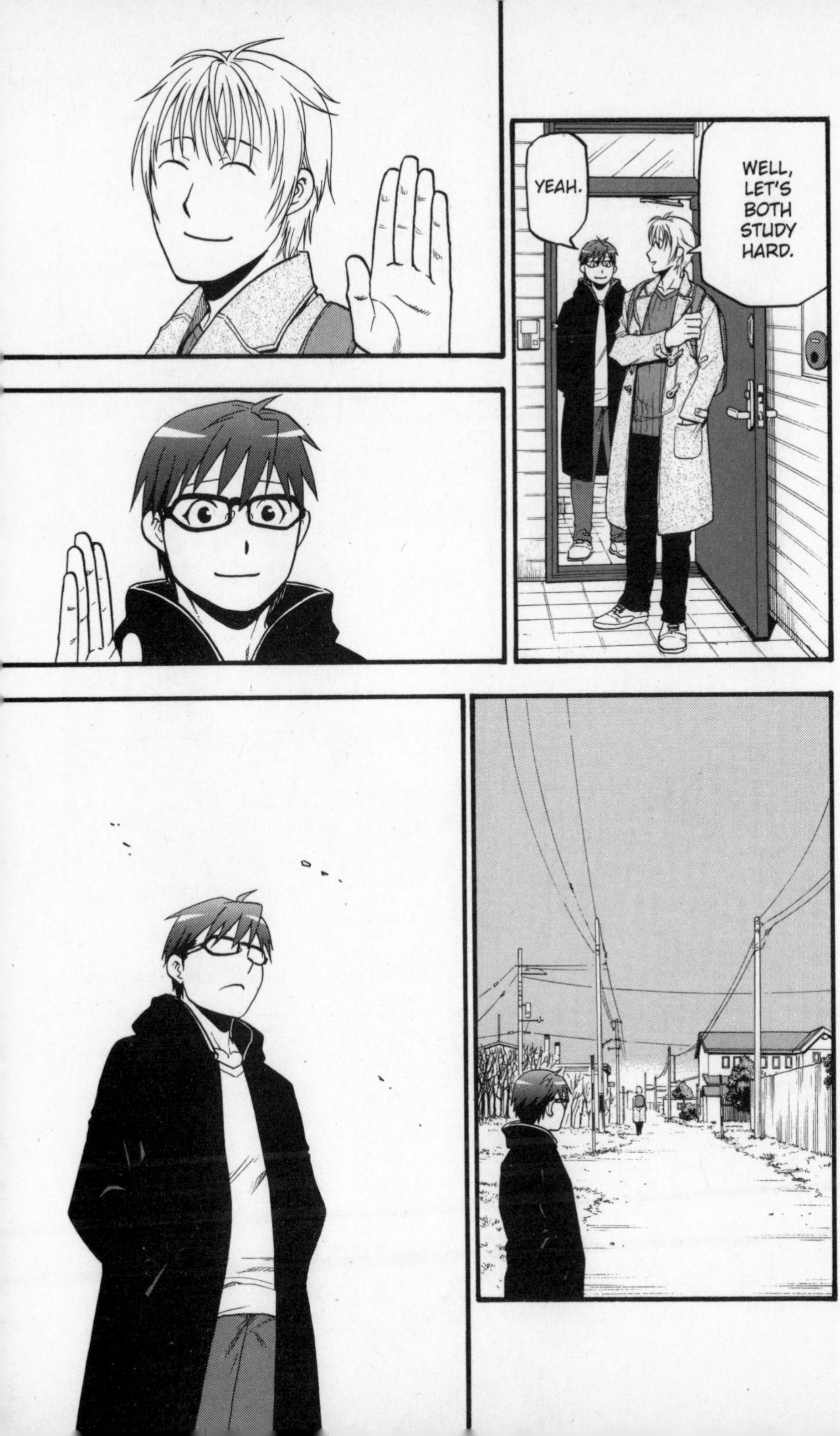
WELL, LET'S BOTH STUDY HARD.
YEAH.

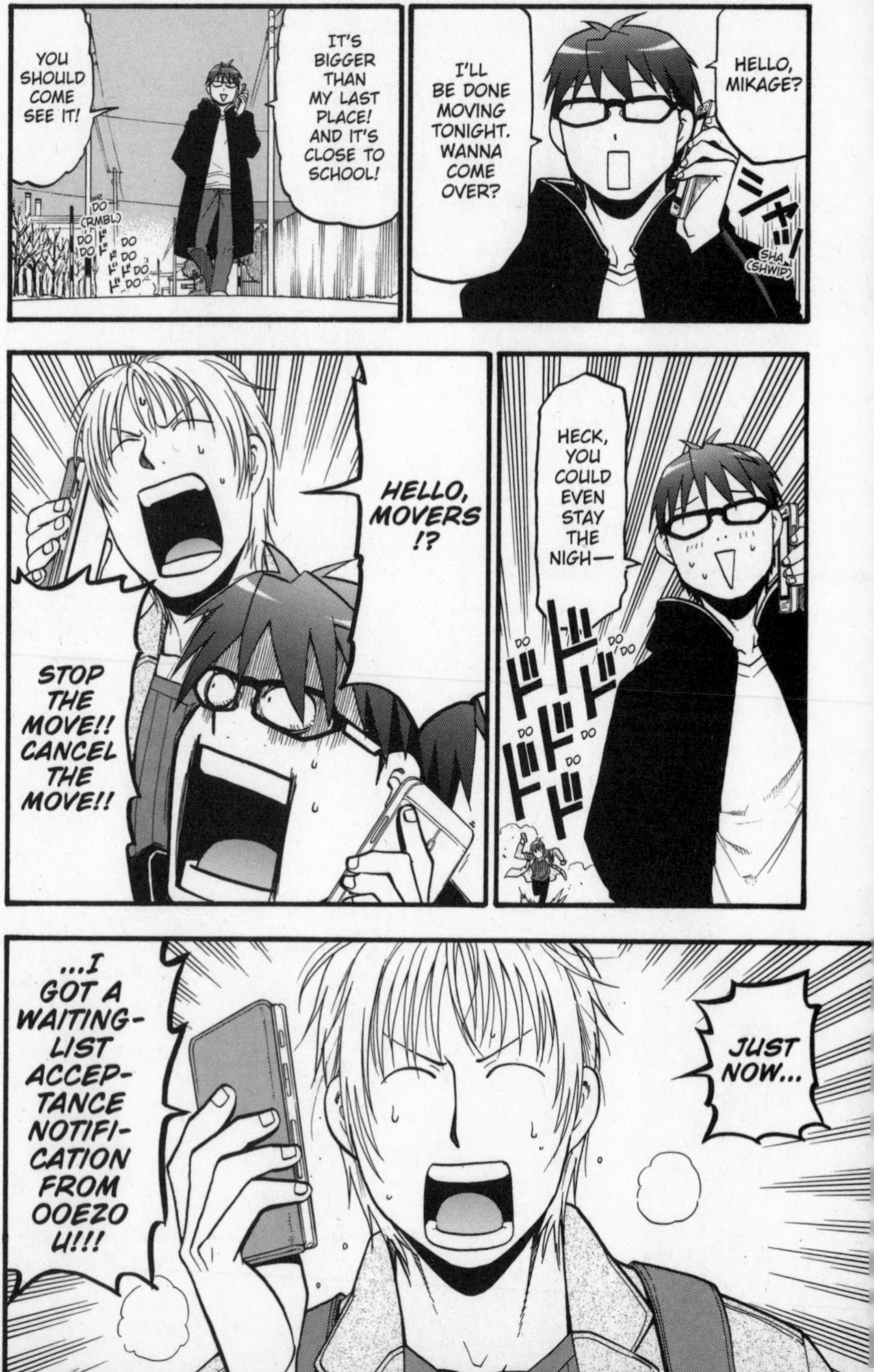
HELLO, MIKAGE?
I'LL BE DONE MOVING TONIGHT. WANNA COME OVER?
SHA (SHWIP)
IT'S BIGGER THAN MY LAST PLACE! AND IT'S CLOSE TO SCHOOL!
YOU SHOULD COME SEE IT!
DO (RMBL) DO DO DO DO DO DO
HECK, YOU COULD EVEN STAY THE NIGH—
DO DO DO DO DO
HELLO, MOVERS!?
STOP THE MOVE!! CANCEL THE MOVE!!
JUST NOW...
...I GOT A WAITING-LIST ACCEPTANCE NOTIFICATION FROM OOEZO U!!!

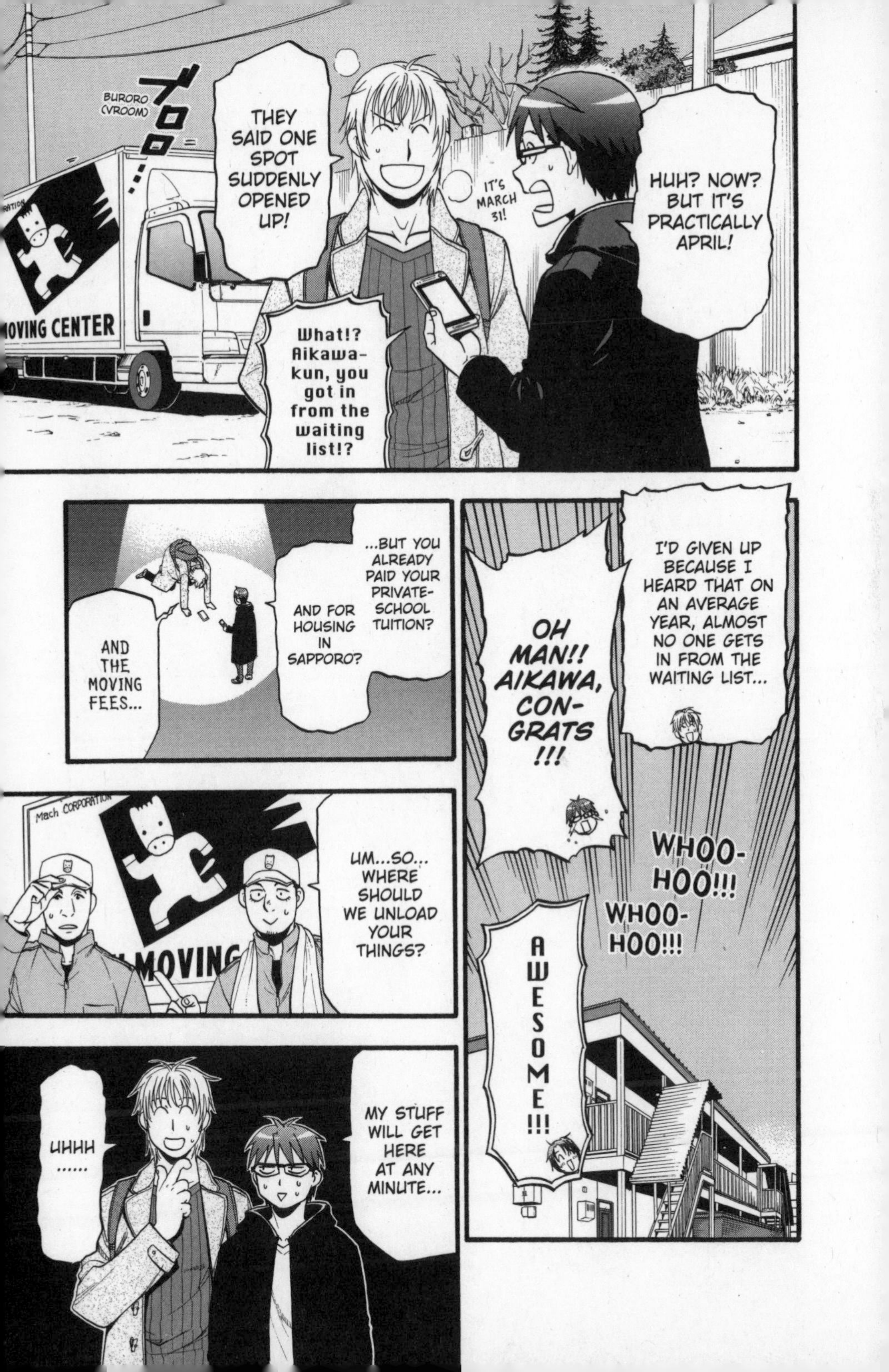
HUH? NOW? BUT IT'S PRACTICALLY APRIL!
IT'S MARCH 31!
THEY SAID ONE SPOT SUDDENLY OPENED UP!
BURORO (VROOM)
MOVING CENTER
What!? Aikawa-kun, you got in from the waiting list!?
I'D GIVEN UP BECAUSE I HEARD THAT ON AN AVERAGE YEAR, ALMOST NO ONE GETS IN FROM THE WAITING LIST...
OH MAN!! AIKAWA, CON-GRATS!!!
WHOO-HOO!!!
WHOO-HOO!!!
AWESOME!!!
...BUT YOU ALREADY PAID YOUR PRIVATE-SCHOOL TUITION?
AND FOR HOUSING IN SAPPORO?
AND THE MOVING FEES...
UM...SO... WHERE SHOULD WE UNLOAD YOUR THINGS?
Mach CORPORATION
MOVING
MY STUFF WILL GET HERE AT ANY MINUTE...
UHHH ......

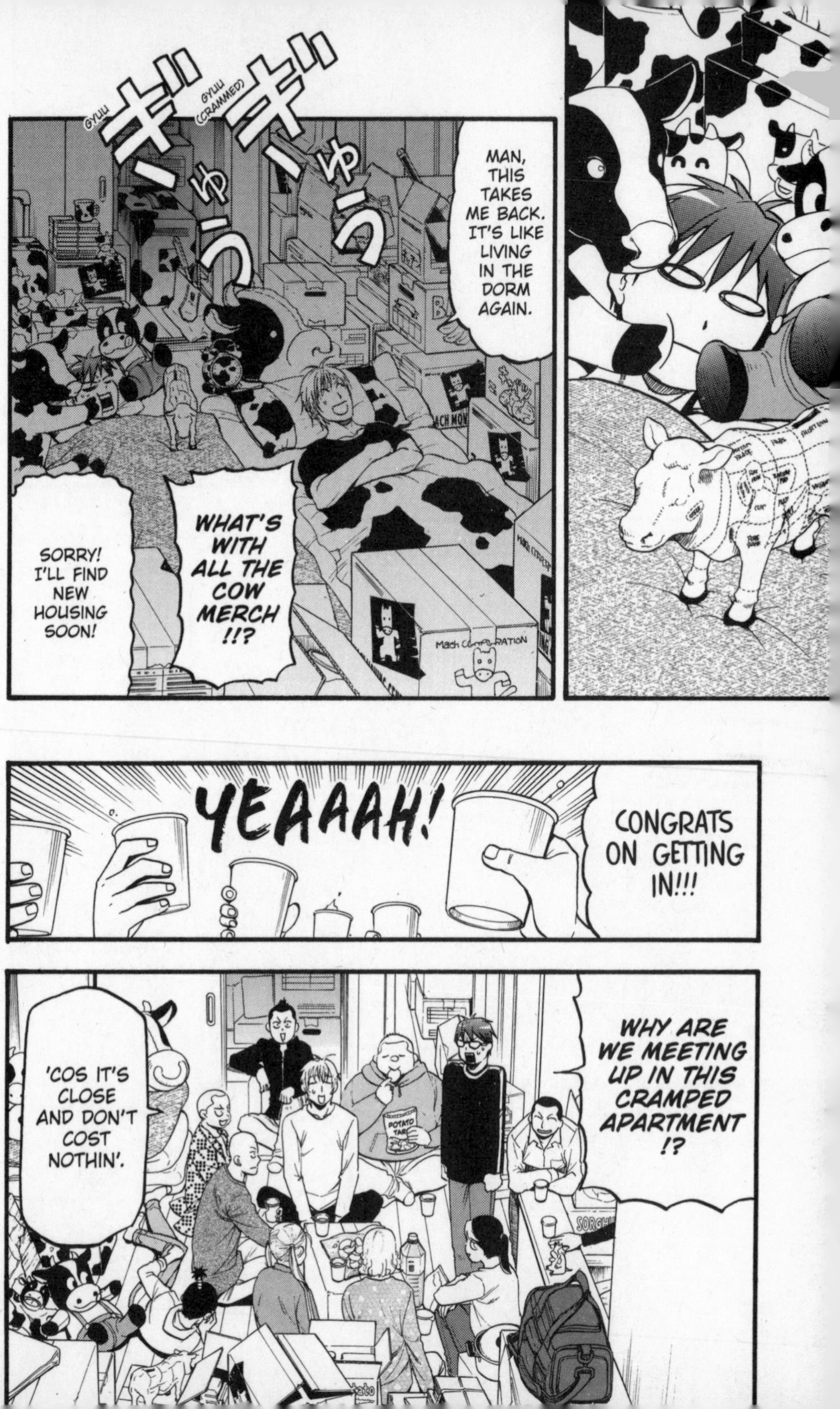
GYUU (CRAMMED)
GYUU
MAN, THIS TAKES ME BACK. IT'S LIKE LIVING IN THE DORM AGAIN.
WHAT'S WITH ALL THE COW MERCH!!?
SORRY! I'LL FIND NEW HOUSING SOON!
CONGRATS ON GETTING IN!!!
YEAAAH!
WHY ARE WE MEETING UP IN THIS CRAMPED APARTMENT!?
'COS IT'S CLOSE AND DON'T COST NOTHIN'.

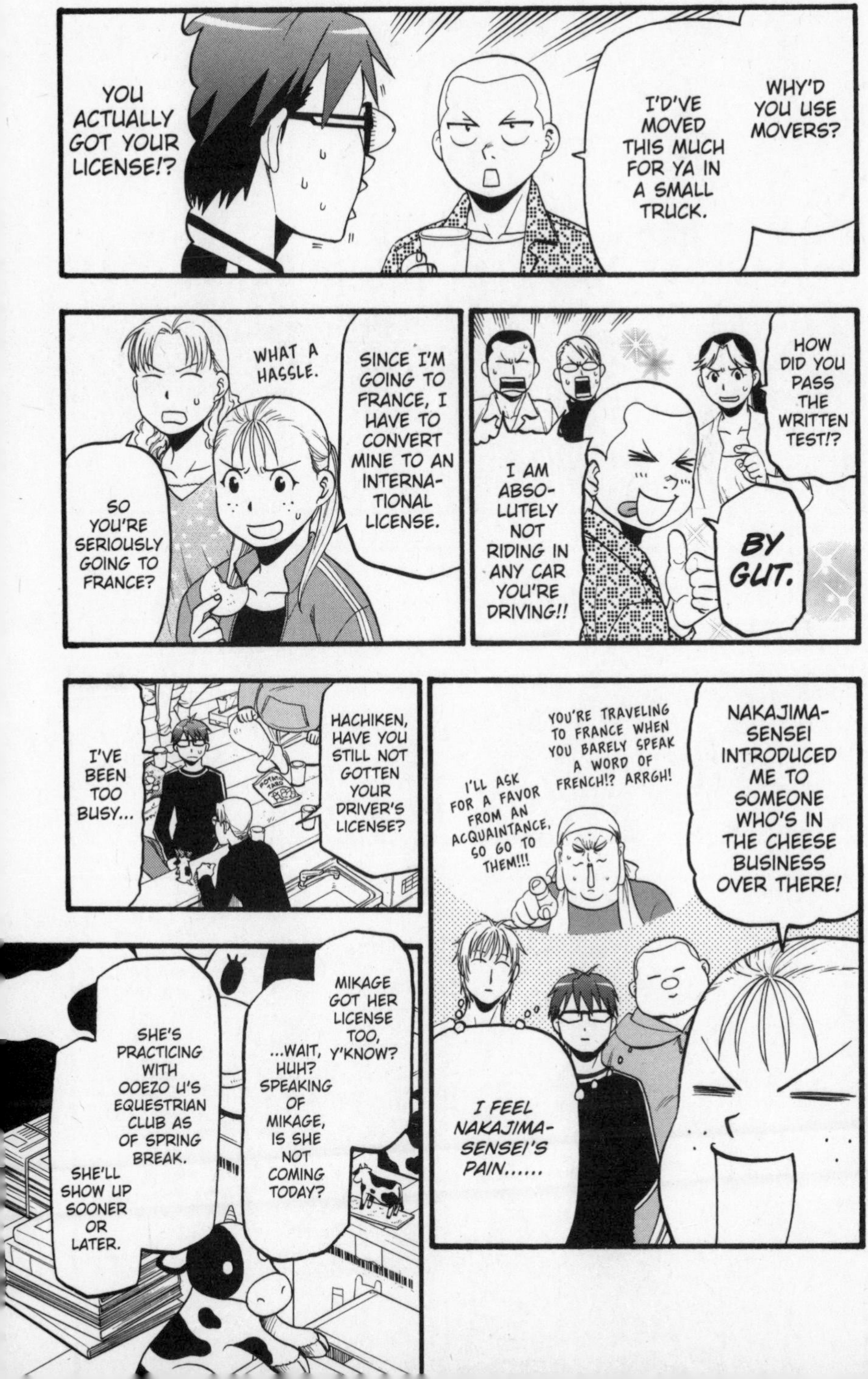
WHY'D YOU USE MOVERS?
I'D'VE MOVED THIS MUCH FOR YA IN A SMALL TRUCK.
YOU ACTUALLY GOT YOUR LICENSE!?
HOW DID YOU PASS THE WRITTEN TEST!?
BY GUT.
I AM ABSOLUTELY NOT RIDING IN ANY CAR YOU'RE DRIVING!!
SINCE I'M GOING TO FRANCE, I HAVE TO CONVERT MINE TO AN INTERNATIONAL LICENSE.
WHAT A HASSLE.
SO YOU'RE SERIOUSLY GOING TO FRANCE?
NAKAJIMA-SENSEI INTRODUCED ME TO SOMEONE WHO'S IN THE CHEESE BUSINESS OVER THERE!
YOU'RE TRAVELING TO FRANCE WHEN YOU BARELY SPEAK A WORD OF FRENCH!? ARRGH!
I'LL ASK FOR A FAVOR FROM AN ACQUAINTANCE, SO GO TO THEM!!!
I FEEL NAKAJIMA-SENSEI'S PAIN......
HACHIKEN, HAVE YOU STILL NOT GOTTEN YOUR DRIVER'S LICENSE?
I'VE BEEN TOO BUSY...
MIKAGE GOT HER LICENSE TOO, Y'KNOW?
...WAIT, HUH? SPEAKING OF MIKAGE, IS SHE NOT COMING TODAY?
SHE'S PRACTICING WITH OOEZO U'S EQUESTRIAN CLUB AS OF SPRING BREAK.
SHE'LL SHOW UP SOONER OR LATER.

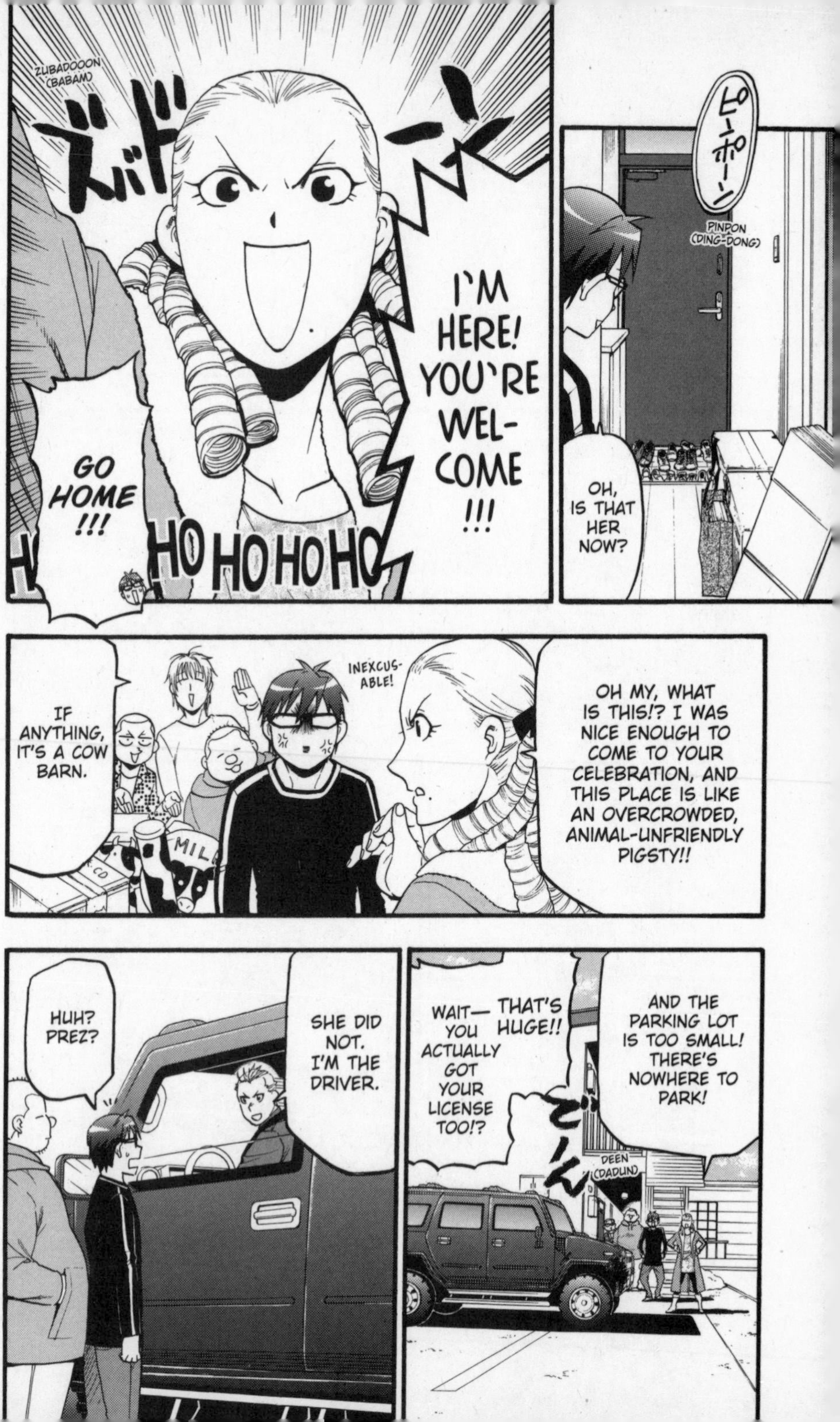

ピーンポーン
PINDON (DING-DONG)
OH, IS THAT HER NOW?
ZUBADOOON (BABAM)
ズバドーン
I'M HERE! YOU'RE WELCOME!!!
HO HO HO HO HO
GO HOME!!!
OH MY, WHAT IS THIS!? I WAS NICE ENOUGH TO COME TO YOUR CELEBRATION, AND THIS PLACE IS LIKE AN OVERCROWDED, ANIMAL-UNFRIENDLY PIGSTY!!
INEXCUSABLE!
IF ANYTHING, IT'S A COW BARN.
AND THE PARKING LOT IS TOO SMALL! THERE'S NOWHERE TO PARK!
どん
DEEN (DADUN)
THAT'S HUGE!!
WAIT— YOU ACTUALLY GOT YOUR LICENSE TOO!?
SHE DID NOT. I'M THE DRIVER.
HUH? PREZ?

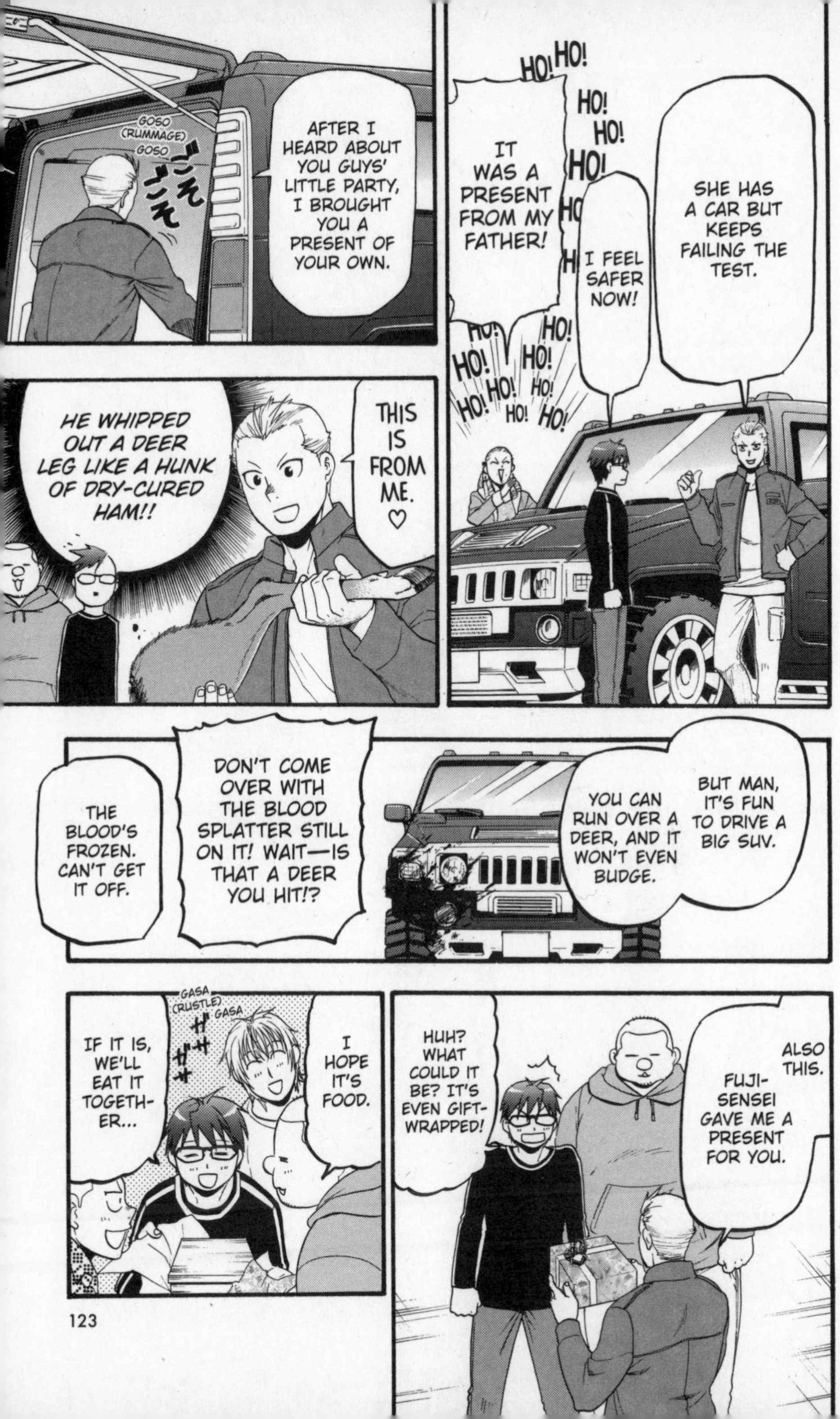
SHE HAS A CAR BUT KEEPS FAILING THE TEST.
I FEEL SAFER NOW!
IT WAS A PRESENT FROM MY FATHER!
HO! HO! HO! HO! HO!
HO! HO! HO! HO! HO! HO! HO! HO!
AFTER I HEARD ABOUT YOU GUYS' LITTLE PARTY, I BROUGHT YOU A PRESENT OF YOUR OWN.
GOSO (RUMMAGE) GOSO
THIS IS FROM ME. ♡
HE WHIPPED OUT A DEER LEG LIKE A HUNK OF DRY-CURED HAM!!
BUT MAN, IT'S FUN TO DRIVE A BIG SUV.
YOU CAN RUN OVER A DEER, AND IT WON'T EVEN BUDGE.
DON'T COME OVER WITH THE BLOOD SPLATTER STILL ON IT! WAIT—IS THAT A DEER YOU HIT!?
THE BLOOD'S FROZEN. CAN'T GET IT OFF.
ALSO THIS.
FUJI-SENSEI GAVE ME A PRESENT FOR YOU.
HUH? WHAT COULD IT BE? IT'S EVEN GIFT-WRAPPED!
I HOPE IT'S FOOD.
GASA (RUSTLE) GASA
IF IT IS, WE'LL EAT IT TOGETHER...

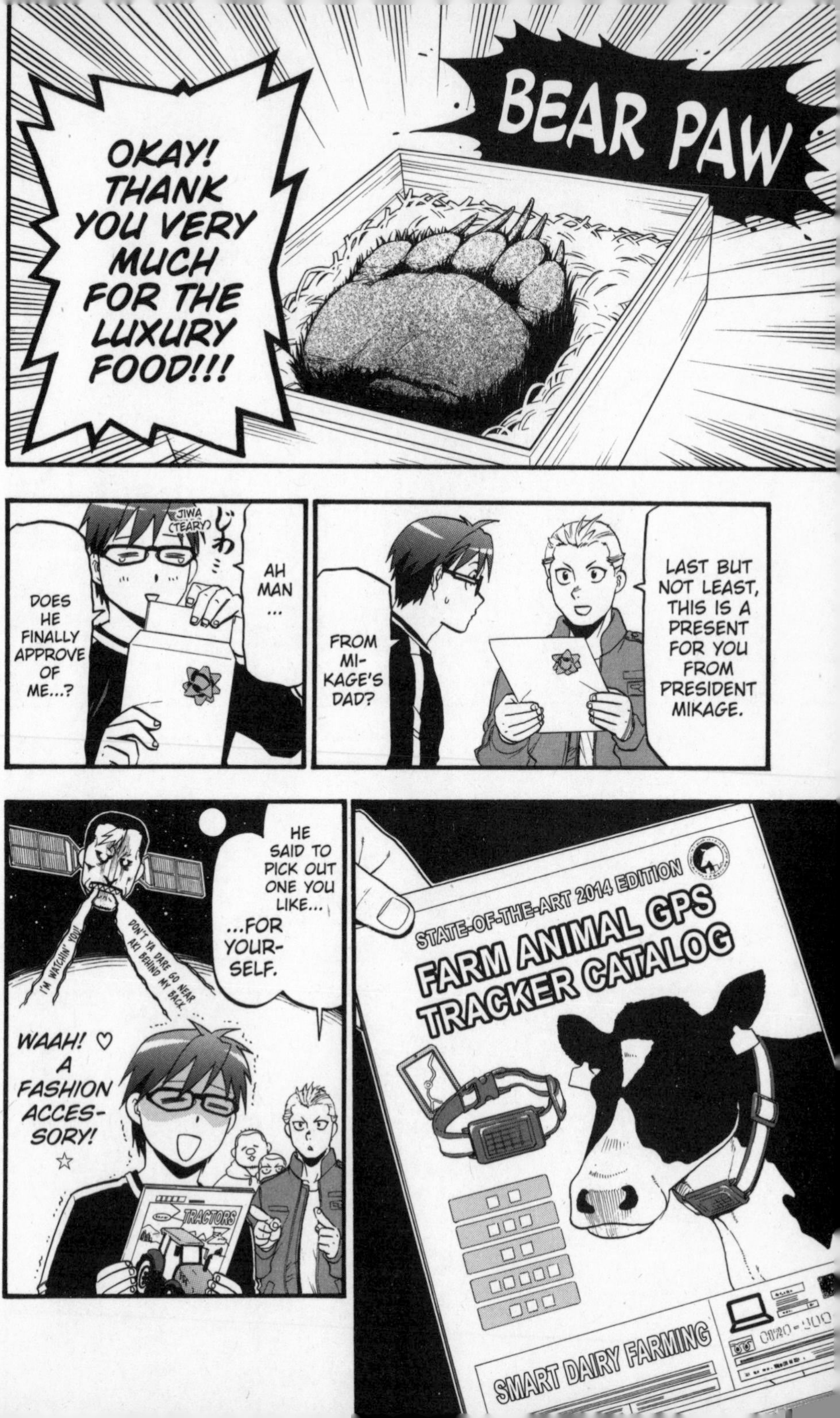
BEAR PAW
OKAY! THANK YOU VERY MUCH FOR THE LUXURY FOOD!!!
LAST BUT NOT LEAST, THIS IS A PRESENT FOR YOU FROM PRESIDENT MIKAGE.
FROM MI-KAGE'S DAD?
JIWA (TEARY)
AH MAN ...
DOES HE FINALLY APPROVE OF ME...?
STATE-OF-THE-ART 2014 EDITION
FARM ANIMAL GPS TRACKER CATALOG
SMART DAIRY FARMING
HE SAID TO PICK OUT ONE YOU LIKE...
...FOR YOUR-SELF.
I'M WATCHIN' YOU!!
DON'T YA DARE GO NEAR AKI BEHIND MY BACK
WAAH! ♡ A FASHION ACCES-SORY! ☆
TRACTORS

Silver Spoon

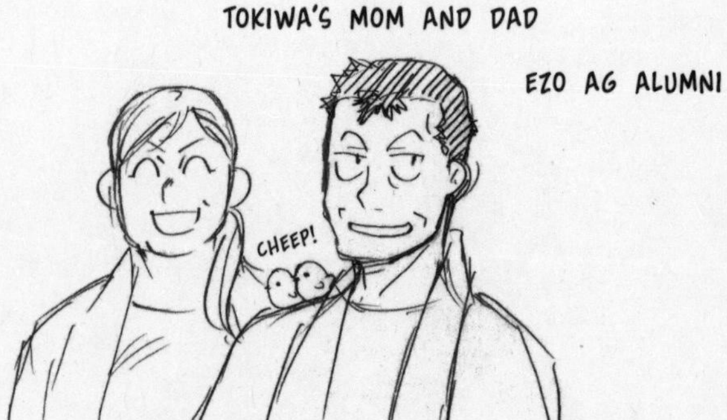
TOKIWA'S MOM AND DAD
EZO AG ALUMNI
CHEEP!

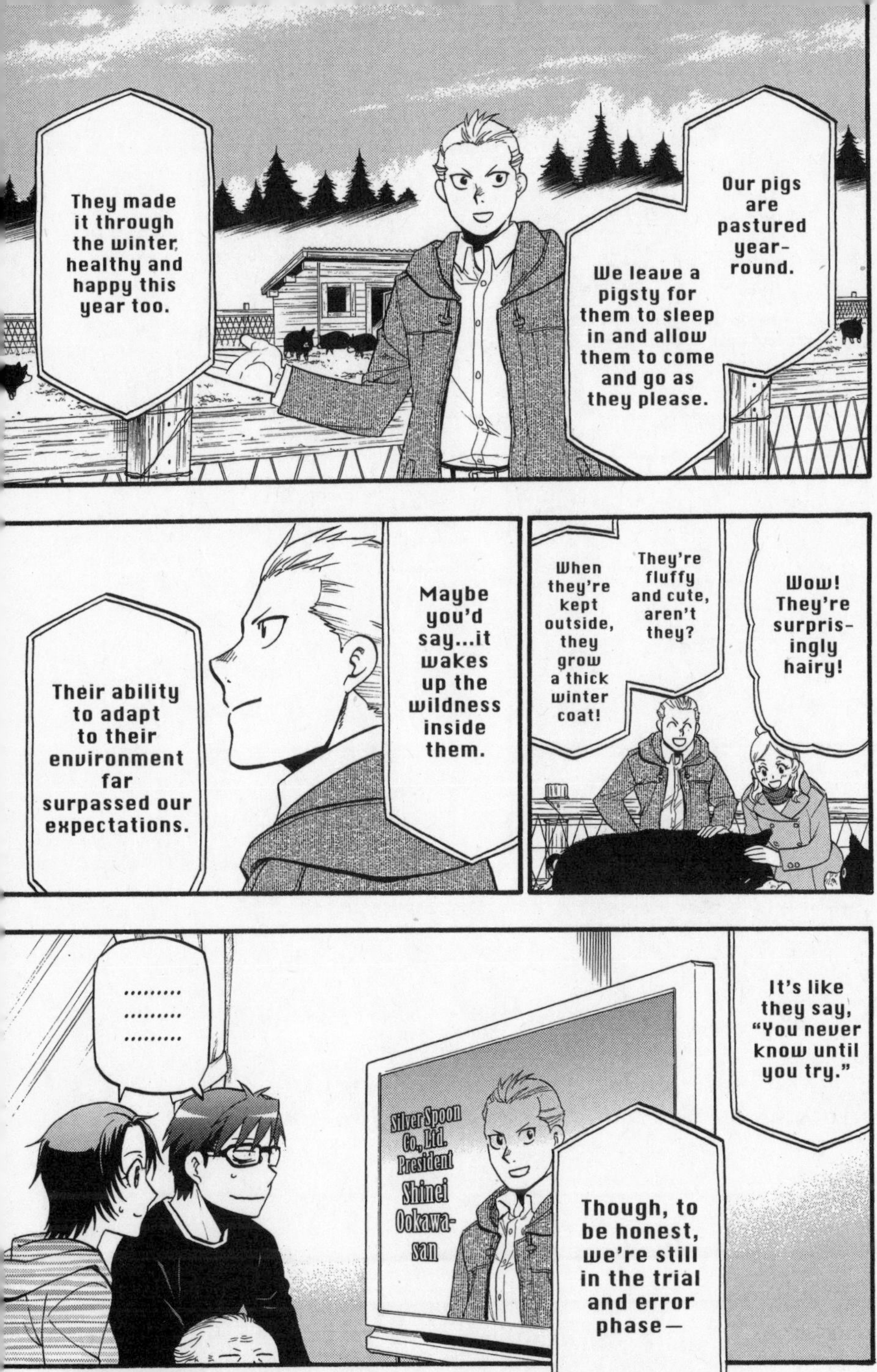
Our pigs are pastured year-round.
We leave a pigsty for them to sleep in and allow them to come and go as they please.
They made it through the winter, healthy and happy this year too.
Wow! They're surpris-ingly hairy!
They're fluffy and cute, aren't they?
When they're kept outside, they grow a thick winter coat!
Maybe you'd say...it wakes up the wildness inside them.
Their ability to adapt to their environment far surpassed our expectations.
It's like they say, "You never know until you try."
Silver Spoon Co., Ltd. President Shinei Ookawa-san
Though, to be honest, we're still in the trial and error phase—
.........
.........
.........

## Chapter 129: Tale of Four Seasons ㉜

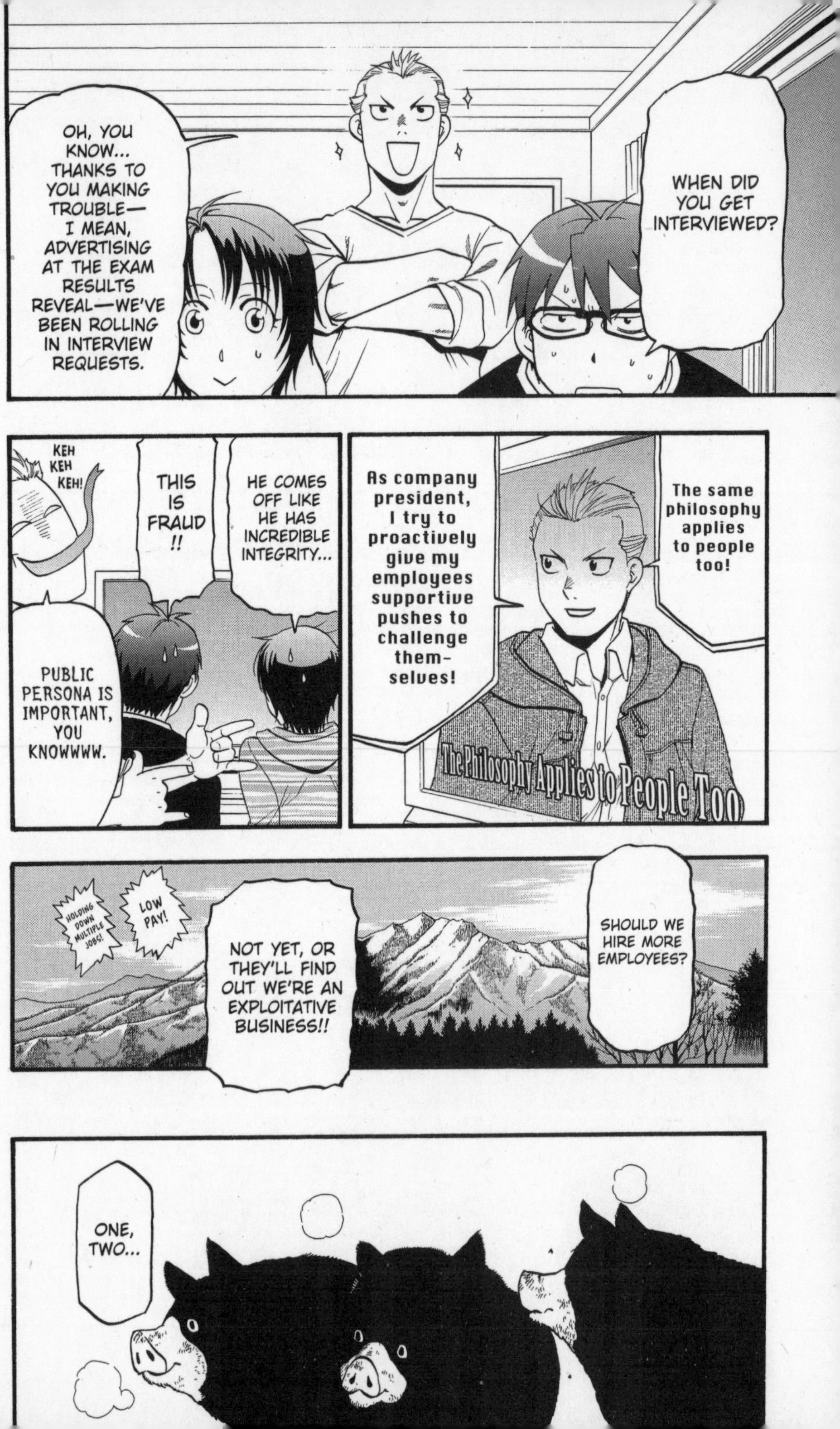
WHEN DID YOU GET INTERVIEWED?
OH, YOU KNOW... THANKS TO YOU MAKING TROUBLE— I MEAN, ADVERTISING AT THE EXAM RESULTS REVEAL—WE'VE BEEN ROLLING IN INTERVIEW REQUESTS.
As company president, I try to proactively give my employees supportive pushes to challenge them-selves!
The same philosophy applies to people too!
The Philosophy Applies to People Too
HE COMES OFF LIKE HE HAS INCREDIBLE INTEGRITY...
THIS IS FRAUD!!
KEH KEH KEH!
PUBLIC PERSONA IS IMPORTANT, YOU KNOWWWW.
SHOULD WE HIRE MORE EMPLOYEES?
NOT YET, OR THEY'LL FIND OUT WE'RE AN EXPLOITATIVE BUSINESS!!
LOW PAY!
HOLDING DOWN MULTIPLE JOBS!
ONE, TWO...

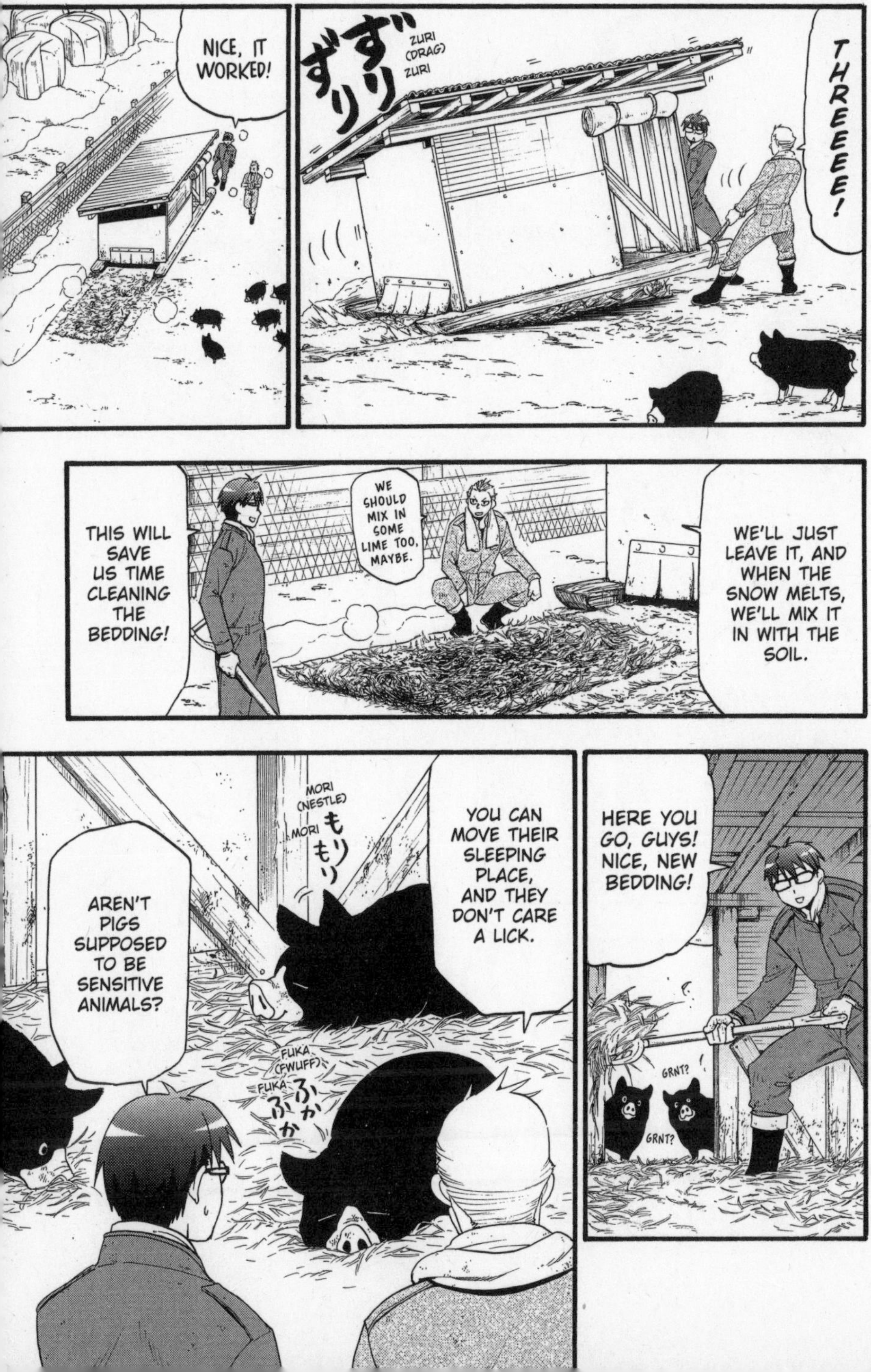
THREEEEE!
ずりずり
ZURI (DRAG) ZURI
NICE, IT WORKED!
WE'LL JUST LEAVE IT, AND WHEN THE SNOW MELTS, WE'LL MIX IT IN WITH THE SOIL.
WE SHOULD MIX IN SOME LIME TOO, MAYBE.
THIS WILL SAVE US TIME CLEANING THE BEDDING!
HERE YOU GO, GUYS! NICE, NEW BEDDING!
GRNT?
GRNT?
YOU CAN MOVE THEIR SLEEPING PLACE, AND THEY DON'T CARE A LICK.
もりもり
MORI (NESTLE) MORI
AREN'T PIGS SUPPOSED TO BE SENSITIVE ANIMALS?
ふかふか
FUKA (FWUFF) FUKA

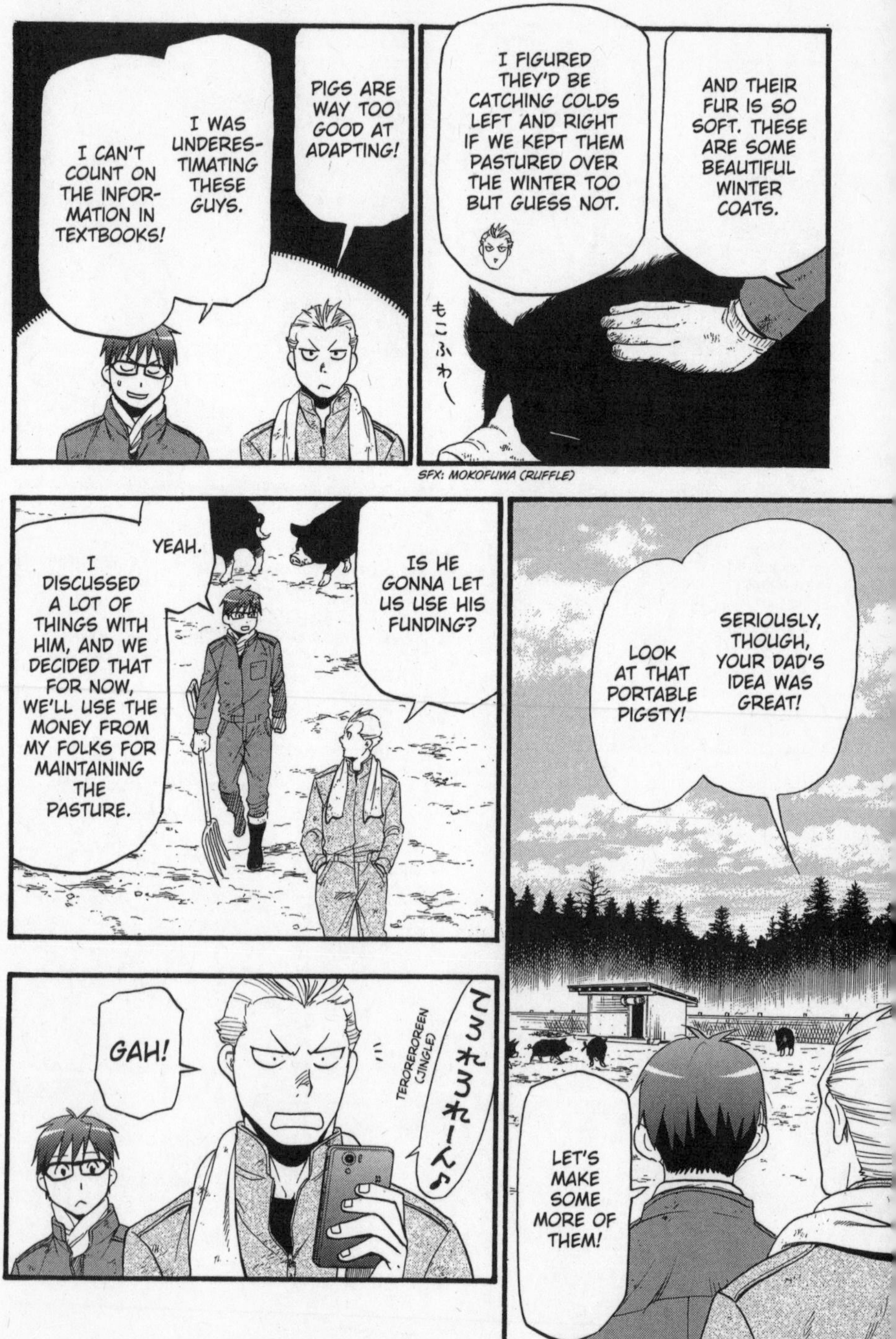
AND THEIR FUR IS SO SOFT. THESE ARE SOME BEAUTIFUL WINTER COATS.
I FIGURED THEY'D BE CATCHING COLDS LEFT AND RIGHT IF WE KEPT THEM PASTURED OVER THE WINTER TOO BUT GUESS NOT.
もこふわ〜
PIGS ARE WAY TOO GOOD AT ADAPTING!
I WAS UNDERES-TIMATING THESE GUYS.
I CAN'T COUNT ON THE INFOR-MATION IN TEXTBOOKS!
SFX: MOKOFUWA (RUFFLE)
SERIOUSLY, THOUGH, YOUR DAD'S IDEA WAS GREAT!
LOOK AT THAT PORTABLE PIGSTY!
LET'S MAKE SOME MORE OF THEM!
IS HE GONNA LET US USE HIS FUNDING?
YEAH.
I DISCUSSED A LOT OF THINGS WITH HIM, AND WE DECIDED THAT FOR NOW, WE'LL USE THE MONEY FROM MY FOLKS FOR MAINTAINING THE PASTURE.
てろれろれ〜ん♪
TERORERUREEN (JINGLE)
GAH!

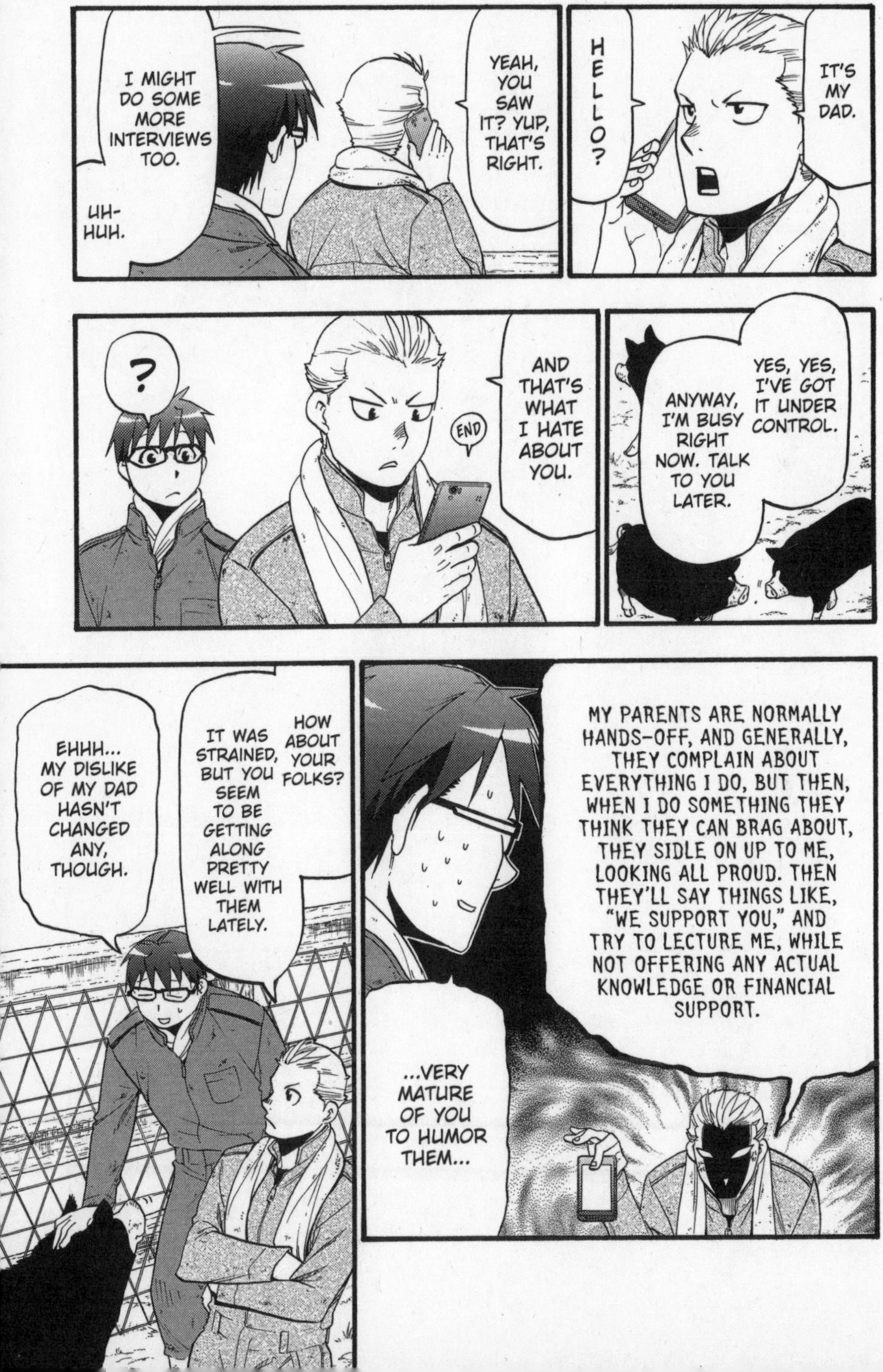

IT'S MY DAD.
HELLO?
YEAH, YOU SAW IT? YUP, THAT'S RIGHT.
I MIGHT DO SOME MORE INTERVIEWS TOO.
UH-HUH.
YES, YES, I'VE GOT IT UNDER CONTROL.
ANYWAY, I'M BUSY RIGHT NOW. TALK TO YOU LATER.
AND THAT'S WHAT I HATE ABOUT YOU.
END
?
MY PARENTS ARE NORMALLY HANDS-OFF, AND GENERALLY, THEY COMPLAIN ABOUT EVERYTHING I DO, BUT THEN, WHEN I DO SOMETHING THEY THINK THEY CAN BRAG ABOUT, THEY SIDLE ON UP TO ME, LOOKING ALL PROUD. THEN THEY'LL SAY THINGS LIKE, "WE SUPPORT YOU," AND TRY TO LECTURE ME, WHILE NOT OFFERING ANY ACTUAL KNOWLEDGE OR FINANCIAL SUPPORT.
...VERY MATURE OF YOU TO HUMOR THEM...
HOW ABOUT YOUR FOLKS?
IT WAS STRAINED, BUT YOU SEEM TO BE GETTING ALONG PRETTY WELL WITH THEM LATELY.
EHHH... MY DISLIKE OF MY DAD HASN'T CHANGED ANY, THOUGH.

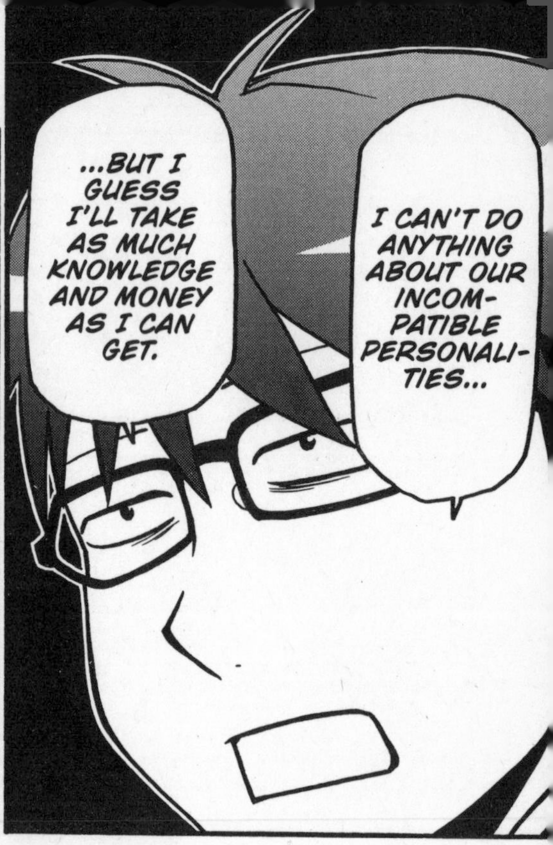
I CAN'T DO ANYTHING ABOUT OUR INCOMPATIBLE PERSONALITIES...
...BUT I GUESS I'LL TAKE AS MUCH KNOWLEDGE AND MONEY AS I CAN GET.

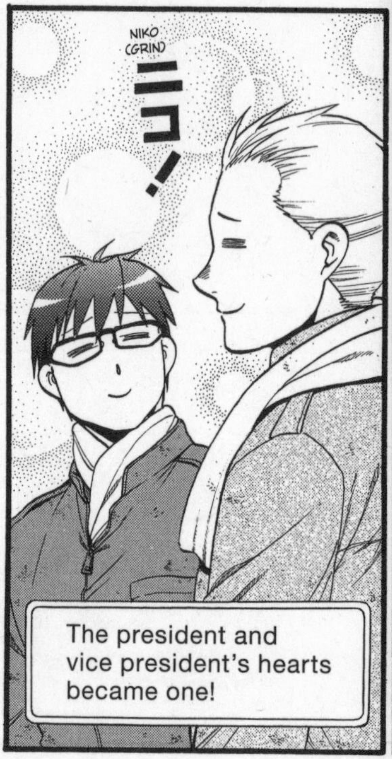
NIKO (GRIN)
ニコ!
The president and vice president's hearts became one!

## Chapter 129:
# Tale of Four Seasons ㉜

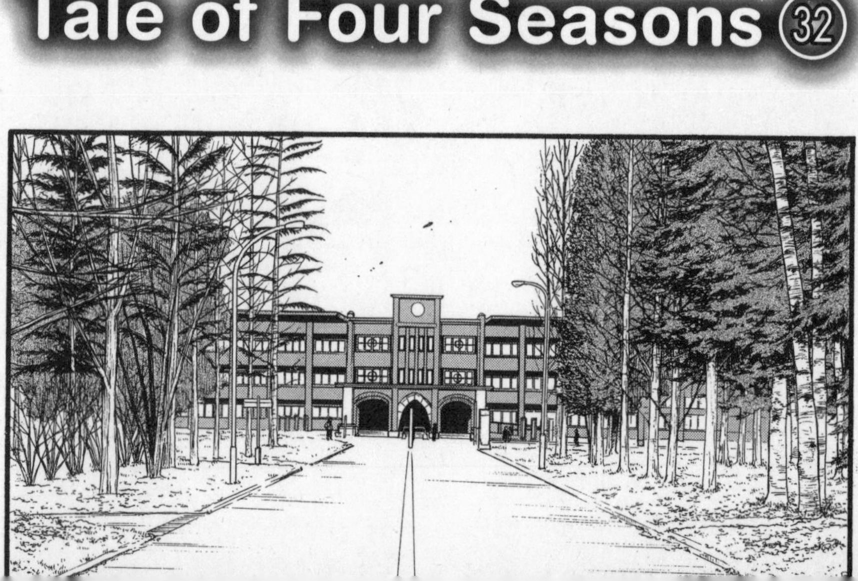

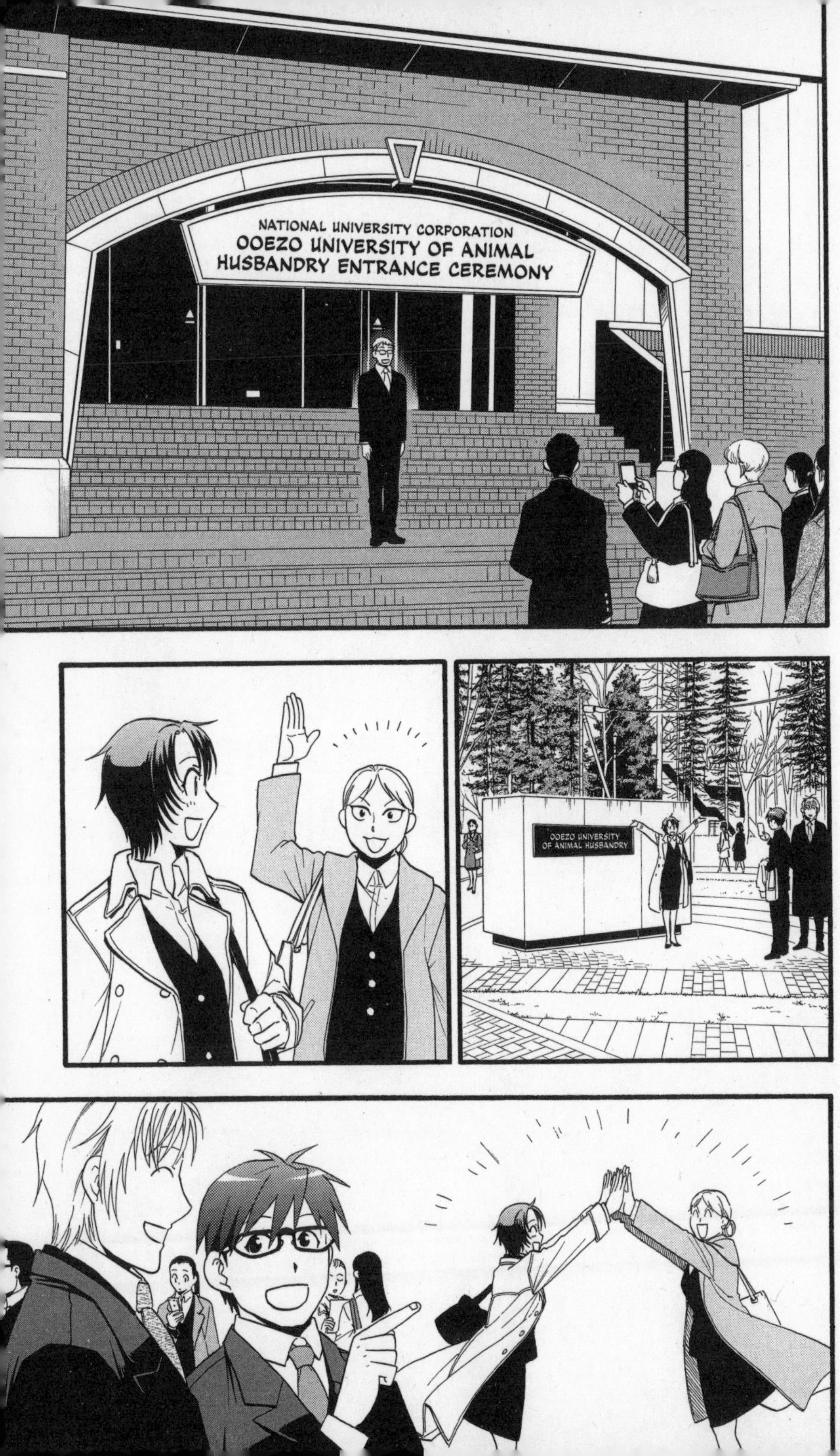
NATIONAL UNIVERSITY CORPORATION
OOEZO UNIVERSITY OF ANIMAL HUSBANDRY ENTRANCE CEREMONY
OOEZO UNIVERSITY OF ANIMAL HUSBANDRY

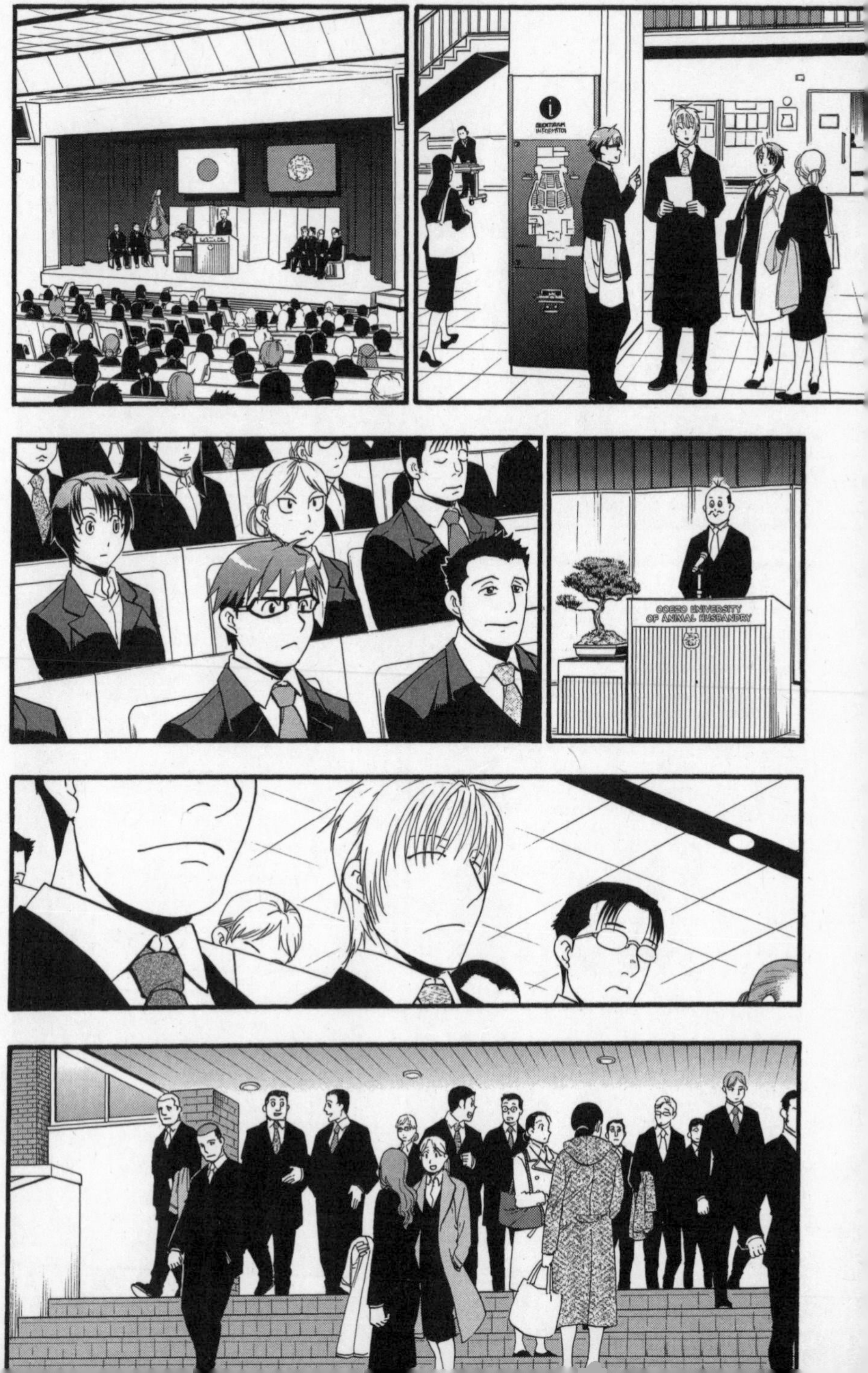
OOEZO UNIVERSITY
OF ANIMAL HUSBANDRY

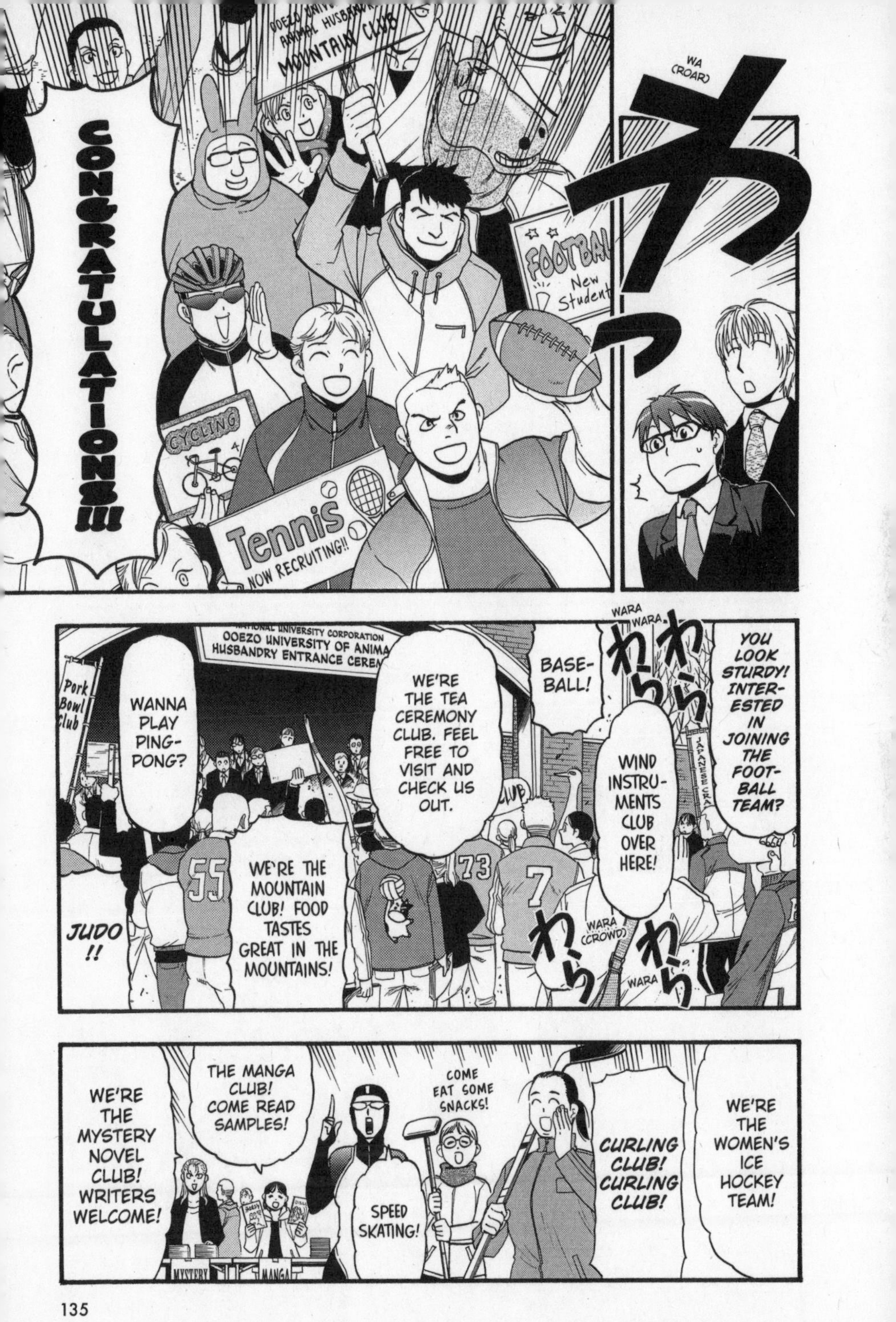
WA (ROAR)
わっ
CONGRATULATIONS!!!
MOUNTAIN CLUB
New Student
CYCLING
Tennis NOW RECRUITING!!
WARA WARA
わらわら
YOU LOOK STURDY! INTERESTED IN JOINING THE FOOTBALL TEAM?
WIND INSTRUMENTS CLUB OVER HERE!
BASEBALL!
WE'RE THE TEA CEREMONY CLUB. FEEL FREE TO VISIT AND CHECK US OUT.
NATIONAL UNIVERSITY CORPORATION OOEZO UNIVERSITY OF ANIMA HUSBANDRY ENTRANCE CEREM
WANNA PLAY PING-PONG?
Pork Bowl Club
WARA (CROWD) WARA
わらわら
WE'RE THE MOUNTAIN CLUB! FOOD TASTES GREAT IN THE MOUNTAINS!
JUDO !!
WE'RE THE WOMEN'S ICE HOCKEY TEAM!
CURLING CLUB! CURLING CLUB!
COME EAT SOME SNACKS!
SPEED SKATING!
THE MANGA CLUB! COME READ SAMPLES!
WE'RE THE MYSTERY NOVEL CLUB! WRITERS WELCOME!
MYSTERY
MANGA

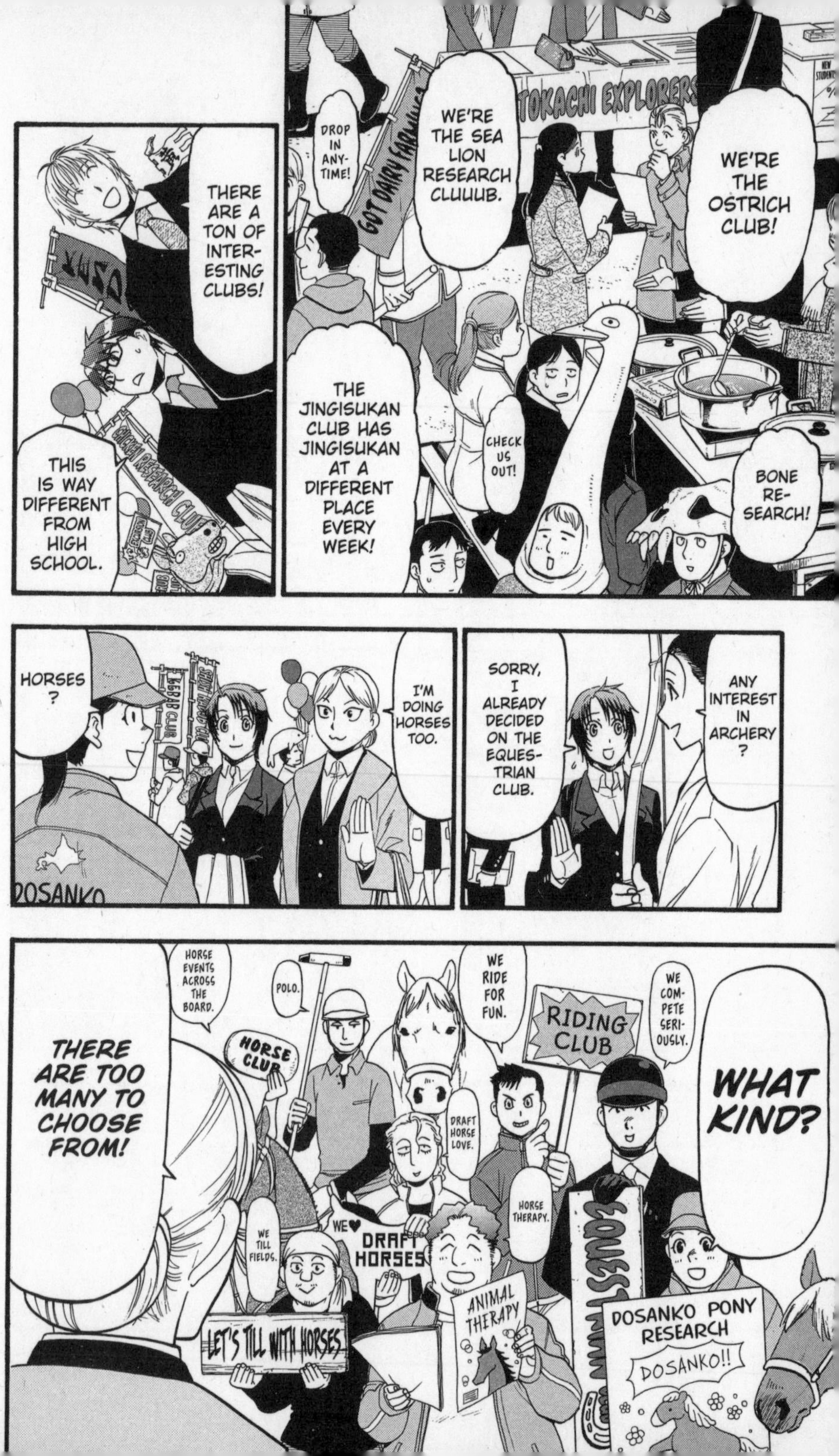
TOKACHI EXPLORERS
WE'RE THE OSTRICH CLUB!
WE'RE THE SEA LION RESEARCH CLUUUB.
DROP IN ANY-TIME!
BONE RE-SEARCH!
CHECK US OUT!
THE JINGISUKAN CLUB HAS JINGISUKAN AT A DIFFERENT PLACE EVERY WEEK!
THERE ARE A TON OF INTER-ESTING CLUBS!
THIS IS WAY DIFFERENT FROM HIGH SCHOOL.
ANY INTEREST IN ARCHERY?
SORRY, I ALREADY DECIDED ON THE EQUES-TRIAN CLUB.
I'M DOING HORSES TOO.
HORSES?
DOSANKO
WHAT KIND?
WE COM-PETE SERI-OUSLY.
RIDING CLUB
WE RIDE FOR FUN.
POLO.
HORSE EVENTS ACROSS THE BOARD.
HORSE CLUB
DRAFT HORSE LOVE.
HORSE THERAPY.
DOSANKO PONY RESEARCH
DOSANKO!!
ANIMAL THERAPY
WE♥ DRAFT HORSES
WE TILL FIELDS.
LET'S TILL WITH HORSES
THERE ARE TOO MANY TO CHOOSE FROM!

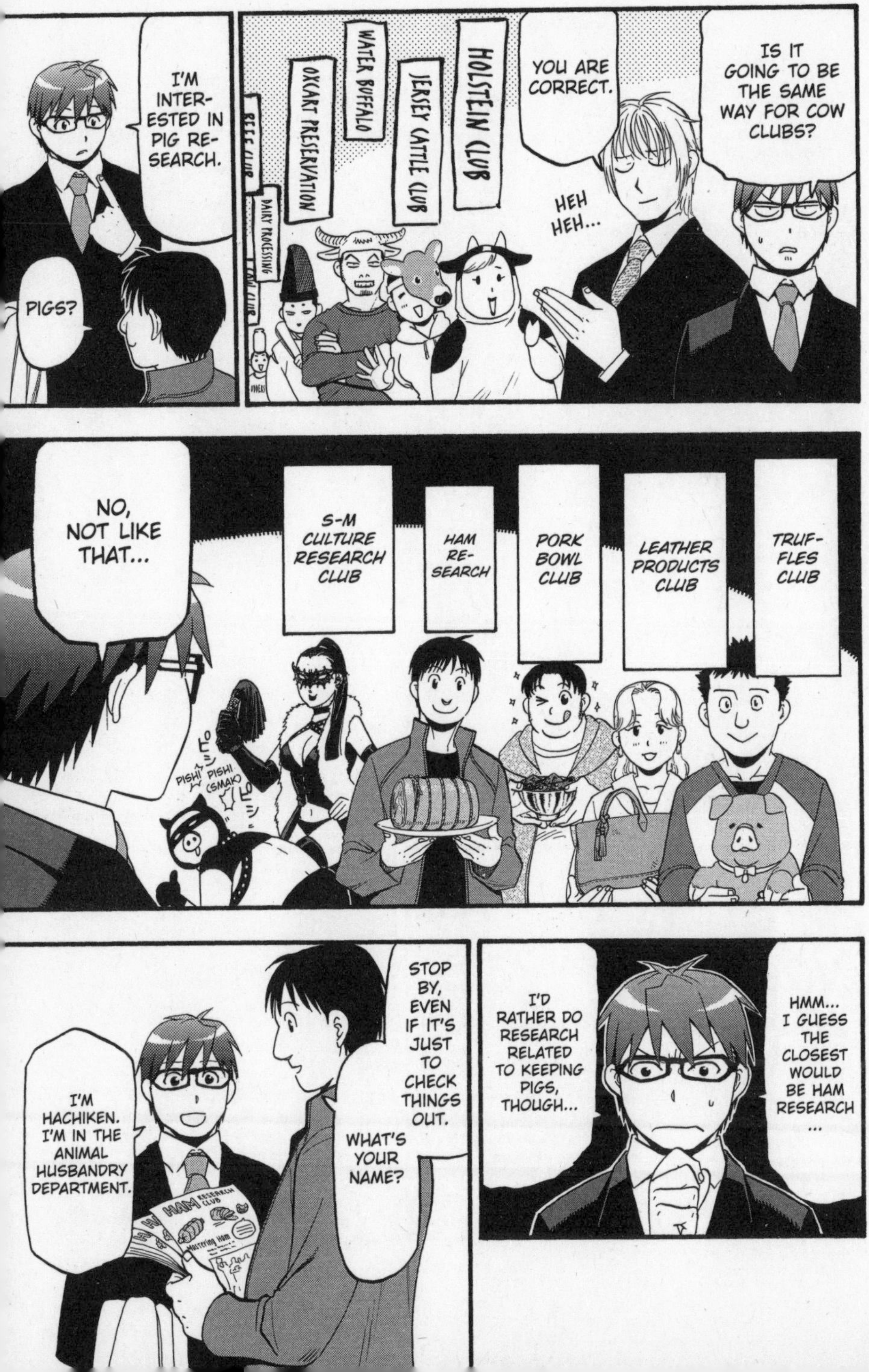
IS IT GOING TO BE THE SAME WAY FOR COW CLUBS?
YOU ARE CORRECT.
HEH HEH...
HOLSTEIN CLUB
JERSEY CATTLE CLUB
WATER BUFFALO
OXCART PRESERVATION
BEEF CLUB
DAIRY PROCESSING
I'M INTERESTED IN PIG RESEARCH.
PIGS?
TRUFFLES CLUB
LEATHER PRODUCTS CLUB
PORK BOWL CLUB
HAM RESEARCH
S-M CULTURE RESEARCH CLUB
NO, NOT LIKE THAT...
PISHI PISHI (SMAK)
HMM... I GUESS THE CLOSEST WOULD BE HAM RESEARCH...
I'D RATHER DO RESEARCH RELATED TO KEEPING PIGS, THOUGH...
STOP BY, EVEN IF IT'S JUST TO CHECK THINGS OUT.
WHAT'S YOUR NAME?
I'M HACHIKEN. I'M IN THE ANIMAL HUSBANDRY DEPARTMENT.
HAM RESEARCH CLUB
Mastering Ham

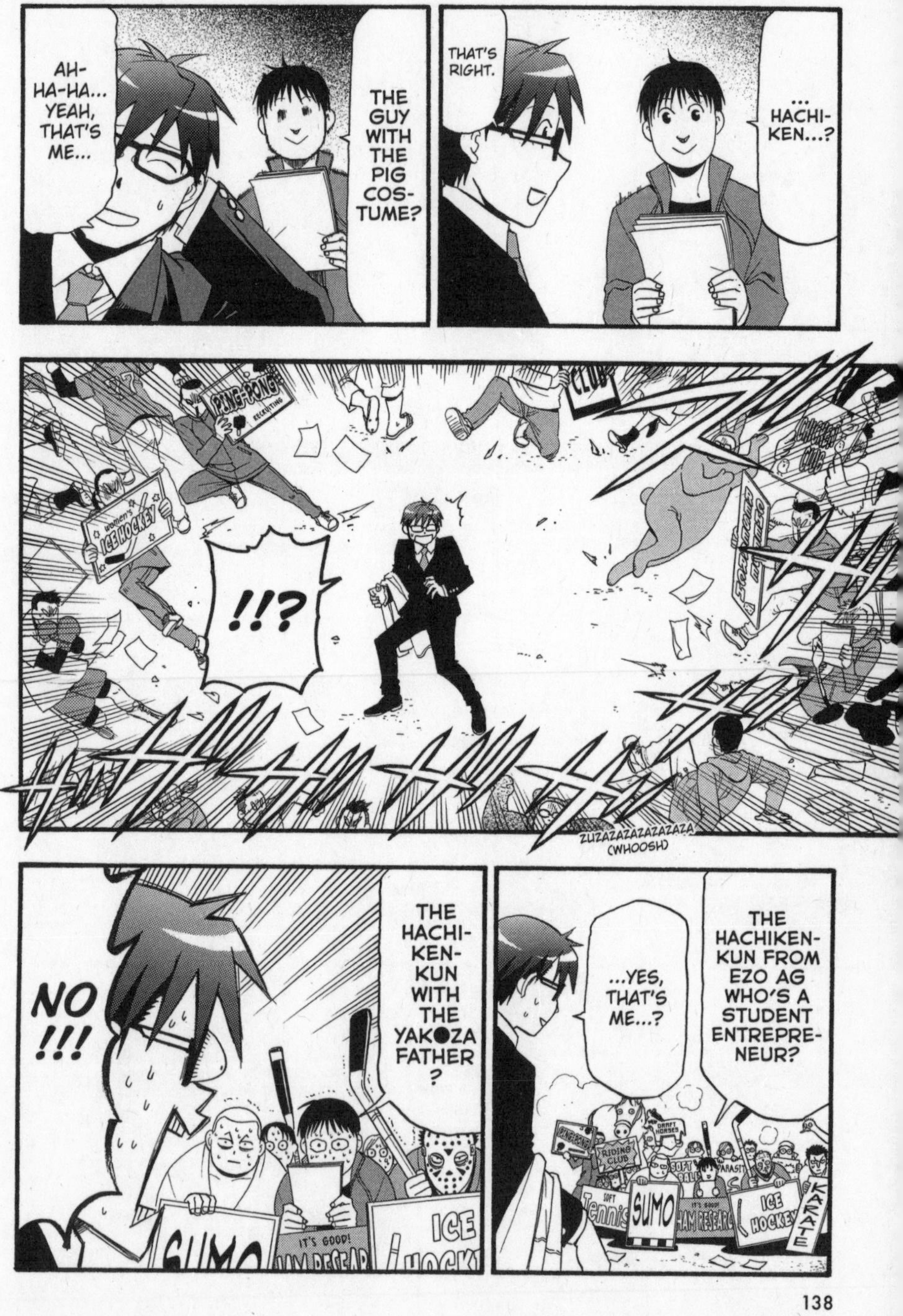
... HACHI-KEN...?
THAT'S RIGHT.
THE GUY WITH THE PIG COS-TUME?
AH-HA-HA... YEAH, THAT'S ME...
CLUB
PING-PONG
RECRUITING
Women's ICE HOCKEY
!!?
ZUZAZAZAZAZAZAZA (WHOOSH)
THE HACHIKEN-KUN FROM EZO AG WHO'S A STUDENT ENTREPRE-NEUR?
...YES, THAT'S ME...?
DRAFT HORSES
RIDING CLUB
SOFT BALL
SOFT Tennis
SUMO
IT'S GOOD!
ICE HOCKEY
KARATE
THE HACHI-KEN-KUN WITH THE YAK●ZA FATHER?
NO!!!
SUMO
IT'S GOOD!
ICE

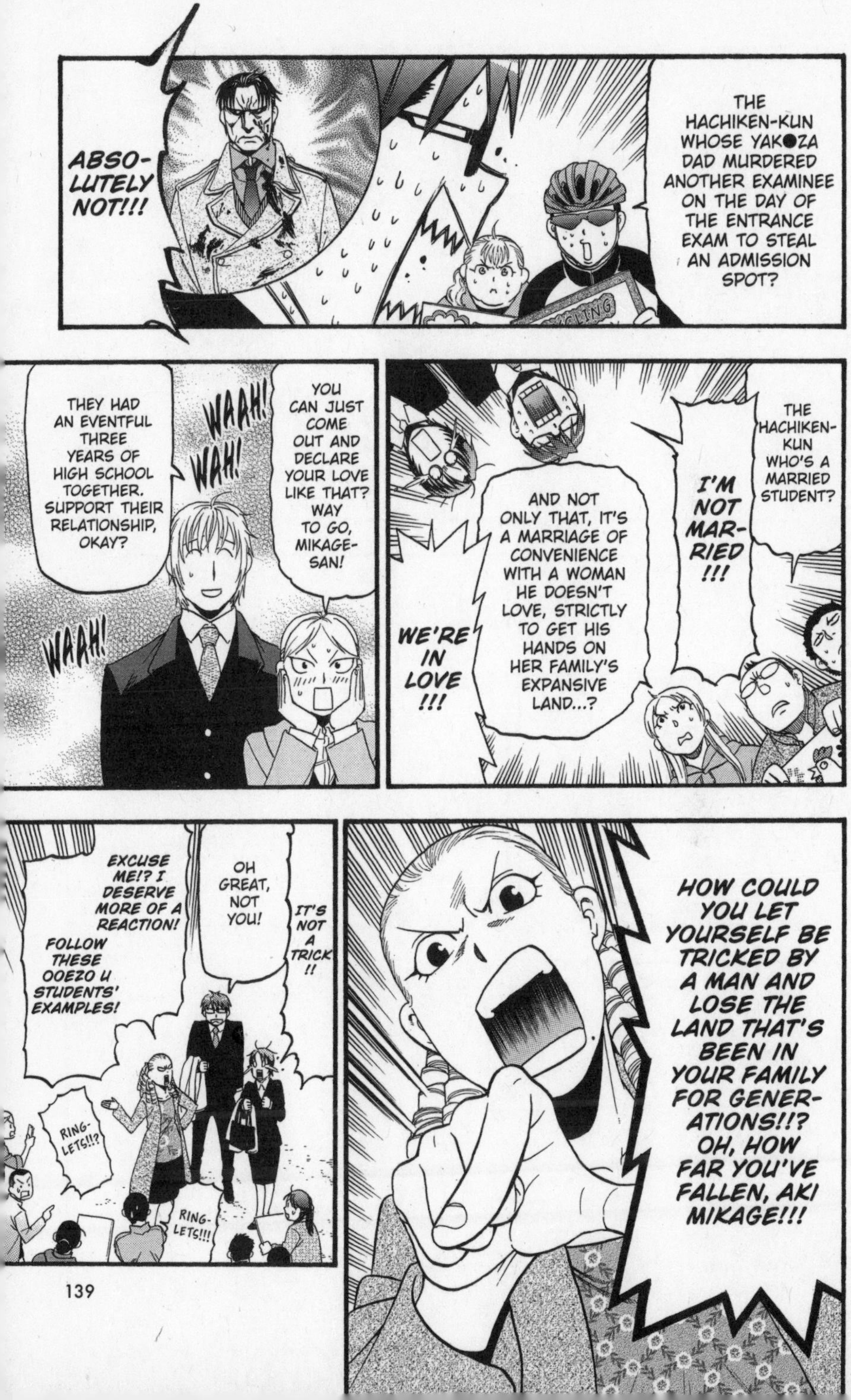
THE HACHIKEN-KUN WHOSE YAK●ZA DAD MURDERED ANOTHER EXAMINEE ON THE DAY OF THE ENTRANCE EXAM TO STEAL AN ADMISSION SPOT?
ABSOLUTELY NOT!!!
THE HACHIKEN-KUN WHO'S A MARRIED STUDENT?
I'M NOT MARRIED!!!
AND NOT ONLY THAT, IT'S A MARRIAGE OF CONVENIENCE WITH A WOMAN HE DOESN'T LOVE, STRICTLY TO GET HIS HANDS ON HER FAMILY'S EXPANSIVE LAND...?
WE'RE IN LOVE!!!
YOU CAN JUST COME OUT AND DECLARE YOUR LOVE LIKE THAT? WAY TO GO, MIKAGE-SAN!
WAAH! WAH!
THEY HAD AN EVENTFUL THREE YEARS OF HIGH SCHOOL TOGETHER. SUPPORT THEIR RELATIONSHIP, OKAY?
WAAH!
HOW COULD YOU LET YOURSELF BE TRICKED BY A MAN AND LOSE THE LAND THAT'S BEEN IN YOUR FAMILY FOR GENERATIONS!!? OH, HOW FAR YOU'VE FALLEN, AKI MIKAGE!!!
OH GREAT, NOT YOU!
IT'S NOT A TRICK!!
EXCUSE ME!? I DESERVE MORE OF A REACTION! FOLLOW THESE OOEZO U STUDENTS' EXAMPLES!
RINGLETS!!?
RINGLETS!!!

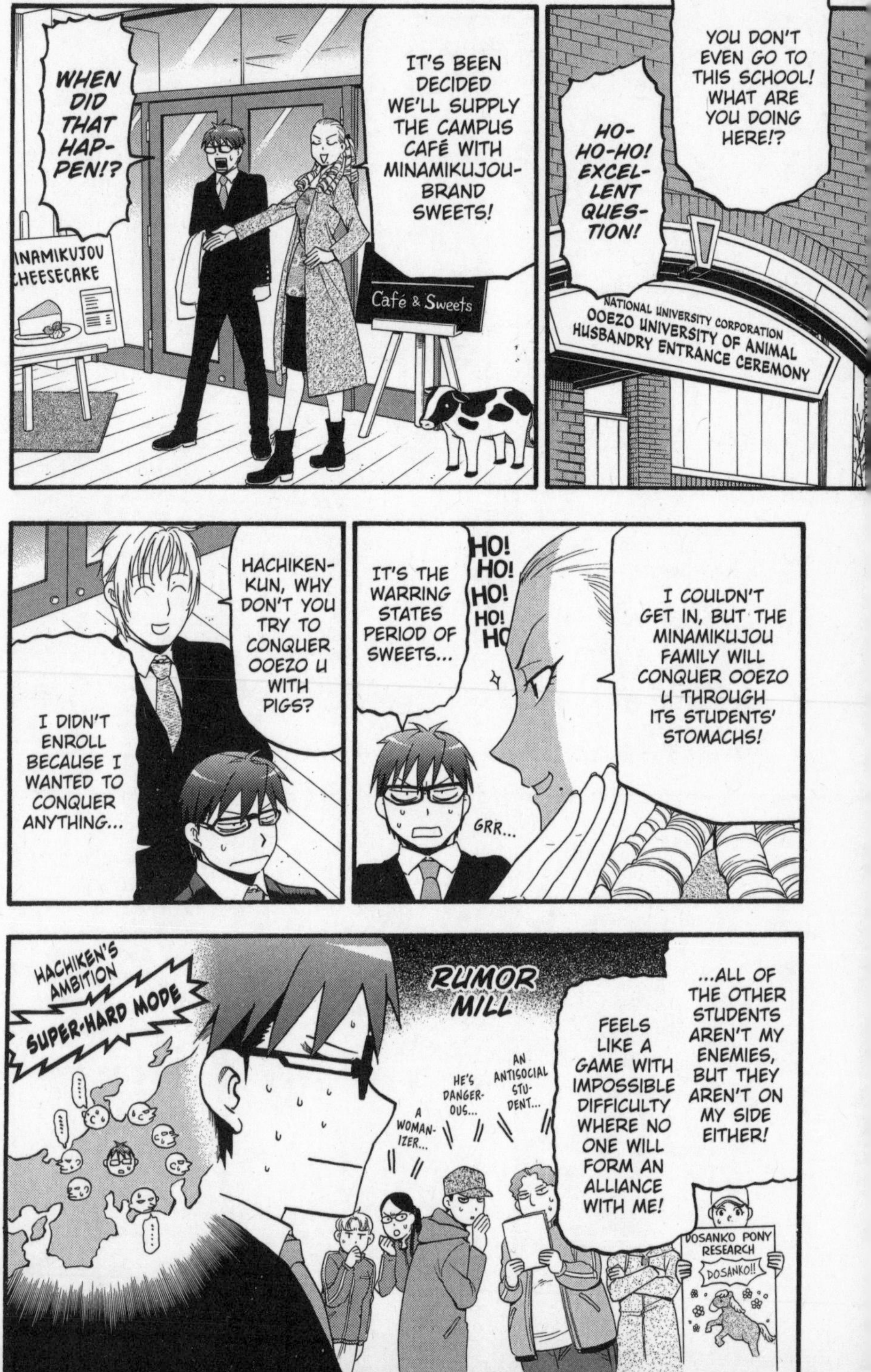
YOU DON'T EVEN GO TO THIS SCHOOL! WHAT ARE YOU DOING HERE!?
HO-HO-HO! EXCEL-LENT QUES-TION!
NATIONAL UNIVERSITY CORPORATION OOEZO UNIVERSITY OF ANIMAL HUSBANDRY ENTRANCE CEREMONY
IT'S BEEN DECIDED WE'LL SUPPLY THE CAMPUS CAFÉ WITH MINAMIKUJOU-BRAND SWEETS!
WHEN DID THAT HAP-PEN!?
Café & Sweets
INAMIKUJOU HEESECAKE
I COULDN'T GET IN, BUT THE MINAMIKUJOU FAMILY WILL CONQUER OOEZO U THROUGH ITS STUDENTS' STOMACHS!
HO! HO! HO! HO! HO
IT'S THE WARRING STATES PERIOD OF SWEETS...
GRR...
HACHIKEN-KUN, WHY DON'T YOU TRY TO CONQUER OOEZO U WITH PIGS?
I DIDN'T ENROLL BECAUSE I WANTED TO CONQUER ANYTHING...
...ALL OF THE OTHER STUDENTS AREN'T MY ENEMIES, BUT THEY AREN'T ON MY SIDE EITHER!
FEELS LIKE A GAME WITH IMPOSSIBLE DIFFICULTY WHERE NO ONE WILL FORM AN ALLIANCE WITH ME!
RUMOR MILL
AN ANTISOCIAL STU-DENT...
HE'S DANGER-OUS...
A WOMAN-IZER...
HACHIKEN'S AMBITION
SUPER-HARD MODE
DOSANKO PONY RESEARCH
DOSANKO!!

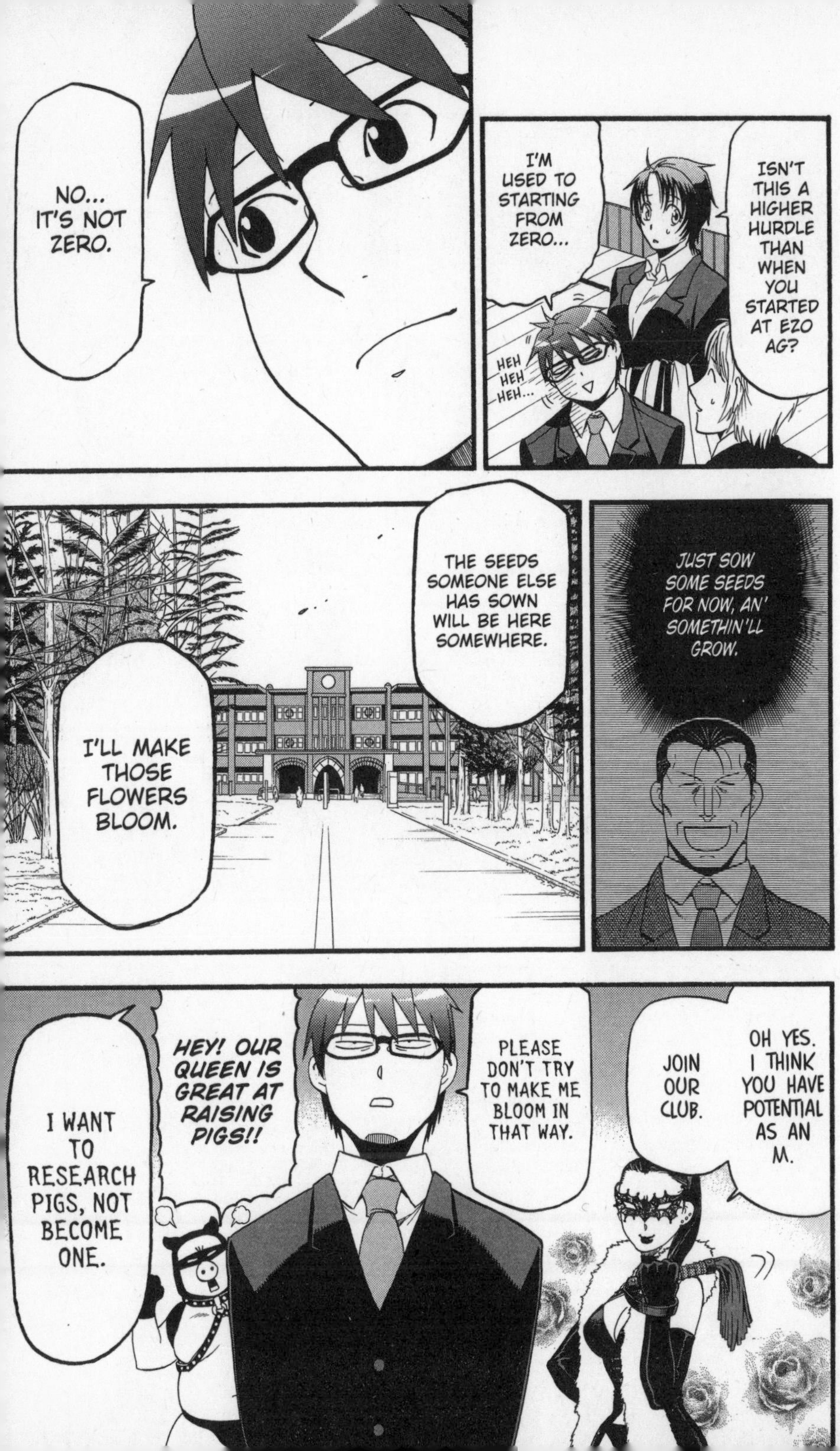
ISN'T THIS A HIGHER HURDLE THAN WHEN YOU STARTED AT EZO AG?
I'M USED TO STARTING FROM ZERO...
HEH HEH HEH...
NO... IT'S NOT ZERO.
JUST SOW SOME SEEDS FOR NOW, AN' SOMETHIN'LL GROW.
THE SEEDS SOMEONE ELSE HAS SOWN WILL BE HERE SOMEWHERE.
I'LL MAKE THOSE FLOWERS BLOOM.
OH YES. I THINK YOU HAVE POTENTIAL AS AN M.
JOIN OUR CLUB.
PLEASE DON'T TRY TO MAKE ME BLOOM IN THAT WAY.
HEY! OUR QUEEN IS GREAT AT RAISING PIGS!!
I WANT TO RESEARCH PIGS, NOT BECOME ONE.

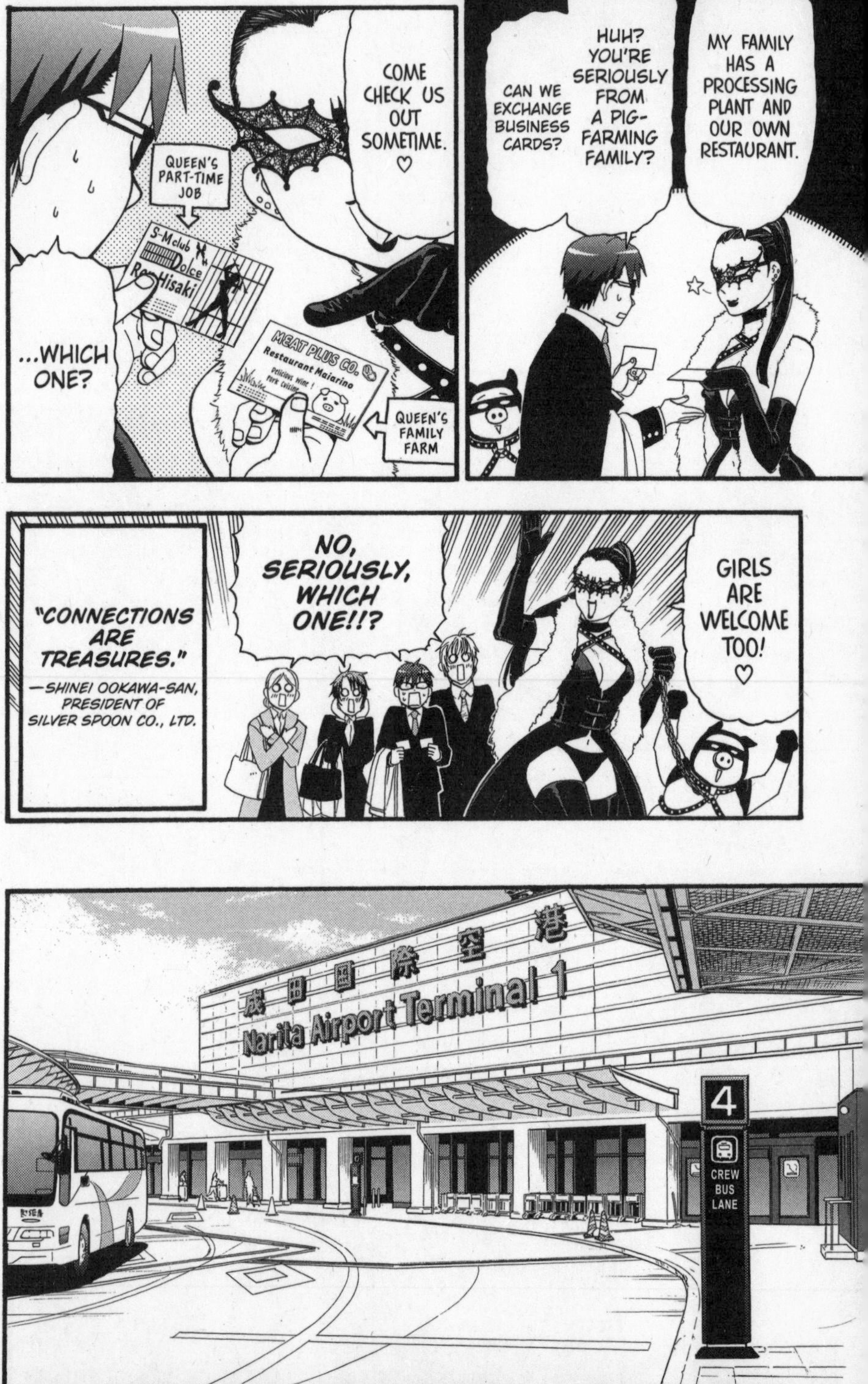
MY FAMILY HAS A PROCESSING PLANT AND OUR OWN RESTAURANT.
HUH? YOU'RE SERIOUSLY FROM A PIG-FARMING FAMILY?
CAN WE EXCHANGE BUSINESS CARDS?
COME CHECK US OUT SOMETIME. ♡
QUEEN'S PART-TIME JOB
S-Mclub
Dolce
Hisaki
...WHICH ONE?
MEAT PLUS CO.
Restaurant Maiarino
QUEEN'S FAMILY FARM
GIRLS ARE WELCOME TOO! ♡
NO, SERIOUSLY, WHICH ONE!!?
"CONNECTIONS ARE TREASURES."
—SHINEI OOKAWA-SAN, PRESIDENT OF SILVER SPOON CO., LTD.
成田国際空港
Narita Airport Terminal 1
4
CREW BUS LANE

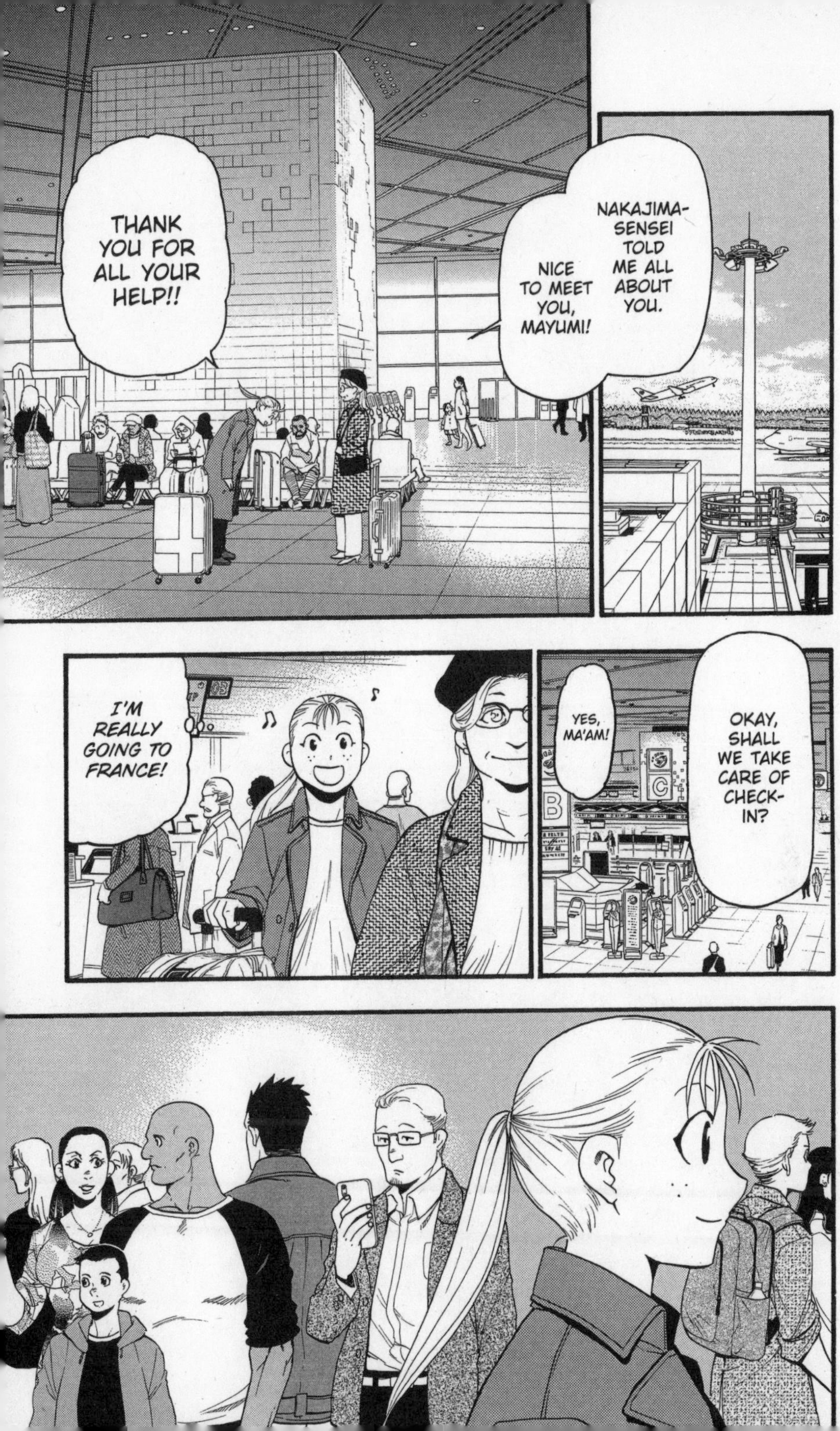
NAKAJIMA-SENSEI TOLD ME ALL ABOUT YOU.
NICE TO MEET YOU, MAYUMI!
THANK YOU FOR ALL YOUR HELP!!
OKAY, SHALL WE TAKE CARE OF CHECK-IN?
YES, MA'AM!
I'M REALLY GOING TO FRANCE!

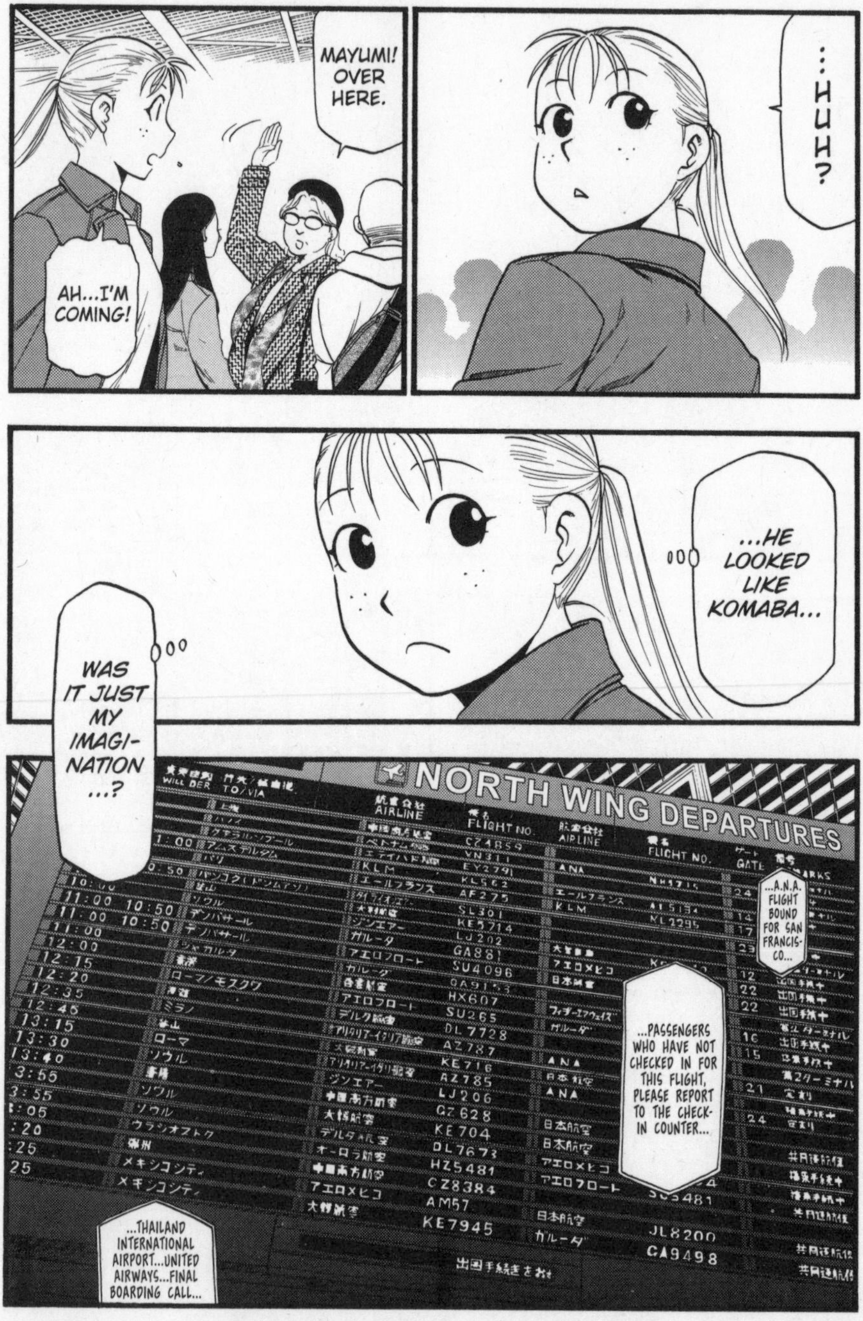
...HUH?
MAYUMI! OVER HERE.
AH...I'M COMING!
...HE LOOKED LIKE KOMABA...
WAS IT JUST MY IMAGINATION...?
NORTH WING DEPARTURES
...A.N.A. FLIGHT BOUND FOR SAN FRANCISCO...
...PASSENGERS WHO HAVE NOT CHECKED IN FOR THIS FLIGHT, PLEASE REPORT TO THE CHECK-IN COUNTER...
...THAILAND INTERNATIONAL AIRPORT...UNITED AIRWAYS...FINAL BOARDING CALL...

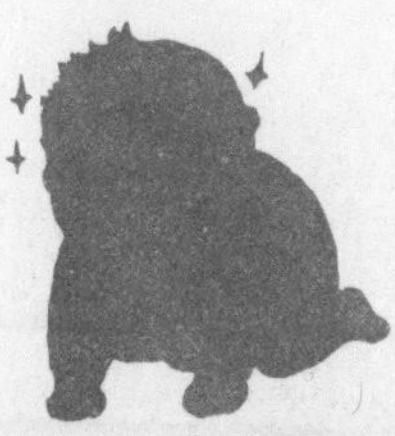

Silver Spoon

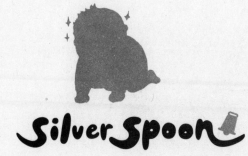

TOKIWA'S
NEW SMARTPHONE
WALLPAPER FOR
WARDING OFF EVIL:
SMILING
HACHIKEN'S DAD

SUPER-RARE!

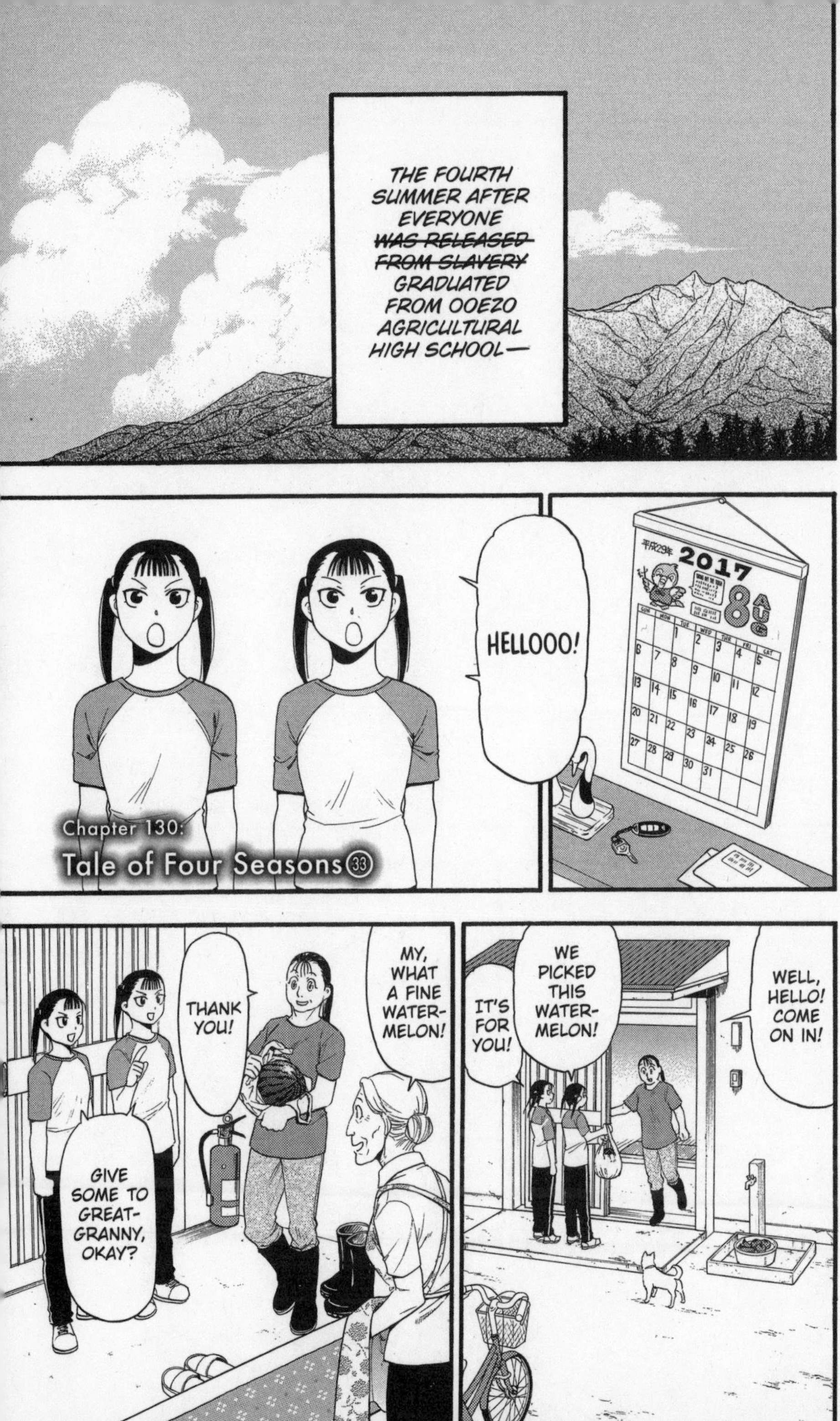
THE FOURTH SUMMER AFTER EVERYONE ~~WAS RELEASED FROM SLAVERY~~ GRADUATED FROM OOEZO AGRICULTURAL HIGH SCHOOL—
HELLOOO!
2017
Chapter 130:
Tale of Four Seasons㉝
WELL, HELLO! COME ON IN!
WE PICKED THIS WATER-MELON!
IT'S FOR YOU!
MY, WHAT A FINE WATER-MELON!
THANK YOU!
GIVE SOME TO GREAT-GRANNY, OKAY?

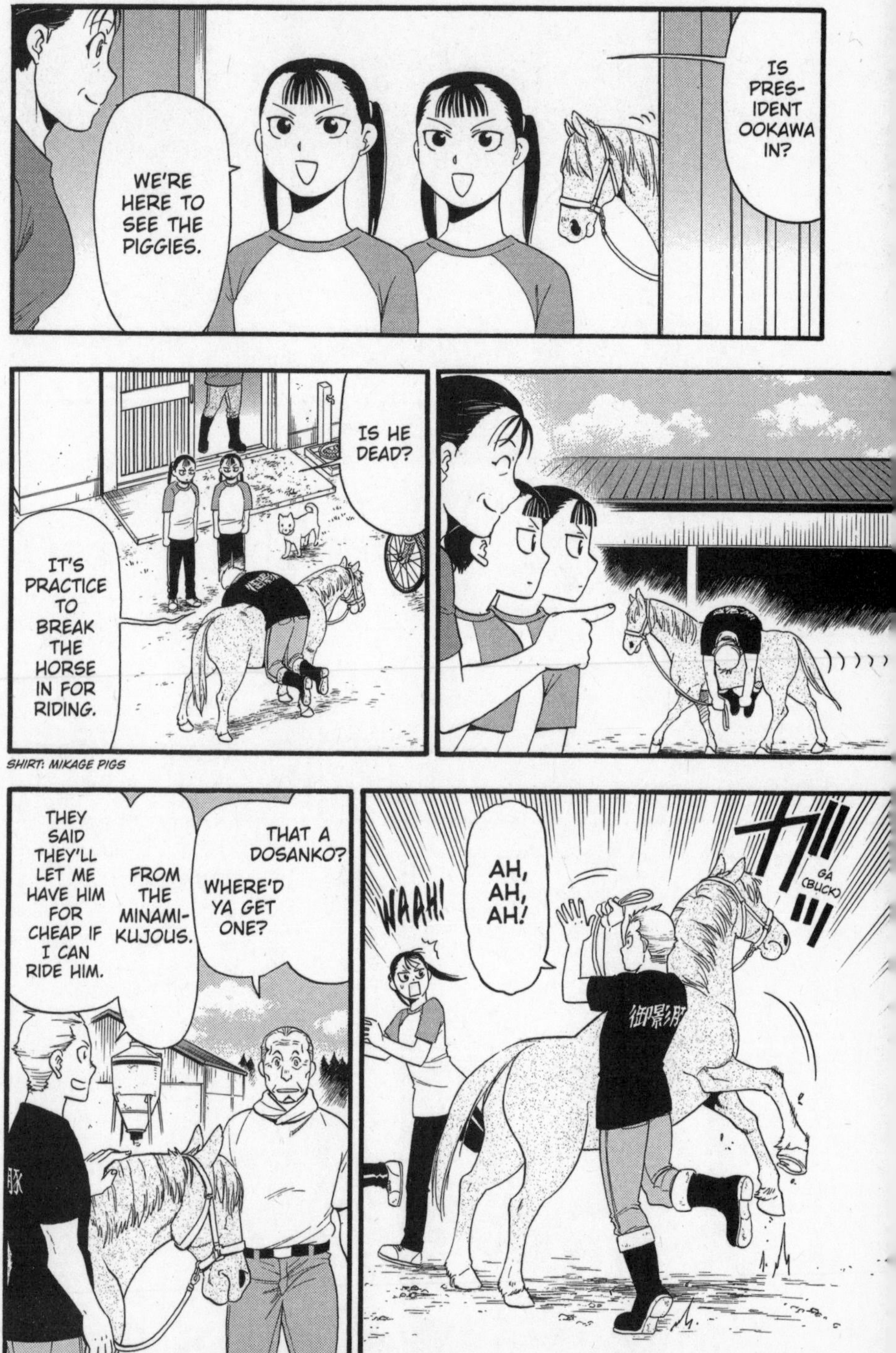
IS PRESIDENT OOKAWA IN?
WE'RE HERE TO SEE THE PIGGIES.
IS HE DEAD?
IT'S PRACTICE TO BREAK THE HORSE IN FOR RIDING.
SHIRT: MIKAGE PIGS
GA (BUCK)
AH, AH, AH!
WAAH!
THAT A DOSANKO? WHERE'D YA GET ONE?
FROM THE MINAMIKUJOUS.
THEY SAID THEY'LL LET ME HAVE HIM FOR CHEAP IF I CAN RIDE HIM.

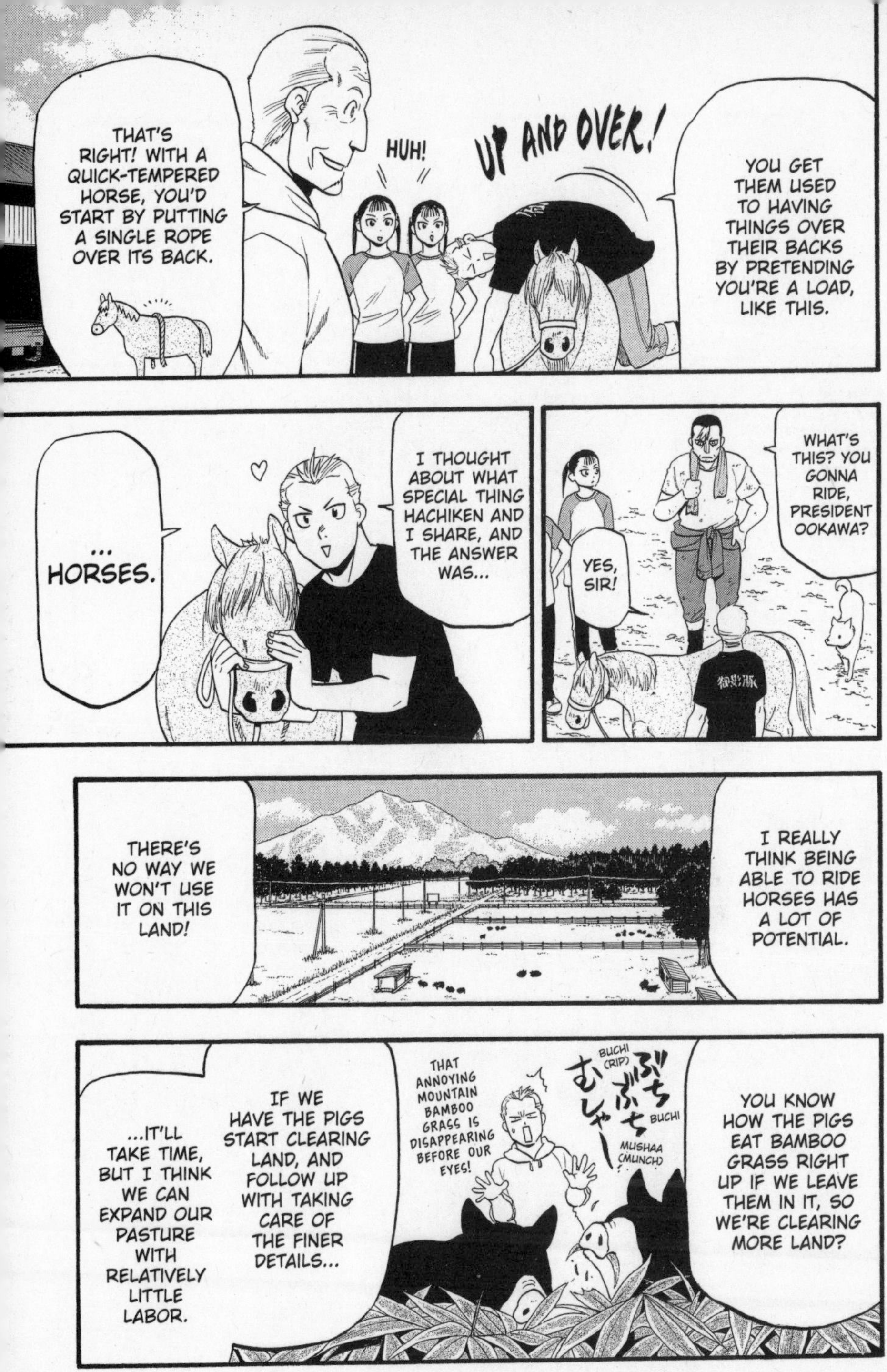
YOU GET THEM USED TO HAVING THINGS OVER THEIR BACKS BY PRETENDING YOU'RE A LOAD, LIKE THIS.
UP AND OVER!
HUH!
THAT'S RIGHT! WITH A QUICK-TEMPERED HORSE, YOU'D START BY PUTTING A SINGLE ROPE OVER ITS BACK.
WHAT'S THIS? YOU GONNA RIDE, PRESIDENT OOKAWA?
YES, SIR!
I THOUGHT ABOUT WHAT SPECIAL THING HACHIKEN AND I SHARE, AND THE ANSWER WAS...
... HORSES.
I REALLY THINK BEING ABLE TO RIDE HORSES HAS A LOT OF POTENTIAL.
THERE'S NO WAY WE WON'T USE IT ON THIS LAND!
YOU KNOW HOW THE PIGS EAT BAMBOO GRASS RIGHT UP IF WE LEAVE THEM IN IT, SO WE'RE CLEARING MORE LAND?
ぶち
BUCHI (RIP)
ぶち
BUCHI
むしゃー
MUSHAA (MUNCH)
THAT ANNOYING MOUNTAIN BAMBOO GRASS IS DISAPPEARING BEFORE OUR EYES!
IF WE HAVE THE PIGS START CLEARING LAND, AND FOLLOW UP WITH TAKING CARE OF THE FINER DETAILS...
...IT'LL TAKE TIME, BUT I THINK WE CAN EXPAND OUR PASTURE WITH RELATIVELY LITTLE LABOR.

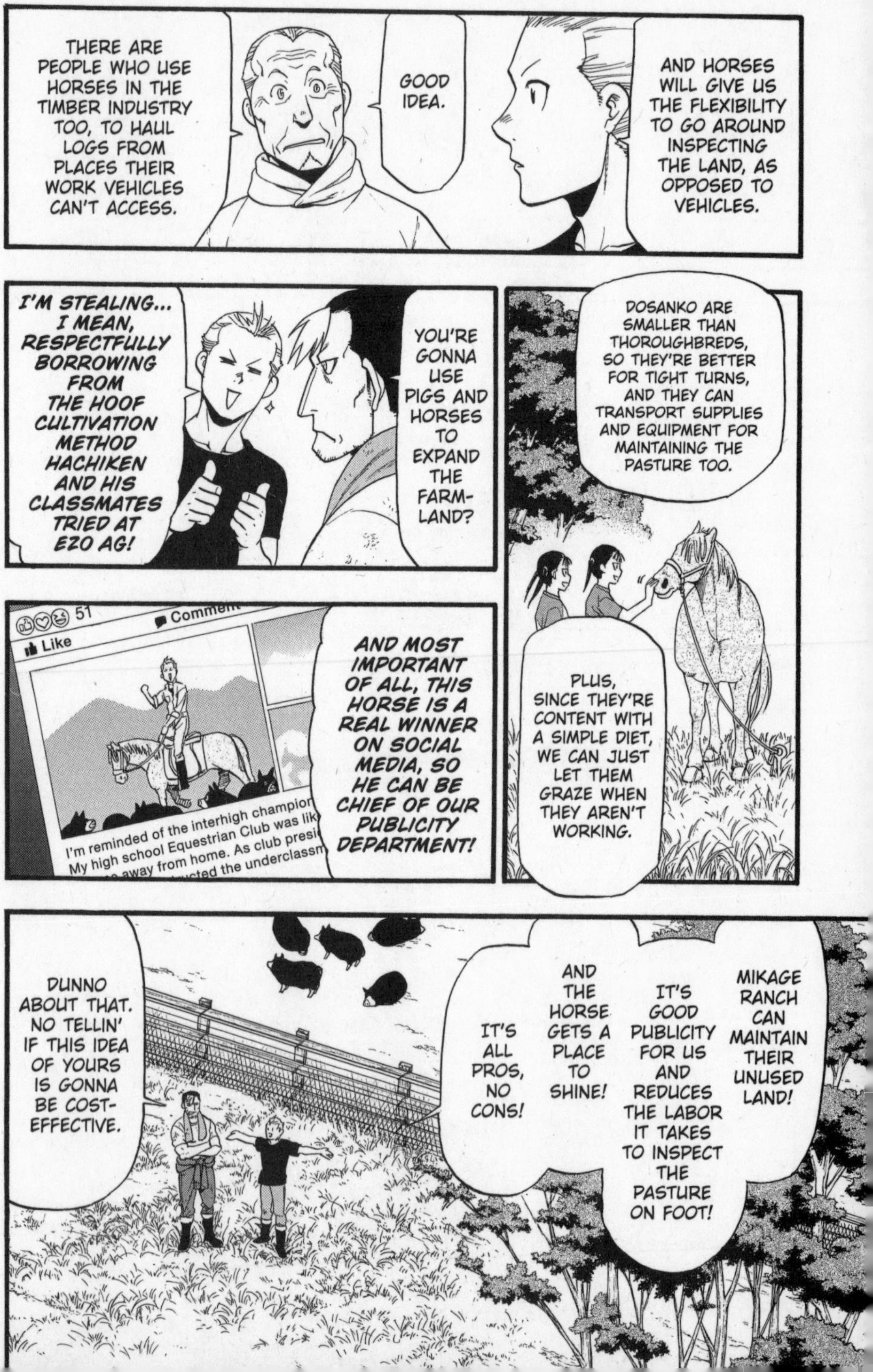
AND HORSES WILL GIVE US THE FLEXIBILITY TO GO AROUND INSPECTING THE LAND, AS OPPOSED TO VEHICLES.
GOOD IDEA.
THERE ARE PEOPLE WHO USE HORSES IN THE TIMBER INDUSTRY TOO, TO HAUL LOGS FROM PLACES THEIR WORK VEHICLES CAN'T ACCESS.
DOSANKO ARE SMALLER THAN THOROUGHBREDS, SO THEY'RE BETTER FOR TIGHT TURNS, AND THEY CAN TRANSPORT SUPPLIES AND EQUIPMENT FOR MAINTAINING THE PASTURE TOO.
PLUS, SINCE THEY'RE CONTENT WITH A SIMPLE DIET, WE CAN JUST LET THEM GRAZE WHEN THEY AREN'T WORKING.
YOU'RE GONNA USE PIGS AND HORSES TO EXPAND THE FARM-LAND?
I'M STEALING... I MEAN, RESPECTFULLY BORROWING FROM THE HOOF CULTIVATION METHOD HACHIKEN AND HIS CLASSMATES TRIED AT EZO AG!
AND MOST IMPORTANT OF ALL, THIS HORSE IS A REAL WINNER ON SOCIAL MEDIA, SO HE CAN BE CHIEF OF OUR PUBLICITY DEPARTMENT!
51
Comment
Like
I'm reminded of the interhigh champio
My high school Equestrian Club was lik
MIKAGE RANCH CAN MAINTAIN THEIR UNUSED LAND!
IT'S GOOD PUBLICITY FOR US AND REDUCES THE LABOR IT TAKES TO INSPECT THE PASTURE ON FOOT!
AND THE HORSE GETS A PLACE TO SHINE!
IT'S ALL PROS, NO CONS!
DUNNO ABOUT THAT. NO TELLIN' IF THIS IDEA OF YOURS IS GONNA BE COST-EFFECTIVE.

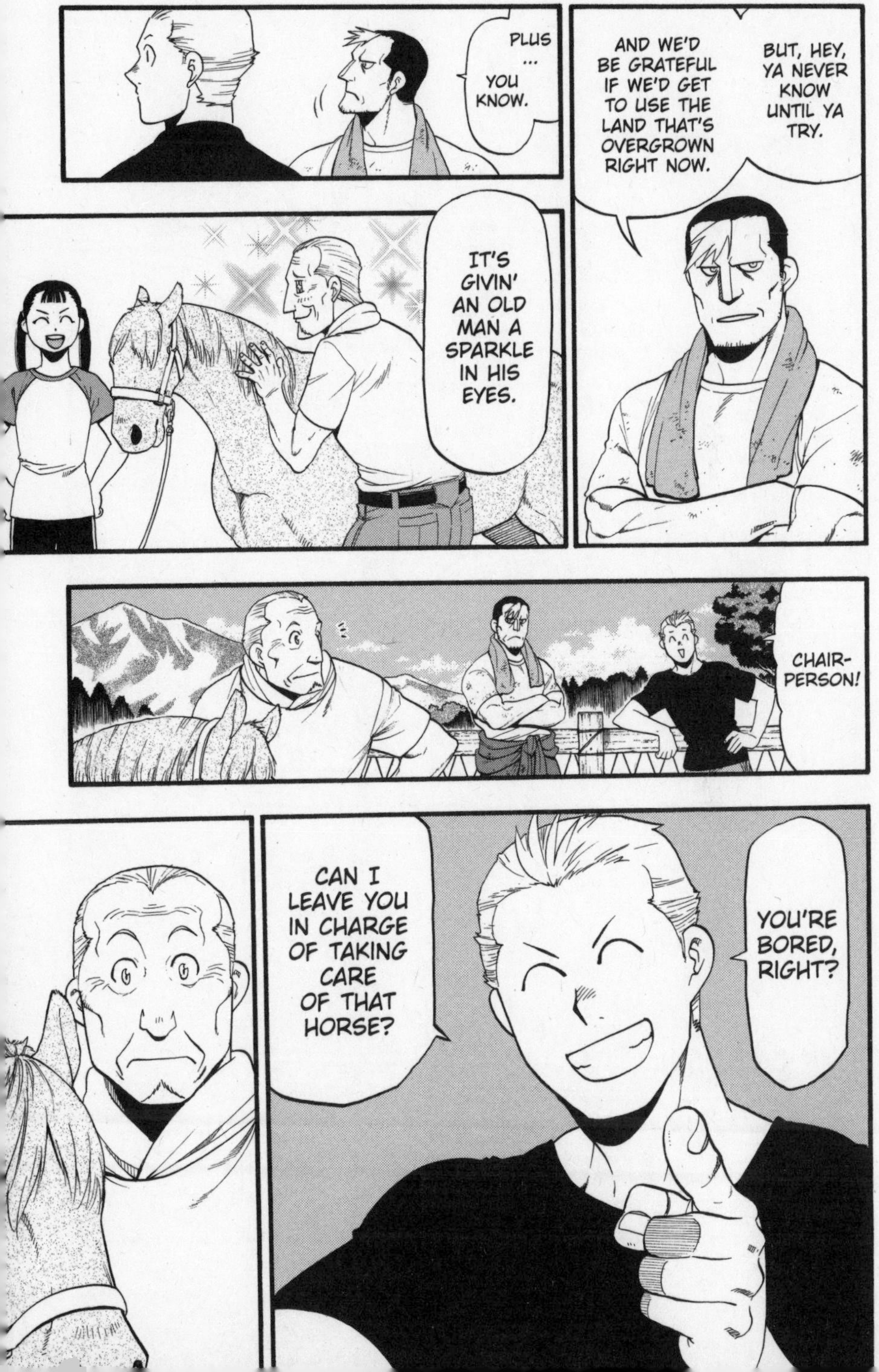
BUT, HEY, YA NEVER KNOW UNTIL YA TRY.
AND WE'D BE GRATEFUL IF WE'D GET TO USE THE LAND THAT'S OVERGROWN RIGHT NOW.
PLUS ... YOU KNOW.
IT'S GIVIN' AN OLD MAN A SPARKLE IN HIS EYES.
CHAIR-PERSON!
YOU'RE BORED, RIGHT?
CAN I LEAVE YOU IN CHARGE OF TAKING CARE OF THAT HORSE?

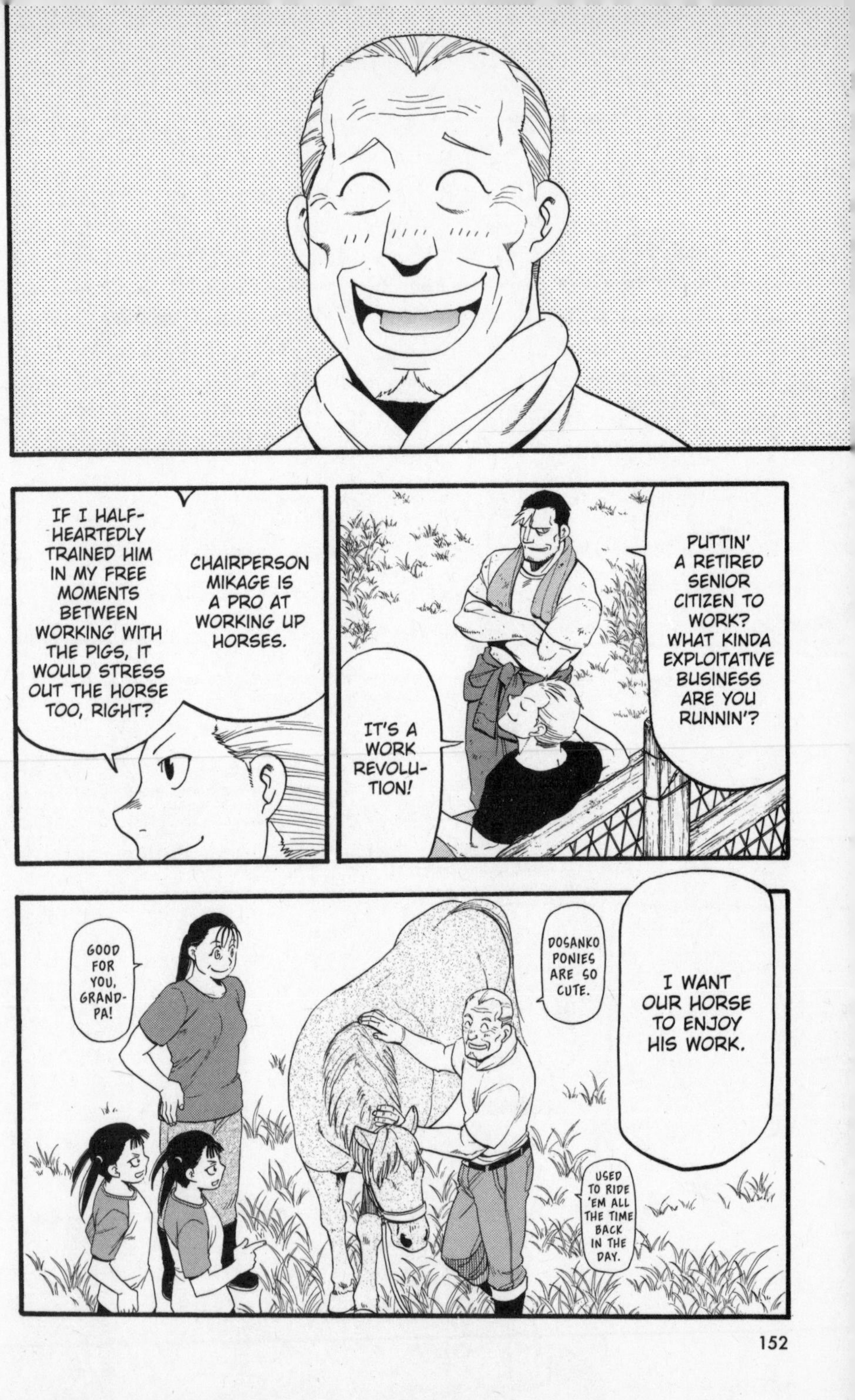
PUTTIN' A RETIRED SENIOR CITIZEN TO WORK? WHAT KINDA EXPLOITATIVE BUSINESS ARE YOU RUNNIN'?
IT'S A WORK REVOLUTION!
CHAIRPERSON MIKAGE IS A PRO AT WORKING UP HORSES.
IF I HALF-HEARTEDLY TRAINED HIM IN MY FREE MOMENTS BETWEEN WORKING WITH THE PIGS, IT WOULD STRESS OUT THE HORSE TOO, RIGHT?
I WANT OUR HORSE TO ENJOY HIS WORK.
DOSANKO PONIES ARE SO CUTE.
USED TO RIDE 'EM ALL THE TIME BACK IN THE DAY.
GOOD FOR YOU, GRANDPA!

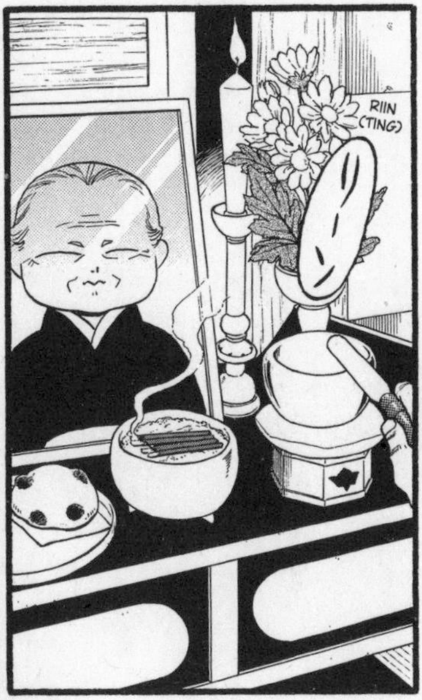
RIIN (TING)

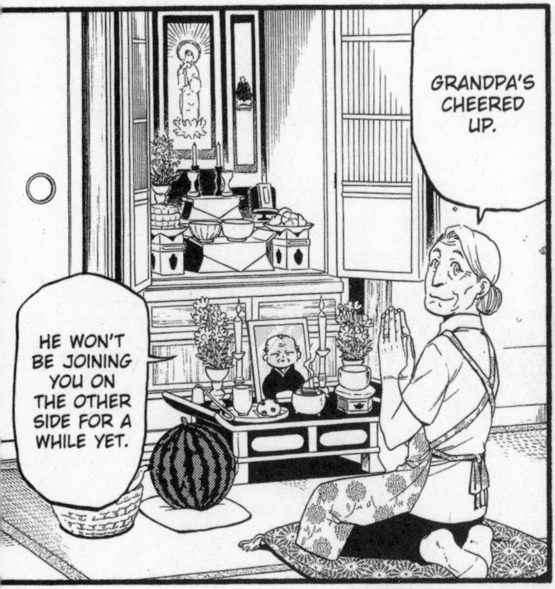
GRANDPA'S CHEERED UP.
HE WON'T BE JOINING YOU ON THE OTHER SIDE FOR A WHILE YET.

## Chapter 130:

# Tale of Four Seasons 33

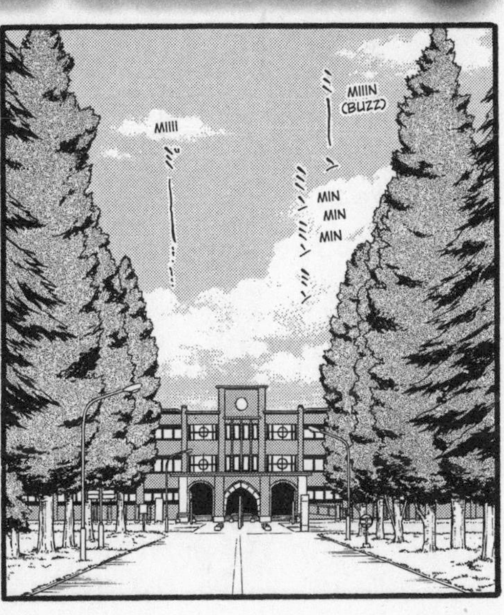
MIIIN (BUZZ)
MIIII
MIN MIN MIN

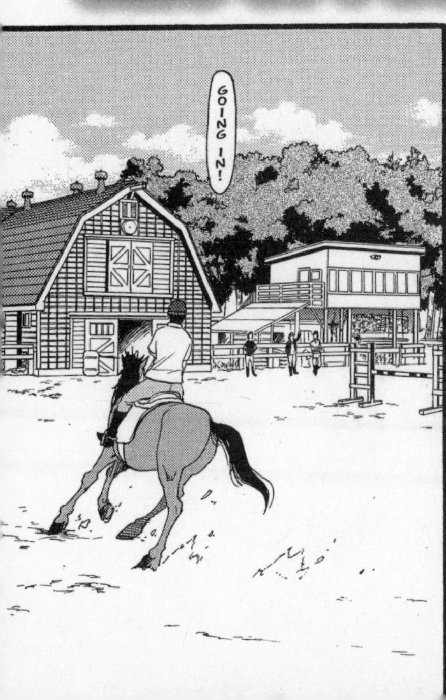
GOING IN!

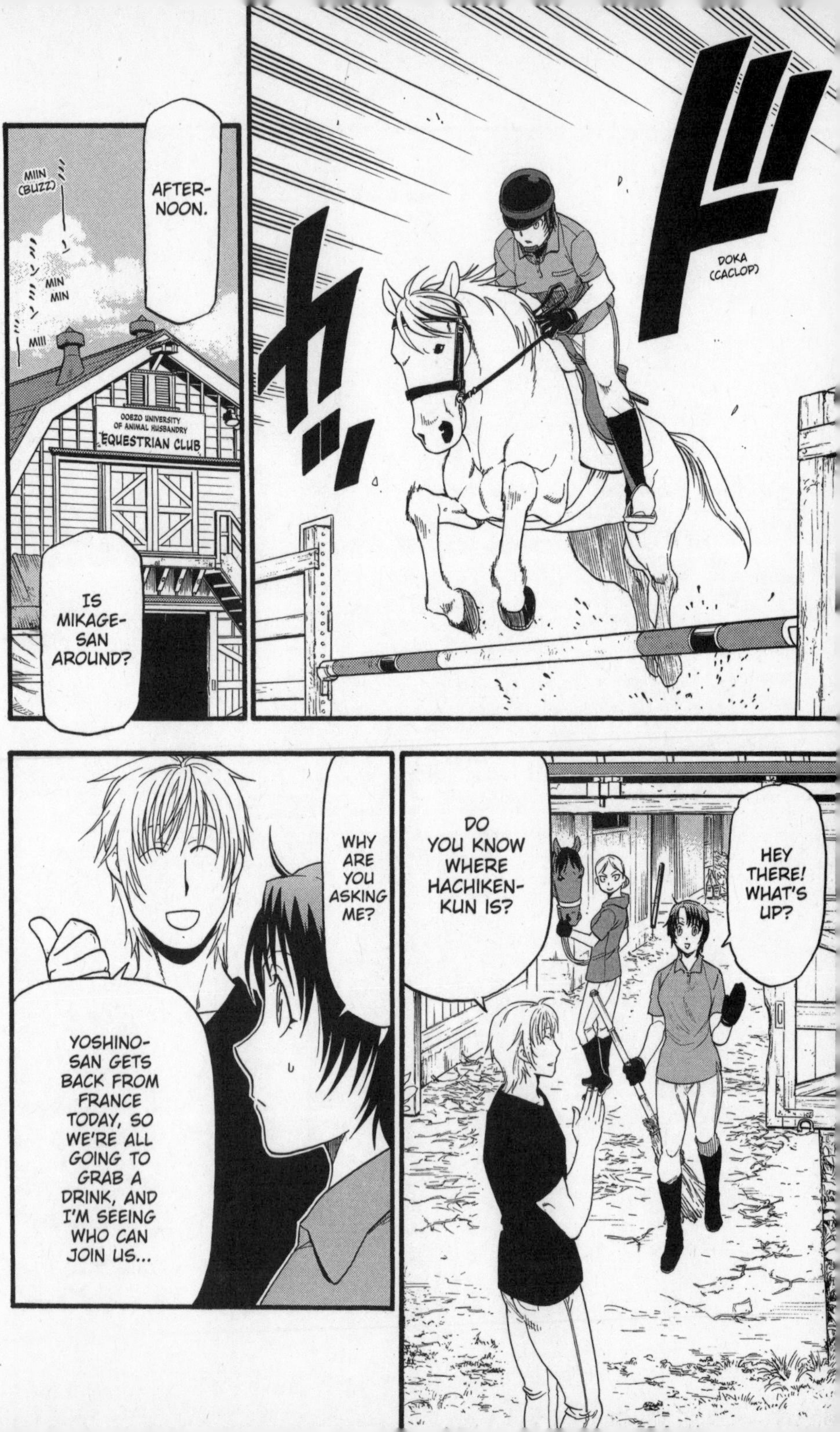
DOKA (CACLOP)
AFTER-NOON.
MIIN (BUZZ)
MIN MIN
MIII
OOEZO UNIVERSITY OF ANIMAL HUSBANDRY
EQUESTRIAN CLUB
IS MIKAGE-SAN AROUND?
HEY THERE! WHAT'S UP?
DO YOU KNOW WHERE HACHIKEN-KUN IS?
WHY ARE YOU ASKING ME?
YOSHINO-SAN GETS BACK FROM FRANCE TODAY, SO WE'RE ALL GOING TO GRAB A DRINK, AND I'M SEEING WHO CAN JOIN US...

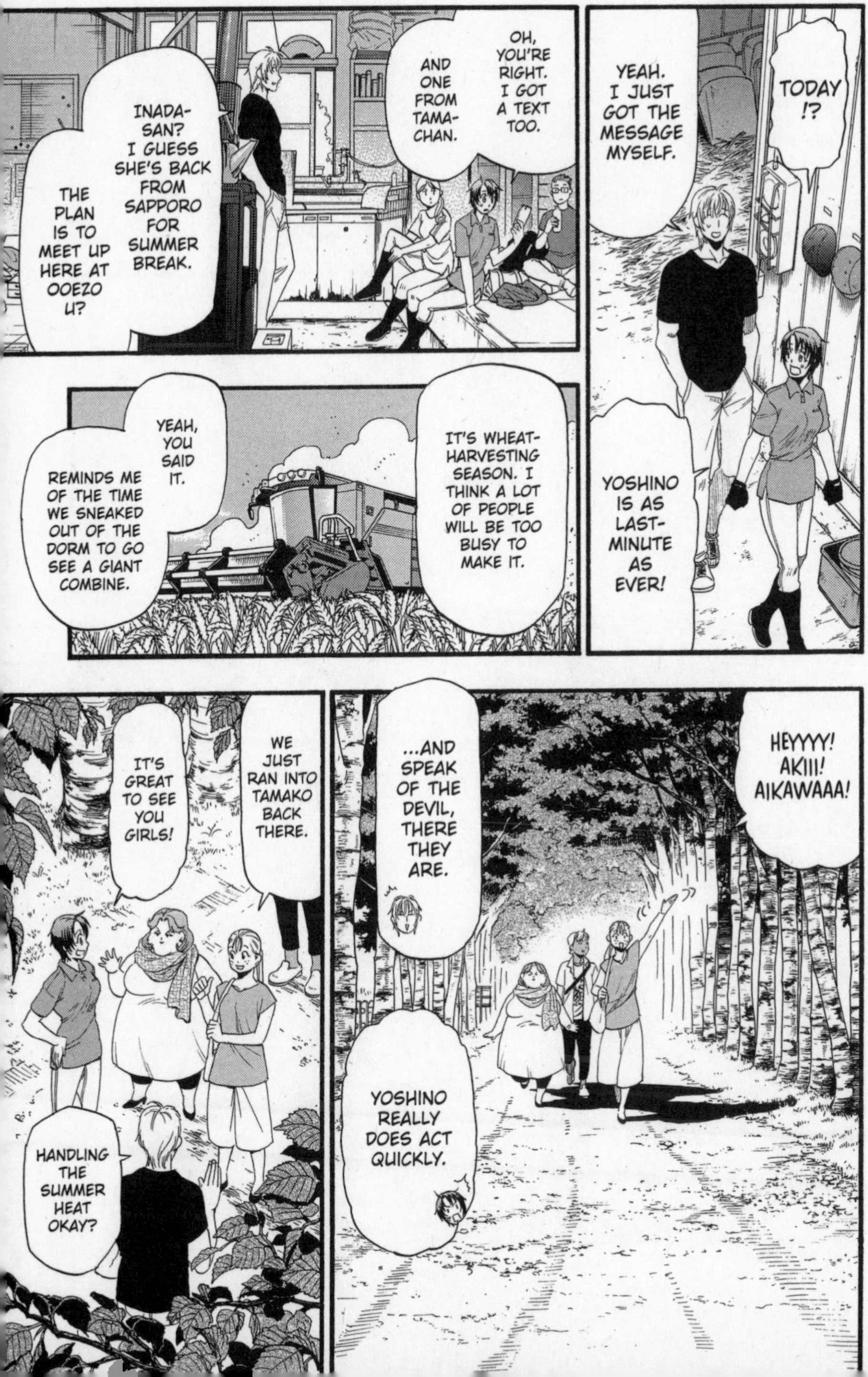
TODAY!?
YEAH. I JUST GOT THE MESSAGE MYSELF.
YOSHINO IS AS LAST-MINUTE AS EVER!
OH, YOU'RE RIGHT. I GOT A TEXT TOO.
AND ONE FROM TAMA-CHAN.
INADA-SAN? I GUESS SHE'S BACK FROM SAPPORO FOR SUMMER BREAK.
THE PLAN IS TO MEET UP HERE AT OOEZO U?
IT'S WHEAT-HARVESTING SEASON. I THINK A LOT OF PEOPLE WILL BE TOO BUSY TO MAKE IT.
YEAH, YOU SAID IT.
REMINDS ME OF THE TIME WE SNEAKED OUT OF THE DORM TO GO SEE A GIANT COMBINE.
HEYYYY! AKIII! AIKAWAAA!
...AND SPEAK OF THE DEVIL, THERE THEY ARE.
YOSHINO REALLY DOES ACT QUICKLY.
WE JUST RAN INTO TAMAKO BACK THERE.
IT'S GREAT TO SEE YOU GIRLS!
HANDLING THE SUMMER HEAT OKAY?

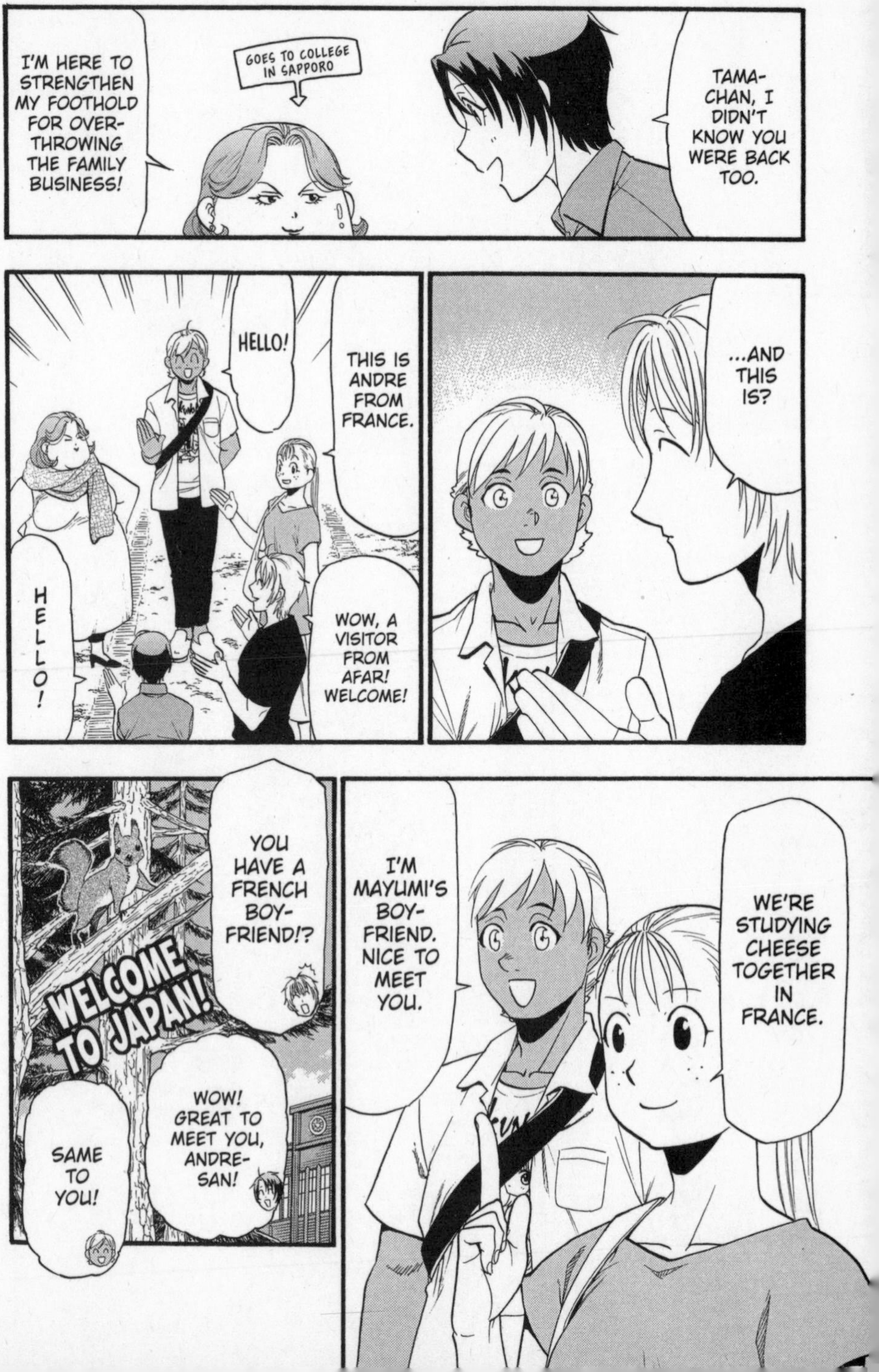
TAMA-CHAN, I DIDN'T KNOW YOU WERE BACK TOO.
GOES TO COLLEGE IN SAPPORO
I'M HERE TO STRENGTHEN MY FOOTHOLD FOR OVER-THROWING THE FAMILY BUSINESS!
...AND THIS IS?
THIS IS ANDRE FROM FRANCE.
HELLO!
WOW, A VISITOR FROM AFAR! WELCOME!
HELLO!
WE'RE STUDYING CHEESE TOGETHER IN FRANCE.
I'M MAYUMI'S BOY-FRIEND. NICE TO MEET YOU.
YOU HAVE A FRENCH BOY-FRIEND!?
WELCOME TO JAPAN!
WOW! GREAT TO MEET YOU, ANDRE-SAN!
SAME TO YOU!

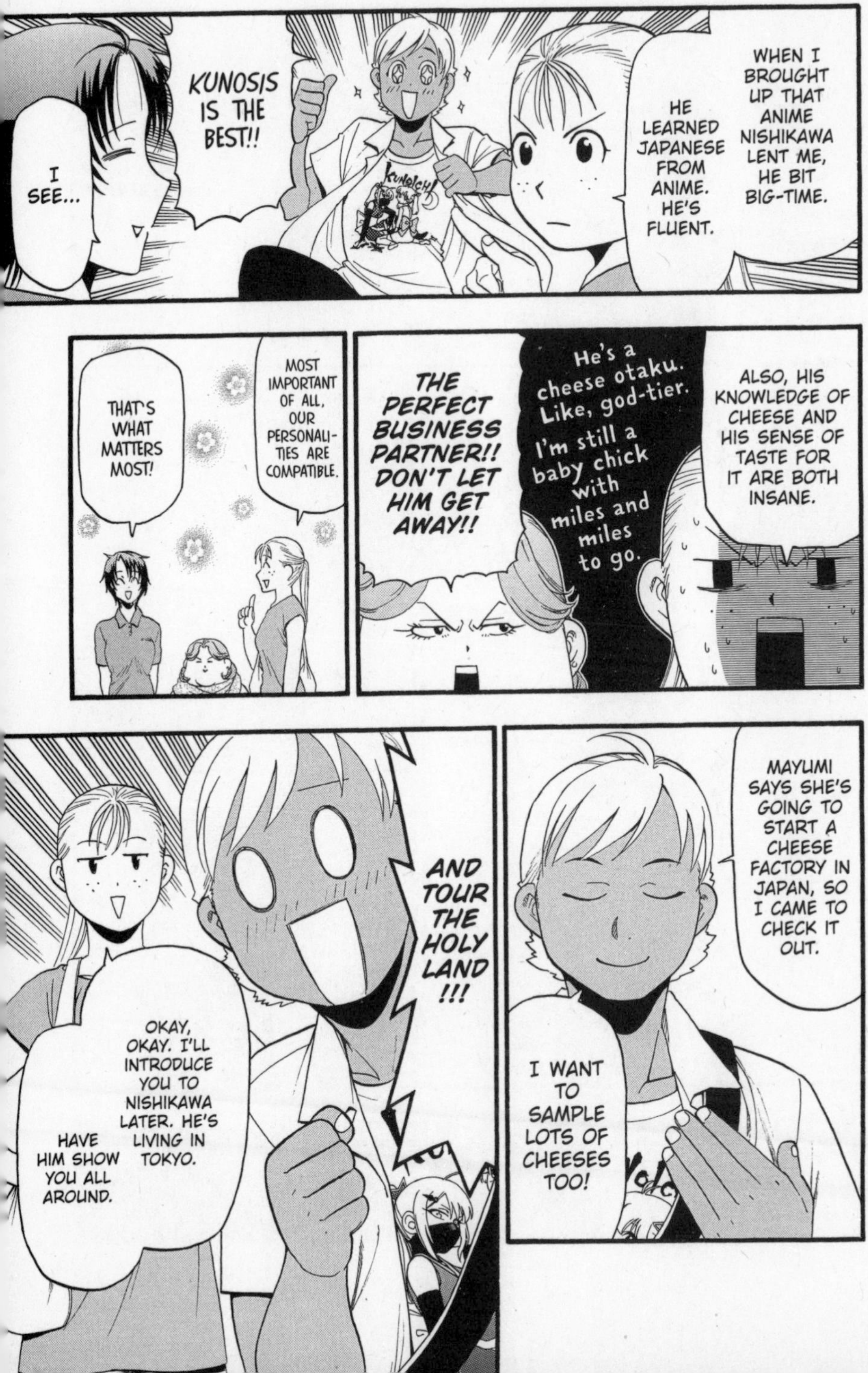
WHEN I BROUGHT UP THAT ANIME NISHIKAWA LENT ME, HE BIT BIG-TIME.
HE LEARNED JAPANESE FROM ANIME. HE'S FLUENT.
KUNOSIS IS THE BEST!!
I SEE...
ALSO, HIS KNOWLEDGE OF CHEESE AND HIS SENSE OF TASTE FOR IT ARE BOTH INSANE.
He's a cheese otaku. Like, god-tier.
I'm still a baby chick with miles and miles to go.
THE PERFECT BUSINESS PARTNER!! DON'T LET HIM GET AWAY!!
MOST IMPORTANT OF ALL, OUR PERSONALITIES ARE COMPATIBLE.
THAT'S WHAT MATTERS MOST!
MAYUMI SAYS SHE'S GOING TO START A CHEESE FACTORY IN JAPAN, SO I CAME TO CHECK IT OUT.
I WANT TO SAMPLE LOTS OF CHEESES TOO!
AND TOUR THE HOLY LAND!!!
OKAY, OKAY. I'LL INTRODUCE YOU TO NISHIKAWA LATER. HE'S LIVING IN TOKYO.
HAVE HIM SHOW YOU ALL AROUND.

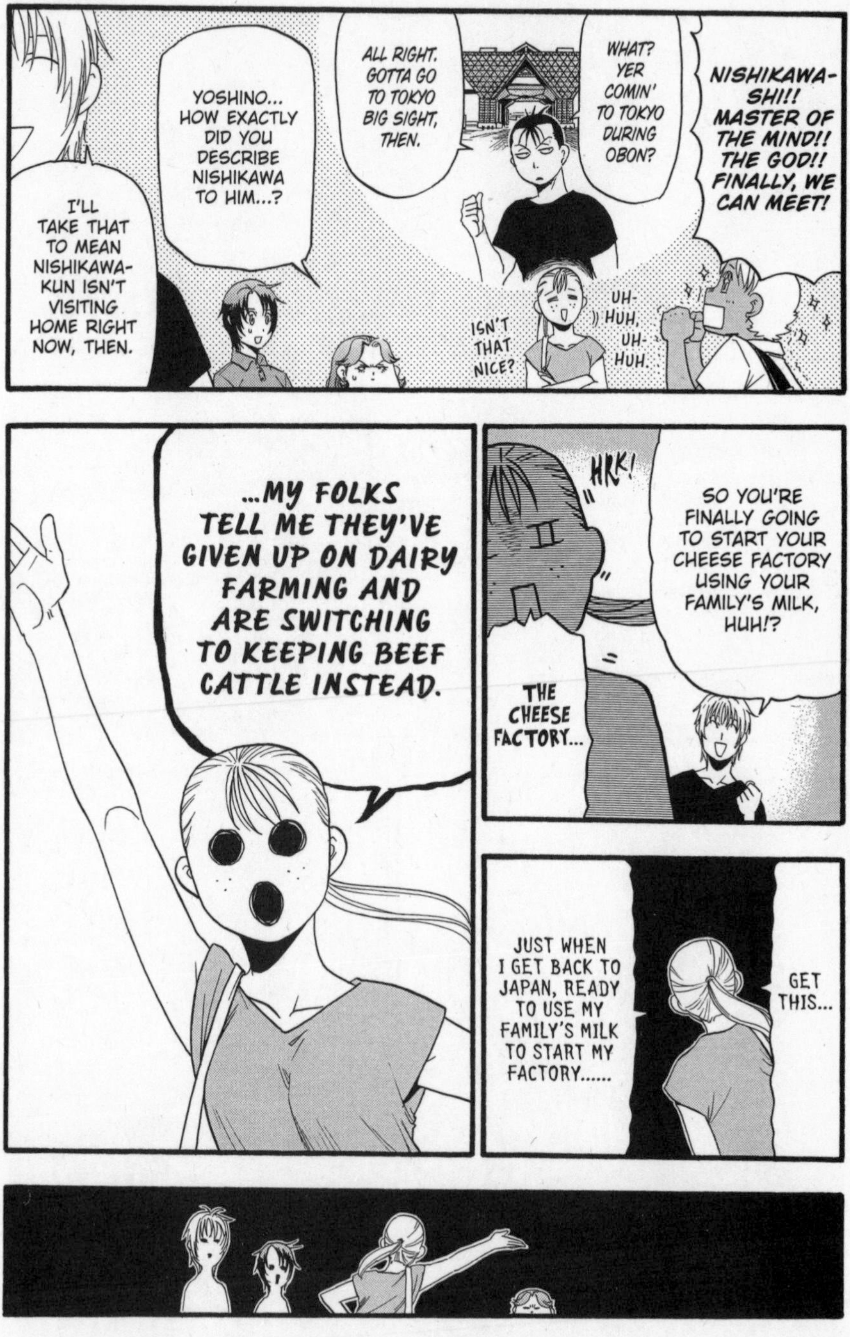
NISHIKAWA-SHI!! MASTER OF THE MIND!! THE GOD!! FINALLY, WE CAN MEET!
WHAT? YER COMIN' TO TOKYO DURING OBON?
ALL RIGHT. GOTTA GO TO TOKYO BIG SIGHT, THEN.
UH-HUH, UH-HUH.
ISN'T THAT NICE?
YOSHINO... HOW EXACTLY DID YOU DESCRIBE NISHIKAWA TO HIM...?
I'LL TAKE THAT TO MEAN NISHIKAWA-KUN ISN'T VISITING HOME RIGHT NOW, THEN.
SO YOU'RE FINALLY GOING TO START YOUR CHEESE FACTORY USING YOUR FAMILY'S MILK, HUH!?
HRK!
THE CHEESE FACTORY...
GET THIS...
JUST WHEN I GET BACK TO JAPAN, READY TO USE MY FAMILY'S MILK TO START MY FACTORY......
...MY FOLKS TELL ME THEY'VE GIVEN UP ON DAIRY FARMING AND ARE SWITCHING TO KEEPING BEEF CATTLE INSTEAD.

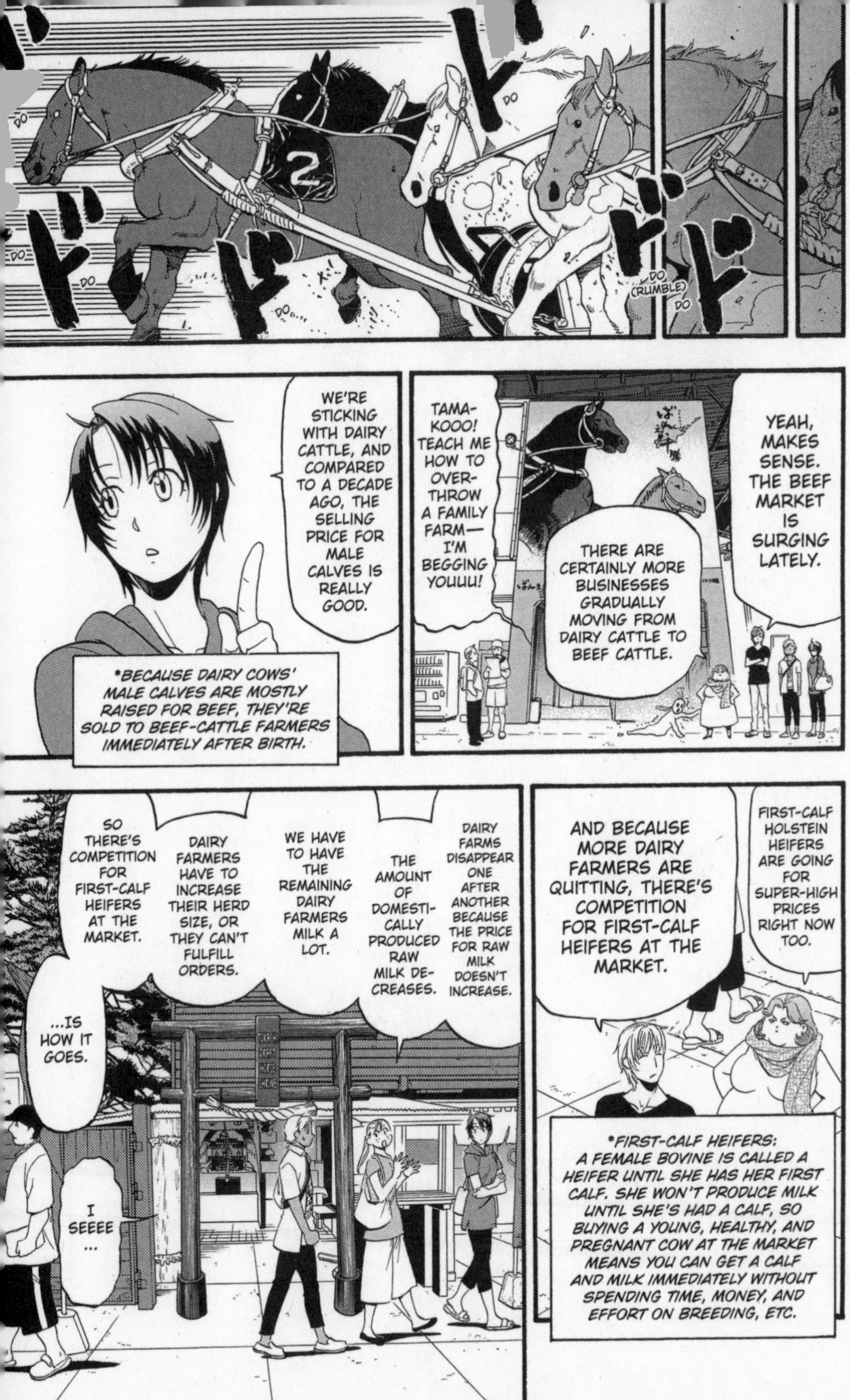
DO (RUMBLE) DO
DO
DO
DO
DO
DO...
WE'RE STICKING WITH DAIRY CATTLE, AND COMPARED TO A DECADE AGO, THE SELLING PRICE FOR MALE CALVES IS REALLY GOOD.
*BECAUSE DAIRY COWS' MALE CALVES ARE MOSTLY RAISED FOR BEEF, THEY'RE SOLD TO BEEF-CATTLE FARMERS IMMEDIATELY AFTER BIRTH.
YEAH, MAKES SENSE. THE BEEF MARKET IS SURGING LATELY.
THERE ARE CERTAINLY MORE BUSINESSES GRADUALLY MOVING FROM DAIRY CATTLE TO BEEF CATTLE.
TAMA-KOOO! TEACH ME HOW TO OVER-THROW A FAMILY FARM—I'M BEGGING YOUUU!
FIRST-CALF HOLSTEIN HEIFERS ARE GOING FOR SUPER-HIGH PRICES RIGHT NOW TOO.
AND BECAUSE MORE DAIRY FARMERS ARE QUITTING, THERE'S COMPETITION FOR FIRST-CALF HEIFERS AT THE MARKET.
*FIRST-CALF HEIFERS: A FEMALE BOVINE IS CALLED A HEIFER UNTIL SHE HAS HER FIRST CALF. SHE WON'T PRODUCE MILK UNTIL SHE'S HAD A CALF, SO BUYING A YOUNG, HEALTHY, AND PREGNANT COW AT THE MARKET MEANS YOU CAN GET A CALF AND MILK IMMEDIATELY WITHOUT SPENDING TIME, MONEY, AND EFFORT ON BREEDING, ETC.
DAIRY FARMS DISAPPEAR ONE AFTER ANOTHER BECAUSE THE PRICE FOR RAW MILK DOESN'T INCREASE.
THE AMOUNT OF DOMESTI-CALLY PRODUCED RAW MILK DE-CREASES.
WE HAVE TO HAVE THE REMAINING DAIRY FARMERS MILK A LOT.
DAIRY FARMERS HAVE TO INCREASE THEIR HERD SIZE, OR THEY CAN'T FULFILL ORDERS.
SO THERE'S COMPETITION FOR FIRST-CALF HEIFERS AT THE MARKET.
...IS HOW IT GOES.
I SEEEE ...

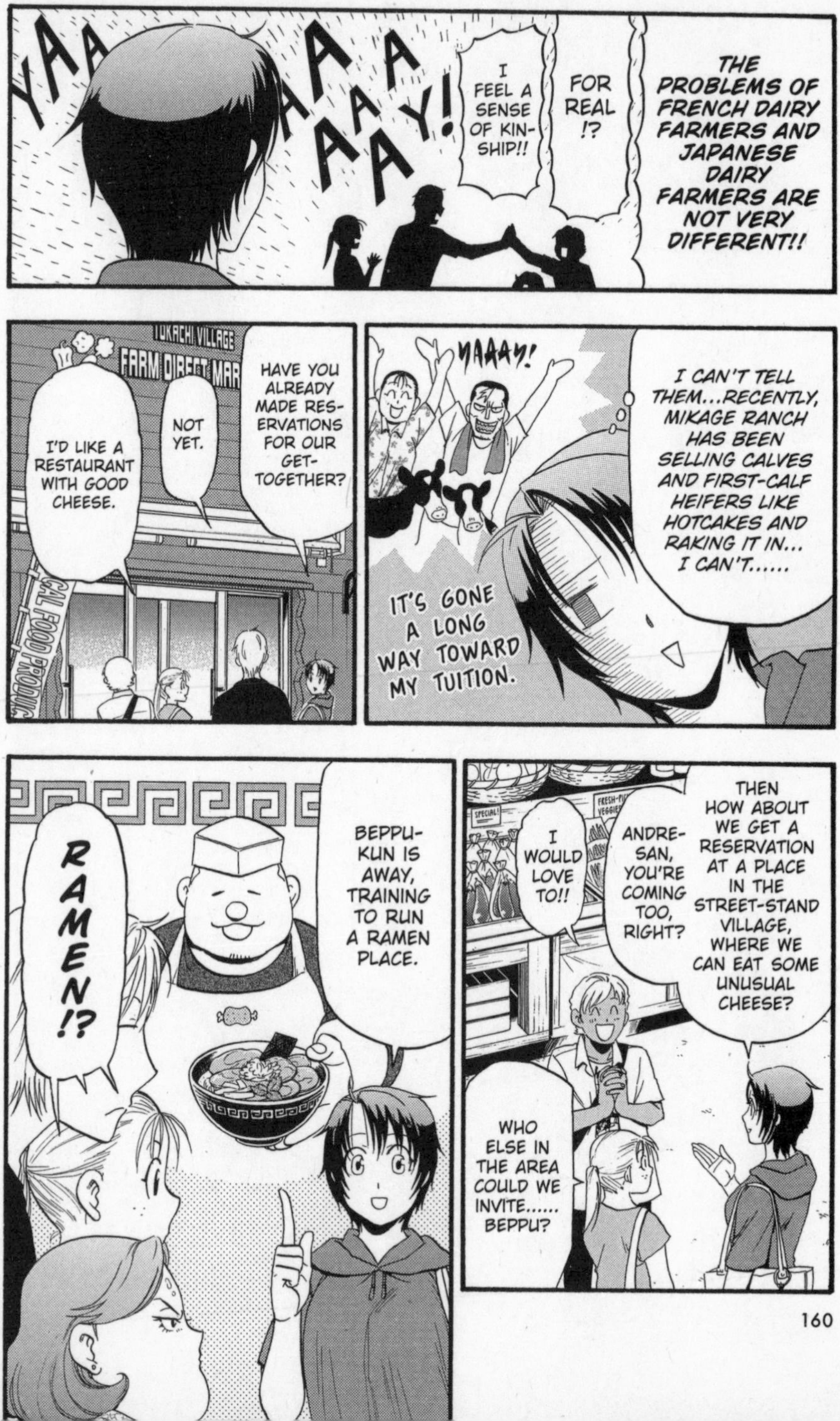
THE PROBLEMS OF FRENCH DAIRY FARMERS AND JAPANESE DAIRY FARMERS ARE NOT VERY DIFFERENT!!
FOR REAL!?
I FEEL A SENSE OF KIN-SHIP!!
YAAAAAAAAY!
I CAN'T TELL THEM...RECENTLY, MIKAGE RANCH HAS BEEN SELLING CALVES AND FIRST-CALF HEIFERS LIKE HOTCAKES AND RAKING IT IN... I CAN'T......
YAAAAY!
IT'S GONE A LONG WAY TOWARD MY TUITION.
TOKACHI VILLAGE
HAVE YOU ALREADY MADE RES-ERVATIONS FOR OUR GET-TOGETHER?
NOT YET.
I'D LIKE A RESTAURANT WITH GOOD CHEESE.
THEN HOW ABOUT WE GET A RESERVATION AT A PLACE IN THE STREET-STAND VILLAGE, WHERE WE CAN EAT SOME UNUSUAL CHEESE?
ANDRE-SAN, YOU'RE COMING TOO, RIGHT?
I WOULD LOVE TO!!
WHO ELSE IN THE AREA COULD WE INVITE...... BEPPU?
BEPPU-KUN IS AWAY, TRAINING TO RUN A RAMEN PLACE.
RAMEN!?

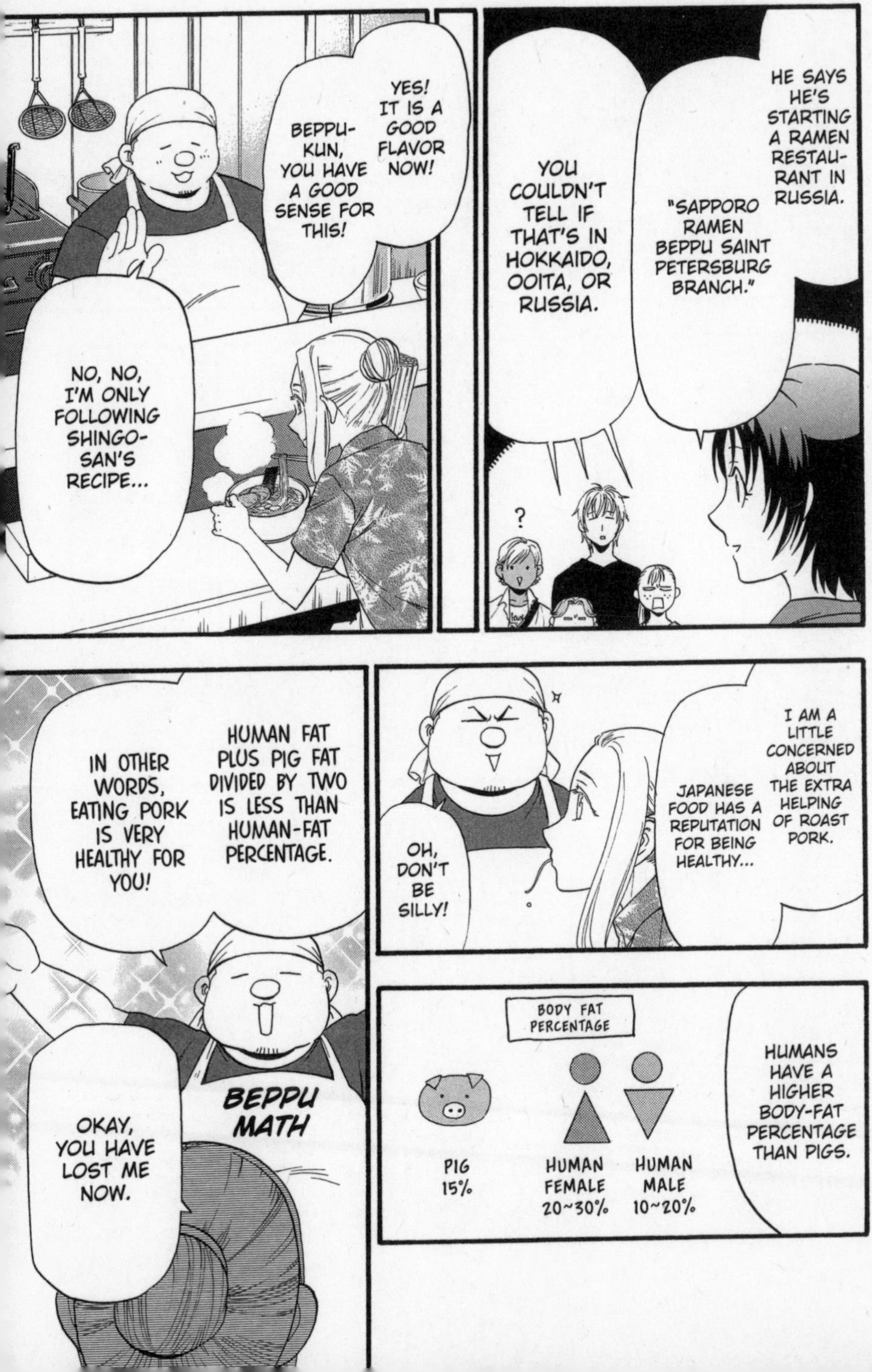
HE SAYS HE'S STARTING A RAMEN RESTAURANT IN RUSSIA.
"SAPPORO RAMEN BEPPU SAINT PETERSBURG BRANCH."
YOU COULDN'T TELL IF THAT'S IN HOKKAIDO, OOITA, OR RUSSIA.
?
YES! IT IS A GOOD FLAVOR NOW!
BEPPU-KUN, YOU HAVE A GOOD SENSE FOR THIS!
NO, NO, I'M ONLY FOLLOWING SHINGO-SAN'S RECIPE...
I AM A LITTLE CONCERNED ABOUT THE EXTRA HELPING OF ROAST PORK.
JAPANESE FOOD HAS A REPUTATION FOR BEING HEALTHY...
OH, DON'T BE SILLY!
HUMANS HAVE A HIGHER BODY-FAT PERCENTAGE THAN PIGS.
BODY FAT PERCENTAGE
PIG 15%
HUMAN FEMALE 20~30%
HUMAN MALE 10~20%
HUMAN FAT PLUS PIG FAT DIVIDED BY TWO IS LESS THAN HUMAN-FAT PERCENTAGE.
IN OTHER WORDS, EATING PORK IS VERY HEALTHY FOR YOU!
BEPPU MATH
OKAY, YOU HAVE LOST ME NOW.

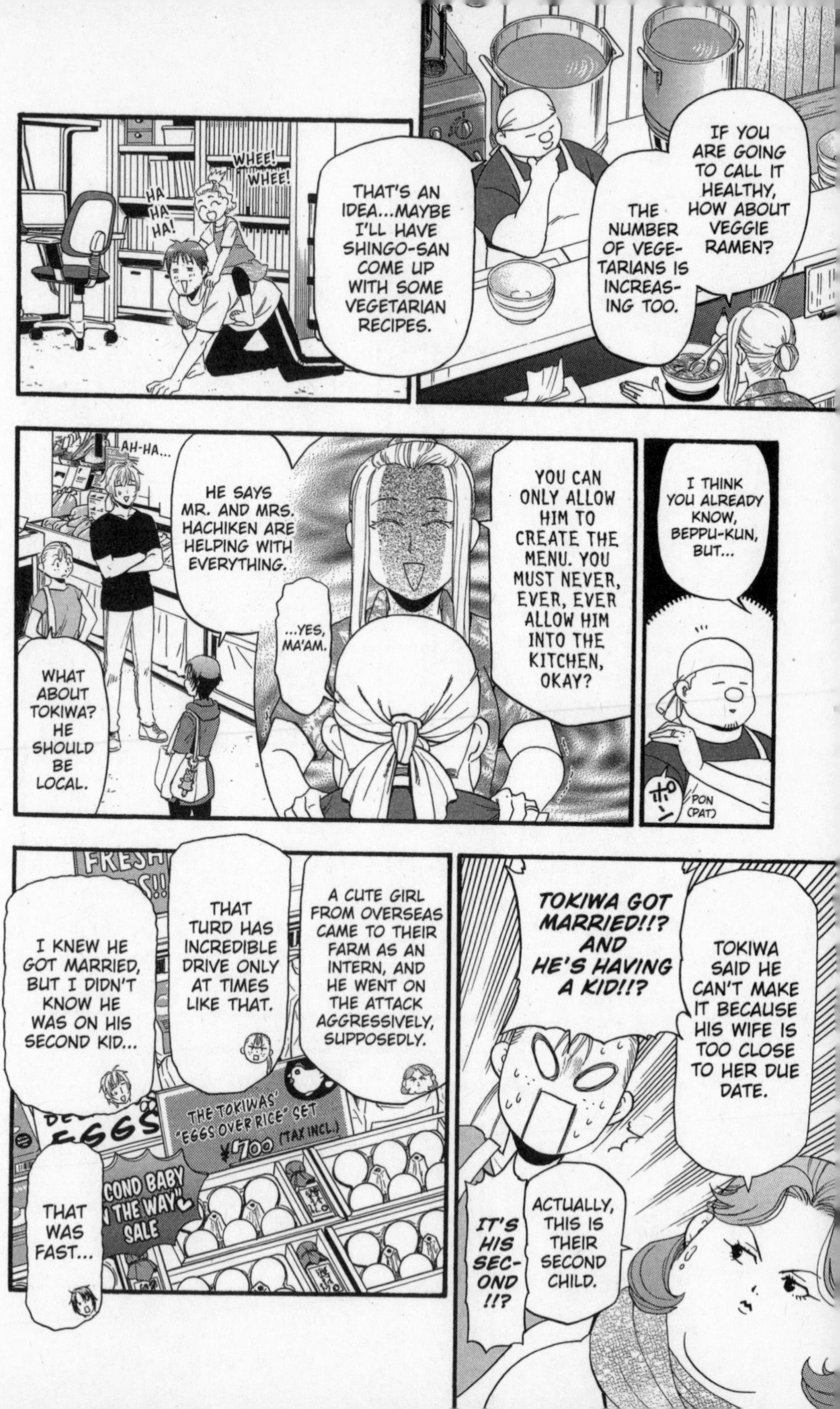
IF YOU ARE GOING TO CALL IT HEALTHY, HOW ABOUT VEGGIE RAMEN?
THE NUMBER OF VEGETARIANS IS INCREASING TOO.
THAT'S AN IDEA...MAYBE I'LL HAVE SHINGO-SAN COME UP WITH SOME VEGETARIAN RECIPES.
WHEE! WHEE!
HA HA HA!
I THINK YOU ALREADY KNOW, BEPPU-KUN, BUT...
PON (PAT)
YOU CAN ONLY ALLOW HIM TO CREATE THE MENU. YOU MUST NEVER, EVER, EVER ALLOW HIM INTO THE KITCHEN, OKAY?
...YES, MA'AM.
HE SAYS MR. AND MRS. HACHIKEN ARE HELPING WITH EVERYTHING.
AH-HA...
WHAT ABOUT TOKIWA? HE SHOULD BE LOCAL.
TOKIWA SAID HE CAN'T MAKE IT BECAUSE HIS WIFE IS TOO CLOSE TO HER DUE DATE.
TOKIWA GOT MARRIED!!? AND HE'S HAVING A KID!!?
ACTUALLY, THIS IS THEIR SECOND CHILD.
IT'S HIS SECOND!!?
A CUTE GIRL FROM OVERSEAS CAME TO THEIR FARM AS AN INTERN, AND HE WENT ON THE ATTACK AGGRESSIVELY, SUPPOSEDLY.
THAT TURD HAS INCREDIBLE DRIVE ONLY AT TIMES LIKE THAT.
I KNEW HE GOT MARRIED, BUT I DIDN'T KNOW HE WAS ON HIS SECOND KID...
THE TOKIWAS' "EGGS OVER RICE" SET
¥700 (TAX INCL.)
COND BABY N THE WAY SALE
THAT WAS FAST...

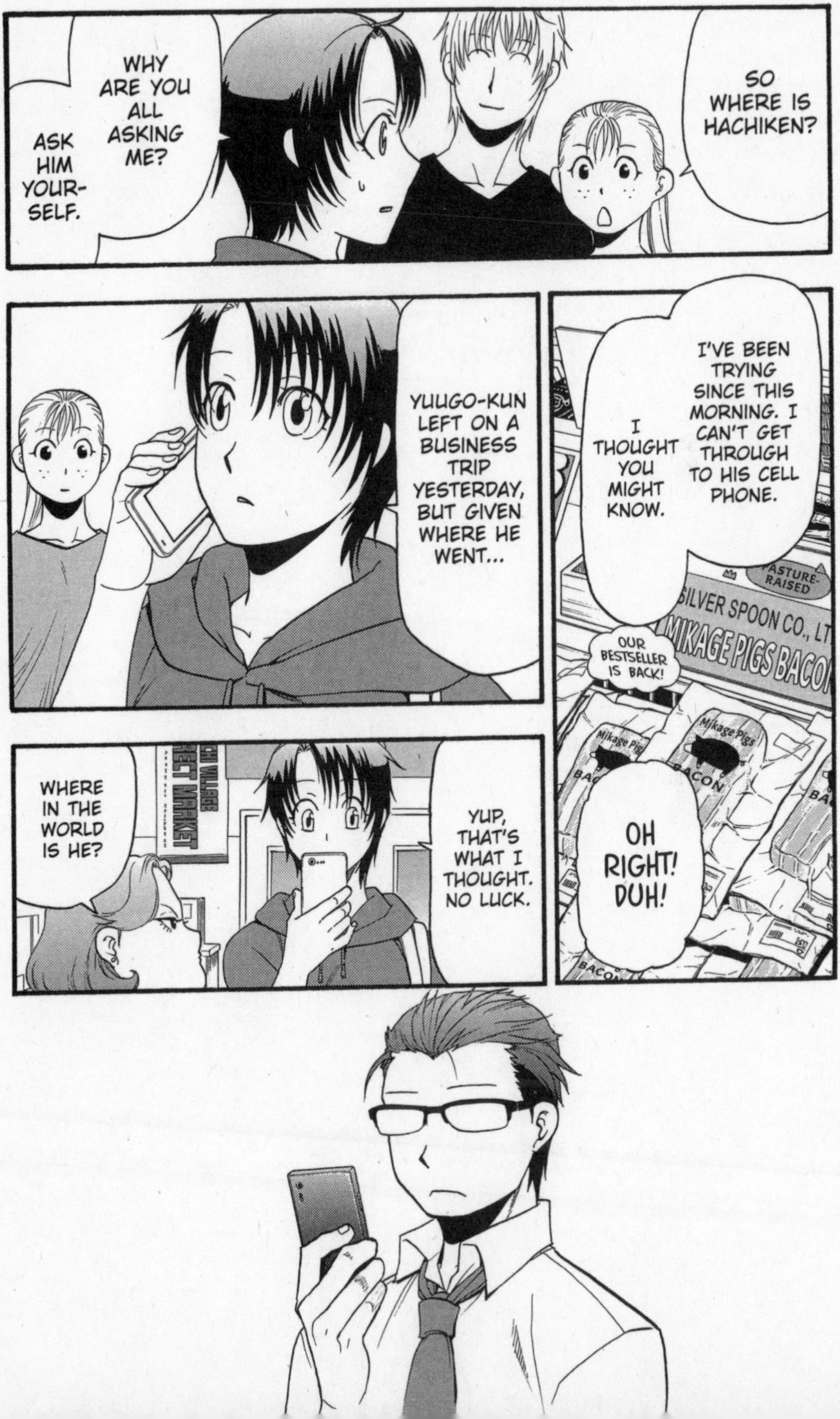
SO WHERE IS HACHIKEN?
WHY ARE YOU ALL ASKING ME?
ASK HIM YOURSELF.
I'VE BEEN TRYING SINCE THIS MORNING. I CAN'T GET THROUGH TO HIS CELL PHONE.
I THOUGHT YOU MIGHT KNOW.
PASTURE-RAISED
SILVER SPOON CO., LT
MIKAGE PIGS BACO
OUR BESTSELLER IS BACK!
Mikage Pigs
BACON
OH RIGHT! DUH!
YUUGO-KUN LEFT ON A BUSINESS TRIP YESTERDAY, BUT GIVEN WHERE HE WENT...
YUP, THAT'S WHAT I THOUGHT. NO LUCK.
WHERE IN THE WORLD IS HE?

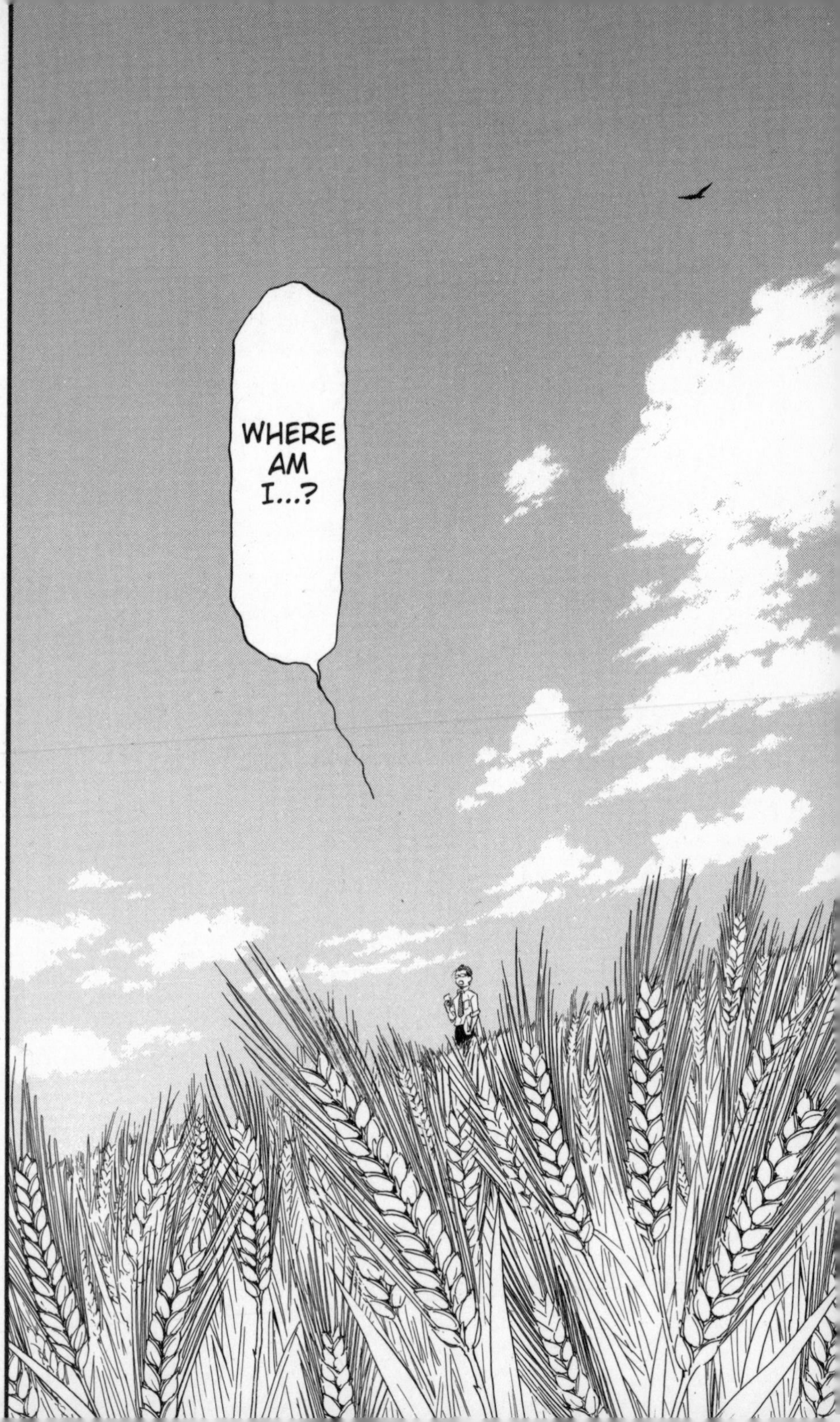
WHERE AM I...?

Silver Spoon

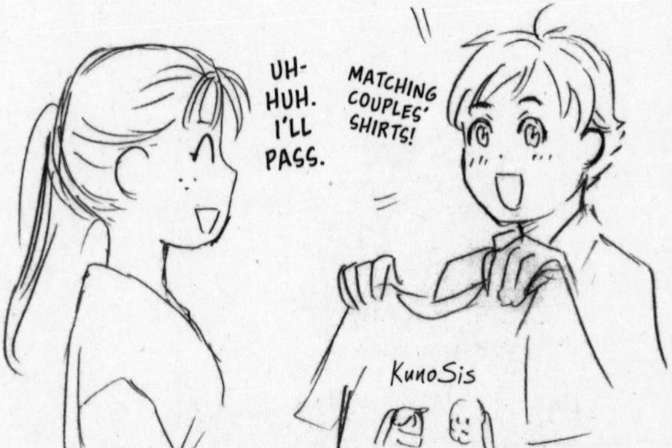
MATCHING COUPLES' SHIRTS!
KunoSis
UH-HUH. I'LL PASS.

## Final Chapter:
# Tale of Yuugo Hachiken

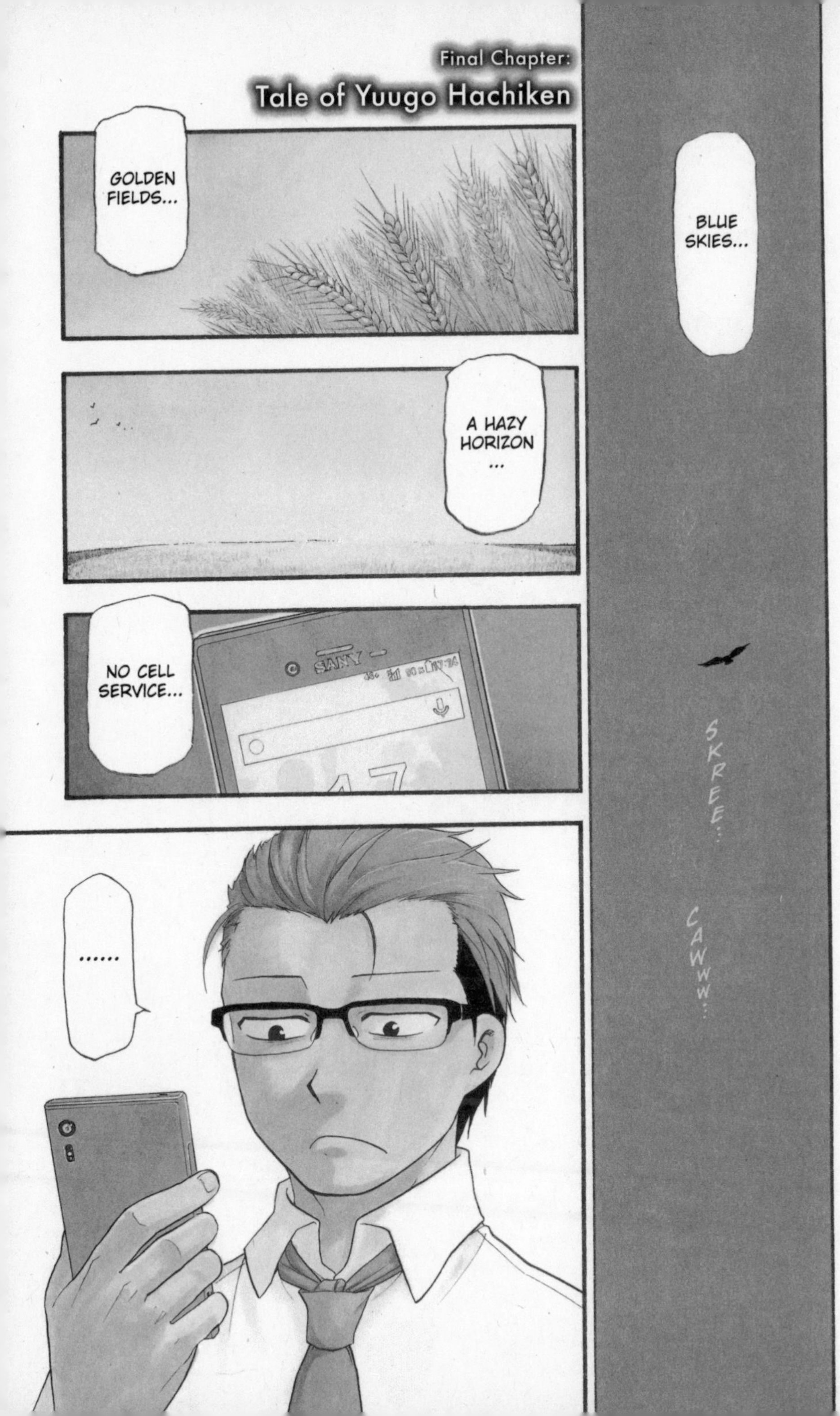
BLUE SKIES...
SKREE...
CAWWW...
GOLDEN FIELDS...
A HAZY HORIZON ...
NO CELL SERVICE...
......

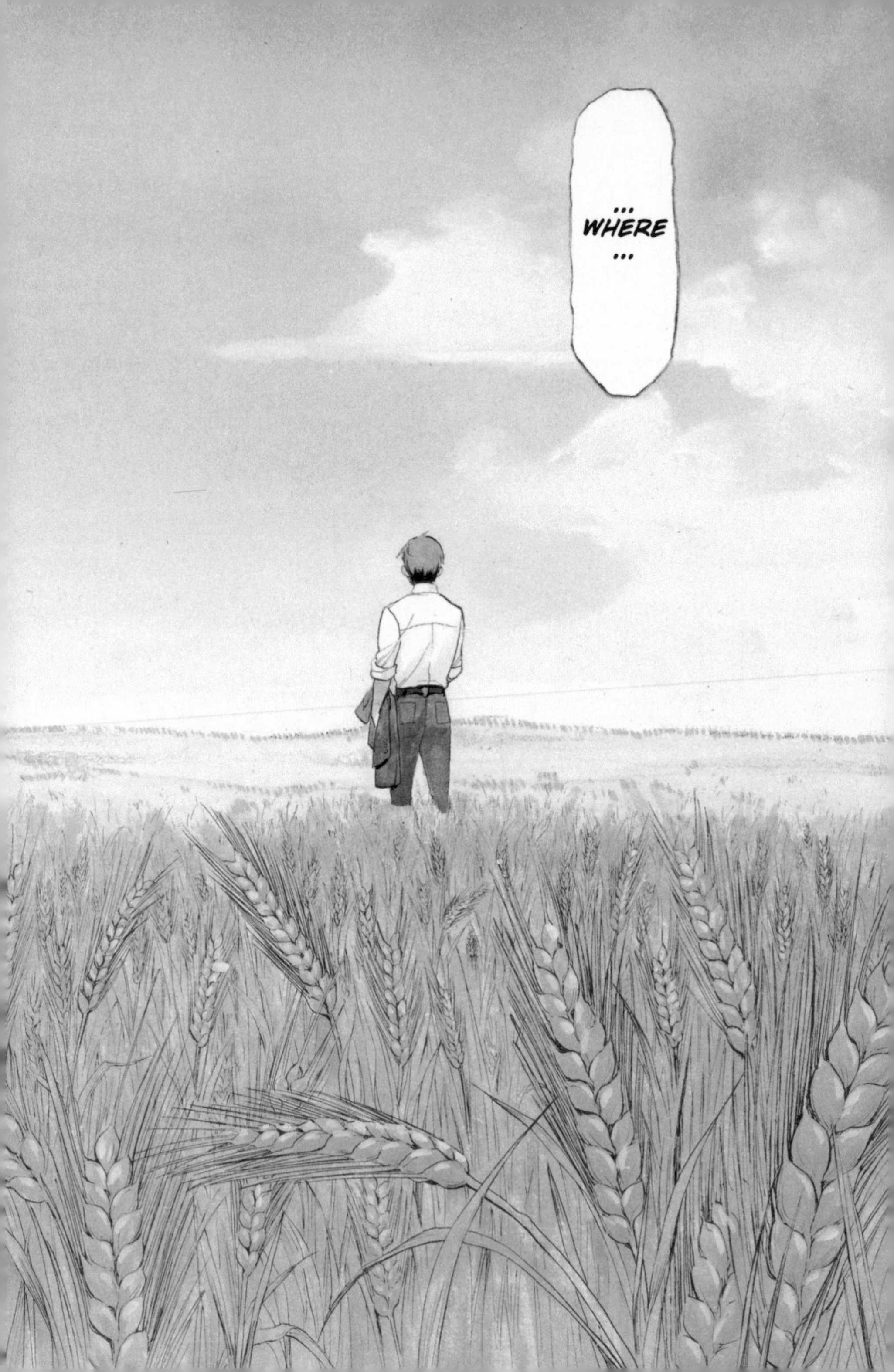
...WHERE...

Final Chapter:
# Tale of Yuugo Hachiken

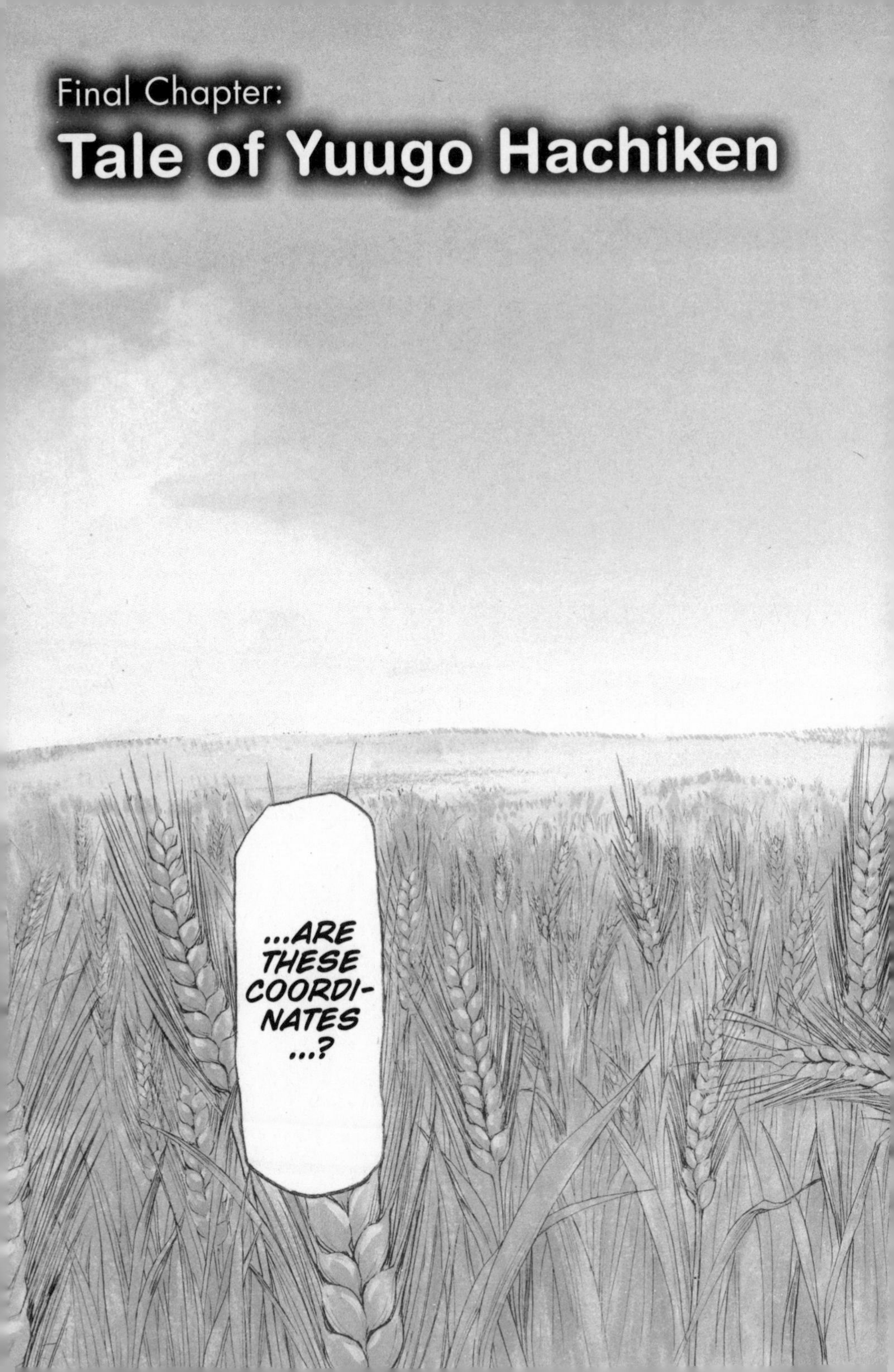
...ARE THESE COORDI-NATES ...?

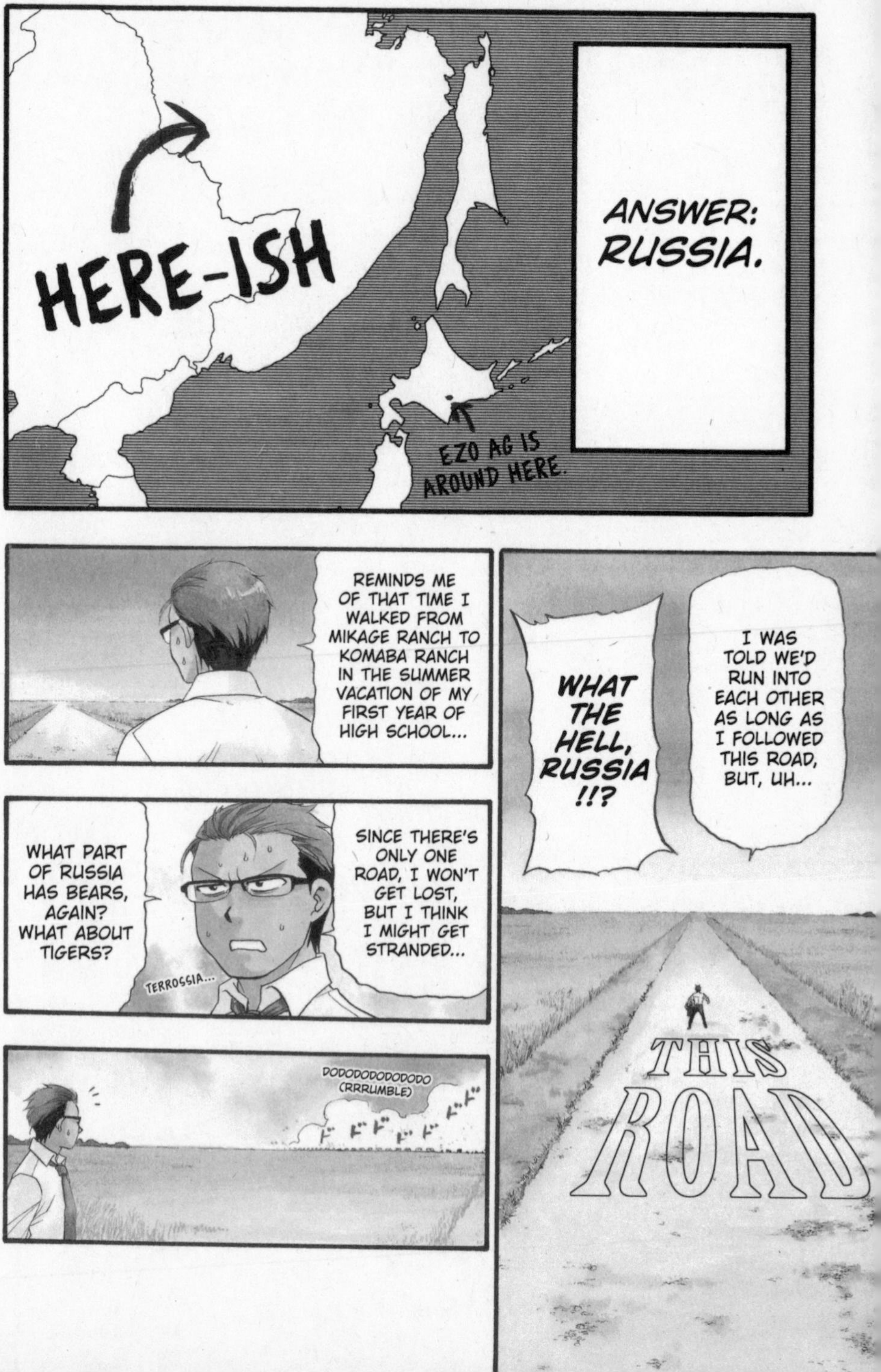
ANSWER: RUSSIA.
HERE-ISH
EZO AG IS AROUND HERE.
I WAS TOLD WE'D RUN INTO EACH OTHER AS LONG AS I FOLLOWED THIS ROAD, BUT, UH...
WHAT THE HELL, RUSSIA !!?
THIS ROAD
REMINDS ME OF THAT TIME I WALKED FROM MIKAGE RANCH TO KOMABA RANCH IN THE SUMMER VACATION OF MY FIRST YEAR OF HIGH SCHOOL...
SINCE THERE'S ONLY ONE ROAD, I WON'T GET LOST, BUT I THINK I MIGHT GET STRANDED...
WHAT PART OF RUSSIA HAS BEARS, AGAIN? WHAT ABOUT TIGERS?
TERROSSIA...
DODODODODODODO (RRRUMBLE)
ドドドドドドド

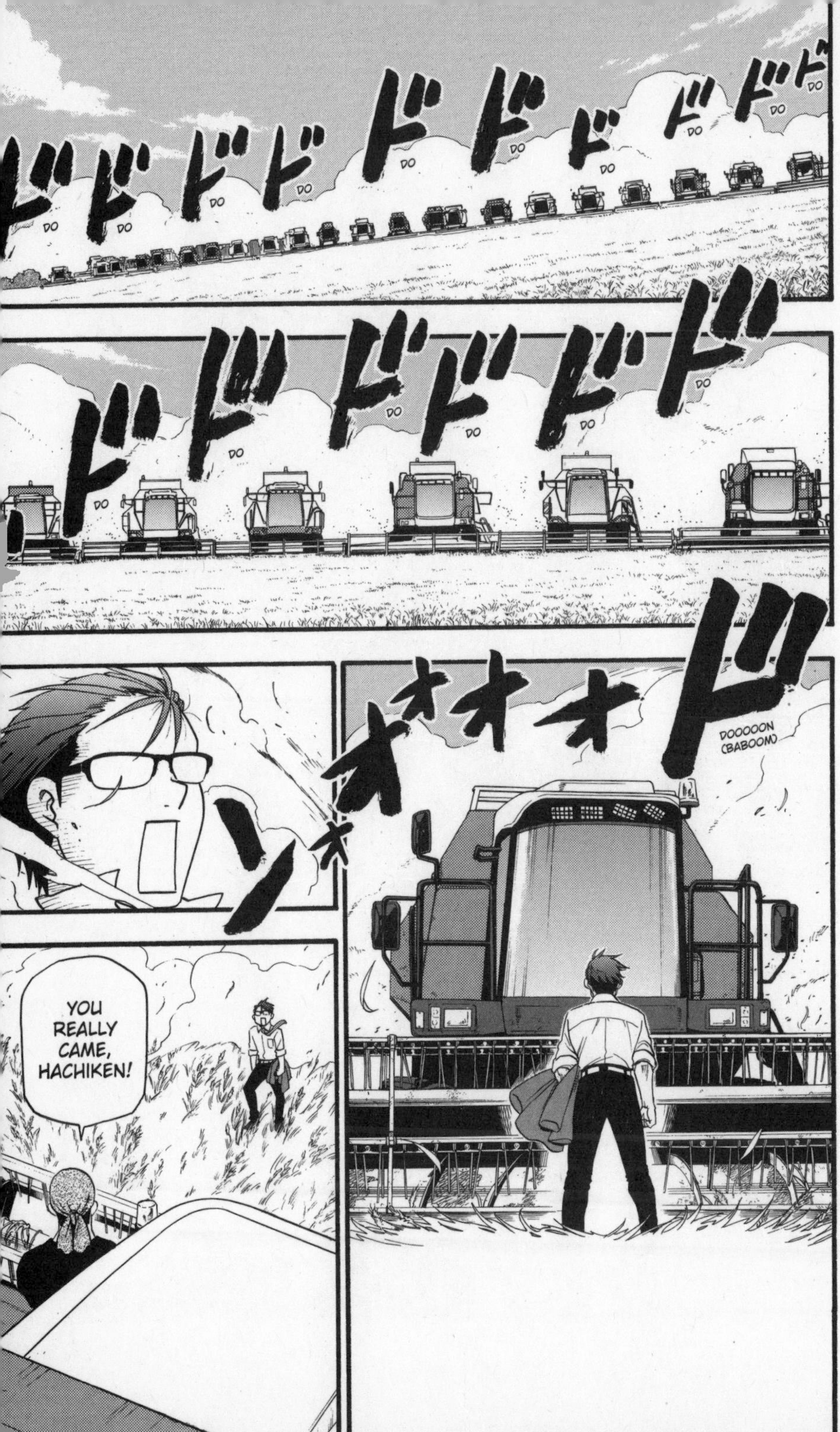
DO DO DO DO DO DO DO DO DO DO DO
DO DO DO DO DO DO
DOOOOON (BABOOM)
YOU REALLY CAME, HACHIKEN!

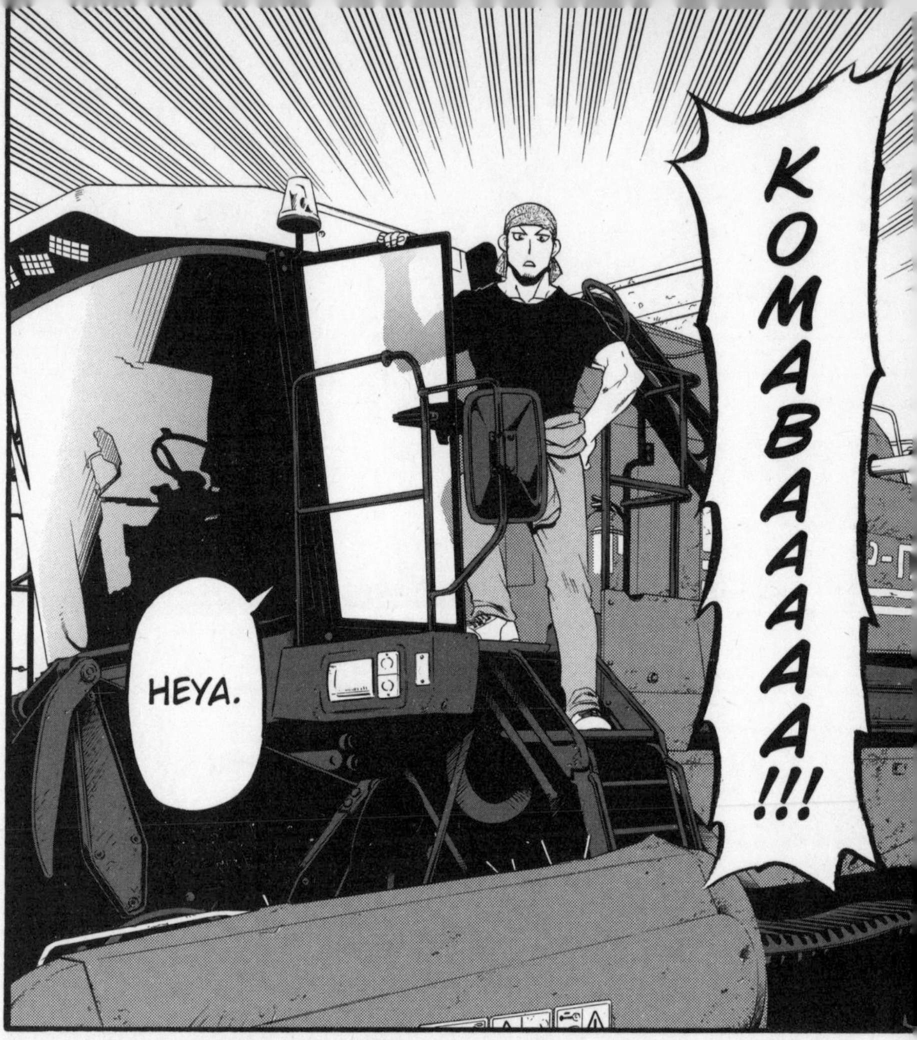
KOMABAAAAAAA!!!
HEYA.

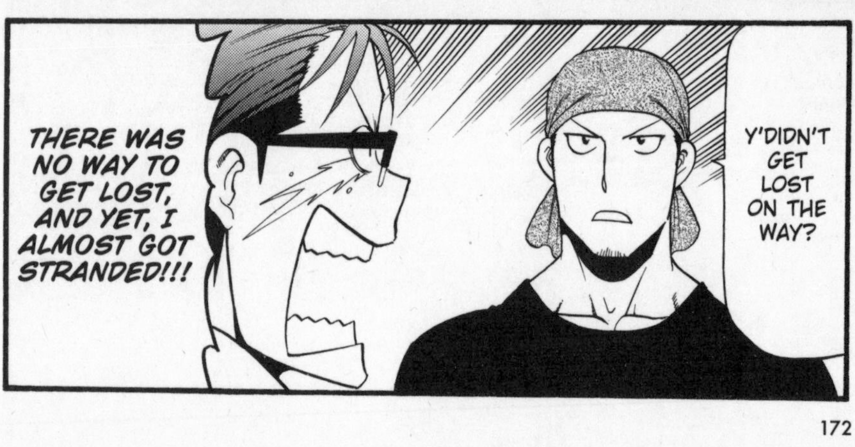
Y'DIDN'T GET LOST ON THE WAY?
THERE WAS NO WAY TO GET LOST, AND YET, I ALMOST GOT STRANDED!!!

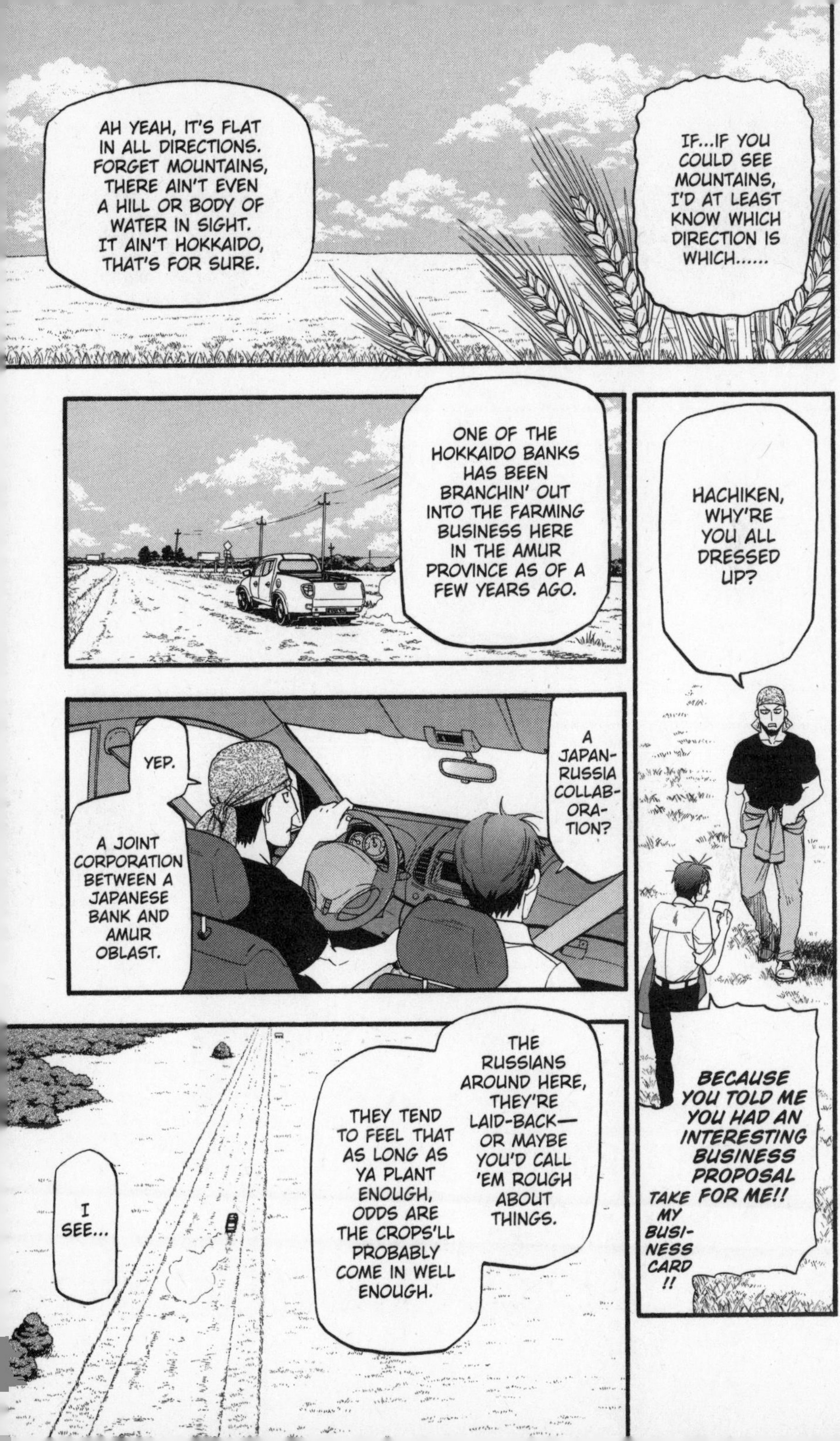
IF...IF YOU COULD SEE MOUNTAINS, I'D AT LEAST KNOW WHICH DIRECTION IS WHICH......
AH YEAH, IT'S FLAT IN ALL DIRECTIONS. FORGET MOUNTAINS, THERE AIN'T EVEN A HILL OR BODY OF WATER IN SIGHT. IT AIN'T HOKKAIDO, THAT'S FOR SURE.
HACHIKEN, WHY'RE YOU ALL DRESSED UP?
BECAUSE YOU TOLD ME YOU HAD AN INTERESTING BUSINESS PROPOSAL FOR ME!!
TAKE MY BUSI-NESS CARD !!
ONE OF THE HOKKAIDO BANKS HAS BEEN BRANCHIN' OUT INTO THE FARMING BUSINESS HERE IN THE AMUR PROVINCE AS OF A FEW YEARS AGO.
A JAPAN-RUSSIA COLLAB-ORA-TION?
YEP.
A JOINT CORPORATION BETWEEN A JAPANESE BANK AND AMUR OBLAST.
THE RUSSIANS AROUND HERE, THEY'RE LAID-BACK— OR MAYBE YOU'D CALL 'EM ROUGH ABOUT THINGS.
THEY TEND TO FEEL THAT AS LONG AS YA PLANT ENOUGH, ODDS ARE THE CROPS'LL PROBABLY COME IN WELL ENOUGH.
I SEE...

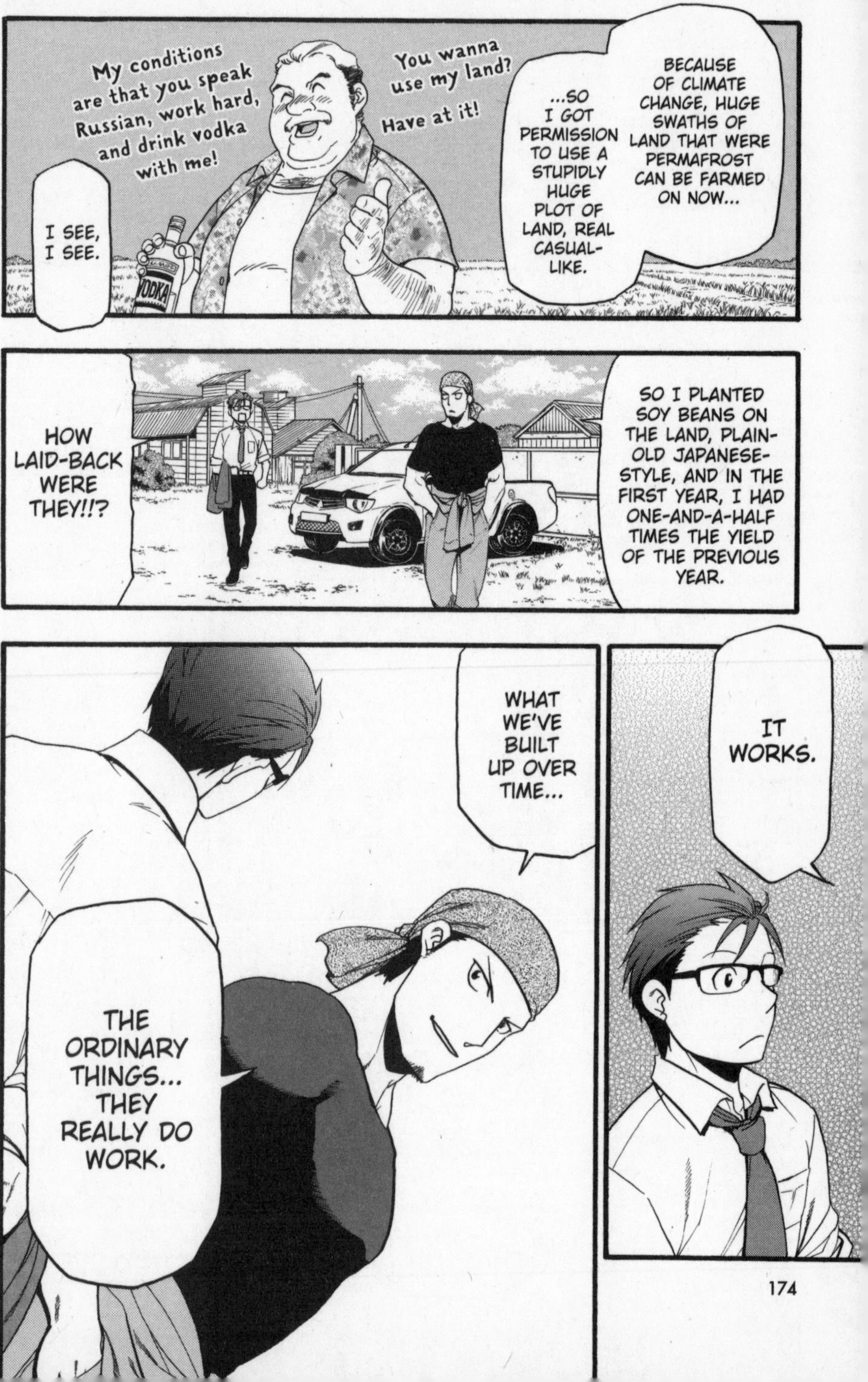
BECAUSE OF CLIMATE CHANGE, HUGE SWATHS OF LAND THAT WERE PERMAFROST CAN BE FARMED ON NOW...
...SO I GOT PERMISSION TO USE A STUPIDLY HUGE PLOT OF LAND, REAL CASUAL-LIKE.
You wanna use my land?
Have at it!
My conditions are that you speak Russian, work hard, and drink vodka with me!
VODKA
I SEE, I SEE.
SO I PLANTED SOY BEANS ON THE LAND, PLAIN-OLD JAPANESE-STYLE, AND IN THE FIRST YEAR, I HAD ONE-AND-A-HALF TIMES THE YIELD OF THE PREVIOUS YEAR.
HOW LAID-BACK WERE THEY!!?
IT WORKS.
WHAT WE'VE BUILT UP OVER TIME...
THE ORDINARY THINGS... THEY REALLY DO WORK.

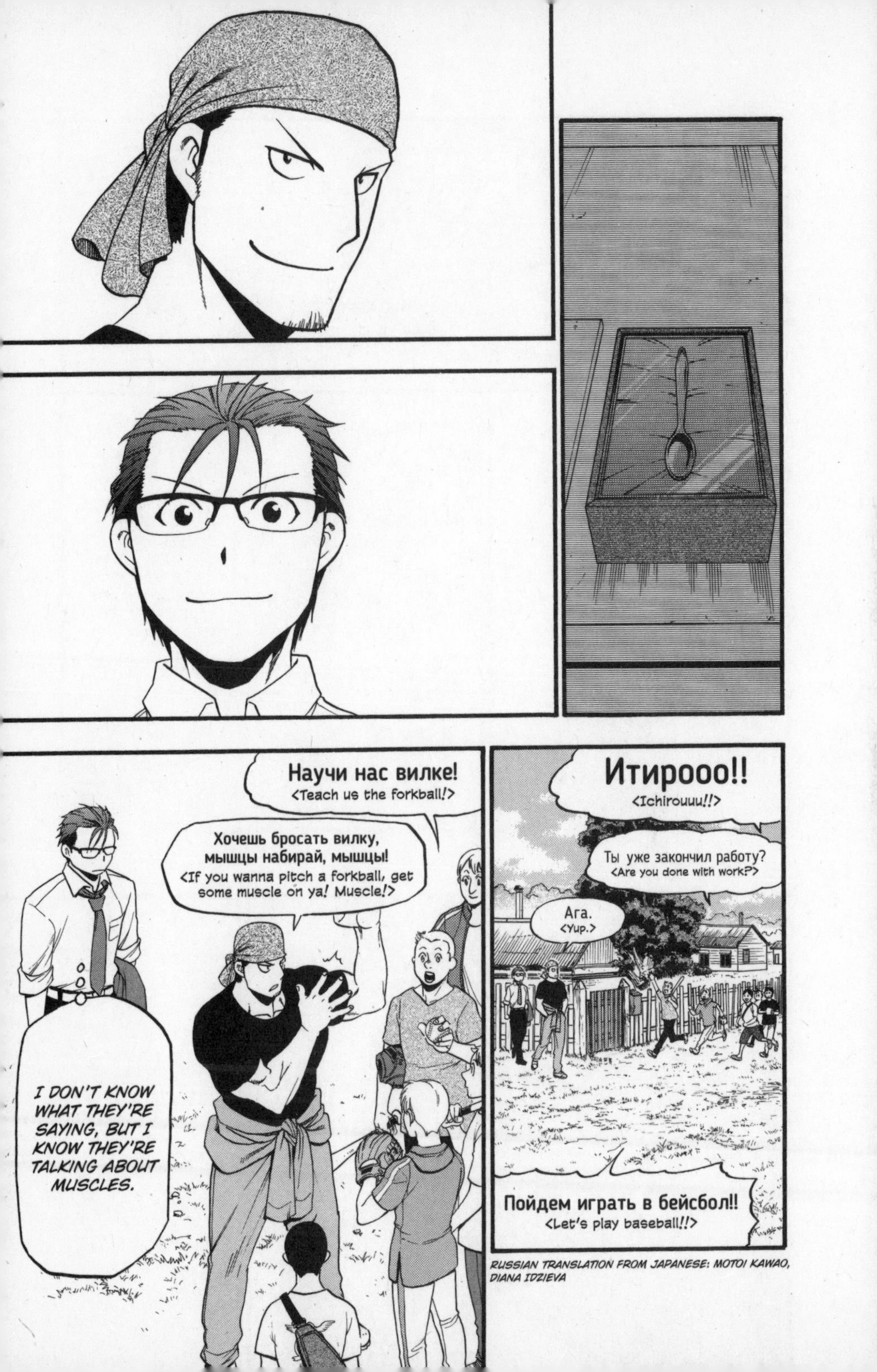
Итирооо!!
<Ichirouuu!!>
Ты уже закончил работу?
<Are you done with work?>
Ага.
<Yup.>
Пойдем играть в бейсбол!!
<Let's play baseball!!>
Научи нас вилке!
<Teach us the forkball!>
Хочешь бросать вилку, мышцы набирай, мышцы!
<If you wanna pitch a forkball, get some muscle on ya! Muscle!>
I DON'T KNOW WHAT THEY'RE SAYING, BUT I KNOW THEY'RE TALKING ABOUT MUSCLES.

*RUSSIAN TRANSLATION FROM JAPANESE: MOTOI KAWAO, DIANA IDZIEVA*

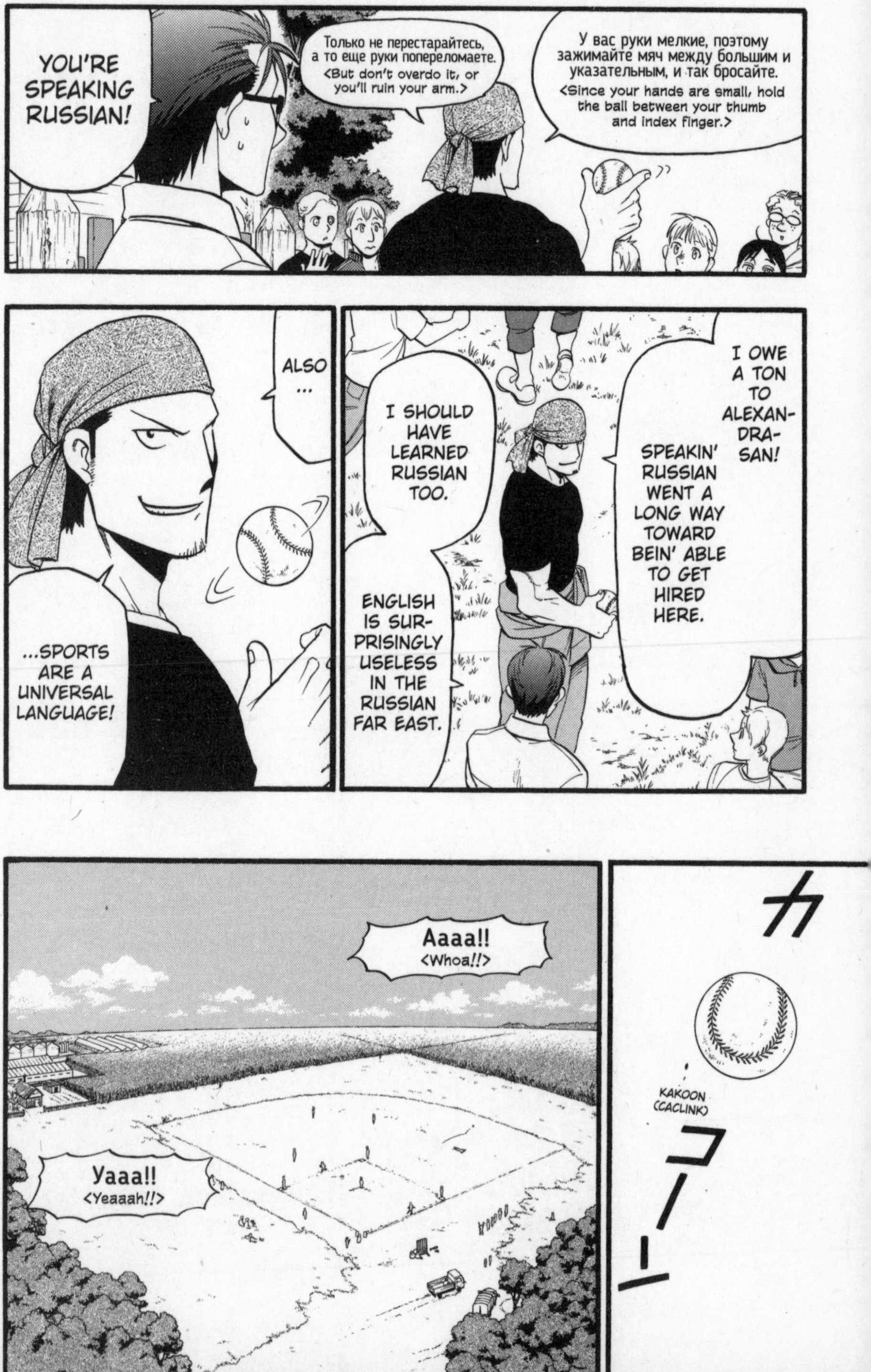
У вас руки мелкие, поэтому зажимайте мяч между большим и указательным, и так бросайте.
<Since your hands are small, hold the ball between your thumb and index finger.>
Только не перестарайтесь, а то еще руки попереломаете.
<But don't overdo it, or you'll ruin your arm.>
YOU'RE SPEAKING RUSSIAN!
I OWE A TON TO ALEXAN-DRA-SAN!
SPEAKIN' RUSSIAN WENT A LONG WAY TOWARD BEIN' ABLE TO GET HIRED HERE.
I SHOULD HAVE LEARNED RUSSIAN TOO.
ENGLISH IS SUR-PRISINGLY USELESS IN THE RUSSIAN FAR EAST.
ALSO ...
...SPORTS ARE A UNIVERSAL LANGUAGE!
KAKOON (CACLINK)
Aaaa!!
<Whoa!!>
Yaaa!!
<Yeaaah!!>

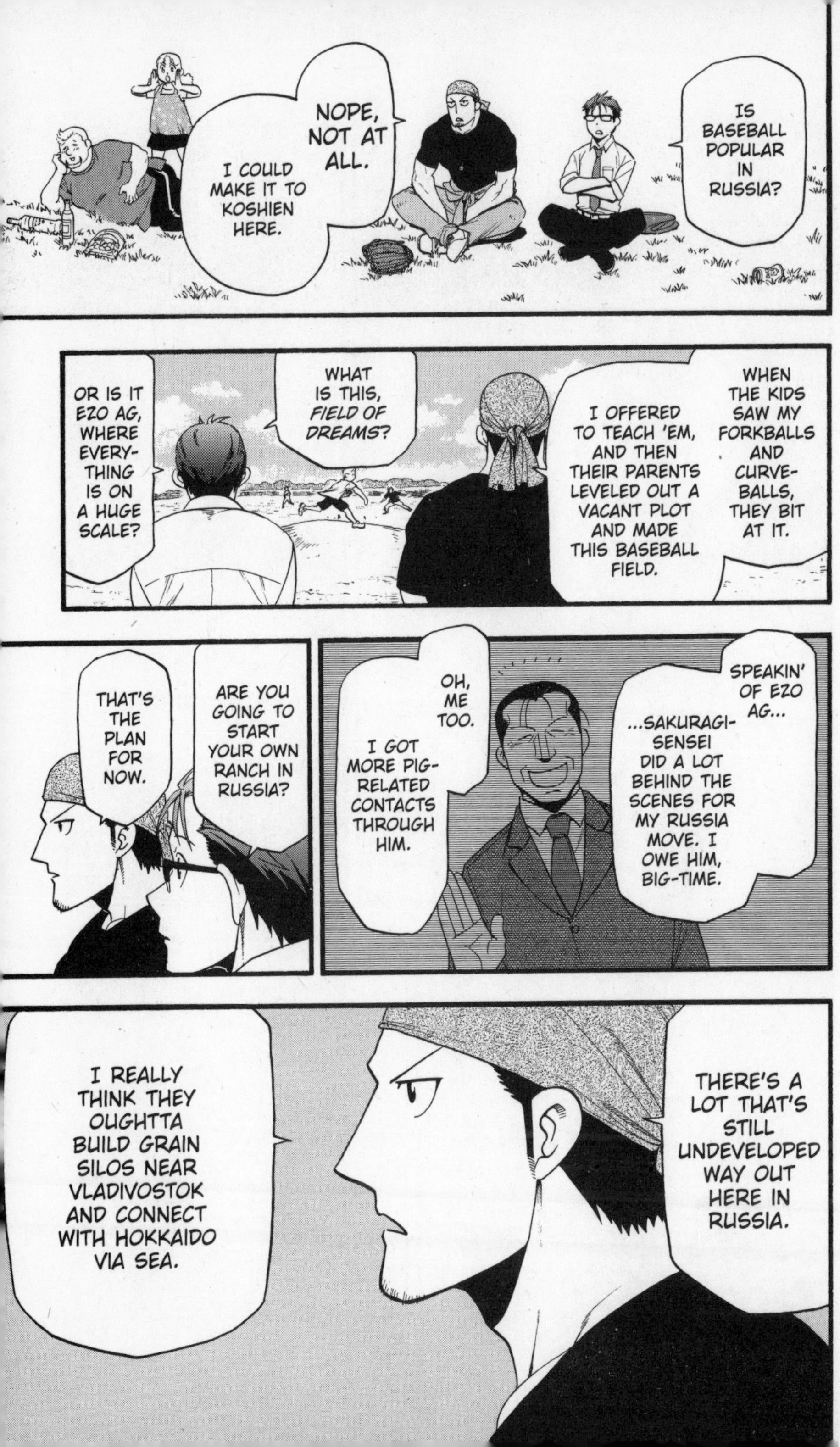
IS BASEBALL POPULAR IN RUSSIA?
NOPE, NOT AT ALL.
I COULD MAKE IT TO KOSHIEN HERE.
WHEN THE KIDS SAW MY FORKBALLS AND CURVE-BALLS, THEY BIT AT IT.
I OFFERED TO TEACH 'EM, AND THEN THEIR PARENTS LEVELED OUT A VACANT PLOT AND MADE THIS BASEBALL FIELD.
WHAT IS THIS, *FIELD OF DREAMS*?
OR IS IT EZO AG, WHERE EVERY-THING IS ON A HUGE SCALE?
SPEAKIN' OF EZO AG...
...SAKURAGI-SENSEI DID A LOT BEHIND THE SCENES FOR MY RUSSIA MOVE. I OWE HIM, BIG-TIME.
OH, ME TOO.
I GOT MORE PIG-RELATED CONTACTS THROUGH HIM.
ARE YOU GOING TO START YOUR OWN RANCH IN RUSSIA?
THAT'S THE PLAN FOR NOW.
THERE'S A LOT THAT'S STILL UNDEVELOPED WAY OUT HERE IN RUSSIA.
I REALLY THINK THEY OUGHTTA BUILD GRAIN SILOS NEAR VLADIVOSTOK AND CONNECT WITH HOKKAIDO VIA SEA.

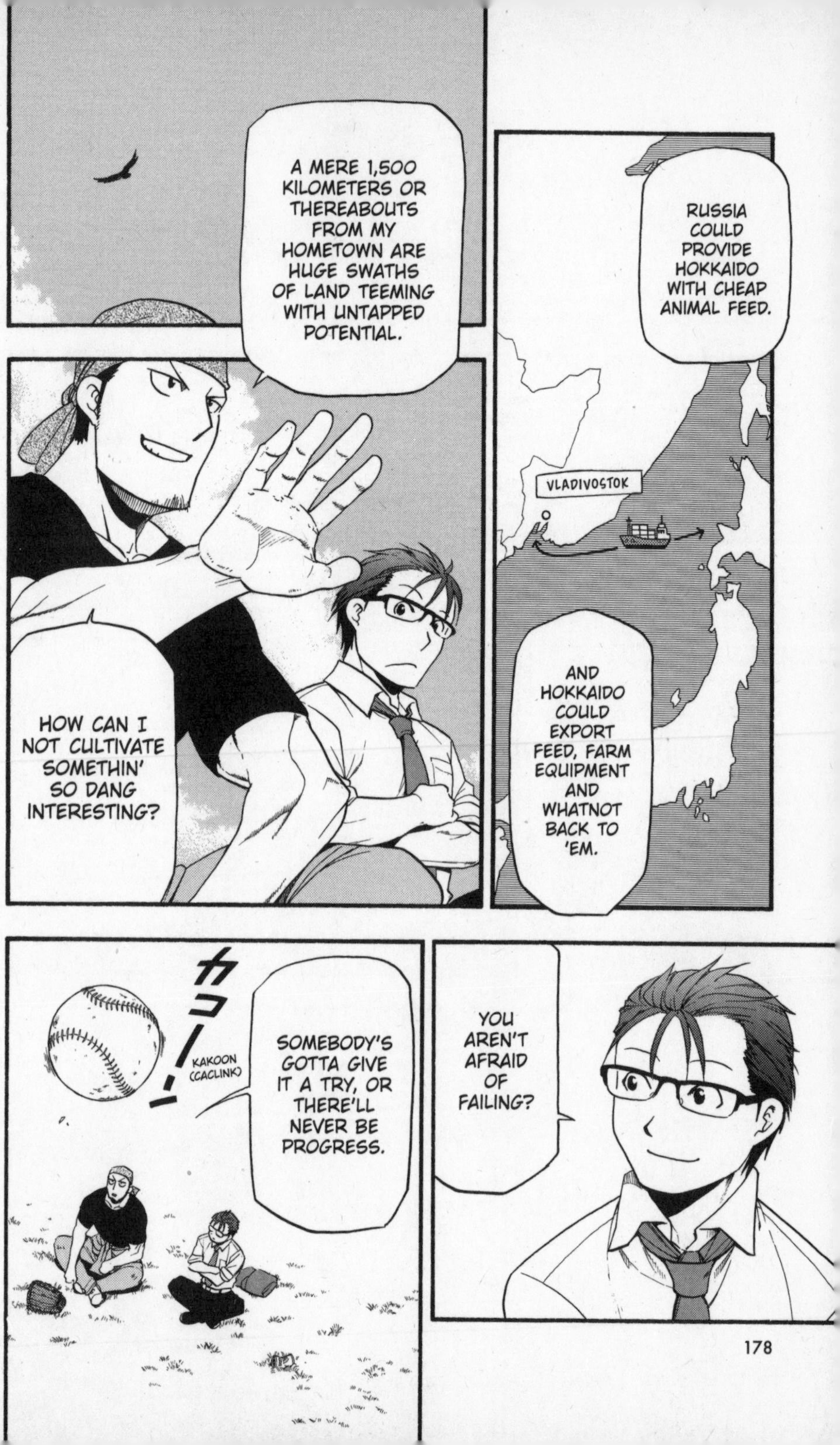
A MERE 1,500 KILOMETERS OR THEREABOUTS FROM MY HOMETOWN ARE HUGE SWATHS OF LAND TEEMING WITH UNTAPPED POTENTIAL.
RUSSIA COULD PROVIDE HOKKAIDO WITH CHEAP ANIMAL FEED.
VLADIVOSTOK
AND HOKKAIDO COULD EXPORT FEED, FARM EQUIPMENT AND WHATNOT BACK TO 'EM.
HOW CAN I NOT CULTIVATE SOMETHIN' SO DANG INTERESTING?
YOU AREN'T AFRAID OF FAILING?
カコーン
KAKOON (CACLINK)
SOMEBODY'S GOTTA GIVE IT A TRY, OR THERE'LL NEVER BE PROGRESS.

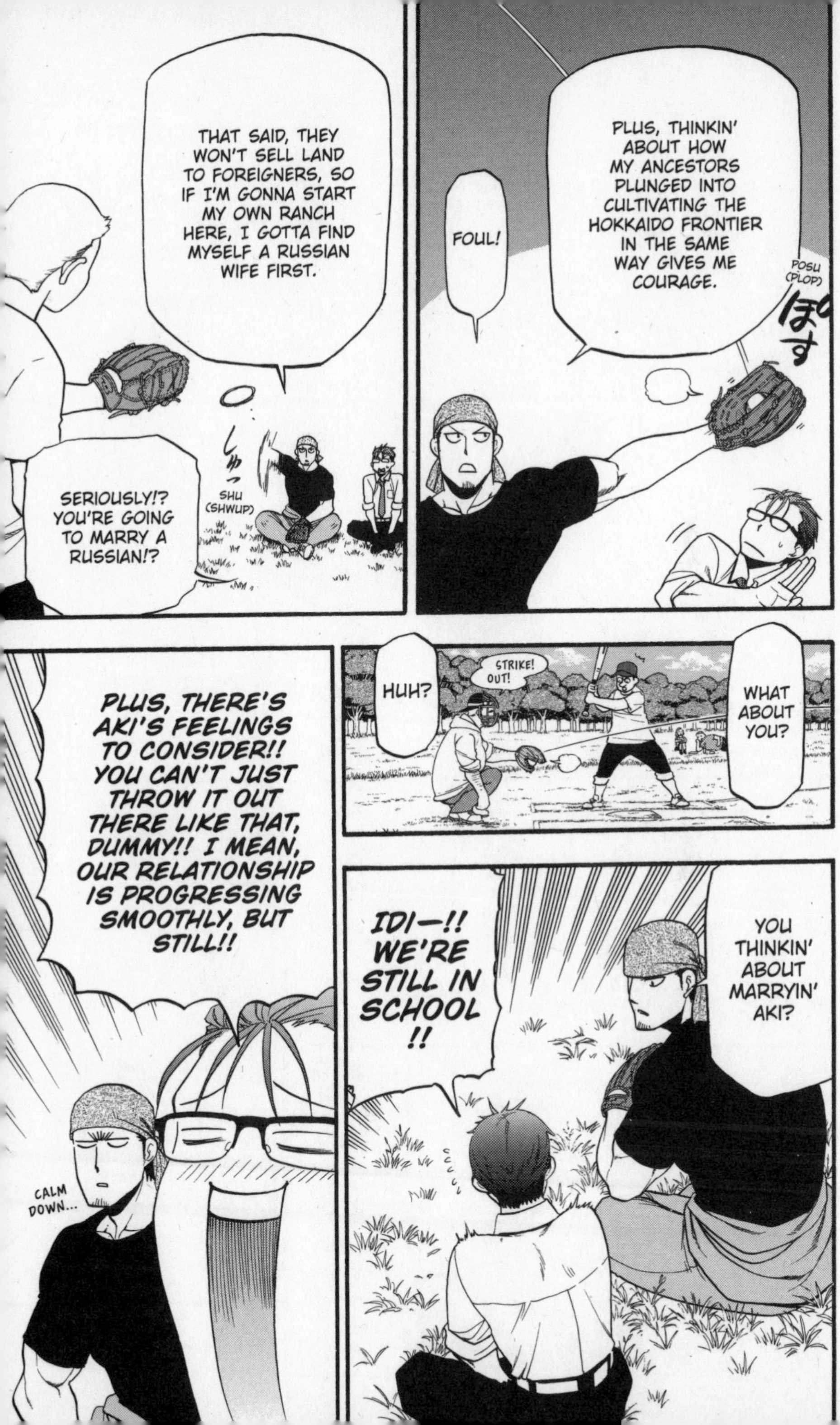
PLUS, THINKIN' ABOUT HOW MY ANCESTORS PLUNGED INTO CULTIVATING THE HOKKAIDO FRONTIER IN THE SAME WAY GIVES ME COURAGE.
POSU (PLOP)
ぽす
FOUL!
THAT SAID, THEY WON'T SELL LAND TO FOREIGNERS, SO IF I'M GONNA START MY OWN RANCH HERE, I GOTTA FIND MYSELF A RUSSIAN WIFE FIRST.
しゅっ
SHU (SHWUP)
SERIOUSLY!? YOU'RE GOING TO MARRY A RUSSIAN!?
WHAT ABOUT YOU?
STRIKE! OUT!
HUH?
YOU THINKIN' ABOUT MARRYIN' AKI?
IDI—!! WE'RE STILL IN SCHOOL !!
PLUS, THERE'S AKI'S FEELINGS TO CONSIDER!! YOU CAN'T JUST THROW IT OUT THERE LIKE THAT, DUMMY!! I MEAN, OUR RELATIONSHIP IS PROGRESSING SMOOTHLY, BUT STILL!!
CALM DOWN...

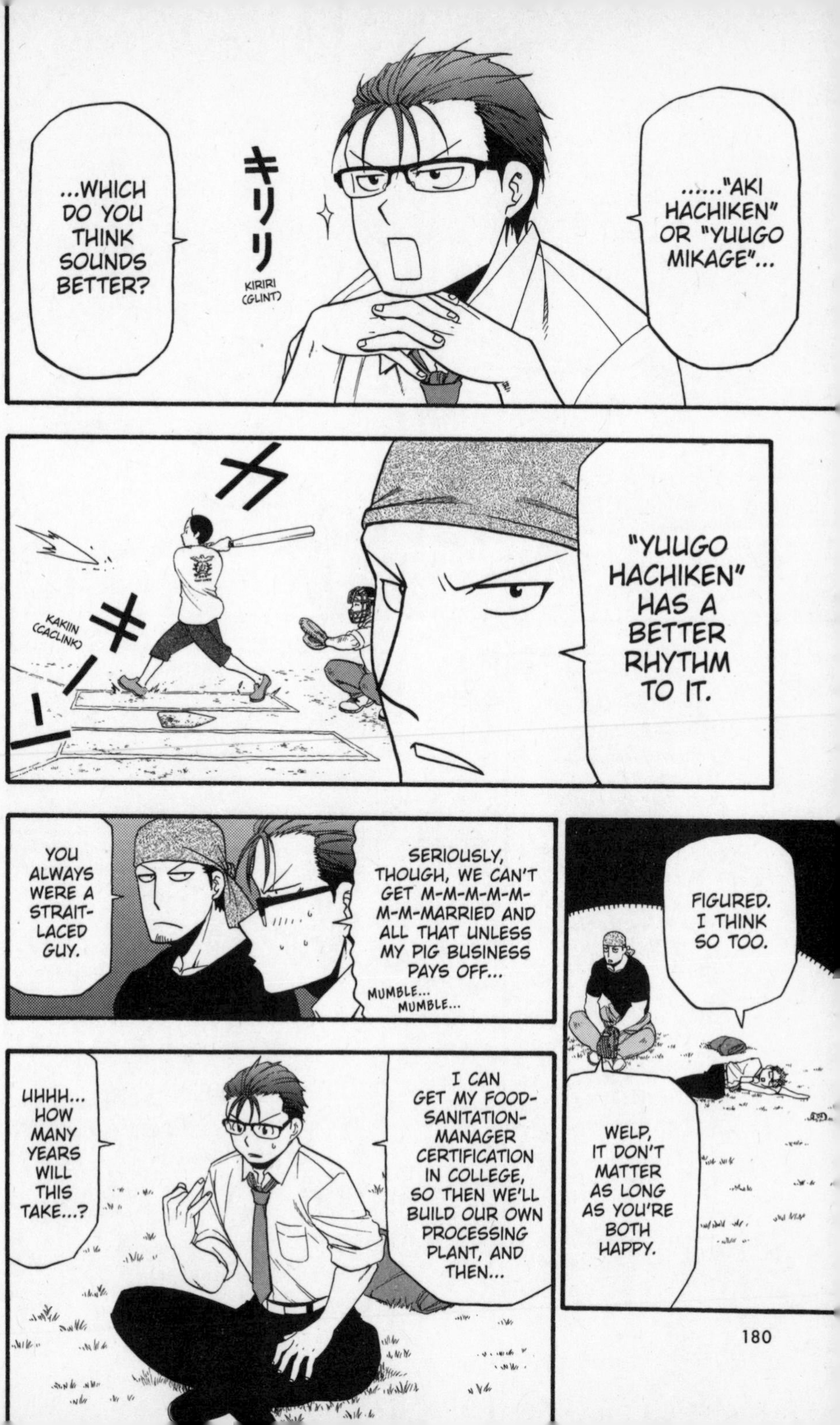
......"AKI HACHIKEN" OR "YUUGO MIKAGE"...
キリリ
KIRIRI (GLINT)
...WHICH DO YOU THINK SOUNDS BETTER?
"YUUGO HACHIKEN" HAS A BETTER RHYTHM TO IT.
カキーン
KAKIIN (CACLINK)
FIGURED. I THINK SO TOO.
WELP, IT DON'T MATTER AS LONG AS YOU'RE BOTH HAPPY.
SERIOUSLY, THOUGH, WE CAN'T GET M-M-M-M-M-M-M-MARRIED AND ALL THAT UNLESS MY PIG BUSINESS PAYS OFF...
MUMBLE... MUMBLE...
YOU ALWAYS WERE A STRAIT-LACED GUY.
I CAN GET MY FOOD-SANITATION-MANAGER CERTIFICATION IN COLLEGE, SO THEN WE'LL BUILD OUR OWN PROCESSING PLANT, AND THEN...
UHHH... HOW MANY YEARS WILL THIS TAKE...?

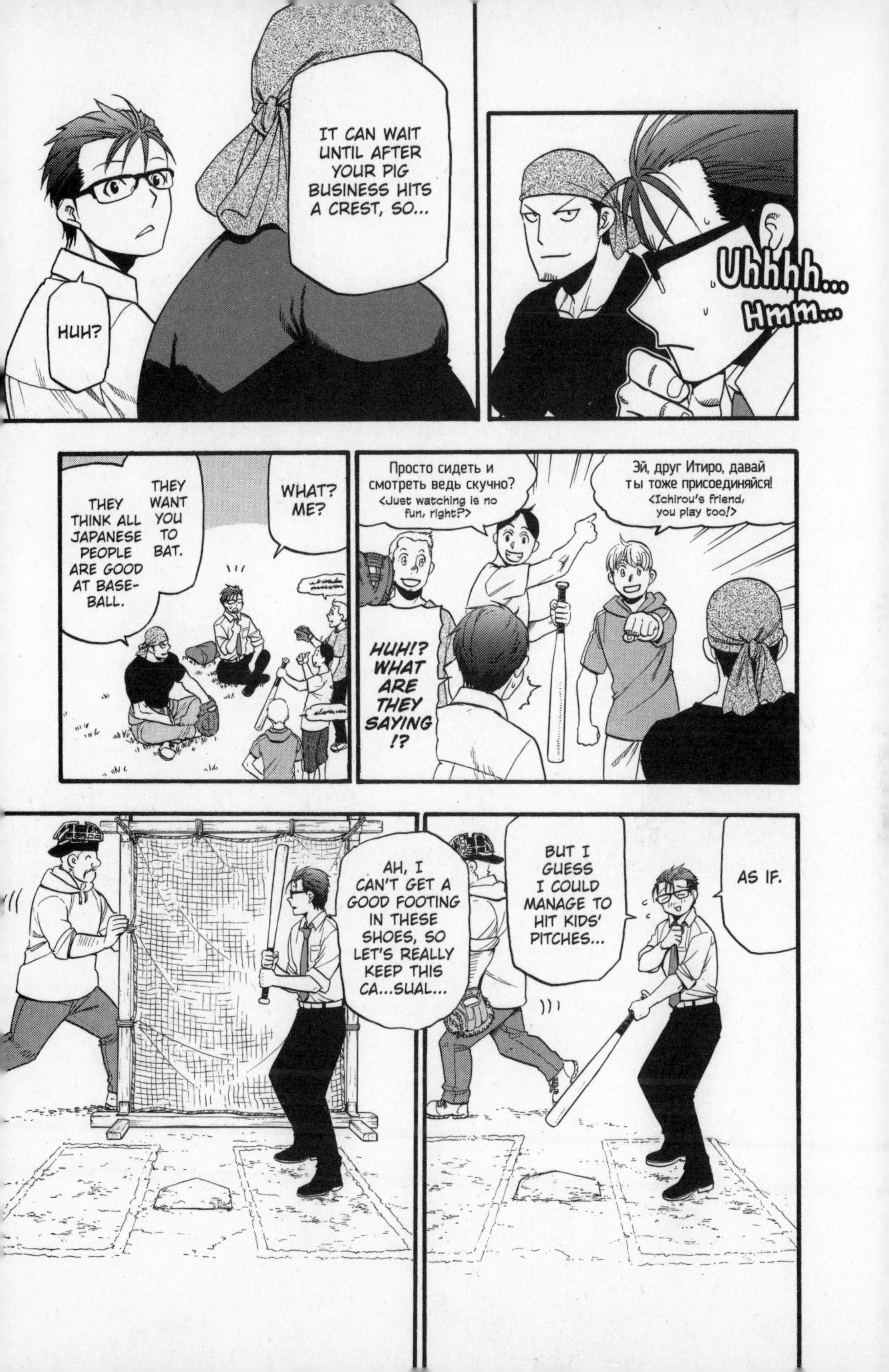
Uhhhh... Hmm...
IT CAN WAIT UNTIL AFTER YOUR PIG BUSINESS HITS A CREST, SO...
HUH?
Эй, друг Итиро, давай ты тоже присоединяйся! <Ichirou's friend, you play too!>
Просто сидеть и смотреть ведь скучно? <Just watching is no fun, right?>
HUH!? WHAT ARE THEY SAYING!?
WHAT? ME?
THEY WANT YOU TO BAT.
THEY THINK ALL JAPANESE PEOPLE ARE GOOD AT BASE-BALL.
AS IF.
BUT I GUESS I COULD MANAGE TO HIT KIDS' PITCHES...
AH, I CAN'T GET A GOOD FOOTING IN THESE SHOES, SO LET'S REALLY KEEP THIS CA...SUAL...

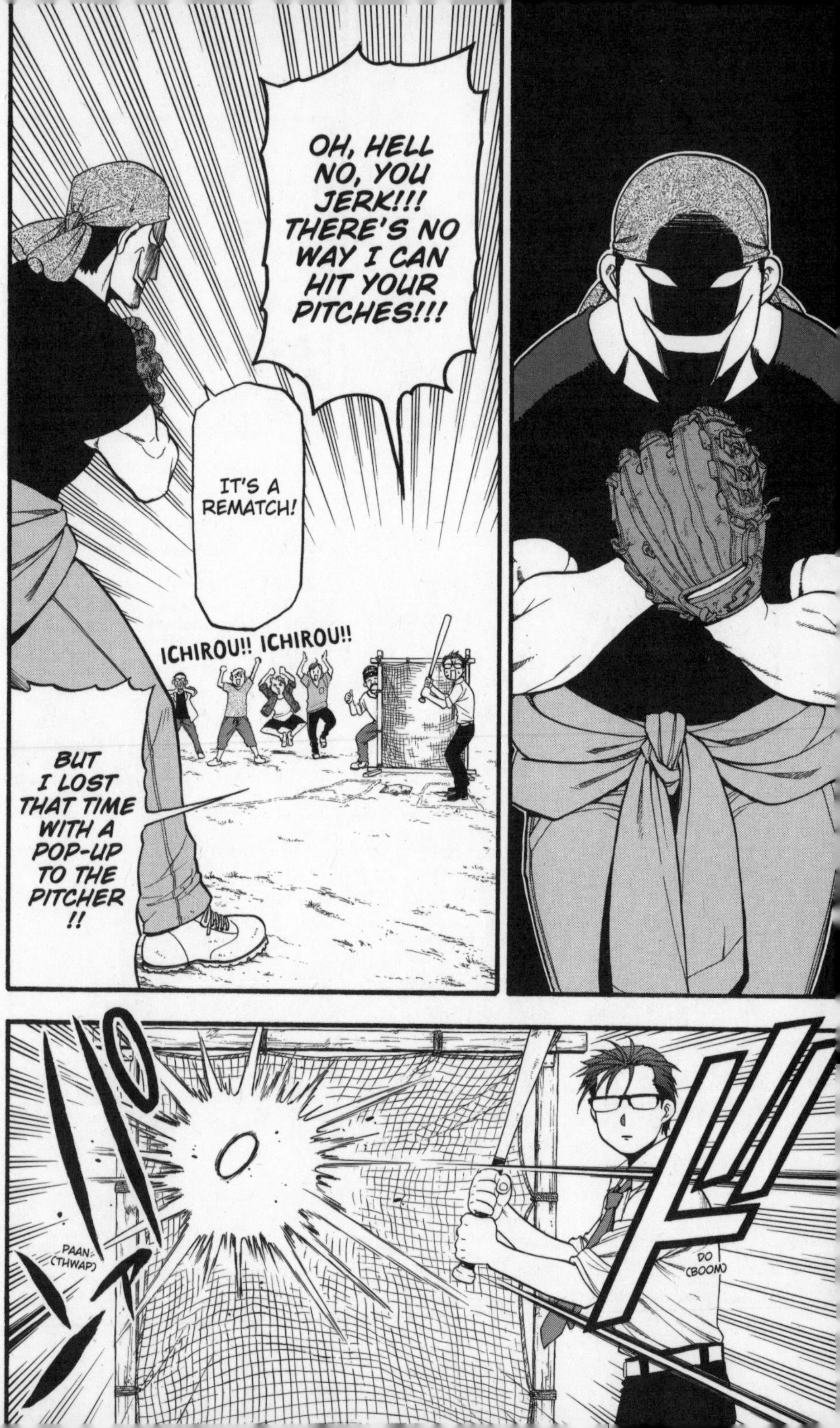
OH, HELL NO, YOU JERK!!! THERE'S NO WAY I CAN HIT YOUR PITCHES!!!
IT'S A REMATCH!
ICHIROU!! ICHIROU!!
BUT I LOST THAT TIME WITH A POP-UP TO THE PITCHER !!
DO (BOOM)
PAAN (THWAP)

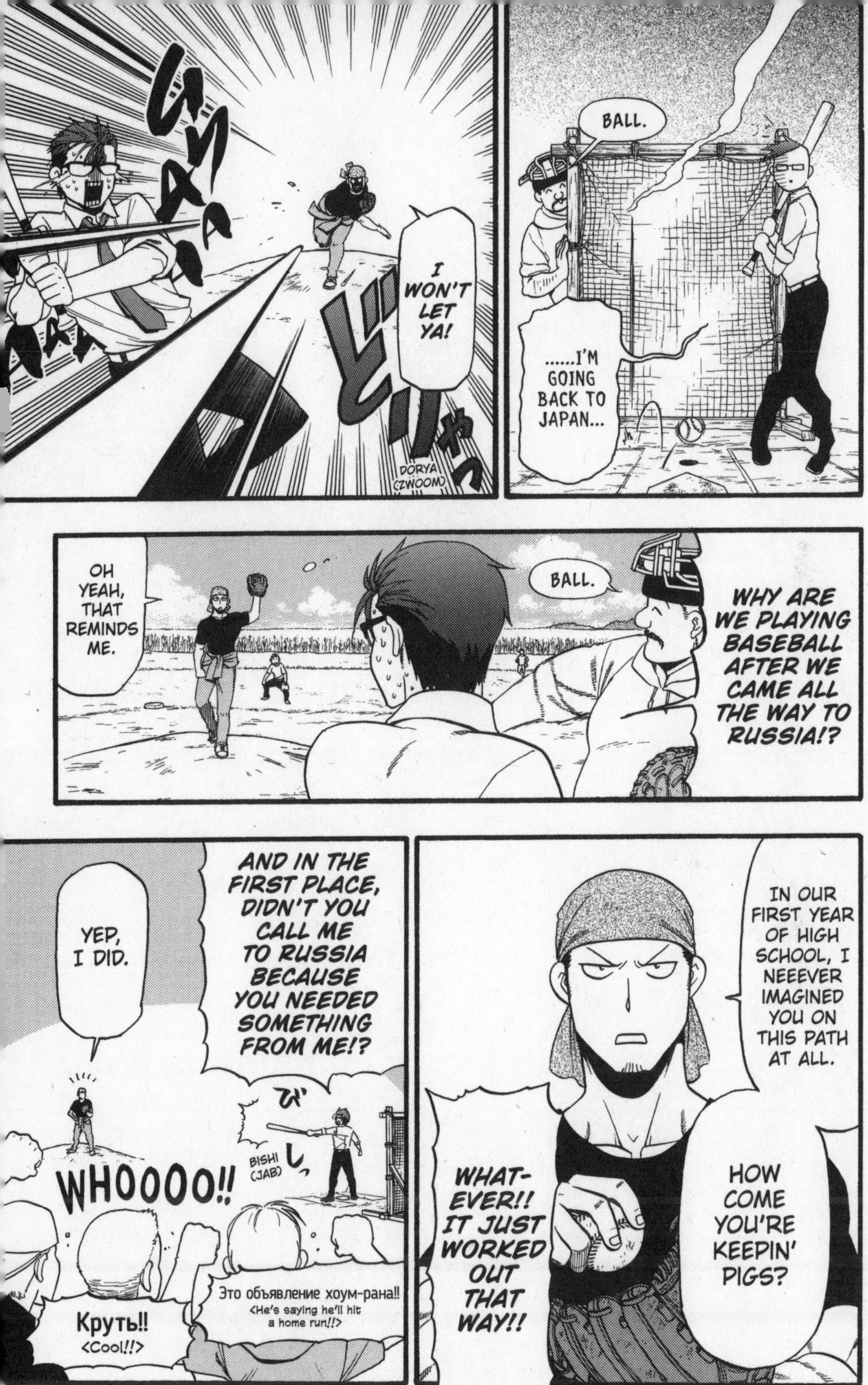
BALL.
......I'M GOING BACK TO JAPAN...
I WON'T LET YA!
DORYA (ZWOOM)
WHY ARE WE PLAYING BASEBALL AFTER WE CAME ALL THE WAY TO RUSSIA!?
BALL.
OH YEAH, THAT REMINDS ME.
IN OUR FIRST YEAR OF HIGH SCHOOL, I NEEEVER IMAGINED YOU ON THIS PATH AT ALL.
HOW COME YOU'RE KEEPIN' PIGS?
WHAT-EVER!! IT JUST WORKED OUT THAT WAY!!
AND IN THE FIRST PLACE, DIDN'T YOU CALL ME TO RUSSIA BECAUSE YOU NEEDED SOMETHING FROM ME!?
YEP, I DID.
BISHI (JAB)
WHOOOO!!
Это объявление хоум-рана!!
<He's saying he'll hit a home run!!>
Круть!!
<Cool!!>

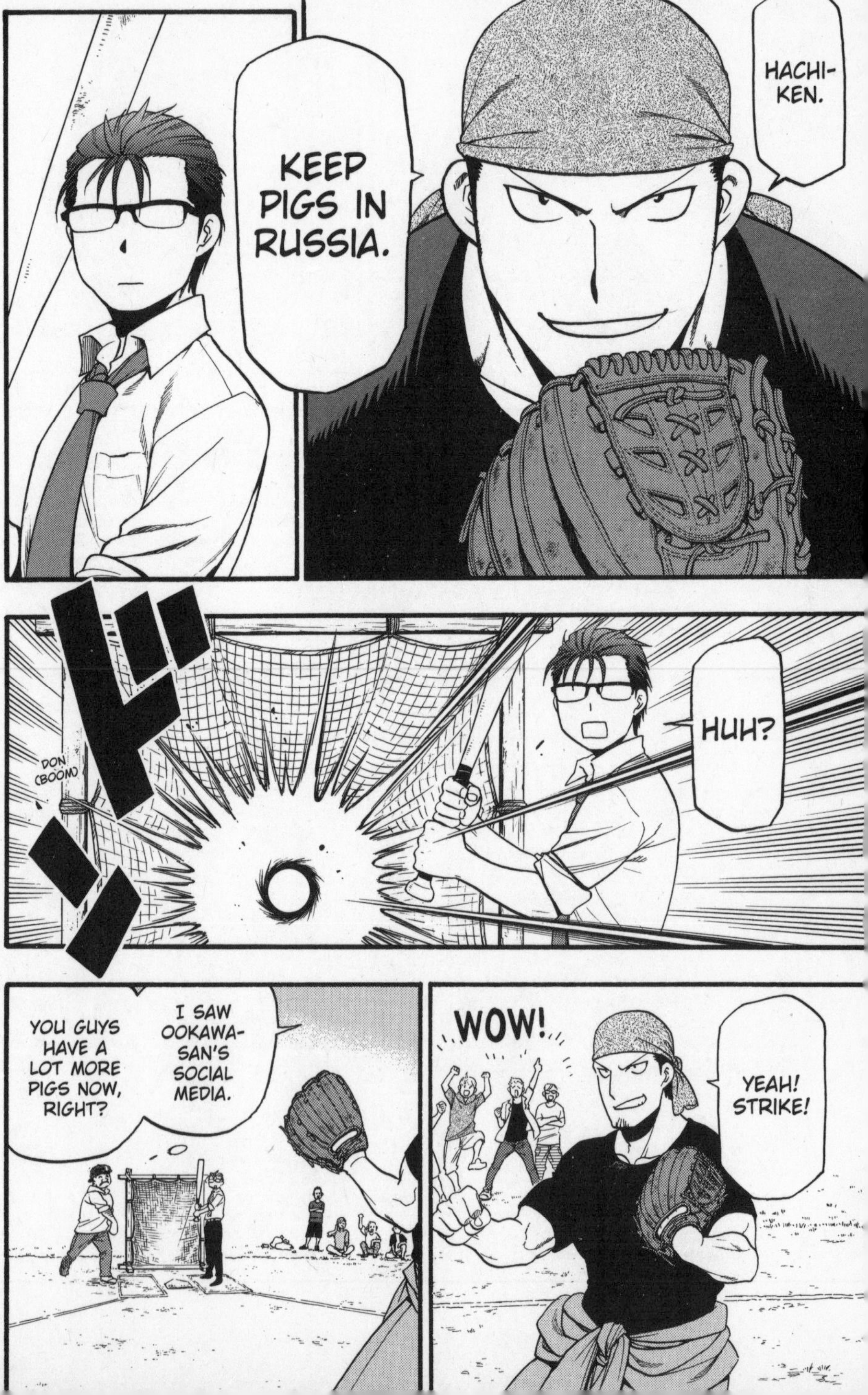
HACHI-KEN.
KEEP PIGS IN RUSSIA.
HUH?
DON (BOOM)
YEAH! STRIKE!
WOW!
I SAW OOKAWA-SAN'S SOCIAL MEDIA.
YOU GUYS HAVE A LOT MORE PIGS NOW, RIGHT?

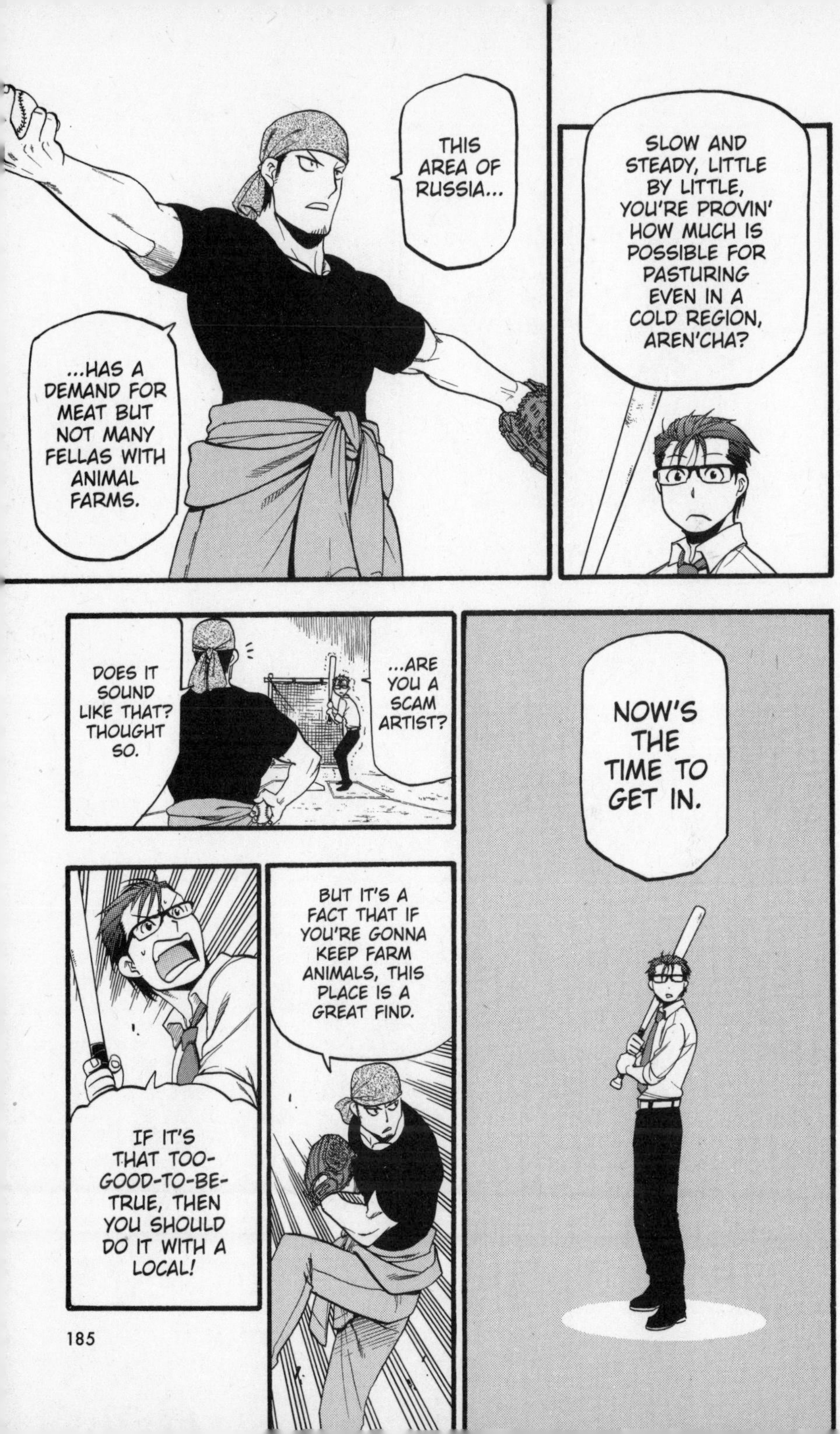
SLOW AND STEADY, LITTLE BY LITTLE, YOU'RE PROVIN' HOW MUCH IS POSSIBLE FOR PASTURING EVEN IN A COLD REGION, AREN'CHA?
THIS AREA OF RUSSIA...
...HAS A DEMAND FOR MEAT BUT NOT MANY FELLAS WITH ANIMAL FARMS.
NOW'S THE TIME TO GET IN.
...ARE YOU A SCAM ARTIST?
DOES IT SOUND LIKE THAT? THOUGHT SO.
BUT IT'S A FACT THAT IF YOU'RE GONNA KEEP FARM ANIMALS, THIS PLACE IS A GREAT FIND.
IF IT'S THAT TOO-GOOD-TO-BE-TRUE, THEN YOU SHOULD DO IT WITH A LOCAL!

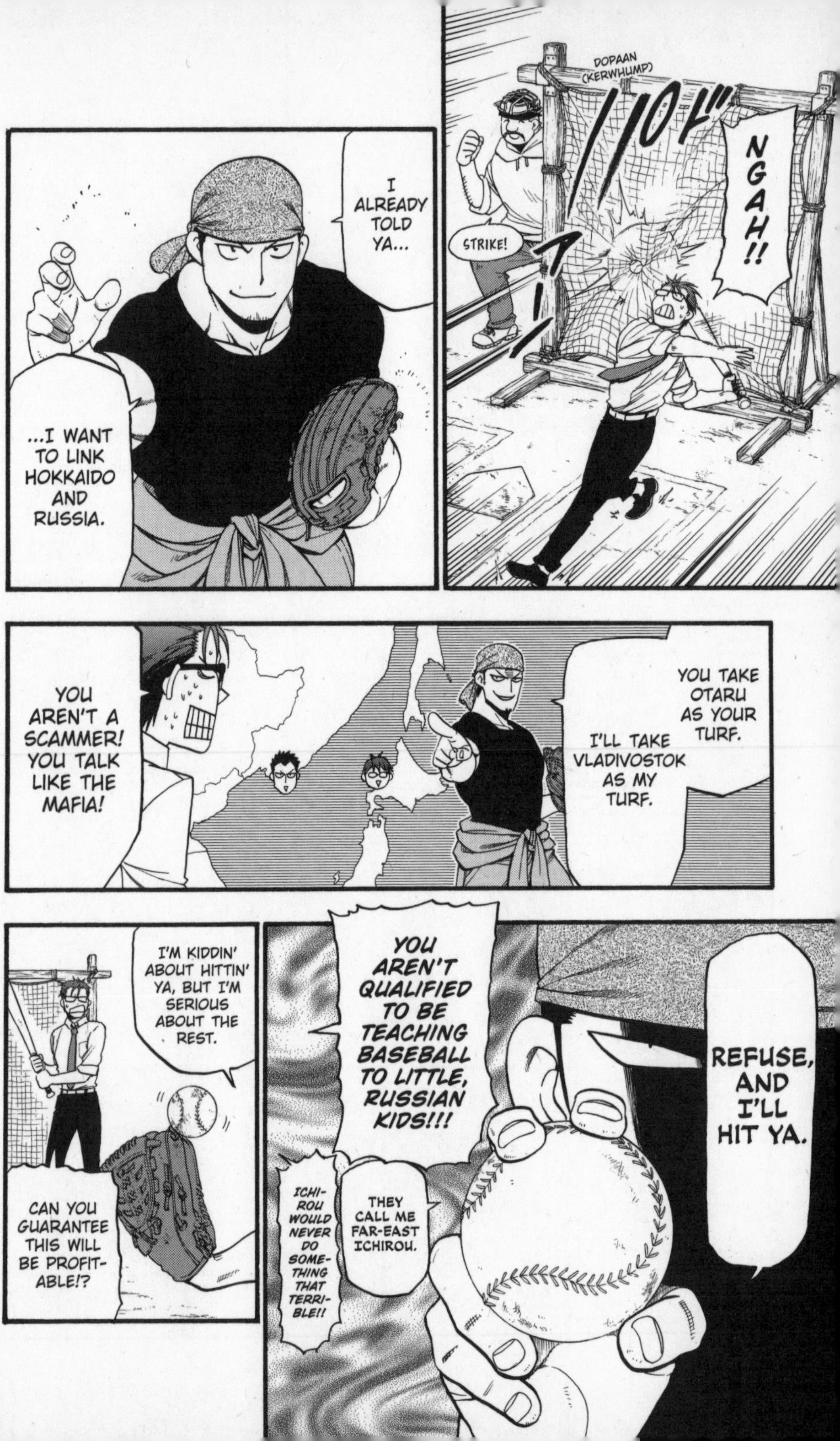
DOPAAN (KERWHUMP)
NGAH!!
STRIKE!
I ALREADY TOLD YA...
...I WANT TO LINK HOKKAIDO AND RUSSIA.
YOU TAKE OTARU AS YOUR TURF.
I'LL TAKE VLADIVOSTOK AS MY TURF.
YOU AREN'T A SCAMMER! YOU TALK LIKE THE MAFIA!
REFUSE, AND I'LL HIT YA.
YOU AREN'T QUALIFIED TO BE TEACHING BASEBALL TO LITTLE, RUSSIAN KIDS!!!
THEY CALL ME FAR-EAST ICHIROU.
ICHIROU WOULD NEVER DO SOMETHING THAT TERRIBLE!!
I'M KIDDIN' ABOUT HITTIN' YA, BUT I'M SERIOUS ABOUT THE REST.
CAN YOU GUARANTEE THIS WILL BE PROFITABLE!?

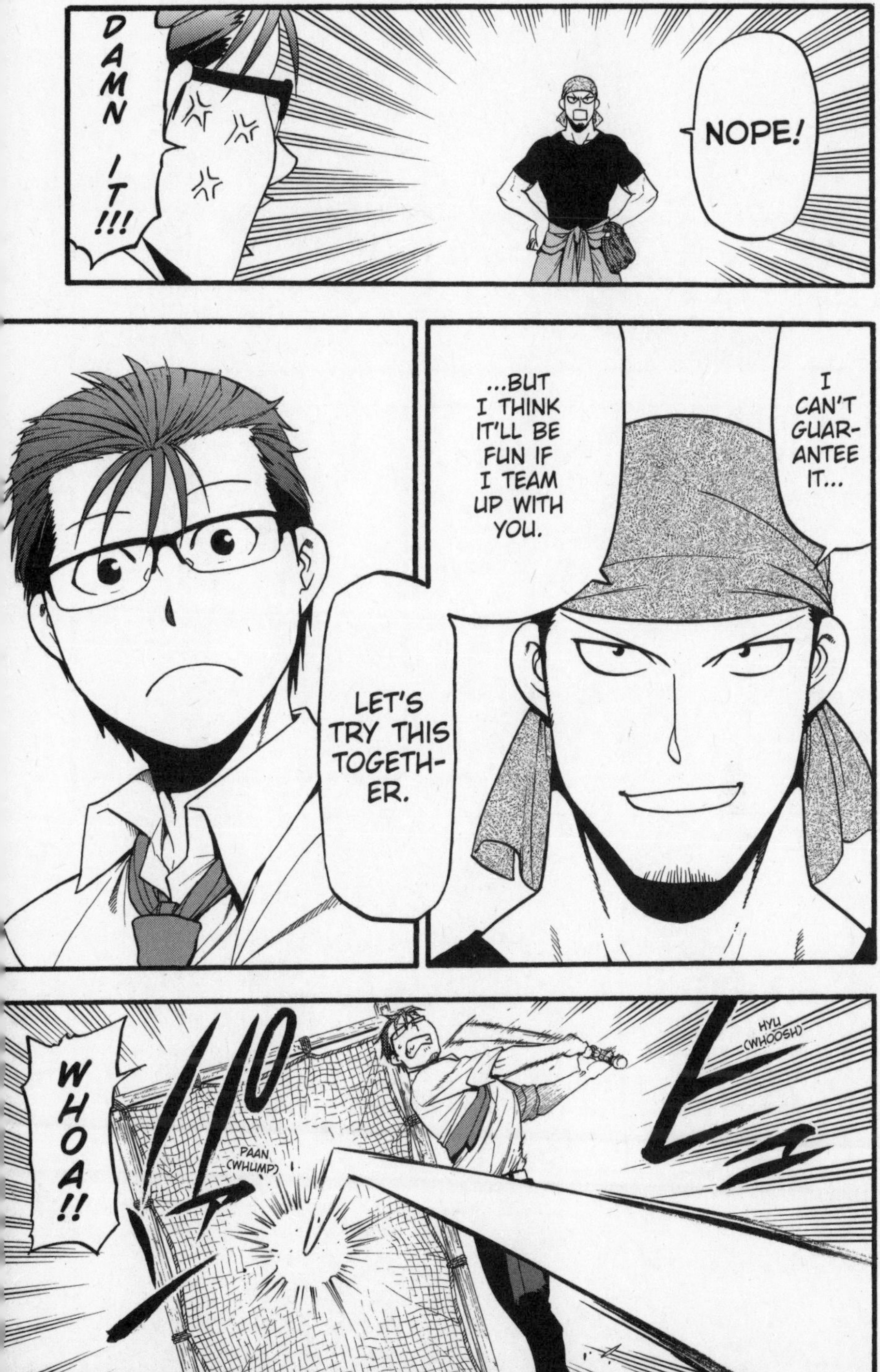
NOPE!
DAMN IT!!!
I CAN'T GUARANTEE IT...
...BUT I THINK IT'LL BE FUN IF I TEAM UP WITH YOU.
LET'S TRY THIS TOGETHER.
HYU (WHOOSH)
PAAN (WHUMP)
WHOA!!

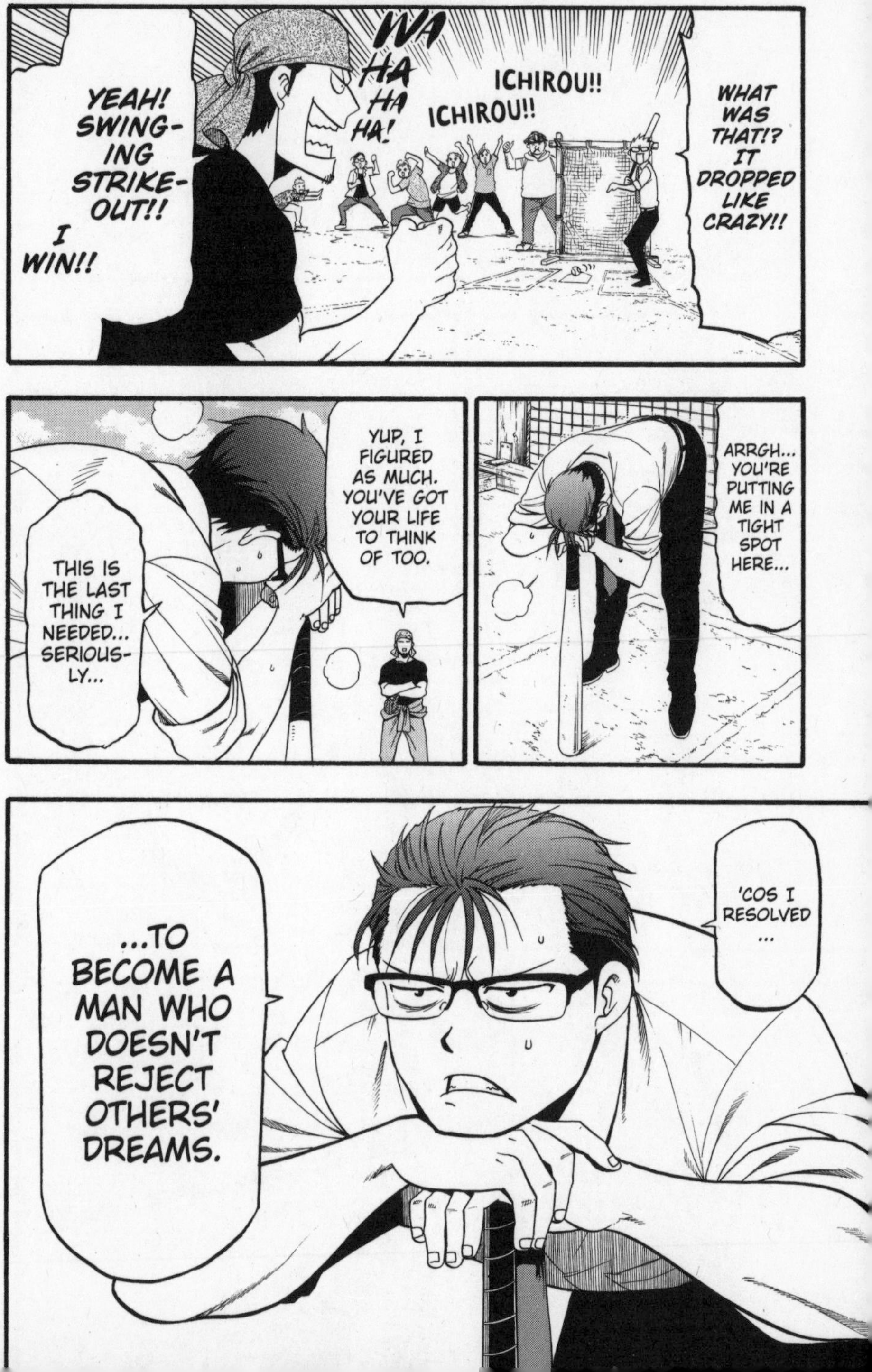
WHAT WAS THAT!? IT DROPPED LIKE CRAZY!!
ICHIROU!!
ICHIROU!!
WA HA HA HA!
YEAH! SWING-ING STRIKE-OUT!!
I WIN!!
ARRGH... YOU'RE PUTTING ME IN A TIGHT SPOT HERE...
YUP, I FIGURED AS MUCH. YOU'VE GOT YOUR LIFE TO THINK OF TOO.
THIS IS THE LAST THING I NEEDED... SERIOUS-LY...
'COS I RESOLVED ...
...TO BECOME A MAN WHO DOESN'T REJECT OTHERS' DREAMS.

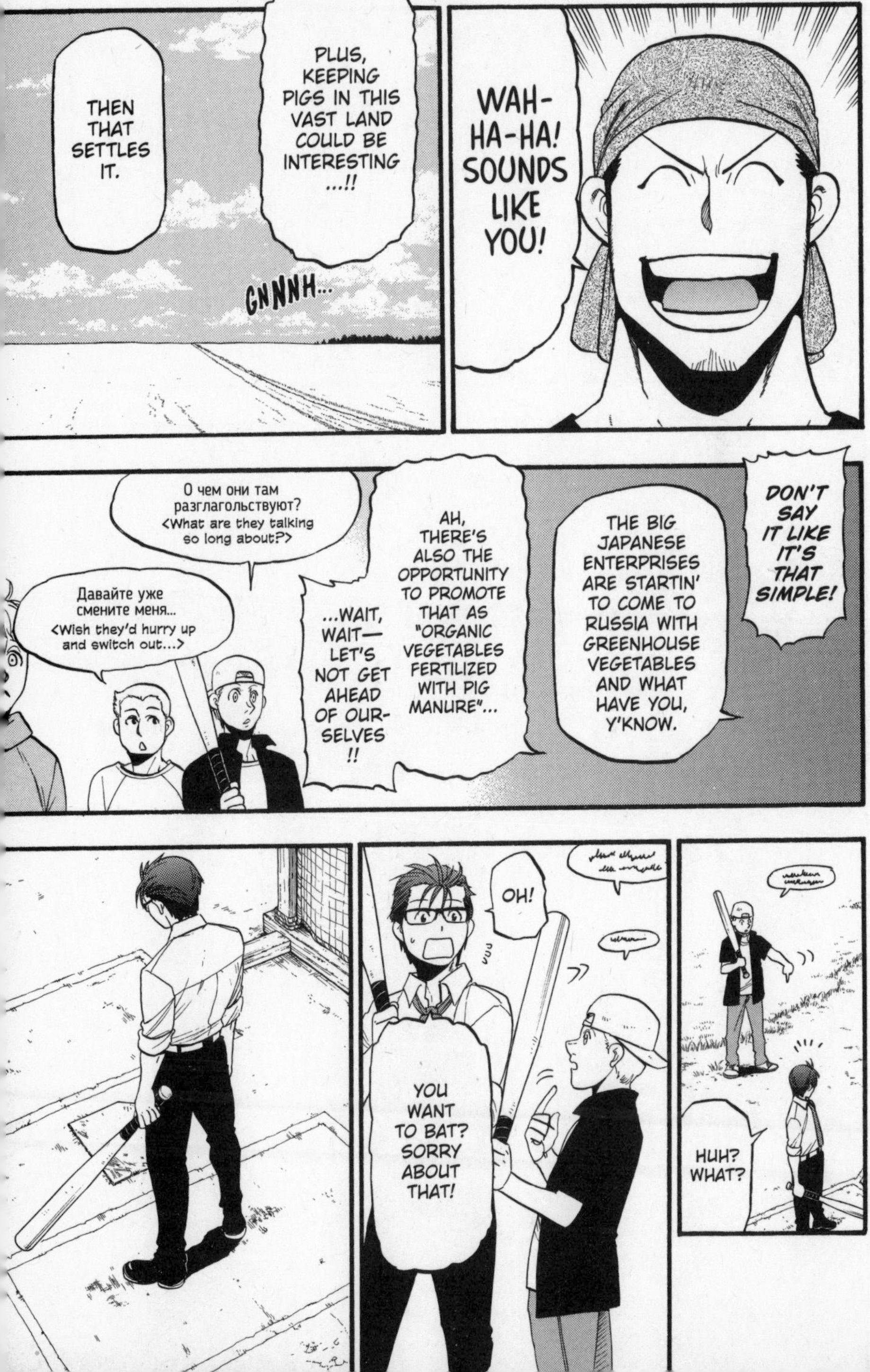
WAH-HA-HA! SOUNDS LIKE YOU!
PLUS, KEEPING PIGS IN THIS VAST LAND COULD BE INTERESTING ...!!
THEN THAT SETTLES IT.
GNNNH...
DON'T SAY IT LIKE IT'S THAT SIMPLE!
THE BIG JAPANESE ENTERPRISES ARE STARTIN' TO COME TO RUSSIA WITH GREENHOUSE VEGETABLES AND WHAT HAVE YOU, Y'KNOW.
AH, THERE'S ALSO THE OPPORTUNITY TO PROMOTE THAT AS "ORGANIC VEGETABLES FERTILIZED WITH PIG MANURE"...
...WAIT, WAIT— LET'S NOT GET AHEAD OF OUR-SELVES !!
О чем они там разглагольствуют? <What are they talking so long about?>
Давайте уже смените меня... <Wish they'd hurry up and switch out...>
HUH? WHAT?
OH!
YOU WANT TO BAT? SORRY ABOUT THAT!

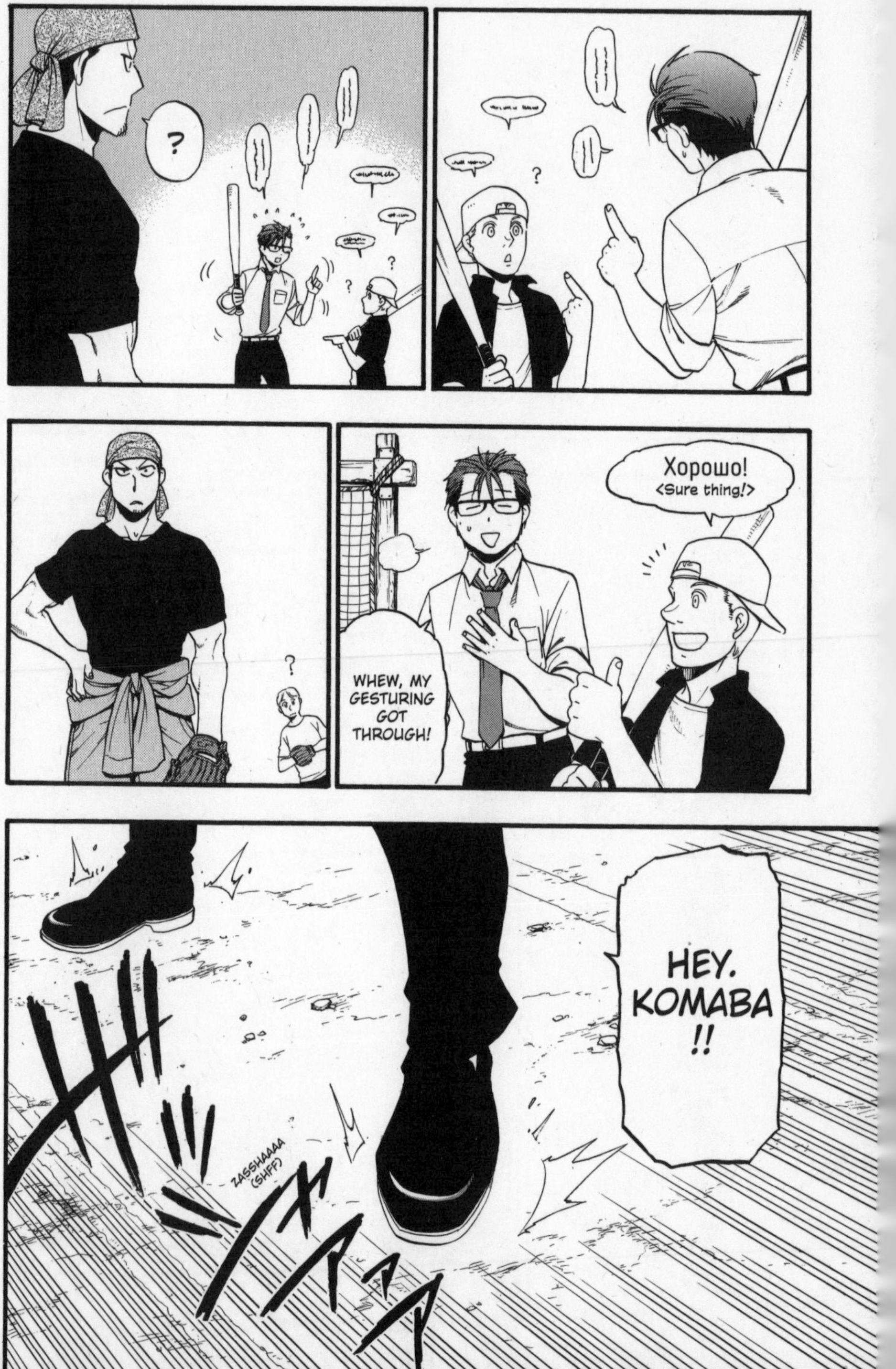
?
?
Хорошо!
<Sure thing!>
WHEW, MY GESTURING GOT THROUGH!
?
HEY. KOMABA!!
ZASSHAAAA (SHFF)

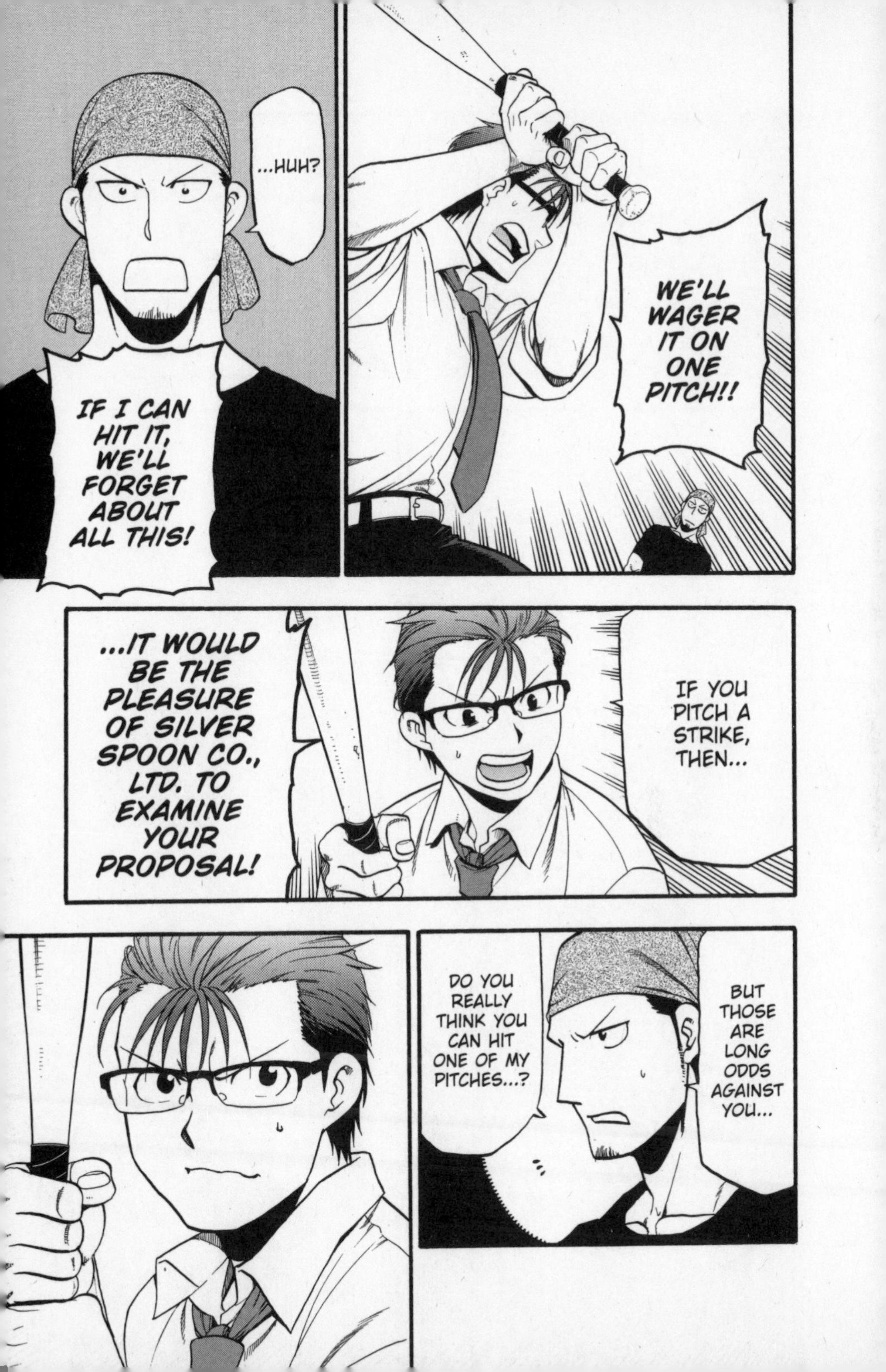
WE'LL WAGER IT ON ONE PITCH!!
...HUH?
IF I CAN HIT IT, WE'LL FORGET ABOUT ALL THIS!
IF YOU PITCH A STRIKE, THEN...
...IT WOULD BE THE PLEASURE OF SILVER SPOON CO., LTD. TO EXAMINE YOUR PROPOSAL!
BUT THOSE ARE LONG ODDS AGAINST YOU...
DO YOU REALLY THINK YOU CAN HIT ONE OF MY PITCHES...?

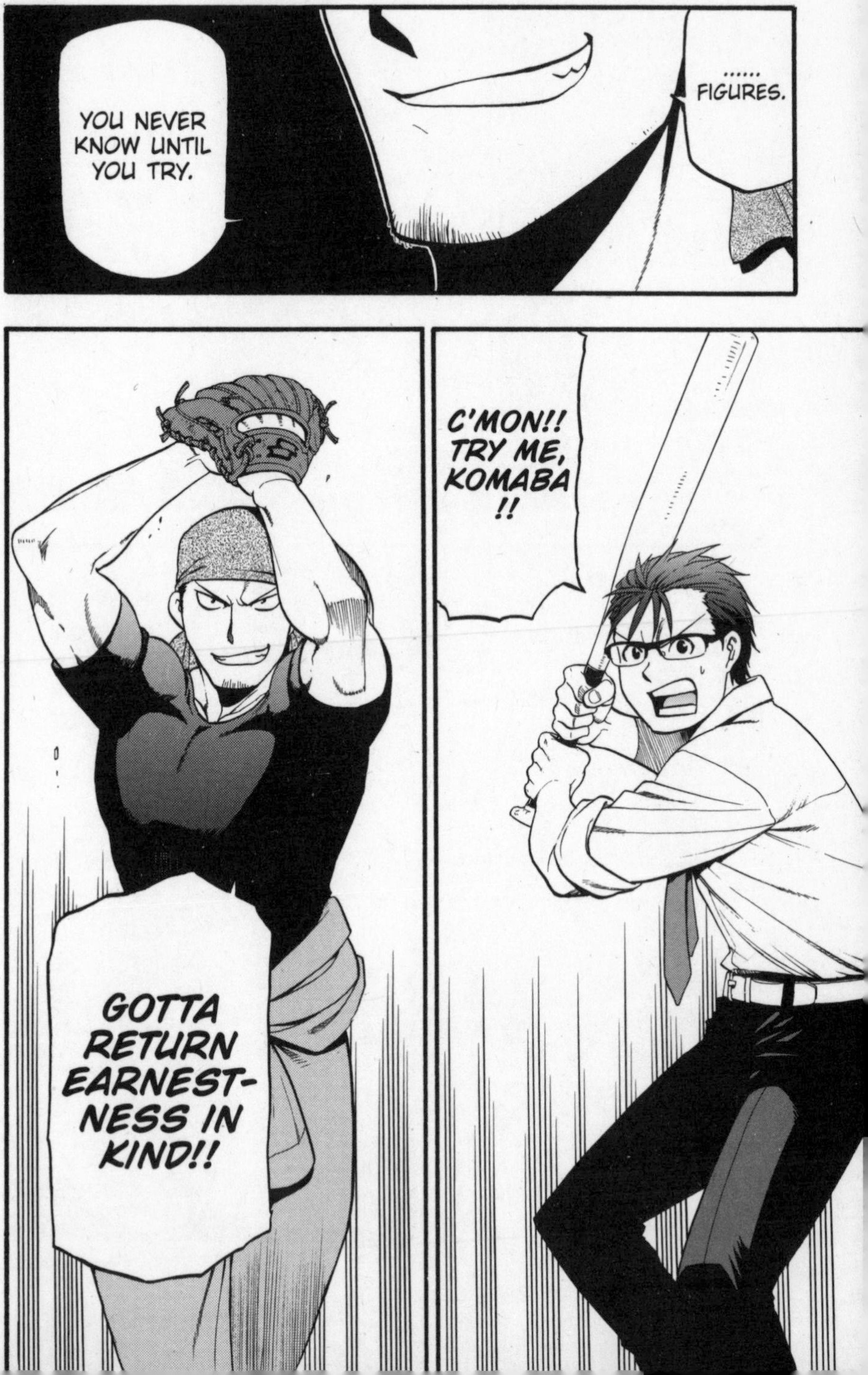
...... FIGURES.
YOU NEVER KNOW UNTIL YOU TRY.
C'MON!! TRY ME, KOMABA!!
GOTTA RETURN EARNESTNESS IN KIND!!

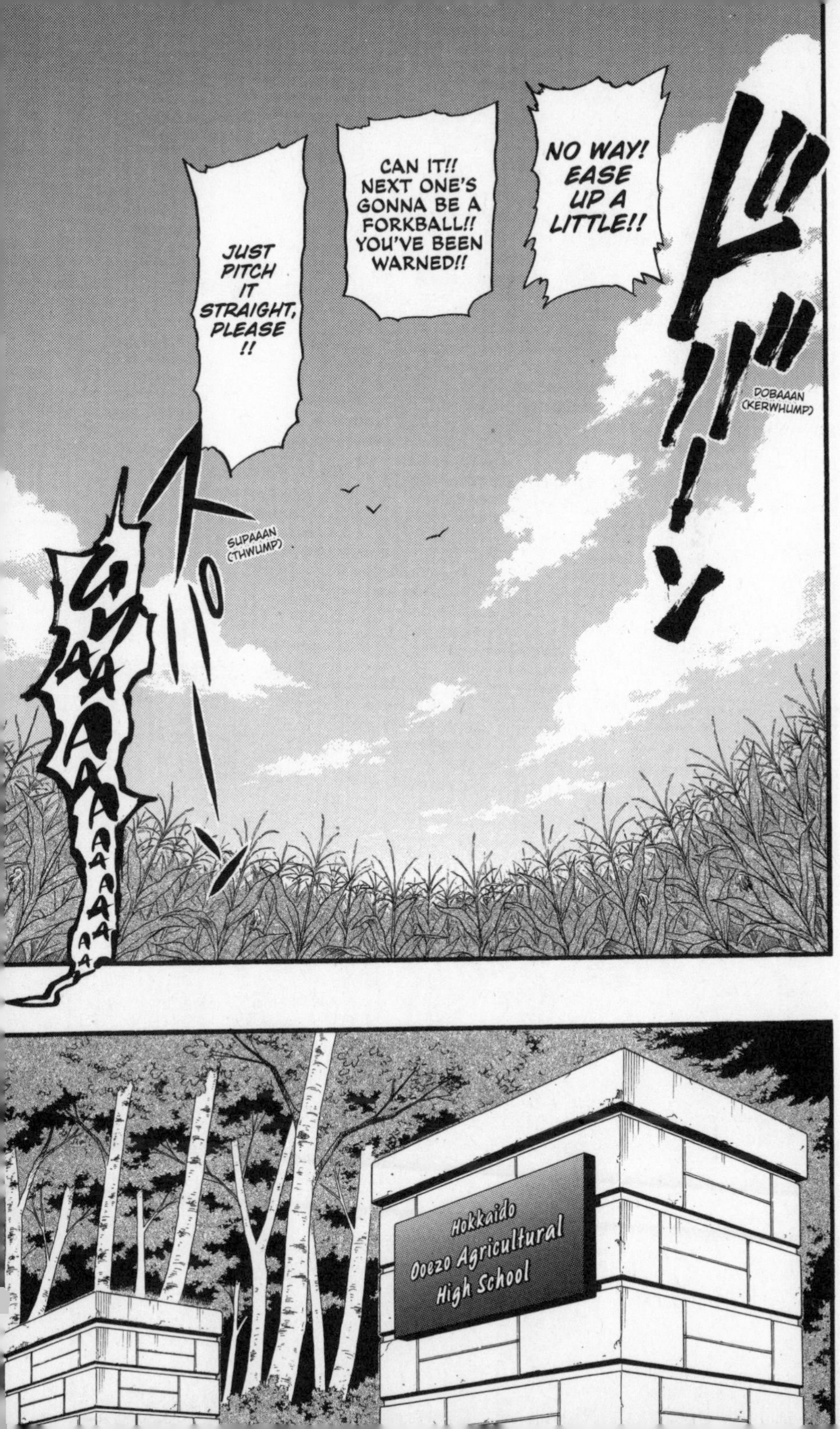
NO WAY! EASE UP A LITTLE!!
CAN IT!! NEXT ONE'S GONNA BE A FORKBALL!! YOU'VE BEEN WARNED!!
JUST PITCH IT STRAIGHT, PLEASE!!
DOBAAAN (KERWHUMP)
SUPAAAN (THWUMP)
Hokkaido Ooezo Agricultural High School

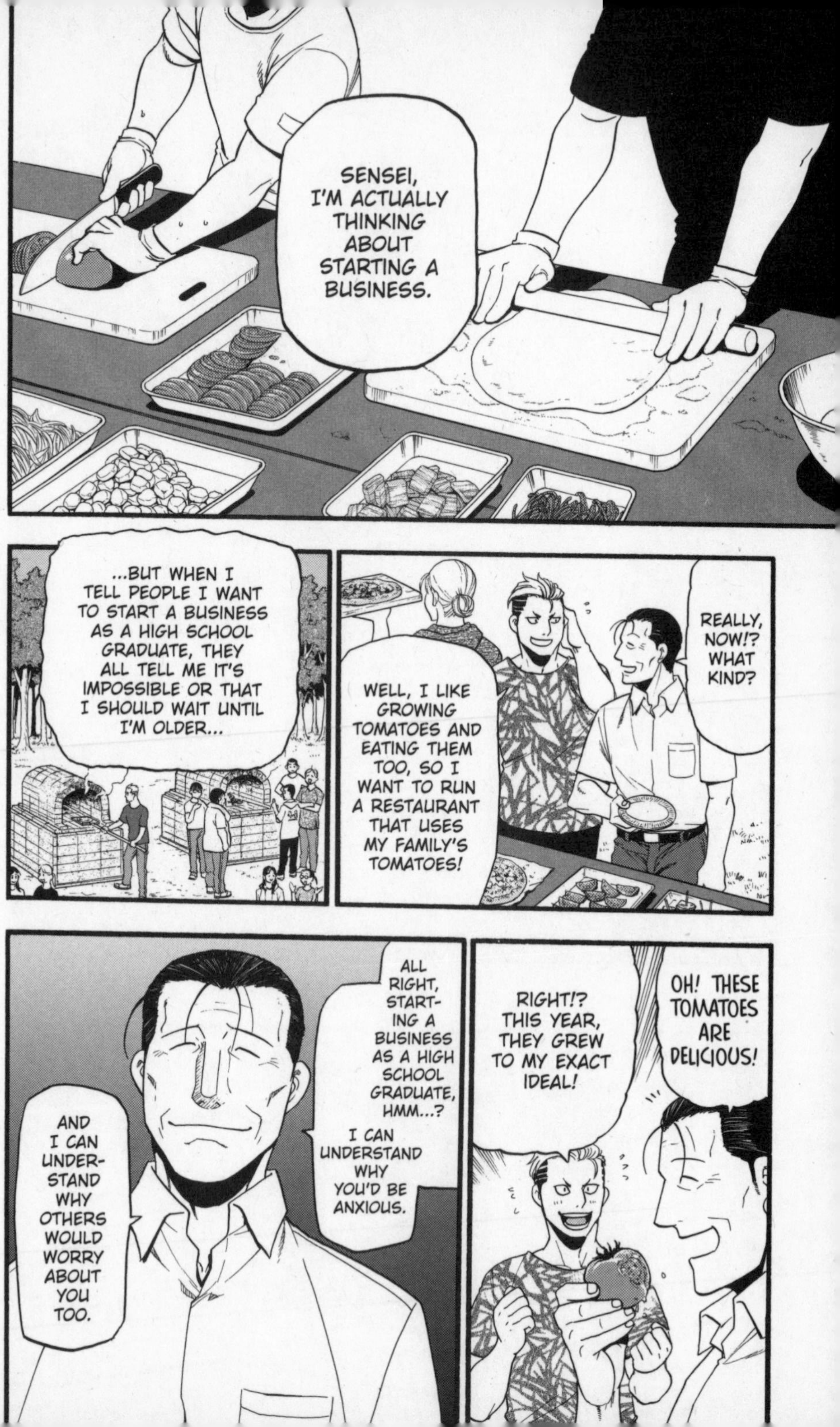
SENSEI, I'M ACTUALLY THINKING ABOUT STARTING A BUSINESS.
REALLY, NOW!? WHAT KIND?
WELL, I LIKE GROWING TOMATOES AND EATING THEM TOO, SO I WANT TO RUN A RESTAURANT THAT USES MY FAMILY'S TOMATOES!
...BUT WHEN I TELL PEOPLE I WANT TO START A BUSINESS AS A HIGH SCHOOL GRADUATE, THEY ALL TELL ME IT'S IMPOSSIBLE OR THAT I SHOULD WAIT UNTIL I'M OLDER...
OH! THESE TOMATOES ARE DELICIOUS!
RIGHT!? THIS YEAR, THEY GREW TO MY EXACT IDEAL!
ALL RIGHT, STARTING A BUSINESS AS A HIGH SCHOOL GRADUATE, HMM...?
I CAN UNDERSTAND WHY YOU'D BE ANXIOUS.
AND I CAN UNDERSTAND WHY OTHERS WOULD WORRY ABOUT YOU TOO.

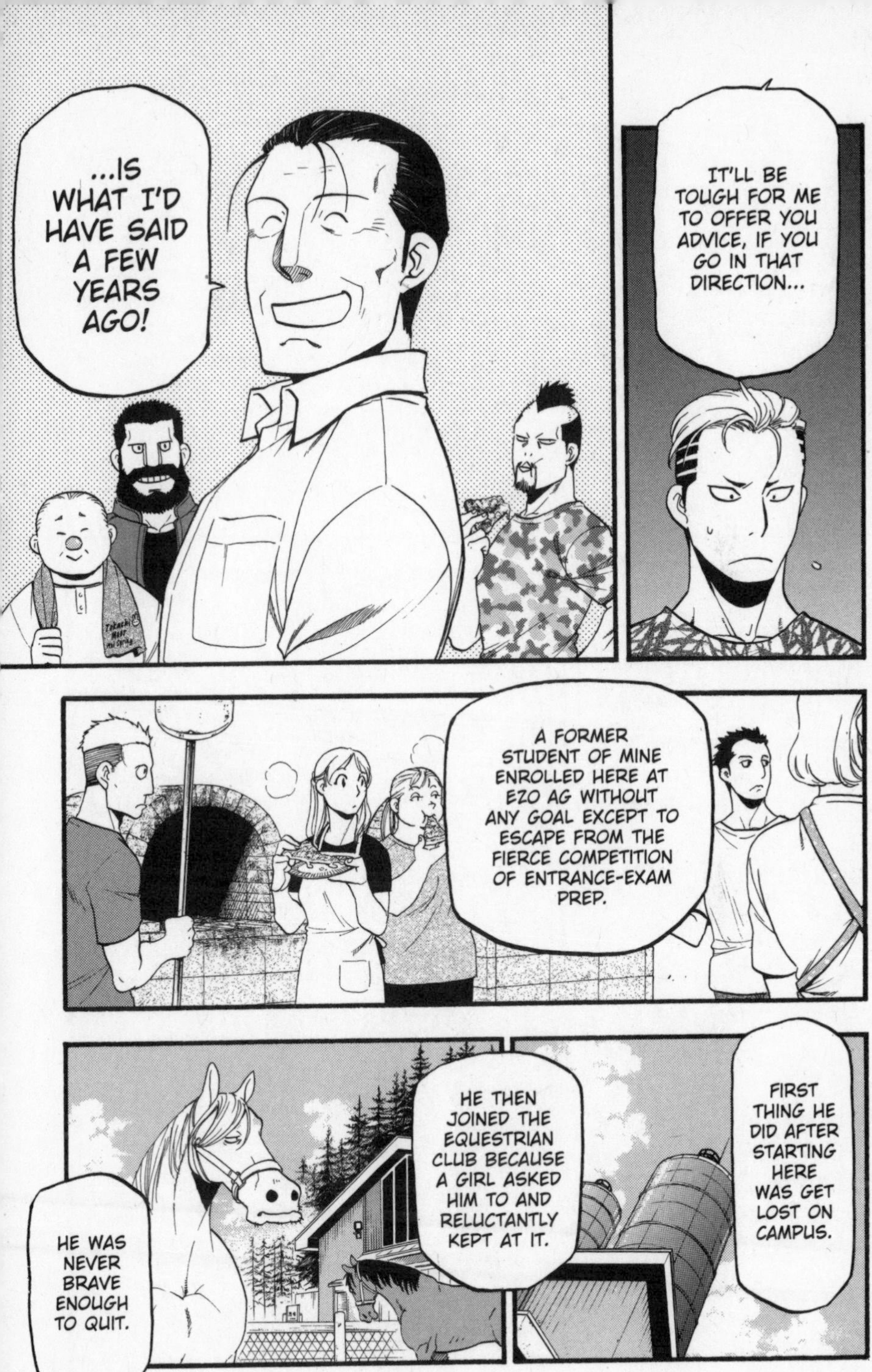
IT'LL BE TOUGH FOR ME TO OFFER YOU ADVICE, IF YOU GO IN THAT DIRECTION...
...IS WHAT I'D HAVE SAID A FEW YEARS AGO!
A FORMER STUDENT OF MINE ENROLLED HERE AT EZO AG WITHOUT ANY GOAL EXCEPT TO ESCAPE FROM THE FIERCE COMPETITION OF ENTRANCE-EXAM PREP.
FIRST THING HE DID AFTER STARTING HERE WAS GET LOST ON CAMPUS.
HE THEN JOINED THE EQUESTRIAN CLUB BECAUSE A GIRL ASKED HIM TO AND RELUCTANTLY KEPT AT IT.
HE WAS NEVER BRAVE ENOUGH TO QUIT.

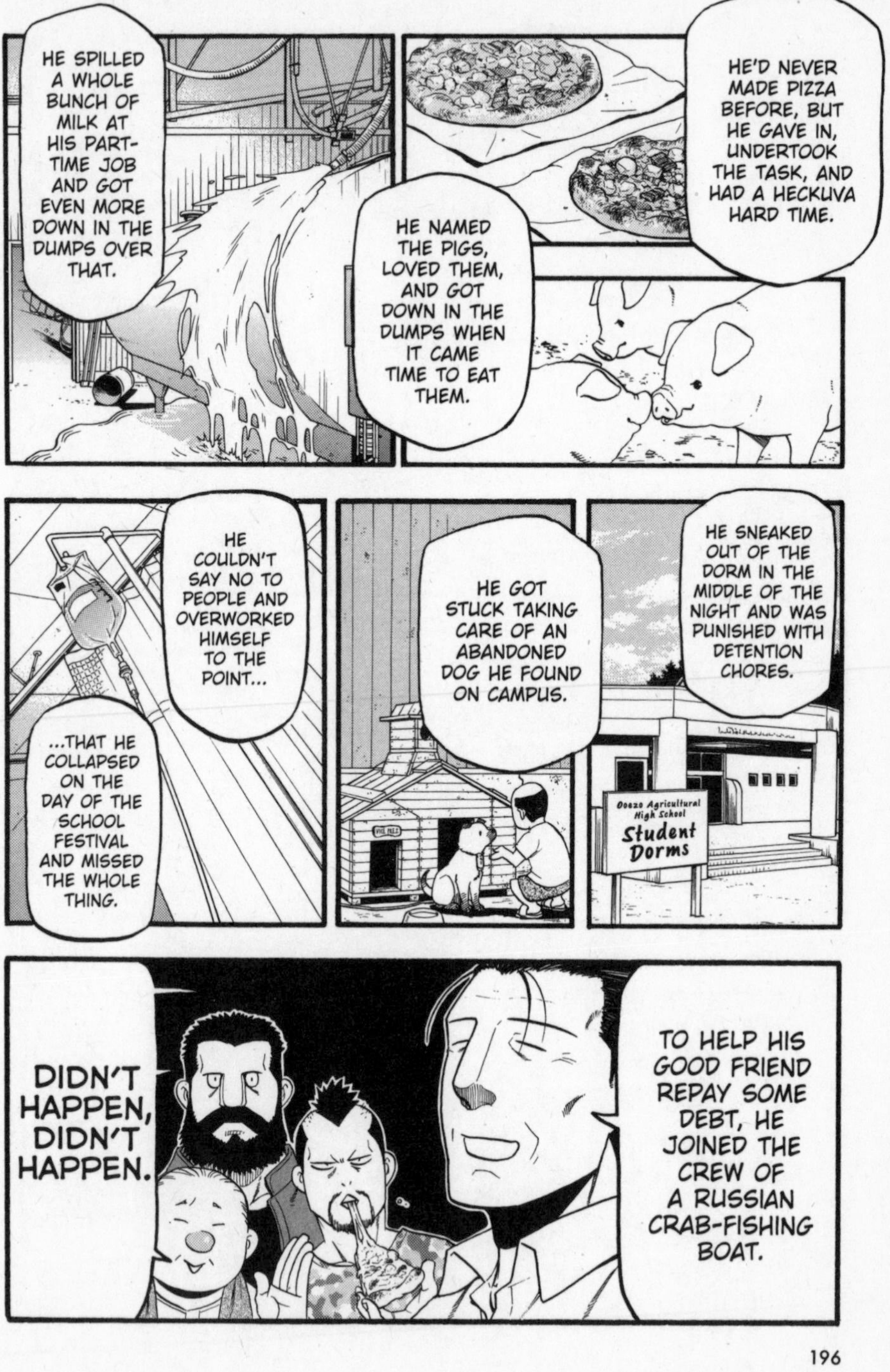
HE'D NEVER MADE PIZZA BEFORE, BUT HE GAVE IN, UNDERTOOK THE TASK, AND HAD A HECKUVA HARD TIME.
HE NAMED THE PIGS, LOVED THEM, AND GOT DOWN IN THE DUMPS WHEN IT CAME TIME TO EAT THEM.
HE SPILLED A WHOLE BUNCH OF MILK AT HIS PART-TIME JOB AND GOT EVEN MORE DOWN IN THE DUMPS OVER THAT.
HE SNEAKED OUT OF THE DORM IN THE MIDDLE OF THE NIGHT AND WAS PUNISHED WITH DETENTION CHORES.
Ooezo Agricultural High School
Student Dorms
HE GOT STUCK TAKING CARE OF AN ABANDONED DOG HE FOUND ON CAMPUS.
HE COULDN'T SAY NO TO PEOPLE AND OVERWORKED HIMSELF TO THE POINT...
...THAT HE COLLAPSED ON THE DAY OF THE SCHOOL FESTIVAL AND MISSED THE WHOLE THING.
TO HELP HIS GOOD FRIEND REPAY SOME DEBT, HE JOINED THE CREW OF A RUSSIAN CRAB-FISHING BOAT.
DIDN'T HAPPEN, DIDN'T HAPPEN.

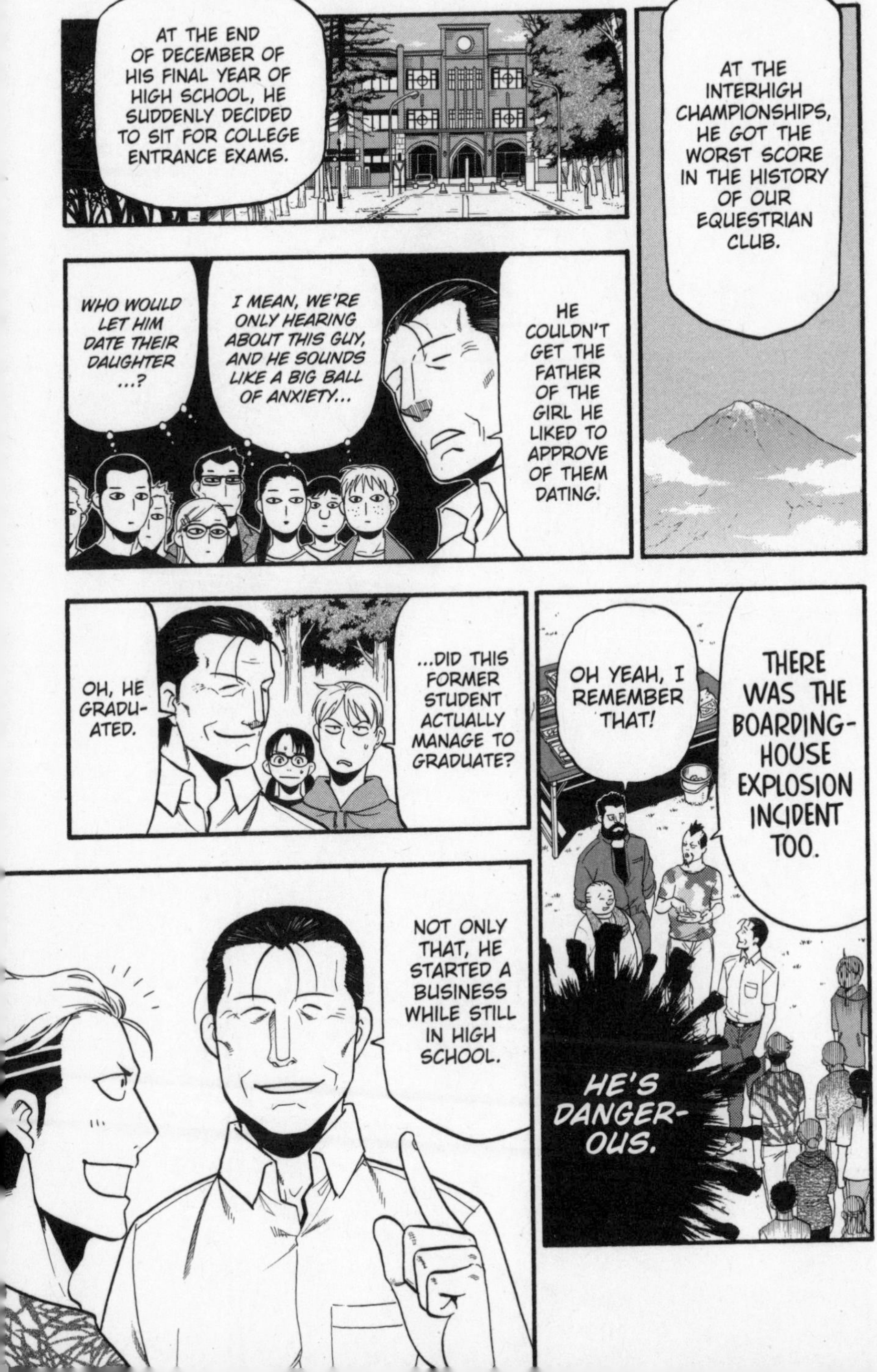
AT THE INTERHIGH CHAMPIONSHIPS, HE GOT THE WORST SCORE IN THE HISTORY OF OUR EQUESTRIAN CLUB.
AT THE END OF DECEMBER OF HIS FINAL YEAR OF HIGH SCHOOL, HE SUDDENLY DECIDED TO SIT FOR COLLEGE ENTRANCE EXAMS.
HE COULDN'T GET THE FATHER OF THE GIRL HE LIKED TO APPROVE OF THEM DATING.
I MEAN, WE'RE ONLY HEARING ABOUT THIS GUY, AND HE SOUNDS LIKE A BIG BALL OF ANXIETY...
WHO WOULD LET HIM DATE THEIR DAUGHTER ...?
THERE WAS THE BOARDING-HOUSE EXPLOSION INCIDENT TOO.
OH YEAH, I REMEMBER THAT!
HE'S DANGER-OUS.
...DID THIS FORMER STUDENT ACTUALLY MANAGE TO GRADUATE?
OH, HE GRADU-ATED.
NOT ONLY THAT, HE STARTED A BUSINESS WHILE STILL IN HIGH SCHOOL.

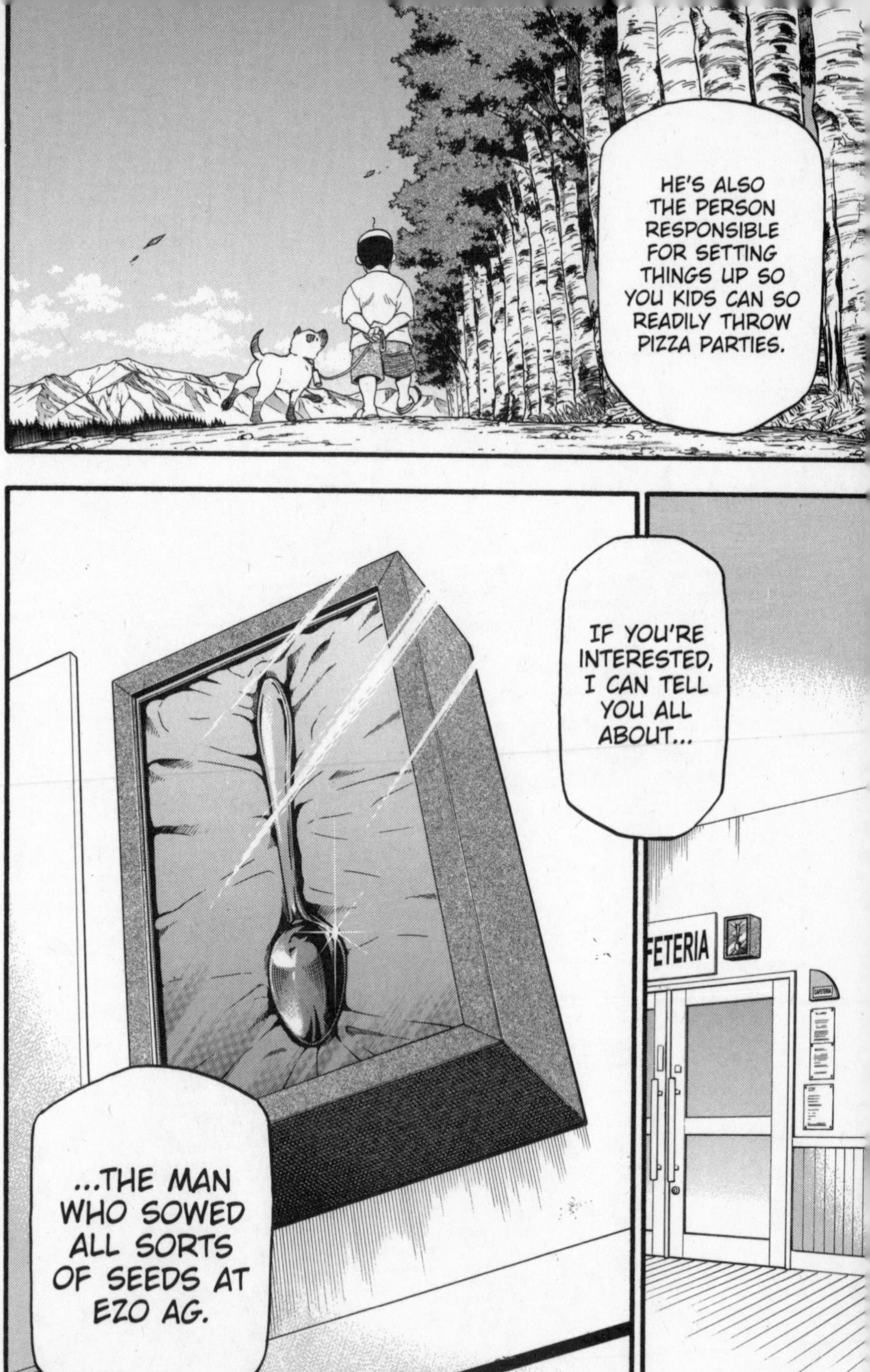
HE'S ALSO THE PERSON RESPONSIBLE FOR SETTING THINGS UP SO YOU KIDS CAN SO READILY THROW PIZZA PARTIES.
IF YOU'RE INTERESTED, I CAN TELL YOU ALL ABOUT...
FETERIA
...THE MAN WHO SOWED ALL SORTS OF SEEDS AT EZO AG.

Silver Spoon • THE END

Silver Spoon

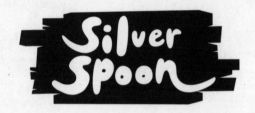

## Cow Shed Diaries: "The Battle With My Editor" Chapter

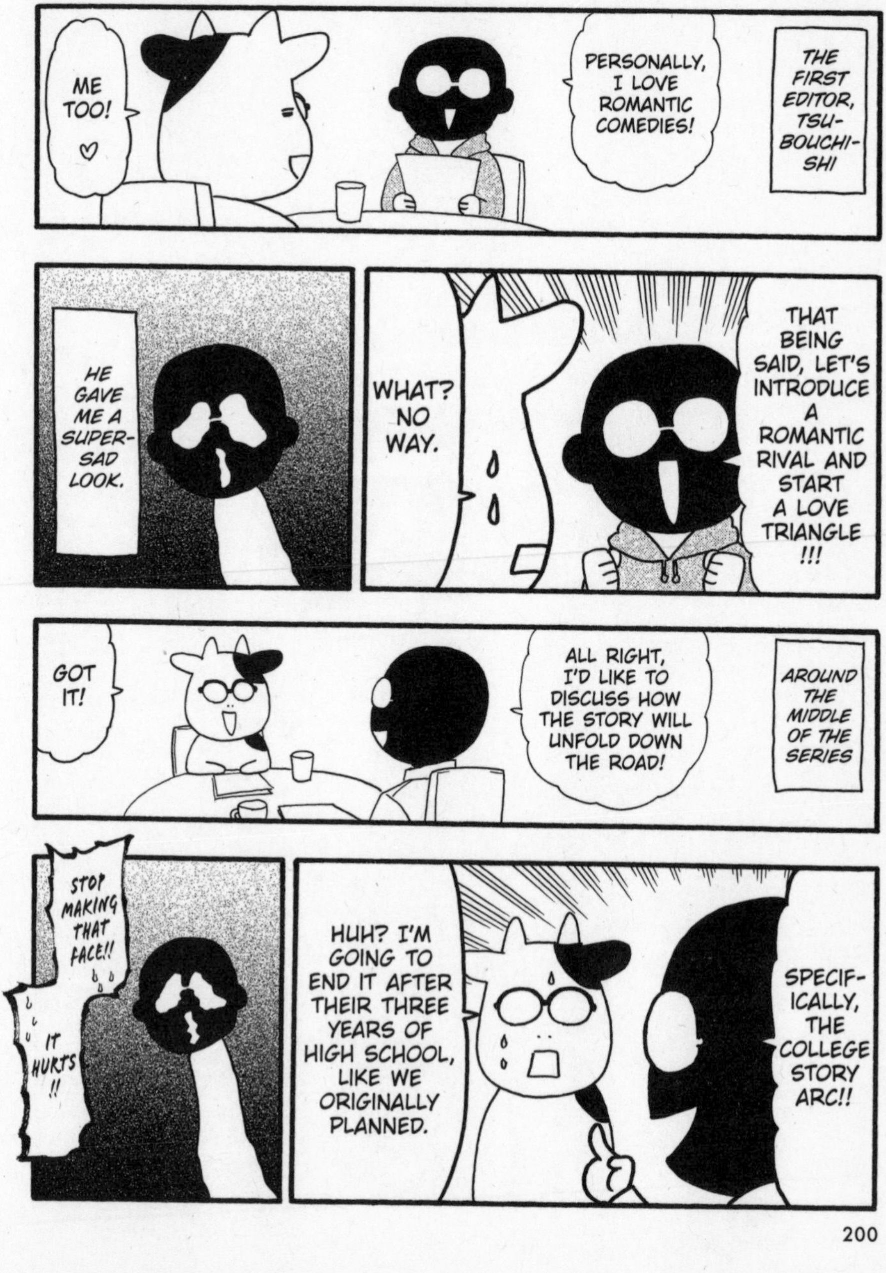
THE FIRST EDITOR, TSUBOUCHI-SHI
PERSONALLY, I LOVE ROMANTIC COMEDIES!
ME TOO! ♡
THAT BEING SAID, LET'S INTRODUCE A ROMANTIC RIVAL AND START A LOVE TRIANGLE!!!
WHAT? NO WAY.
HE GAVE ME A SUPER-SAD LOOK.
AROUND THE MIDDLE OF THE SERIES
ALL RIGHT, I'D LIKE TO DISCUSS HOW THE STORY WILL UNFOLD DOWN THE ROAD!
GOT IT!
SPECIFICALLY, THE COLLEGE STORY ARC!!
HUH? I'M GOING TO END IT AFTER THEIR THREE YEARS OF HIGH SCHOOL, LIKE WE ORIGINALLY PLANNED.
STOP MAKING THAT FACE!!
IT HURTS!!

## An Instant Fail

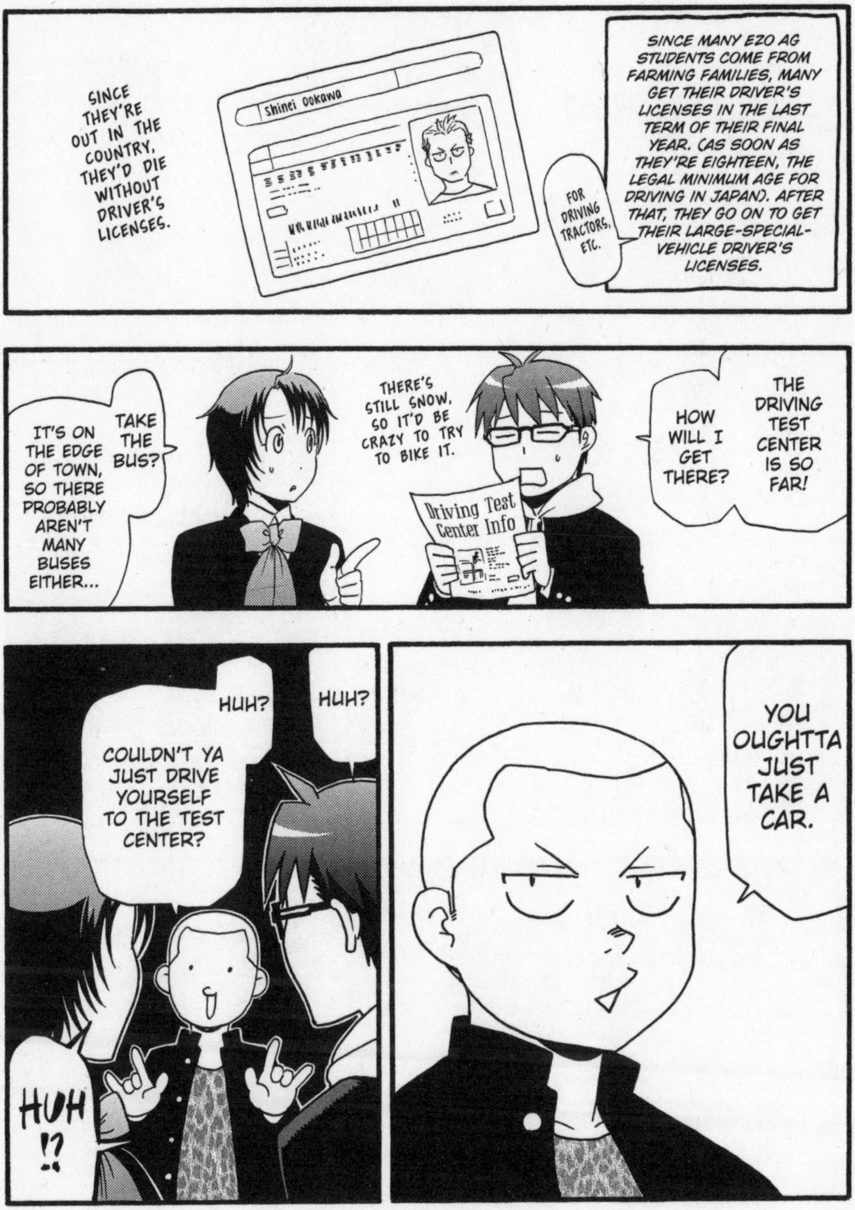
SINCE MANY EZO AG STUDENTS COME FROM FARMING FAMILIES, MANY GET THEIR DRIVER'S LICENSES IN THE LAST TERM OF THEIR FINAL YEAR. (AS SOON AS THEY'RE EIGHTEEN, THE LEGAL MINIMUM AGE FOR DRIVING IN JAPAN). AFTER THAT, THEY GO ON TO GET THEIR LARGE-SPECIAL-VEHICLE DRIVER'S LICENSES.
FOR DRIVING TRACTORS, ETC.
Shinei Ookawa
SINCE THEY'RE OUT IN THE COUNTRY, THEY'D DIE WITHOUT DRIVER'S LICENSES.
THE DRIVING TEST CENTER IS SO FAR!
HOW WILL I GET THERE?
Driving Test Center Info
THERE'S STILL SNOW, SO IT'D BE CRAZY TO TRY TO BIKE IT.
TAKE THE BUS?
IT'S ON THE EDGE OF TOWN, SO THERE PROBABLY AREN'T MANY BUSES EITHER...
YOU OUGHTTA JUST TAKE A CAR.
HUH?
HUH?
COULDN'T YA JUST DRIVE YOURSELF TO THE TEST CENTER?
HUH!?

## Got a Grandchild

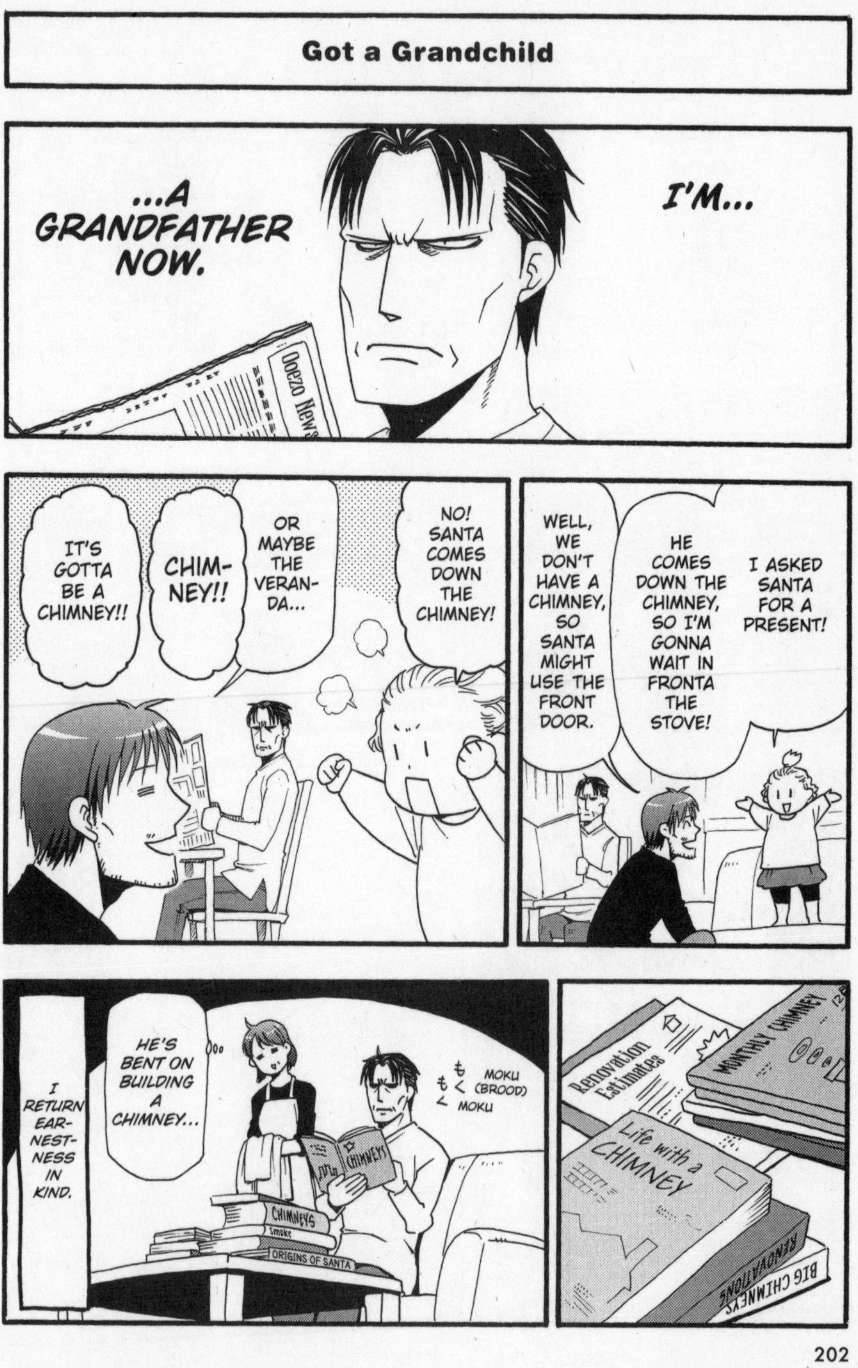
I'M...
...A GRANDFATHER NOW.
Oezo News
I ASKED SANTA FOR A PRESENT!
HE COMES DOWN THE CHIMNEY, SO I'M GONNA WAIT IN FRONTA THE STOVE!
WELL, WE DON'T HAVE A CHIMNEY, SO SANTA MIGHT USE THE FRONT DOOR.
NO! SANTA COMES DOWN THE CHIMNEY!
OR MAYBE THE VERANDA...
CHIMNEY!!
IT'S GOTTA BE A CHIMNEY!!
MONTHLY CHIMNEY
Renovation Estimates
Life with a CHIMNEY
RENOVATIONS
BIG CHIMNEYS
もくもく
MOKU MOKU (BROOD)
HE'S BENT ON BUILDING A CHIMNEY...
CHIMNEYS
Smoke
ORIGINS OF SANTA
I RETURN EARNESTNESS IN KIND.

## Got a Grandchild 2

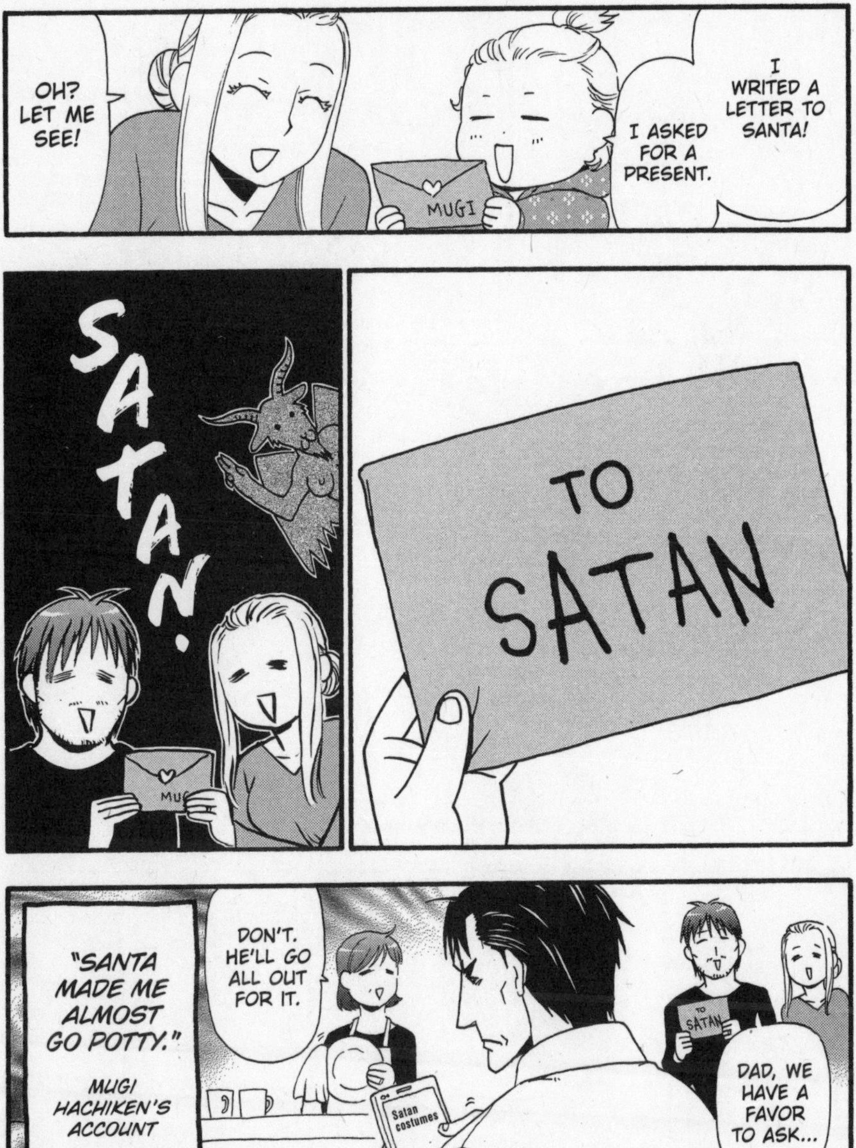
I WRITED A LETTER TO SANTA!
I ASKED FOR A PRESENT.
MUGI
OH? LET ME SEE!
TO SATAN
SATAN!
MUGI
DAD, WE HAVE A FAVOR TO ASK...
TO SATAN
Satan costumes
DON'T. HE'LL GO ALL OUT FOR IT.
"SANTA MADE ME ALMOST GO POTTY."
MUGI HACHIKEN'S ACCOUNT

## Got a Niece

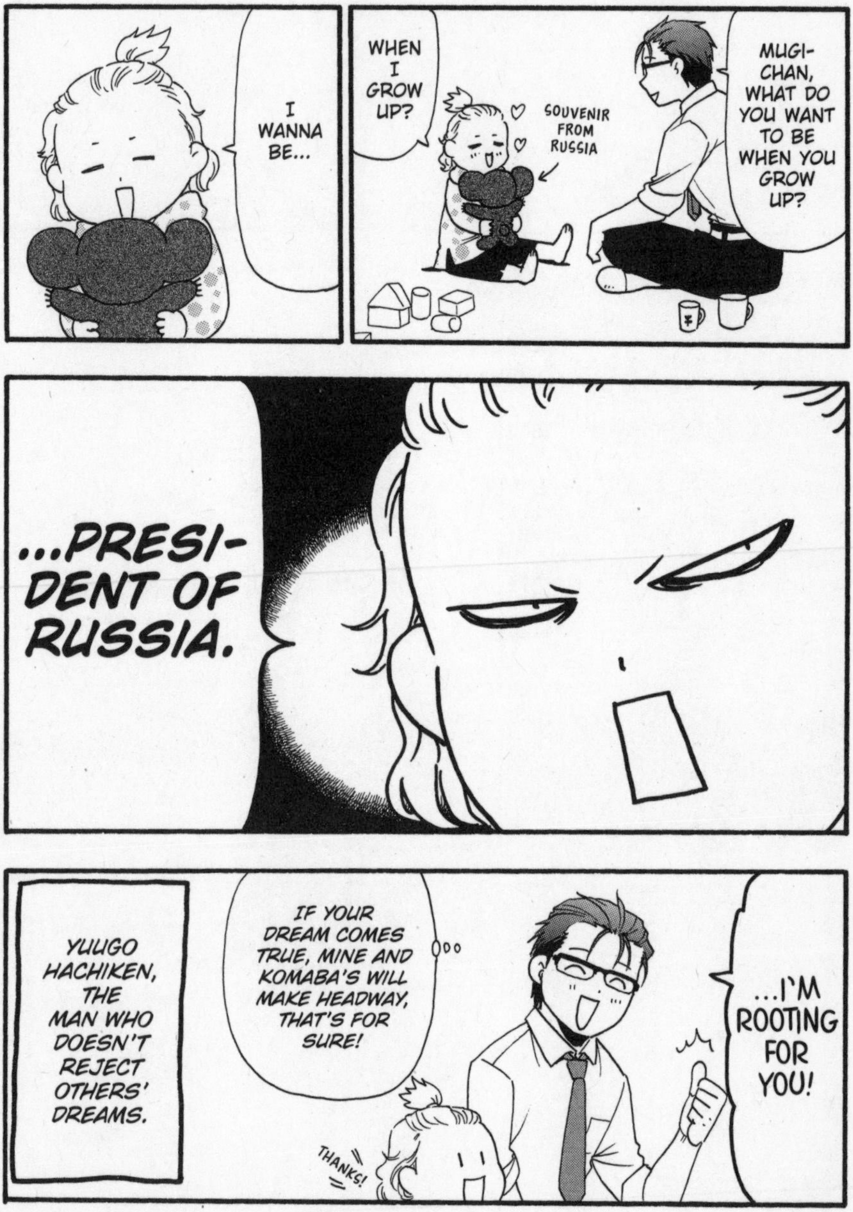
MUGI-CHAN, WHAT DO YOU WANT TO BE WHEN YOU GROW UP?
WHEN I GROW UP?
SOUVENIR FROM RUSSIA
I WANNA BE...
...PRESI-DENT OF RUSSIA.
...I'M ROOTING FOR YOU!
IF YOUR DREAM COMES TRUE, MINE AND KOMABA'S WILL MAKE HEADWAY, THAT'S FOR SURE!
THANKS!
YUUGO HACHIKEN, THE MAN WHO DOESN'T REJECT OTHERS' DREAMS.

## Advertising!!!

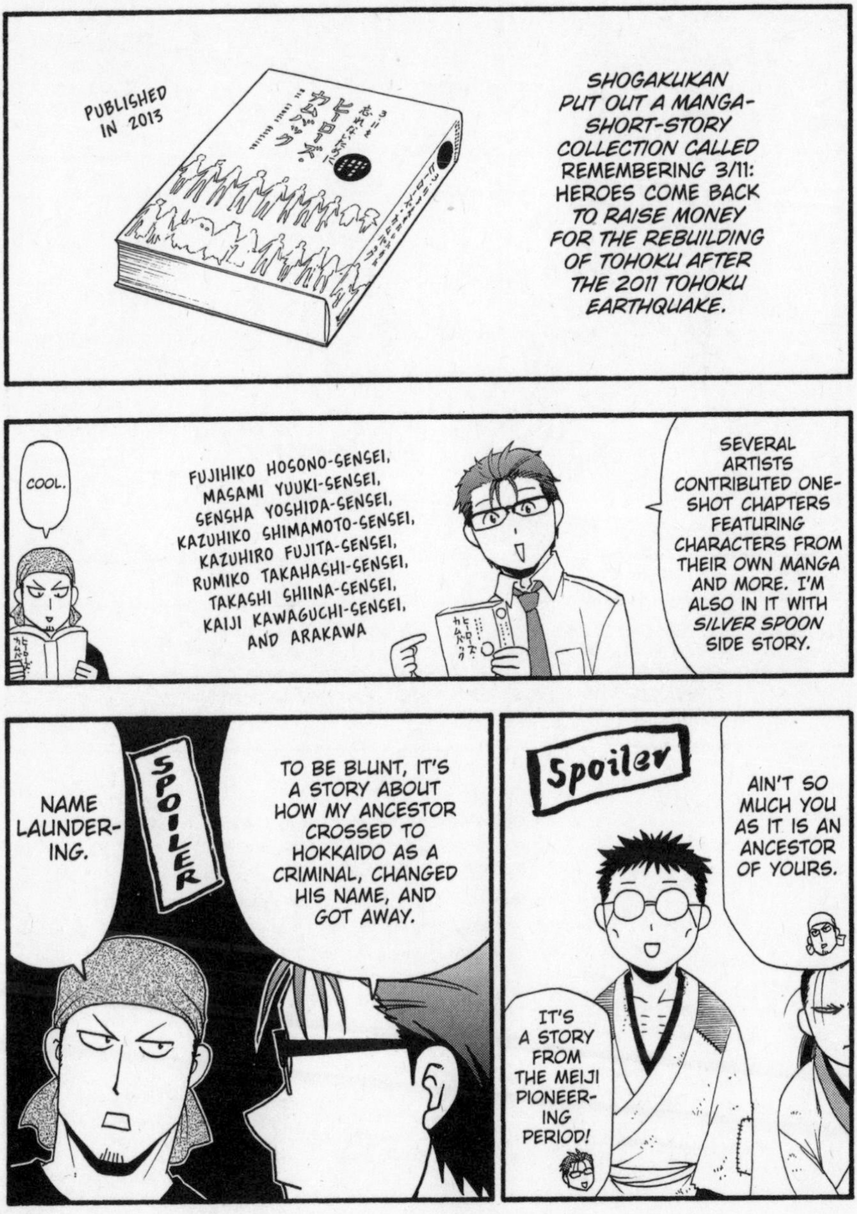
SHOGAKUKAN PUT OUT A MANGA-SHORT-STORY COLLECTION CALLED REMEMBERING 3/11: HEROES COME BACK TO RAISE MONEY FOR THE REBUILDING OF TOHOKU AFTER THE 2011 TOHOKU EARTHQUAKE.
PUBLISHED IN 2013
SEVERAL ARTISTS CONTRIBUTED ONE-SHOT CHAPTERS FEATURING CHARACTERS FROM THEIR OWN MANGA AND MORE. I'M ALSO IN IT WITH *SILVER SPOON* SIDE STORY.
FUJIHIKO HOSONO-SENSEI, MASAMI YUUKI-SENSEI, SENSHA YOSHIDA-SENSEI, KAZUHIKO SHIMAMOTO-SENSEI, KAZUHIRO FUJITA-SENSEI, RUMIKO TAKAHASHI-SENSEI, TAKASHI SHIINA-SENSEI, KAIJI KAWAGUCHI-SENSEI, AND ARAKAWA
COOL.
Spoiler
AIN'T SO MUCH YOU AS IT IS AN ANCESTOR OF YOURS.
IT'S A STORY FROM THE MEIJI PIONEERING PERIOD!
SPOILER
TO BE BLUNT, IT'S A STORY ABOUT HOW MY ANCESTOR CROSSED TO HOKKAIDO AS A CRIMINAL, CHANGED HIS NAME, AND GOT AWAY.
NAME LAUNDERING.

MAN, SO THE HACHIKENS ARE DESCENDED FROM CRIMINALS, HUH?

HOW 'BOUT THAT?

DON'T SAY IT LIKE WE'RE ALL CROOKS!!

YOU MAKE ME SOUND BAD!!

SO GIVEN THOSE CIRCUMSTANCES, I THINK "YUUGO MIKAGE" IS BETTER THAN "AKI HACHIKEN," AFTER ALL.

HUH? WAS THAT A MARRIAGE PROPOSAL!? ON A BONUS JOKES PAGE!?

NAME LAUNDER-ING, TAKE TWO.

IF YOU CAN'T FIND *REMEMBERING 3/11: HEROES COME BACK* (PUBLISHED BY SHOGAKUKAN) IN BOOKSTORES, *SILVER SPOON SIDE STORY* CAN CURRENTLY BE READ FOR FREE (IN JAPANESE) ON SUNDAY WEB EVERY! (HTTPS://WWW.SUNDAY-WEBRY.COM/DETAIL.PHP?TITLE_ID=624)

### Silver Spoon is!

The original candidate for the location of the final chapter was Ukraine (which also has a demand for more farm animals). As I was planning out the story, unbelievably, Ukraine turned into a war zone, and I could no longer use that idea. Instead, we set the finale in our second candidate, the Amur region. It freaked me out...War is wrong!! No doubt about it!! There were some bumps along the way, but I managed to get the final volume safely into your hands. Now I can breathe a sigh of relief! Thank you so very much for sticking with *Silver Spoon* until the end. May we meet again somewhere!!

**Special Thanks**
Everyone who helped with collecting material and interviews, all of my assistants, all of the consultants, the first editor, Tsubouchi-san, the second editor, Yamada-san, the Shounen Sunday editorial department, Araseki-san, without whom there wouldn't have been convincing pictures,

### AND YOU!!

# Translation Notes

## Common Honorifics

**no honorific:** Indicates familiarity or closeness; if used without permission or reason, addressing someone in this manner would constitute an insult.

*-san:* The Japanese equivalent of Mr./Mrs./Miss. This is the fail-safe honorific if politeness is required.

*-sama:* Conveys great respect; may indicate the speaker's social status is lower than the addressee's.

*-kun:* Used most often when referring to boys, this honorific indicates affection or familiarity. Occasionally used by older men among their peers, but it may also be used by anyone referring to a person of lower standing.

*-chan, -tan:* An affectionate honorific indicating familiarity used mostly in reference to girls; also used in reference to cute persons or animals of either gender.

*-sensei:* A respectful term for teachers, artists, or high-level professionals.

*-niisan, nii-san, aniki,* etc.: A term of endearment meaning "big brother" that may be more widely used to address any young man who is like a brother, regardless of whether he is related or not.

*-neesan, nee-san, aneki,* etc.: The female counterpart of the above, meaning "big sister."

## Currency Conversion

While conversion rates fluctuate, an easy estimate for Japanese yen conversion is ¥100 to 1 USD.

**Page 6** • In Japan, it's customary to go on a New Year's cleaning spree of your living space in preparation for the year ahead (like spring-cleaning).

**Page 19** • *The Red-White Singing Contest* is a staple New Year's Eve program featuring the most popular music artists competing in two teams (Red and White). The New Year's Eve countdown program referenced here is *Yuku Toshi Kuru Toshi* ("the passing year and the coming year"), which features scenes from temples or shrines as people gather waiting for midnight.

**Page 42** • A perfect Center Test score would be 900. Ayame's score of 222 is abysmal...

**Page 88** • The song sung at the ceremony is a well-known graduation song called "Aogeba Toutoshi."

**Page 96** • Yoshino is imitating a statue of William S. Clark, an American professor who was invited to Japan to establish an agricultural college in Hokkaido. "Boys, be ambitious," were his parting words to his Japanese students, and the motto is well known throughout Japan.

**Page 119** • The Japanese school year begins in April, so a March 31 acceptance is extremely last-minute.

**Page 140** • The Warring States period (also known as the Sengoku period, 1467–1603) was an age of military conflict as different factions fought for power. *Hachiken's Ambition* is a play on Nobunaga's Ambition, a strategy video game series set in the Warring States period.

**Page 158** • *Obon,* or just *Bon,* is a family-reunion holiday for honoring the spirits of one's ancestors. The dates vary depending on the lunar calendar, but it generally takes place sometime between mid-August and early September.

Tokyo Big Sight is the largest convention and exhibition center in Japan. It is also where the Comic Market convention (Comiket) is held. Nishikawa is likely planning on taking Andre to Summer Comiket.

**Page 161** • Beppu is also the name of a city and famous hot-spring resort in Ooita Prefecture.

**Page 163** • Aki addressing Hachiken by his given name—Yuugo—implies they are closer than before.

**Page 186** • Otaru is a port city on Hokkaido.

# Silver Spoon 15

## HIROMU ARAKAWA

Translation: **Amanda Haley** Lettering: **Abigail Blackman**

This book is a work of fiction. Names, characters, places, and incidents are the product of the author's imagination or are used fictitiously. Any resemblance to actual events, locales, or persons, living or dead, is coincidental.

GIN NO SAJI SILVER SPOON Vol. 15
by Hiromu ARAKAWA
© 2011 Hiromu ARAKAWA
All rights reserved.
Original Japanese edition published by SHOGAKUKAN.
English translation rights in the United States of America, Canada, the United Kingdom, Ireland, Australia and New Zealand arranged with SHOGAKUKAN through Tuttle-Mori Agency, Inc.

English translation © 2020 by Yen Press, LLC

Yen Press
150 West 30th Street, 19th Floor
New York, NY 10001

Visit us at yenpress.com
facebook.com/yenpress
twitter.com/yenpress
yenpress.tumblr.com
instagram.com/yenpress

First Yen Press Edition: September 2020

Yen Press is an imprint of Yen Press, LLC.
The Yen Press name and logo are trademarks of Yen Press, LLC.

The publisher is not responsible for websites (or their content) that are not owned by the publisher.

Library of Congress Control Number: 2017959207

ISBNs: 978-1-9753-5365-0 (paperback)
978-1-9753-1224-4 (ebook)

10 9 8 7 6 5 4 3 2 1

WOR

Printed in the United States of America